W0079773

SQL Server CE Database Development with the .NET Compact Framework

ROB TIFFANY

APress Media, LLC

SQL Server CE Database Development with the .NET Compact Framework
Copyright ©2003 by Rob Tiffany
Originally published by Apress in 2003

ISBN 978-1-59059-119-2   ISBN 978-1-4302-0785-6 (eBook)
DOI 10.1007/978-1-4302-0785-6

Trademarked names may appear in this book. Rather than use a trademark symbol with every occurrence of a trademarked name, we use the names only in an editorial fashion and to the benefit of the trademark owner, with no intention of infringement of the trademark.

Technical Reviewer: Darren Flatt

Editorial Board: Dan Appleman, Craig Berry, Gary Cornell, Tony Davis, Steven Rycroft, Julian Skinner, Martin Streicher, Jim Sumser, Karen Watterson, Gavin Wray, John Zukowski

Assistant Publisher: Grace Wong

Project Manager: Nate McFadden

Copy Editor: Ami Knox

Production Manager: Kari Brooks

Production Editor: Lori Bring

Proofreader: Lori Bring

Compositor: Argosy Publishing

Indexer: Ron Strauss

Cover Designer: Kurt Krames

Manufacturing Manager: Tom Debolski

To Cathy, Caroline, Nicholas, and Michael.
You're everything I've ever wanted or needed in this world.

Contents at a Glance

Contents

Chapter 9   Remote Data Access 311

Chapter 10 Replication 361

Appendix   The .NET Compact Framework Class Libraries 395

Foreword

WELCOME TO *SQL Server CE Database Development with the .NET Compact Framework*! Back in 1998, I moved off of working on the Jet database engine and started investigating what was to become Microsoft SQL Server Windows CE Edition. There was a lot of excitement behind working on a V1 product and building a new team that was to tackle an area that Microsoft had not yet embraced. Of course, with all of this came some incredible challenges to create a robust database to work in the confines of a different OS that had very limited CPU and RAM resources. I distinctly remember waking up at night, worrying how we would ever get a database engine to initialize, let alone have good performance on a MIPS 48 MHz CPU with 16MB total RAM! On top of that, we still had to get management approval and contend with the fact that we were the last of the "big" database vendors to come to market for the mobile space.

For the V1 product, we had some design goals that would differentiate us from the competition in the mobile database arena. First, we decided that being an in-process DLL would be a competitive advantage over the embedded database and server model in terms of having tight integration with eMbedded Visual Tools. Second, we decided that we had to have a very strong sync model, as we believed our customer base was primarily disconnected. Third, we knew that we had to be very competitive in performance against our competitors, even though we would provide more features in a larger footprint. Finally, we knew that we had to have a very efficient QP that could come up with good query plans, even with limited CPU power.

As part of any Microsoft project, the team needed to investigate all possibilities before starting on the project and doing the Bill G review. This meant investigating all angles on how to create a small but still feature-rich database engine. We looked at everything from buying technology, to porting native SQL Server, to using existing technology, to starting from scratch. Amazingly, the first release was a combination of everything that eventually made the SQL Server CE product.

As is the case with any V1 product, there was a lot of blood, sweat, and tears. Big features had to be cut because of time constraints (having a componentized engine was one feature that was hard to cut), and there were a host of inner team dependencies. It certainly didn't help that the tools (eMbedded Visual Tools) were in V1 mode and SQL Server 2000 was in beta. Nothing is as challenging as having every component that the product relies on also be in beta. This led to many interesting challenges, one being when a group of us stayed up for three straight days trying to get a demo to work for the Windows DNA 2000 Readiness Conference. It's amazing, when an objective needs to be achieved, how sleep can become irrelevant and one can watch cars come and go from the adjacent parking garage three times straight! Even with all the all-nighters and 14+-hour work days, the team pulled together and launched the V1.0 version of the product in October 2000 with Nabisco for their "cookies and crackers" direct store delivery application.

Amazingly, the V1.0 project didn't have an internal code name, something that never happens at Microsoft. We got with the times for our V1.1 release and formed an official committee to come up with a set of code names that would define the product future releases. We determined that beaches should be the theme, and V1.1 was christened "Pebble."

We then focused our sights on V2.0, code-named Daytona, and concentrated primarily on improving the developer experience from eMbedded Visual Tools to VS .NET and integration with the super cool functionality that came with .NET CF. Again, the whole dependency of other products caused us some strain and forced us to ship the product twice, once for eMbedded Visual Tools on Sept 19, 2002, and then again with VS .NET 2003 on April 19, 2003.

Currently we are working on our next release of SQL Server CE, code named Laguna, and we have an incredibly valuable set of features and functionality.

Even working at a technology company, I am still amazed at how fast technology improves. Since the inception of SQL Server CE, the CPU speeds have dramatically increased from the days of the MIPS 48 MHz PPC device to the latest Intel XScale PXA255 running at 400 MHz, with a data bus that runs twice the speed of the previous XScale device. The OS in Pocket PC 2003 has moved from the 3.0 code base of Windows CE .NET to a 4.2 code base, which among many things has introduced significant performance improvements and the removal of the 64MB RAM limitation. Most importantly has been the widespread adoption and standardization of wireless data protocols. GPRS has finally caught on with Europe and has widespread deployment in the U.S., and the latest generation of CDMA, providing over 100KB throughput speeds, has dramatically increased the options available to developers to deploy truly interesting mobile applications. The exciting mobile applications that come from this and tight integration of wireless data into the device is something I still find amazing.

What all of these technology advances have done is increased the widespread adoption of mobile databases, especially SQL Server CE. We now have a large number of successful corporate rollouts, with many customers rolling out large deployments of devices. For example, one customer will have a 90,000-device deployment.

With all of this technology and large deployments, one of the things that I do hear from customers is "When is a book on SQL Server CE coming out?" I'm very happy to say that *SQL Server CE Database Development with the .NET Compact Framework* is the first book of its kind to focus on SQL Server CE, data access to SQL Server CE, and synchronization with SQL Server 2000. This lends credence to the increased growth of mobile devices in both the consumer and corporate space. Rob's book does a great job of covering all the basics that a developer would need to know to start developing an application and moving forward to a final product, while still keeping everything interesting to read.

I know I can speak for the entire SQL Server CE team that we are very pleased to see a book finally come out that is focused on SQL Server CE.

Kevin Collins
Microsoft Senior Program Manager for SQL Server CE

About the Author

Rob Tiffany is cofounder and chief technology officer of Hood Canal Systems, where he's focused on providing exceptional wireless and handheld products and solutions for his clients. In addition, Rob is also a speaker, editor, columnist, and author of articles that have appeared in a variety of trade magazines, including *Java Developer's Journal* and *Visual Basic Developer,* on topics ranging from PersonalJava to wireless development. *SQL Server CE Database Development with the .NET Compact Framework* is Rob's second book to be published by Apress. Rob's first book, *Pocket PC Database Development with eMbedded Visual Basic,* is still popular with eVB programmers. You can contact Rob at rob.tiffany@hoodcanalsystems.com.

About the Technical Reviewer

Darren Flatt is the cofounder and chief operating officer of Hood Canal Systems. Darren's current focus is determining how to best leverage mobile technology in the enterprise. Darren has participated in startup ventures with focuses ranging from enterprise network management software to consulting services. While Darren has a business degree, he can code with the best of them. You can contact Darren at darren.flatt@hoodcanalsystems.com.

Acknowledgments

TO THE DREAM TEAM at Apress, Gary Cornell, Dan Appleman, and Karen Watterson, thanks for all your support over the years. Back when you gave me the opportunity to write my first book, Apress was the little publishing company that could. Apress isn't little anymore.

To the .NET Compact Framework and SQL Server CE teams at Microsoft, the next phase of the Information Age belongs to you. The wires are gone and the computers have gotten a lot smaller.

Introduction

Remembering 9/11

THE TRAGIC EVENTS of September 11, 2001, have affected everyone very deeply. Seeing those airplanes fly into the Twin Towers was almost surreal. In utter shock, I watched the World Trade Center collapse and witnessed thousands of people running and screaming. Until that moment, I thought something of this magnitude only happened in science fiction movies, when Earth found herself on the verge of extinction at the hands of an alien race. I remember thinking that this couldn't be happening; my denial was probably coming from that part of the human psyche that prevents the brain from being overwhelmed when faced with a previously unimaginable horror. Like many people, I was at the office, in a skyscraper, with my coworkers, watching the events unfold on television. I remember a strange silence in the office; I remember a common look of disbelief on the faces of my friends; I remember looking out the window and noticing an eerily empty sky once the president had cleared the U.S. airspace of commercial aircraft.

How Can I Help?

Later that day, I received an e-mail from my former boss on the USS *Alaska*, Senior Chief Sexton. The subject line of the e-mail read, "Get Ready." I served my country during the Gulf War in the Naval Submarine Service, first on a SEAL team delivery vehicle, and later on a Trident submarine. I assumed that I'd be getting a phone call from the United States Navy within the next few weeks recalling me to submarine duty to go fight World War III. Well, the call never came, so I kept going to work, kept writing software, and spent as much time as possible with my family. President Bush launched the War on Terrorism and invaded Afghanistan. I seem to recall a Sunday football game being interrupted to announce the beginning of this new conflict. There were lots of football fans cheering the soldiers on to war. Since the call to once again serve my country didn't come, I felt like I was sitting on the sidelines, unable to contribute. How could I help? I can navigate oceans and evade torpedoes. I can keep a submarine perfectly level at launch depth in order to fire her ICBMs. I even used to have a pretty high security clearance.

Getting Ready for This Book

In the meantime, I'd been planning to write a book that taught programmers how to create database applications on the Pocket PC using the .NET Compact Framework and SQL Server CE 2.0. You know, something that would allow employees working in the field to enter relevant data into their handheld and then replicate it back to corporate headquarters. I'd previously written a book with similar goals that taught developers to how to build Pocket PC database applications using eMbedded Visual Basic and Pocket Access. This new technology from Microsoft looked to be a giant leap forward, so I knew it was time to teach readers a new technology to help them solve problems and streamline business processes. While making the corporate world run more efficiently is an important goal, with all that was going on in the world, I couldn't help but wonder if there was a higher purpose for this new technology.

Not Connecting the Dots

In the spring of 2002, I started hearing news reports of FBI agents working in Phoenix and Minneapolis who seemed to know something about the terrorists who hijacked those airplanes on 9/11. These agents had picked up on the fact that several young foreign men with expired visas were taking flying lessons all around the country, paying with cash. They noted their suspicions in field memos, which they sent to their superiors in Washington D.C. Some memos were rejected by mid-level bureaucrats, while others were lost in mounds of paperwork. Congressmen and senators started pointing fingers and wondering why senior FBI officials didn't connect the dots. Why wasn't data shared amongst the various government agencies? Why weren't the FBI and CIA working together? Some time later, reports surfaced that the CIA had two of the terrorists who flew the plane into the Pentagon under surveillance when they were attending an al-Qaida meeting overseas. The CIA had plenty of information on these two guys in their databases, and yet the two terrorists entered the United States without incident. Why didn't the INS get this information so they could stop these terrorists from entering the U.S.? Is the company you work for made up of a bunch of departments that don't talk to each other?

We Have the Technology

When President Bush addressed the nation to announce his desire to form a cabinet-level homeland security department to coordinate this tangled web of government agencies, people, and data, I knew what I had to do. I had to harness my knowledge of the Pocket PC, wireless data networks, security, the .NET Compact Framework, and both SQL Server 2000 and CE to help solve the problems faced by those FBI field agents. In the future, field agents will be able to use a secure Pocket PC to rapidly enter their intelligence data into a Visual Basic .NET or C# application. That data will then be safely stored in an encrypted SQL Server CE database until it is replicated back to a master SQL Server 2000 database via an SSL tunnel. This multi-petabyte SQL Server 2000 database of electronic field memos will contain the combined data of the FBI, CIA, and the Department of Homeland

Security. Intelligent software agents can then mine this data in order to connect the dots and present the president with a more accurate daily threat assessment.

What to Expect from This Book

Readers of this book will learn about the technologies necessary to build the important system I just described. If you're thinking I'm crazy, and that this line of thinking is a little "out there" for a computer book, go take a look at the new HP iPAQ, which has a biometric fingerprint reader. Who do you think HP made that Pocket PC for? Anyone with highly sensitive data who can't afford to have that information fall into the wrong hands. That applies to federal agents, military personnel, government scientists, defense contractors, and yes, corporate executives. Who knows, maybe this kind of security will become mainstream one day.

Don't worry, you don't have to build software designed to save the world from terrorism in order to benefit from what you're about to read. In a nutshell, you'll learn what it takes to build powerful Pocket PC database applications that utilize SQL Server CE 2.0. Remember all those stand-alone desktop applications you built with Visual Basic and Access? You'll be able to build those same applications on the Pocket PC. Need to have your Pocket PC application synchronize with SQL Server 2000 over a wired or wireless network? I'll show you how to do that as well. I'll even show you how to make those network data connections secure. You'll have the tools needed to empower a mobile workforce. Whether you need to provide your sales force with freshly updated information at their fingertips or you need to give your insurance claims adjusters a way to capture data, this book has you covered.

Probably much like yourself, I am a business software developer. Sometimes, problems can be solved and efficiencies can be gained through the use of technology. Technology for technology's sake doesn't fly in the corporate world. When you're on a project, you're expected to work quickly, and in many cases you're figuring out the appropriate technology on the fly. That's where I'm coming from, and that's what you'll get from this book. My style is very succinct, so you get your questions answered without a lot of fluff. This book will serve as both a tutorial and a reference for you to keep on hand whenever a solution requires a Pocket PC database application. At no time when you read this book will you ever get the impression that I'm a computer scientist. I will not spend a single sentence teaching you "what's under the hood" or "the low-level guts" of the .NET Compact Framework technology. If you're looking for volumes of information on how to build Pocket PC applications using just the Microsoft Intermediate Language, Notepad, and a command-line compiler, you'll be extremely disappointed. On the other hand, if you're looking for a book that will make you productive in the shortest amount of time possible, then you've come to the right place. The chapter summaries later in this introduction will give you a better feel for what to expect from this book.

Who This Book Is For

Normally, this is the part where you find out if you're qualified to read this book. I certainly don't want to come off sounding like a stock analyst who's in the back pocket of an investment bank by throwing out erroneous buy, sell, or hold recommendations. So instead of telling you that this book targets either beginner, intermediate, or advanced developers, I'm going to throw you a little curve. In today's .NET Compact Framework environment, there's no requirement for advanced embedded C++ coding experience to build powerful Pocket PC applications. In fact, those advanced embedded C++ developers are going to find that life has gotten a lot easier for them in this arena. By the same token, beginning .NET developers are going to find out how straightforward Pocket PC database development truly is with the .NET Compact Framework. I will make the most complex topics appear simple so that this book doesn't go over the head of a single developer. All .NET developers who have a need to build Pocket PC database applications are invited to this party.

Chapter Summaries

In order to get a quick glimpse of what's to come in this book, I've included brief summaries of each chapter. As you will see, this book takes you from the ground floor of learning how to use the Smart Device Extensions, to teaching you about ADO.NET, and then diving into the inner workings of SQL Server CE 2.0.

Chapter 1: Getting Started

In this chapter, I'll give you an overview of the new Smart Device Extensions for Visual Studio .NET 2003 as well as what to expect in SQL Server CE 2.0. You'll be taken from start to finish with a visual walkthrough of building your first Pocket PC application with the .NET Compact Framework.

Chapter 2: ADO.NET

In this chapter, you'll see which .NET Compact Framework classes are needed to connect to and manipulate SQL Server CE databases. You'll examine data providers as well as all the nuances of both connected and disconnected database access.

Chapter 3: Query Analyzer

In this chapter, I'll give you a visual tour of a useful tool that lets you work with SQL Server CE databases in a graphical manner. You'll learn how to point-and-click your way through data retrieval as well as database and table creation and manipulation.

Chapter 4: SQL Server CE Data Definition Language

In this chapter, I'll teach you how to create and manipulate SQL Server CE database objects using a combination of SQL and .NET code. Through extensive examples, you'll gain the skills necessary to construct any of kind of SQL Server CE data structure.

Chapter 5: Metadata

In this chapter, you'll learn how to view database objects and their metadata using the SQL Server CE Information Schema views. Once you've completed this chapter, you'll no longer need to use Query Analyzer to view the data structures you've created with DDL.

Chapter 6: Data Manipulation Language

In this chapter, I'll show you how to add, modify, retrieve, and remove data from SQL Server CE databases. You'll learn the ins and outs of filtering, grouping, and ordering data in your queries. Additionally, I'll describe the various types of table joins that are now available to you in SQL Server CE 2.0.

Chapter 7: Operator Reference

In this chapter, you'll see how to use SQL Server CE's operators to build powerful queries. This example-filled chapter will serve as an indispensable reference for the use of logical, unary, mathematical, bitwise, and comparison operators.

Chapter 8: Function Reference

In this chapter, you'll explore the dozens of built-in functions supported by SQL Server CE. Whether you're looking for mathematical, aggregate, date/time, system, or string functions, this chapter will answer all your questions with detailed examples.

Chapter 9: Remote Data Access

In this chapter, you'll learn about the easy way to connect your .NET Compact Framework/SQL Server CE applications to SQL Server 2000. I'll show you how to pull data down to your Pocket PC, where you can manipulate it, track the changes you made, and then push those changes back to SQL Server. You'll also learn how to submit INSERT, UPDATE, and DELETE statements against a remote SQL Server.

Chapter 10: Replication

In this chapter, you'll learn how to work with the powerful merge replication feature of SQL Server 2000. I'll show you how to subscribe and synchronize with a SQL Server 2000 publication containing a collection of articles.

Appendix: The .NET Compact Framework Class Libraries

This appendix provides you with a complete reference to all the .NET Compact Framework class libraries. This reference includes all namespaces, classes, structures, enumerations, delegates, and interfaces.

Hood Canal Systems

To keep up with what's going on in the world of handheld and wireless development, frequent trips to http://www.hoodcanalsystems.com will keep you current. This site provides you with resources such as the latest handheld and wireless news, training courses, articles, newsgroups, and links to other important Web sites. Additionally, Hood Canal Systems sells commercial applications, components, and consulting services to make your wireless, handheld, barcoding, and RFID projects a success. Feel free to contact me about these services at rob.tiffany@hoodcanalsystems.com.

CHAPTER 1

Getting Started

IN OUR LAST EPISODE, back in the 2000–2001 timeframe, I described how we were entering a new phase of computing that would be dominated by small, handheld devices designed to make your life easier. The dynamic duo of eMbedded Visual Basic (eVB) and Pocket Access seemed like a godsend to the millions of Visual Basic and Access programmers who would be instantly productive in this familiar environment. With old friends like ActiveX controls and ADO along for the ride, a new wave of powerful Pocket PC 2000 applications would storm onto the scene. With handheld devices containing 32MB of RAM running at speeds of over 200 MHz, I always found it amusing when Microsoft told us eVB programmers that we were working in a severely constrained environment. Did everybody forget that in the early '90s we were building similar Windows applications using Visual Basic 3.0 and Access 2.0 with only 4MB of RAM available to us? As we fast-forward to 2003, handheld devices are everywhere, and they're more powerful than ever. That being said, your 400 MHz XScale Pocket PC with 64MB of RAM, a 256MB SD card, and an 802.11x compact flash card is still considered a resource-constrained device <g>. I hope the true embedded programmers who are slinging just a few KBs of C code and burning EPROMs don't feel slighted. Oh well, memory and processors are now small and cheap and that's why smart devices of all kinds are taking over the market and even outselling PCs.

What This Book Is All About

The decision by Microsoft to introduce a subset of the .NET Framework to run on these devices could not have come at a better time. The .NET Compact Framework takes the eMbedded Visual Basic, PersonalJava, or eMbedded Visual C++ developer to the next level with built-in support for things like networking, custom controls, ADO.NET, Visual Basic .NET, C#, threading, compiled code, Web services, and structured error handling. Not bad for something that weighs in at just under 1.5MB. This power is only matched by the ease with which you can build .NET Compact Framework applications in Visual Studio .NET 2003 utilizing the Smart Device Extensions (SDE). SDE empowers the developer to build Pocket PC, and Windows CE applications using the same IDE, forms designer, and wizards that desktop and server .NET Framework developers use. You're even provided with an emulator to aid in debugging your applications. Sharing the stage with the .NET Compact Framework is SQL Server CE 2.0. Just when you thought you were going to get an upgrade to the Pocket Access (cdb) database you've been using all these years, Microsoft decides to cram their server database into a constrained device and allows it to work with the .NET Compact Framework via ADO.NET. SQL Server CE is an amazing database that runs in-process as a DLL with your .NET Compact Framework application and is a giant leap forward over Pocket Access. Believe it or not, SQL Server CE shares many of the same features as SQL Server 2000. Some of these features include the following:

- 249 indexes per table (same as SQL Server 2000)

- Both inner and outer joins

- Query Analyzer

- The union operator (plus 30 more operators where that came from)

- Support for parameterized queries

- 128-bit file-level encryption

- Full referential integrity including cascading updates and deletes

- Merge replication and remote data access

- Over 50 built-in functions

SQL Server CE packs an unbelievable amount of functionality for a product that takes up no more than 1.33MB of memory on your handheld. Of course, don't let its small size fool you, as it supports databases up to 2GB in size. As you make your way through this book, you'll see lots of Visual Basic .NET and C# code examples. Since the primary focus of this book is to describe all the aspects of SQL Server CE 2.0, keep in mind that this .NET Compact Framework code is there only to demonstrate what can be done with SQL Server CE.

System Requirements

As I mentioned previously, .NET Compact Framework applications are created with Visual Studio .NET 2003. This is possible through the use of a Visual Studio Integration Package (VSIP) that plugs into Visual Studio. This VSIP is called Smart Device Extensions and allows you to target Pocket PC and Windows CE .NET devices.

Development

The requirements to create .NET Compact Framework applications are the same as the requirements to run Visual Studio .NET 2003. You need one of the following:

- Windows Server 2003

- Windows XP Professional

- Windows XP Home

- Windows 2000 Server

- Windows 2000 Professional

One interesting caveat is that you won't be able to debug your applications in the included emulator unless your computer is on a network with an active connection. If you find yourself without a network, you'll need to install the Microsoft Loopback Adapter in order to fool the emulator into believing that you're on a network. The following steps will get you up and running with the Loopback Adapter.

Windows Server 2003/Windows XP

Follow these steps to install the Microsoft Loopback Adapter on a Windows Server 2003 or Windows XP system:

1. Go to the Control Panel and double-click the Add Hardware applet.

2. Click Next until you get to the Is the hardware connected? screen. Select Yes and then click Next.

3. Select Add a new hardware device from the Installed hardware list and then click Next.

4. Select the Install the hardware that I manually select from a list (Advanced) radio button and then click Next.

5. Select Network Adapters from the Common hardware types list and then click Next.

6. Select Microsoft from the Manufacturer list, select Microsoft Loopback Adapter from the Network Adapter list, and then click Next.

7. Click Next to initiate the installation process and then click Finish.

Windows 2000

If you have a Windows 2000 system, follow these steps to install the Microsoft Loopback Adapter:

1. Go to the Control Panel and double-click the Add/Remove Hardware applet.

2. Click Next until you get to the Choose a Hardware Task screen. Select Add/ Troubleshoot a device and then click Next.

3. Select Add a new device from the Devices list and then click Next.

4. Select the No, I want to select the hardware from a list radio button and then click Next.

5. Select Network adapters from the Hardware types list and then click Next.

6. Select Microsoft from the Manufacturers list, select Microsoft Loopback Adapter from the Network Adapter list, and then click Next.

7. Click Next to initiate the installation process and then click Finish.

Deployment

Your .NET Compact Framework applications can be targeted at a number of different devices:

- Pocket PC 2000

- Pocket PC 2002

- Pocket PC 2002 Phone Edition

- Windows CE 4.x

Later on in 2003, you'll get a few other devices to choose from, including Pocket PC 2003 and Smartphone 2003, based on the latest version of Windows CE 4.x. Support for these forthcoming devices will come from Web downloadable SDKs. By the time you read this, the Pocket PC 2003 SDK should be available for download at http://microsoft.com/downloads/details.aspx?FamilyId=9996B314-0364-4623-9EDE-0B5FBB133652&displaylang=en. The future looks bright for the Pocket PC, but you may have to look for other database alternatives on the forthcoming version of Smartphone, since it won't support SQL Server CE.

ActiveSync All Over Again

Now that the Pocket PC is a first-class, enterprise network client, you're probably thinking that ActiveSync is now a thing of the past. After all, your device has virtually all of the capabilities that a laptop does, and can connect directly to Internet and intranet resources like databases and Web services. Don't forget, consumers who don't know what the enterprise is and just want to keep track of their everyday life purchase millions of Pocket PCs. The reason you still need to care about ActiveSync is for debugging and deploying your .NET Compact Framework applications.

Installation

Based on my experience over the years working with the eMbedded Visual Tools and now the Smart Device Extensions in Visual Studio .NET 2003, it's important to have ActiveSync installed and working on a machine before installing the development environment. Don't ask me why, it's just a chicken-and-egg thing. I've tried it the other way around, and the result was that I had to reinstall Visual Studio in order to get anything to work. Microsoft Knowledge Base article 813579 describes the inability to deploy a Smart Device Application once ActiveSync is uninstalled and then reinstalled. In fact, our esteemed technical editor validated just this situation the hard way and lost a day of editing in the process. Therefore, I'm going to walk you through the ActiveSync Setup Wizard to ensure that you get it installed properly. To get the latest and greatest version of ActiveSync, surf on over to the Pocket PC downloads page at http://www.microsoft.com/mobile/pocketpc/downloads/. As of the writing of this book, the latest version is 3.7. Double-clicking msasync.exe will get things installed and shouldn't require a reboot.

Get Connected

Once ActiveSync is installed, it's time to get your device connected. Plug the USB cable that came with your Pocket PC into your computer's USB port as well as the Pocket PC itself. Most likely, you should hear a musical chime from both your Pocket PC and your desktop computer when the two connect. Once the connection is made, you'll be prompted to create a new partnership as shown in Figure 1-1.

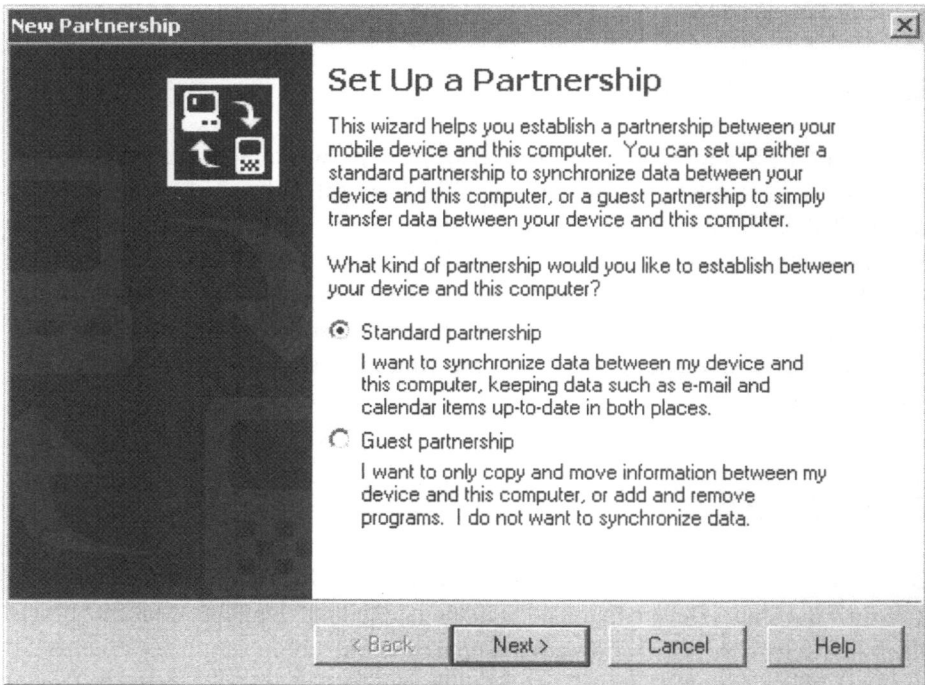

Figure 1-1. Setting up a partnership

Creating a Partnership

As you can see in Figure 1-1, you need to choose between setting up a Standard or Guest partnership. A Standard partnership allows you to move data between the desktop and device, debug with Visual Studio .NET, and synchronize items such as Outlook calendars, Pocket Access databases, and e-mail. This is the most widely used type of partnership, and it creates a permanent relationship between your computer and your device. On the other hand, a Guest partnership is more of a transient type of relationship. An example would be where many different devices need to connect to a single computer. A Guest partnership allows you to debug with Visual Studio .NET and move data back and forth between the desktop and device, but it doesn't allow any kind of synching.

Data Synchronization

It used to be that the only thing you had to worry about synching with was your desktop computer. Now you have some other options to concern yourself with. As shown in Figure 1-2, you can choose to synchronize either with your desktop computer and/or with the Microsoft Mobile Information Server. Very shortly, the technology found in the Mobile Information Server will be merged into Microsoft Exchange 2003 to give you even more choices when synchronizing your data.

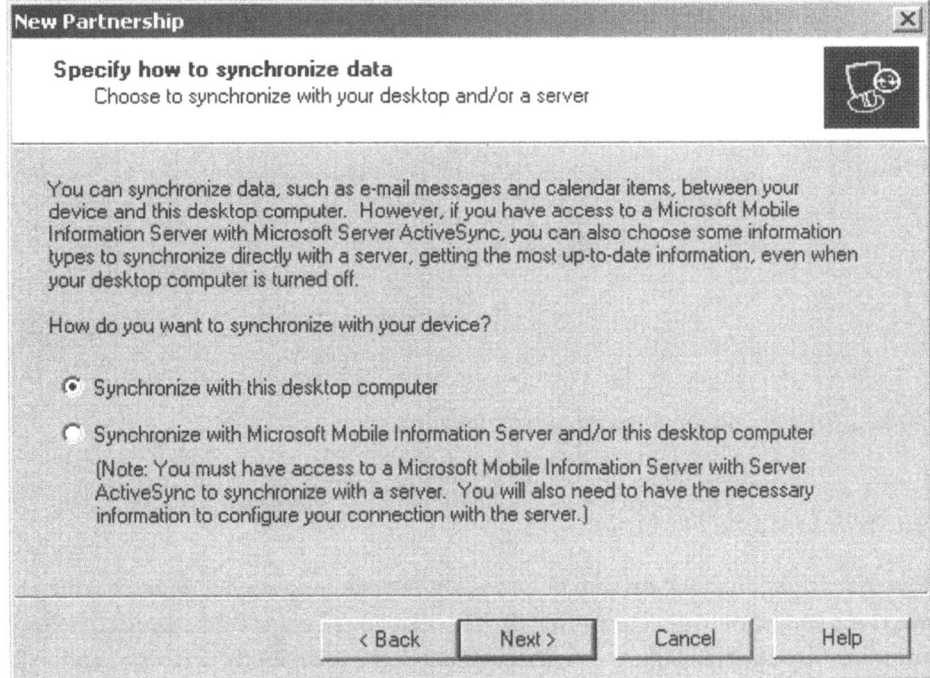

Figure 1-2. Specifying how to synchronize data

How Many Partnerships?

At this point, you need to decide if you want to create a partnership with just one or two computers. If you don't have a partnership in place with another computer that you want to keep and you only want to sync with a single desktop, select Yes as shown in Figure 1-3. Otherwise, select No to maintain an existing partnership while still being able to sync with the current computer you're installing ActiveSync on. It's very common to have partnerships set up at both your home and office computers.

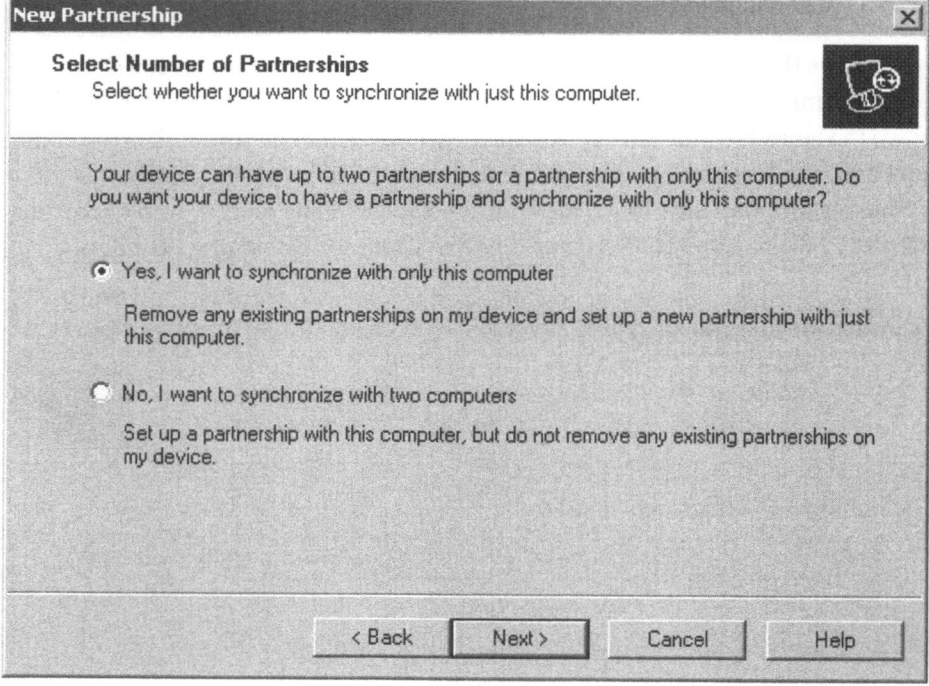

Figure 1-3. Selecting the number of partnerships

Synchronization Settings

Now that you've decided on one or two partnerships, you need to choose which programs you want to synchronize with between your Pocket PC and your desktop computer as shown in Figure 1-4. These choices are completely up to you and will have no impact on your ability to debug and deploy .NET Compact Framework applications from Visual Studio .NET. Alas, we've moved on from Pocket Access, so you won't have to select it this time around.

With your synchronization setting decided upon, the creation of your ActiveSync partnership is now complete, and the ActiveSync setup is finished. The ActiveSync software now serves as the primary conduit between your Pocket PC and your desktop computer. In addition to USB, ActiveSync can also communicate with your Pocket PC via serial cable, infrared, Ethernet, and wireless 802.11x. Some notable features found in ActiveSync include the following:

- A File Explorer that allows you to drag and drop files between your desktop computer and your Pocket PC

- A Backup and Restore program to keep your Pocket PC data safe

- The ability to add and remove Pocket PC programs in the same manner as Windows on the desktop

- The ability to import and export databases and tables

- The ability to synchronize with various desktop and Internet applications

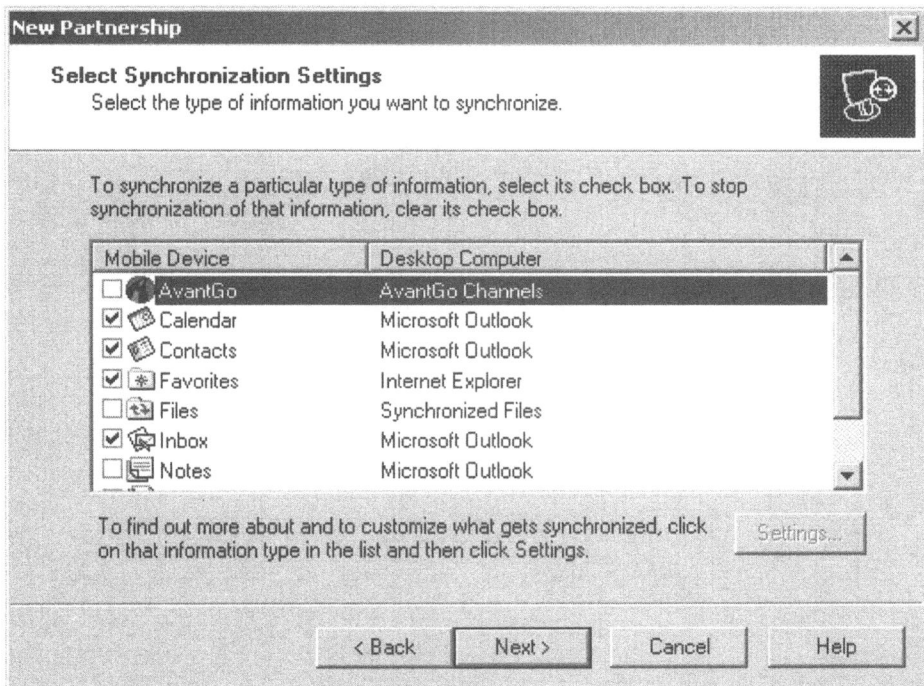

Figure 1-4. Selecting synchronization settings

I personally think the most important element of ActiveSync is the pass-through feature that allows your device to connect to either the Internet or network resources in the enterprise when it's in the cradle. This allows you to test applications that utilize TCP/IP networks even if your device doesn't have a wireless network card. This feature will be very important later in the book when I show you how to replicate data across the network with SQL Server 2000.

Smart Device Extensions Walkthrough

By now, you're probably anxious to build your first .NET Compact Framework application with Visual Studio .NET 2003 and the Smart Device Extensions. To get started with your first Smart Device Application project, you'll need to click the

New Project button on the Start Page. Alternatively, you can go to the File menu, and select New | Project to achieve the same result. Either way, you'll be presented with the New Project dialog box as shown in Figure 1-5. In the Project Types pane, you can choose which language you'd like to use. In the Templates pane, you get to select a particular project template based on whether you want to build a Windows or Web application among other things. In this case, you're going to choose a Visual Basic Project and a Smart Device Application, specify a clever name for your project, and then click OK.

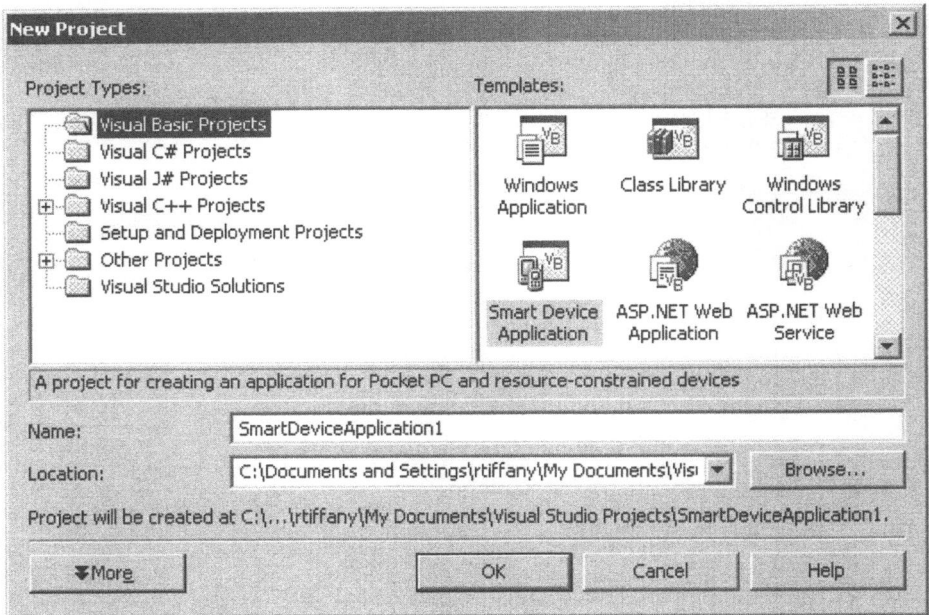

Figure 1-5. New Project dialog box

Smart Device Application Wizard

You are now presented with a dialog box that allows you to choose the platform you wish to target as well as the type of project you want to create as shown in Figure 1-6. As you can see, you're currently allowed to target Pocket PCs and Windows CE .NET devices. In the near future, you'll be able to target the Smartphone as well.

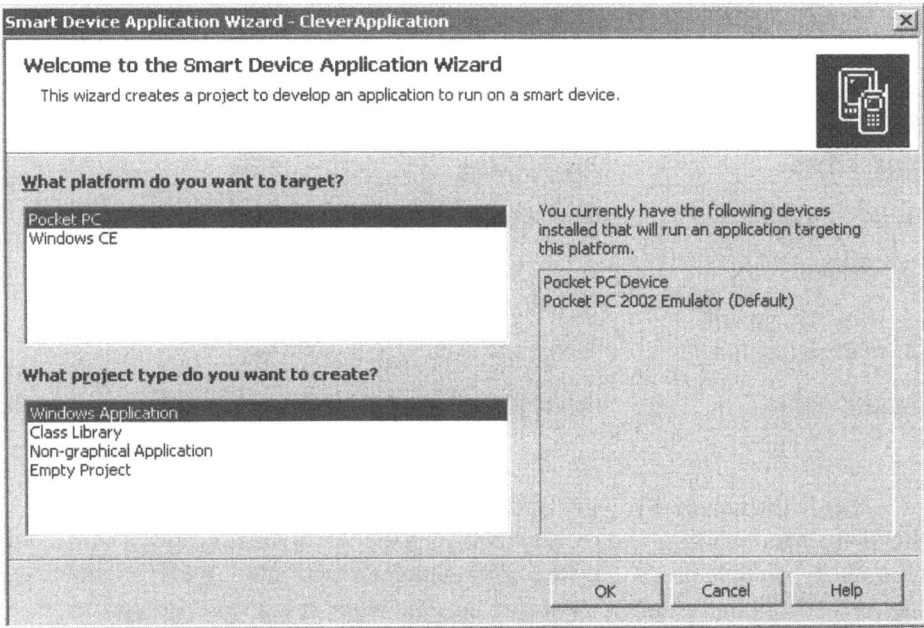

Figure 1-6. Smart Device Application Wizard

The four project types listed in Table 1-1 are available to the Pocket PC 2000 and Pocket PC 2002.

Table 1-1. Pocket PC 2000/2002 Project Types

PROJECT TYPE	DESCRIPTION
Windows Application	An application that utilizes Windows Forms
Class Library	A DLL containing classes and methods that may be used by other applications
Non-graphical Application	An application that has no user interface and doesn't require user interaction
Empty Project	A project without any files

Likewise, Table 1-2 describes the four project types that are available for Windows CE .NET.

Table 1-2. Windows CE .NET Project Types

PROJECT TYPE	DESCRIPTION
Windows Application	An application that utilizes Windows Forms
Class Library	A DLL containing classes and methods that may be used by other applications
Console Application	A command-line application like DOS
Empty Project	A project without any files

Despite the fact that you get all these great choices, I want you to select a Pocket PC Windows Application and then click OK. After your computer thinks for a moment, you'll be presented with your Pocket PC Windows project as shown in Figure 1-7. It's time to start dragging, dropping, referencing, and coding.

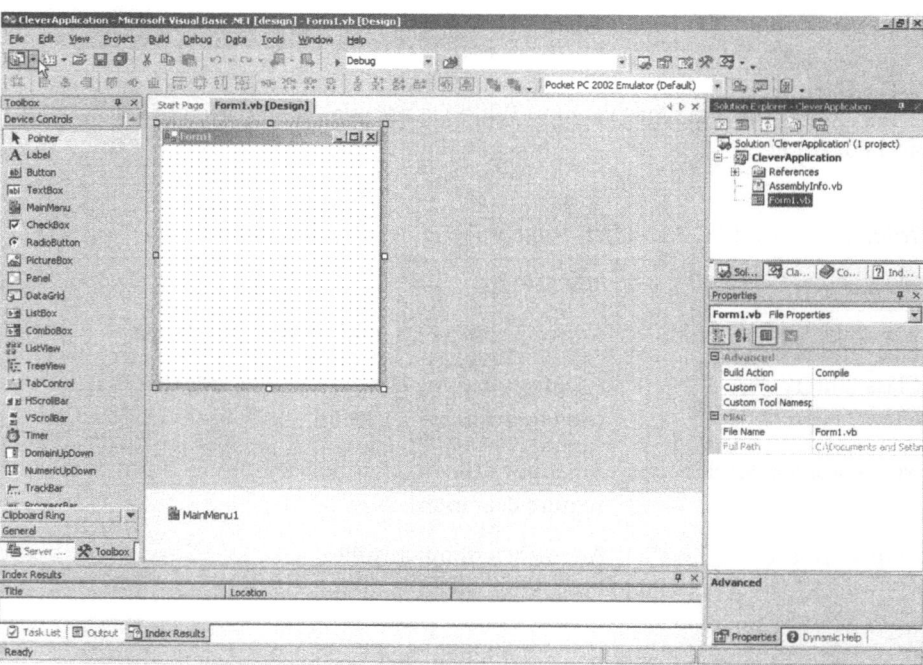

Figure 1-7. Smart Device Project running inside Visual Studio .NET

Forms Designer

As you can see, your Pocket PC project looks just like a standard Windows Forms project that you'd expect to see on the desktop. The only difference is that your form is only 295 pixels high by 246 pixels wide. On the left side of the IDE, you can see the familiar Toolbox containing almost 30 different controls to help you build rich graphical user interfaces. These controls can be added to your form either by double-clicking the control or by clicking and drawing the control on your form's surface. Controls with a runtime user interface include the following:

- Button

- CheckBox

- ComboBox

- DataGrid

- DomainUpDown

- HscrollBar

- Label

- ListBox

- ListView

- NumericUpDown

- Panel

- PictureBox

- ProgressBar

- RadioButton

- StatusBar

- TabControl

- TextBox

- ToolBar

- TrackBar

- TreeView

- VscrollBar

You also have a number of controls without any kind of runtime or design-time user interface. Instead, these controls display themselves in the panel below your form:

- ContextMenu

- ImageList

- InputPanel

- MainMenu

- OpenFileDialog

- SaveFileDialog

- Timer

Thinking back in time, I don't recall either Visual Basic 3 or 4 having this many controls. Since the purpose of this walkthrough is to get you up and running with the Smart Device Extensions, go ahead and drop a Button control anywhere on the form you like. Normally, you might be asked to display "Hello World" when you click on the button. Since this book targets SQL Server CE specifically, I'll have you do things a little differently. Double-click the Button control to bring up the code window for the button's click event. Inside that click event, type MessageBox.Show("Hello SQL") as shown in Figure 1-8.

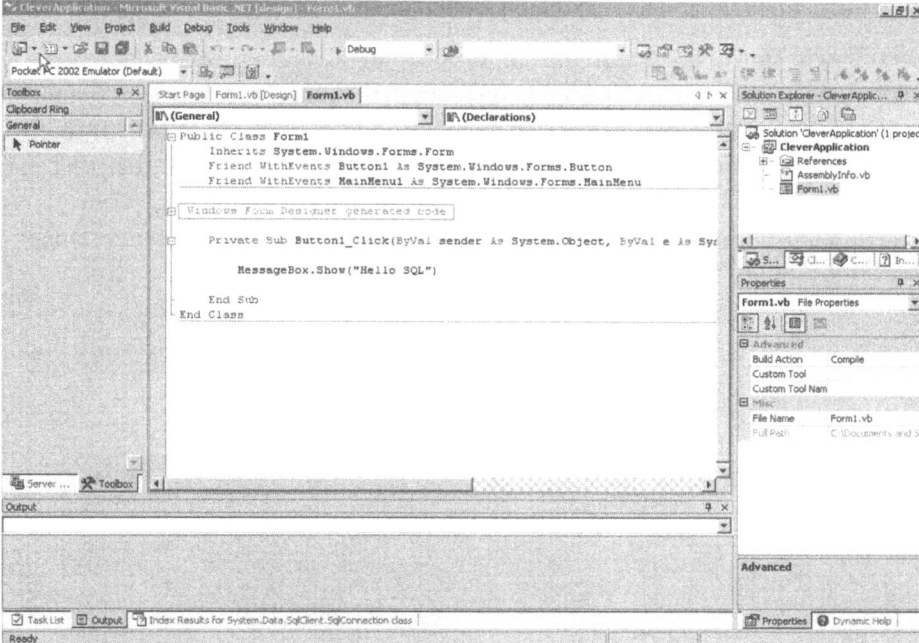

Figure 1-8. Visual Studio .NET code window

Before you move on, I have one little adjustment I'd like you to make while you're working with the Forms Designer. One of my personal pet peeves deals with the familiar circle with an X or OK in the middle that you find in the upper-right corner of your application. Presumably, you tap on this to close your application. You might be surprised to know that this is actually a minimize button. Under normal circumstances, when you tap on this button, your program disappears, but it's actually still running in the background, taking up resources. This behavior might be fine for some applications, but it's not a good idea when your application has an open connection to a SQL Server CE database. Luckily, there is a way to fix this problem. With your form displayed in the Forms Designer, go to the MinimizeBox property and set it to False. Problem solved. Tapping on the X or OK will now close your application and return its resources back to the operating system.

References

On the right side of the IDE in the Solution Explorer, you've probably noticed a folder labeled References. The items beneath the References folder signify that special functionality has been added to your application. For instance, the fact that you see System.XML beneath the References folder means that the ability to work with XML has been added to your application. If you need to give your program more capabilities, doing so is as easy as adding a new reference. Since this book is about SQL Server CE, you'll find yourself needing to add additional references to get the job done. Practice this task by right-clicking the References folder and then selecting Add Reference. The Add Reference dialog box will pop up, displaying a list of .NET components as shown in Figure 1-9.

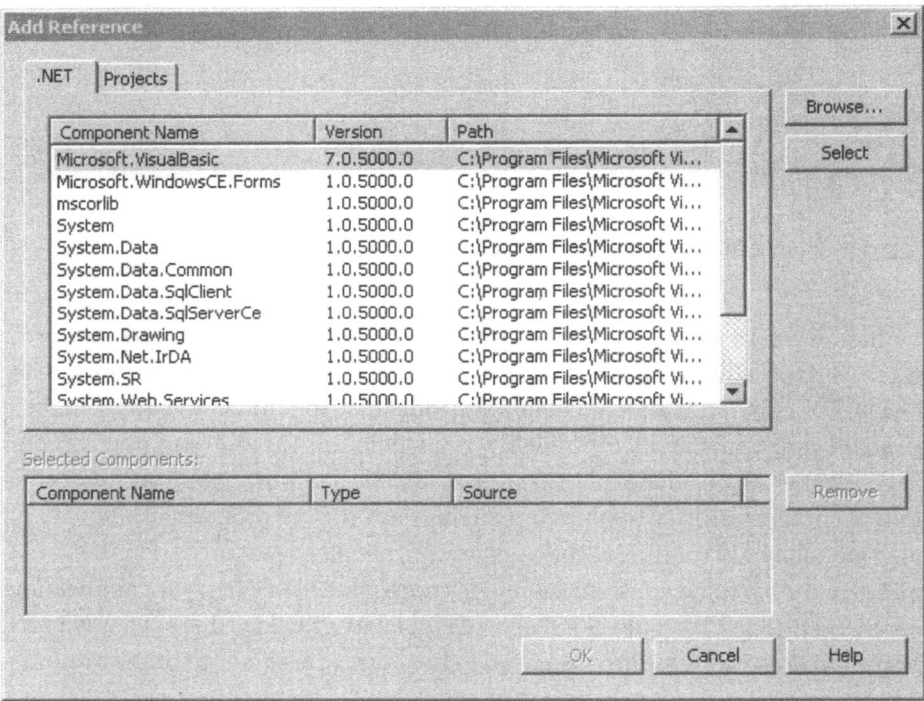

Figure 1-9. Add Reference dialog box

Double-click both System.Data.Common and System.Data.SqlServerCe and then click OK, since those are the two most frequently needed references in this book. The reference to System.Data.Common allows you to work with things like DataSets. These XML-based structures will be utilized later in the book when you want to bind the results of your queries to a DataGrid. Referencing

System.Data.SqlServerCe gives you the power to communicate with SQL Server CE via ADO.NET. Any time you need to work with SQL Server CE, you must have this reference added to your project if you want your applications to work. Additionally, having System.Data.SqlServerCe referenced tells Visual Studio .NET that it needs to copy and install SQL Server CE to either the emulator or your device when the time comes to debug or deploy.

Project Properties

As you might imagine, your Smart Device Extension applications have all kinds of properties that can be set through the Project Property Pages dialog box. This dialog box can be activated by clicking the Project menu and then selecting the <Application Name> Properties menu item. As shown in Figure 1-10, you can set properties to optimize your application, alter the assembly name, and modify how the compiler performs type conversions.

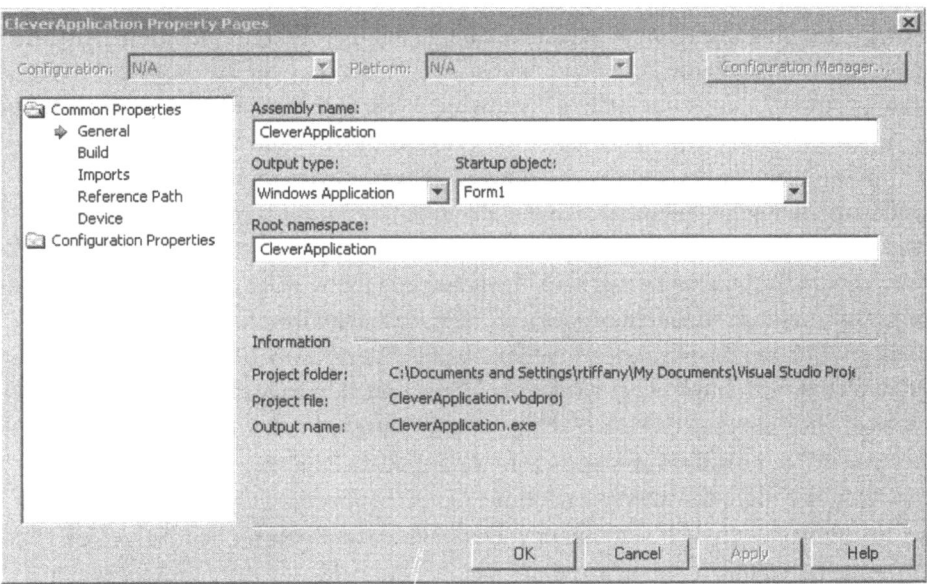

Figure 1-10. Property Pages dialog box

For this walkthrough, I'm only interested in showing you how to control where your application is deployed and how to give it an icon. If you click Device under Common Properties, you'll see a textbox called Output file folder. This is the key to making sure your application ends up where you intend it to go. If you want your application to show up on the Start Menu, type \Windows\Start Menu into the textbox. If, on the other hand, you want it to show up with all the other programs like Pocket Word and Excel, type in \Windows\Start Menu\Programs. With your output path set the way you want it, click Build under Common Properties in Visual Basic .NET or General in C# to display the Application Icon combo box. Click the ellipsis button to the right of the combo box in order to browse for an icon. The icons included with Visual Studio .NET can be found at C:\Program Files\Microsoft Visual Studio .NET 2003\Common7\Graphics\icons. Once you've chosen an icon, you'll see that its filename has been added to the Solution Explorer if you're using Visual Basic .NET. In order to prevent the icon from being sent along as just an additional file, you need to highlight the filename, drop down to the Properties area below the Solution Explorer, and set the Build Action property to Embedded Resource. In C#, you won't see the icon in the Solution Explorer.

Sending Extra Files

In the last section, I showed you how to prevent your icon from being deployed with your application as an extra file. Sometimes, there is a good reason to send along extra files with your application during debugging or deployment. Anyone who's ever worked with Microsoft Access or SQL Server over the years has definitely heard of a database called Northwind. Well, SQL Server CE is no exception, as a version of this database comes with your copy of Visual Studio .NET.

In order to get this database deployed to your device or emulator, I'll have to walk you through a few steps. First of all, go to the Solution Explorer, right-click your application name (just below the Solution name), select Add, and then click Add Existing Item. This brings up a file dialog box that will let you search your computer for the desired file. Navigate to C:\Program Files\Microsoft Visual Studio .NET 2003\CompactFrameworkSDK\v1.0.5000\Windows CE\Samples\VB\Pocket PC\NorthwindCE and select NorthwindDemo.sdf. You may need to adjust the file types of your file dialog box to (*.*) in order to find it. Once you've selected it, NorthwindDemo.sdf should appear in the Solution Explorer. This time around, highlight the filename and set the Build Action property to Content. Getting this set properly will ensure that this new Northwind database for SQL Server CE gets deployed to your device and/or emulator. It's important to note that following these steps to get NorthwindDemo.sdf deployed to your device or emulator is not just a request. Most of the examples found throughout the book rely on the fact that this database has been deployed. Without it, the rest of this book won't be nearly as delightful.

Let's Run It

The wait is now over. If you've followed my instructions carefully, then your new .NET Compact Framework application is ready to go. Unfortunately, there are just a few more steps to follow. First of all, you need to tell Visual Studio .NET where to deploy your application when you run it. This is accomplished by going to the Deployment Device combo box on the toolbar and selecting either Pocket PC Device as shown in Figure 1-11 or Pocket PC 2002 Emulator as shown in Figure 1-12. Remember, your device must be connected to your desktop via ActiveSync in order to successfully deploy your application to your device.

Figure 1-11. Deploying to a Pocket PC device

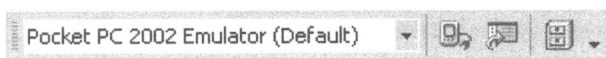

Figure 1-12. Deploying to the emulator

One other choice you can make before running your program is to select either Debug or Release from the Solution Configurations combo box found on the toolbar. If you choose Debug, you'll be able to set breakpoints and utilize the full debugging capabilities of Visual Studio .NET regardless of whether you're deploying to the emulator or to your Pocket PC. If you choose Release, Visual Studio .NET will build an optimized executable for deployment. For our purposes, select Pocket PC 2002 Emulator and Debug, and then click the Start button on the toolbar as shown in Figure 1-13 in order to get things going.

▶   *Figure 1-13. Start button*

A Deploy dialog box will pop up immediately after clicking the Start button, as shown in Figure 1-14. This dialog box is somewhat redundant to the choices you've already made, but it gives you a second chance to change your mind in regards to your deployment target. It also reminds you that if your device doesn't already have the .NET Compact Framework installed, it will take care of that task for you automatically.

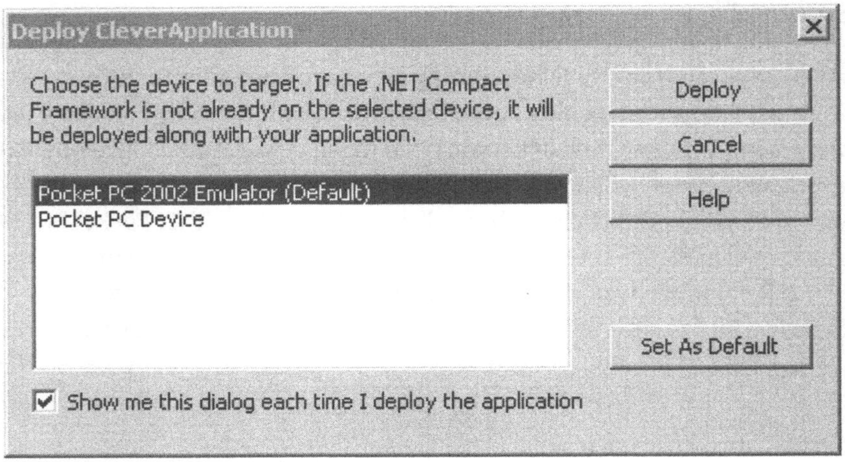

Figure 1-14. Deploy dialog box

Once you hit the Deploy button, the emulator should load in anticipation of your application being deployed to it, as shown in Figure 1-15.

Those of you who worked with the emulators that came with the eMbedded Visual Tools should be pleasantly surprised. Whereas the unreliable older emulators were a close approximation to a Pocket PC, the new emulator in Visual Studio .NET is an exact device image. This means that testing your application in the emulator will yield the same results as testing on an actual device, which is especially good news if you don't own a Pocket PC but want to develop applications for them anyway. A final look at your emulator as illustrated in Figure 1-16 should show your Hello SQL application running in all its glory. If this is the first time you've built and deployed a .NET Compact Framework application, then congratulations.

I have one bit of housekeeping left for you to do before moving on. When you deployed your Hello SQL application to your emulator (or device if your weren't following directions), you also sent along a copy of the NorthwindDemo.sdf database. This database file now resides in the same folder as your application. What I need for you to do now is launch the Pocket PC File Explorer, navigate to your application's directory, and then copy and paste NorthwindDemo.sdf from there to the \My Documents folder. All my examples will utilize the \My Documents folder throughout the book.

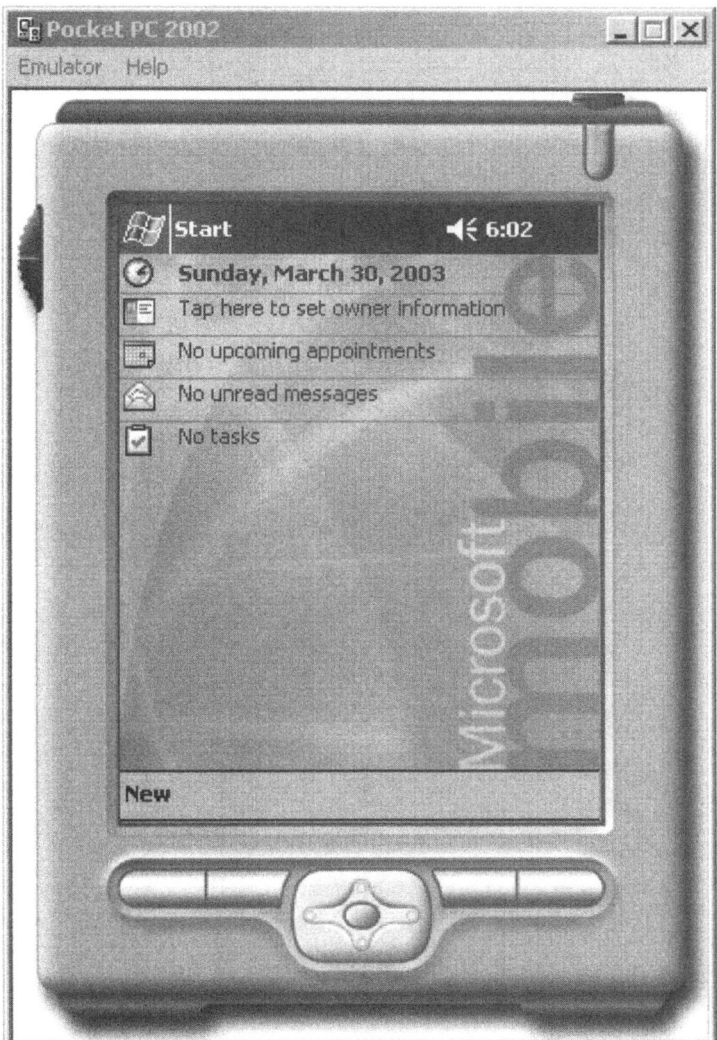

Figure 1-15. The Pocket PC 2002 emulator

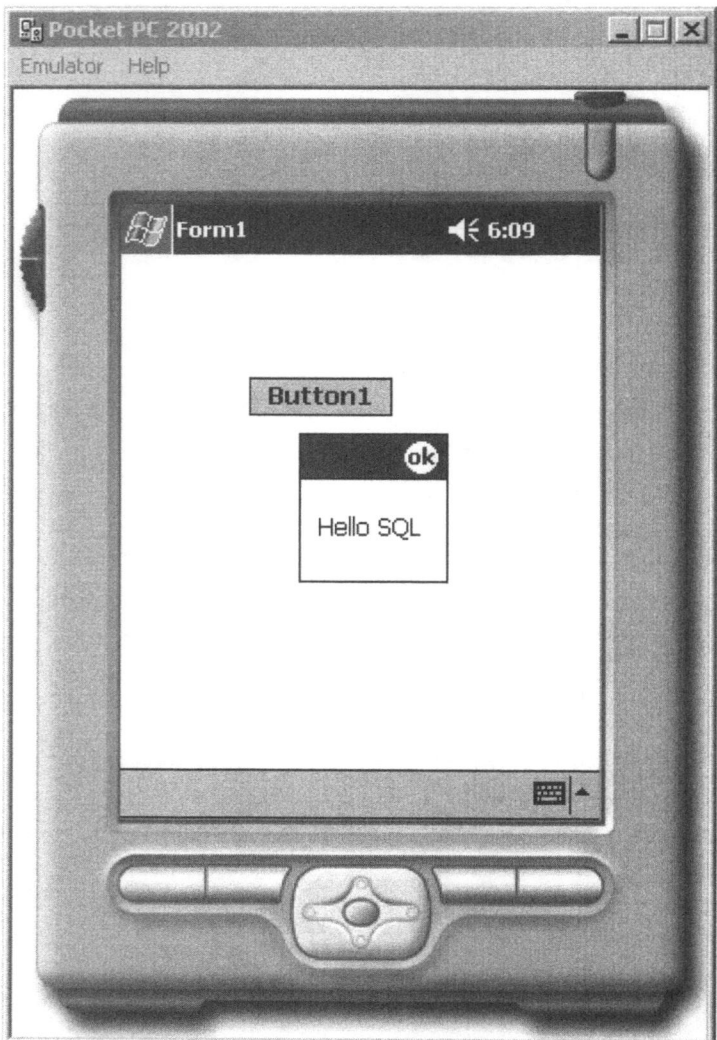

Figure 1-16. Hello SQL application

Security Considerations

In this day and age, it's not enough to just teach the reader how to write code and create useful applications. There are too many groups and individuals out there who have nothing better to do than wreak havoc on today's computer systems and software applications. This might include an anarchist who just wants to deface a Web site, a thief who wants to steal credit cards numbers, or a disgruntled corporate insider who wants to find out everything he or she can about his or her fellow employees from an HR database.

 NOTE *In 2002, the GIGA Information Group stated that mobile devices are the most severe and overlooked security threats to the enterprise.*

Device Security

When the Pocket PC first came out, your security options were either a 4-digit PIN or nothing at all. Initially targeted at individual consumers where Palm reigned supreme, security wasn't really an important issue to anyone. The Pocket PC soon began to grow in market share by leaps and bounds in the corporate world due to its superior processor power, larger amounts of memory, multithreading, and support for enterprise applications. As the numbers of Pocket PCs grew inside corporations and government agencies, so too did the amount of sensitive data residing on their RAM drives. A lost or stolen Pocket PC that hasn't been secured can lead to devastating consequences depending on the data that's compromised. You do have a few options available to you when it comes to securing data on your Pocket PC. When the Pocket PC 2002 operating system was released, the devices finally had support for stronger, alphanumeric passwords. I strongly recommend that anyone using a Pocket PC with data that musn't be compromised use a strong password.

What's not a strong password?

- One that uses any part of your name or login name

- One that uses consecutive letters or numbers

- One that uses an actual name or word from any language

- One that uses numbers in place of similar letters

- One that uses repeating sequences or letters or numbers

- One that uses adjacent keys on the keyboard

What is a strong password?

- One that's at least seven characters in length or longer

- One that includes upper- and lowercase letters, numbers, and symbols

- One that looks like a sequence of random letters and numbers

- One that has at least four different characters with no repeats

It goes without saying that the password must be easy to remember but hard to guess. Biometrics has arrived on the scene with the release of the HP iPAQ h5450. This device already supports strong passwords and then layers on a fingerprint reader to effectively double the amount of security for the operating system. Keep in mind, though, that neither of these protective measures will save you if your sensitive data is residing on a secure digital or compact flash card. Unless you've somehow encrypted these files using the Pocket PC's built-in Crypto API, you'll be out of luck. The Crypto API is not supported in the .NET Compact Framework, but it can be accessed via native code.

Database Security

Pocket Access has no security features, so don't use it to store sensitive data. SQL Server CE 2.0 is the smart choice when your databases must remain secure. For starters, SQL Server CE supports the use of strong passwords on database files. That's a great first line of defense, so use it. But what if an unsavory character decides to open the database file using a hex editor? Luckily, SQL Server CE supports 128-bit encryption on its database files. Problem solved. Even if your database is stored on a removable card, the information inside the database will never be compromised. This brings up an interesting point. Don't just assume that you can only protect your rows and columns of Integers and NVarchars. SQL Server CE is also capable of storing binary data. That means you can safely store your sensitive Word documents and Excel spreadsheets in the database as well. It should be noted that not all OEMs include the necessary files for SQL Server CE to do encryption. Therefore, it may be necessary to download the high encryption pack from Microsoft at http://www.microsoft.com/downloads/details.aspx?displaylang=en&familyid=DA49D0CF-EF96-4567-B817-215E24668F75. The last thing to remember about database security relates to the use of remote data access and replication with SQL Server 2000. Since your Pocket PC is potentially interacting with IIS over the public Internet, don't forget to secure that connection with SSL.

Future Issues

More and more Pocket PC devices are becoming wireless enabled. Whether through Bluetooth, CDPD, 802.11x, GPRS (2.5G), or CDMA/1xRTT (3G), a greater number of devices are able to interact with the world around them. Increasingly, that also means that the world surrounding the Pocket PC will begin to probe these devices in the same way a hacker uses a port scanner against a router or firewall. For now, most of the wireless-enabled Pocket PC devices are operating behind the corporate firewall. While they're most likely safe from Internet-based attacks, they aren't safe from prying corporate insiders. Today, we can't even imagine what kinds of network-aware applications will be built for the Pocket PC in the future. One thing's for sure: As more devices find their way on to the public Internet, they will be susceptible to the same issues faced by any other type of computer that finds itself on the wrong side of the DMZ.

Deployment

You're probably thinking that I already covered deployment earlier in this chapter. As long as you're only deploying to the device that's connected to your development computer, you'd be correct. Visual Studio .NET has made you lazy by taking care of things like installing the .NET Compact Framework, SQL Server CE, and your application on your development device or emulator. When the time comes to deploy these various elements to a thousand Pocket PCs that will be used throughout your company, you'll need to know how to get the job done on a much wider scale. The good news is that Visual Studio .NET provides you with all these different components packaged up in Cab files that target specific processors.

Deploying the .NET Compact Framework and SQL Server CE

Everything you need to get the .NET Compact Framework and SQL Server CE deployed to a device is included in Visual Studio .NET, packaged up as Cab files. All you have to do is copy the appropriate Cab file to the device, and tap on the file with your stylus to have everything installed for you. The self-installing Cab files even delete themselves after the installation is complete. Cab files for Windows CE 3.0 devices can be found in C:\Program Files\Microsoft Visual Studio .NET 2003\CompactFrameworkSDK\v1.0.5000\Windows CE\wce300. Cab files for Windows CE 4.x devices can be found in C:\Program Files\Microsoft Visual Studio .NET 2003\CompactFrameworkSDK\v1.0.5000\Windows CE\wce400. The subdirectories you find beneath the paths to Windows CE 3 and 4.x devices are labeled according to their processor type. Examples include arm, sh3, x86, and mips. Inside those processor-specific folders are the actual Cab files that you'll want to deploy. The .NET Compact Framework Cab files start with netcf, whereas the SQL Server CE Cab files start with sqlce. Since there are two sqlce files found in every processor folder, it's important to know that the ones with dev included in their filename are only needed if you want to install Query Analyzer on the target device.

Deploying Your Application

Since all Pocket PC installations are based on Cab files, it only makes sense that you'll have to create one for your application once it's complete. For starters, make sure that you switch the Solution Configurations combo on the toolbar from Debug to Release and then do a build of your application. Now all you have to do is go to the Build menu and select the Build Cab File menu item to create your Cab file. A series of console windows will pop up as Visual Studio .NET builds the appropriate Cab files. These files will be saved in the \cab\Release subdirectory beneath your project folder. Once you've ensured that your target devices already have the .NET Compact Framework and/or SQL Server CE installed, you can feel free to go ahead with your own installation.

Deployment Options

The key thing you've learned in this section on deployment is to get the appropriate Cab file on the target device and then initiate the installation process by tapping on the Cab file. What I haven't talked about is how best to get those Cab files on your device. The first option that comes to mind is to use ActiveSync to transfer the files to the device. This method is fine if there are only a few devices to deploy to. A better way to go would be to put the necessary Cabs on either compact flash or smart digital cards and hand them out to the users of the target devices for installation. This is especially good for an offline environment with the added bonus that users have the original installation files in case something goes wrong with their Pocket PC. If you have a well-connected environment, you should consider a Web-based installation. Using Pocket Internet Explorer, Pocket PC users could navigate to an appropriate Web page that contains hyperlinks that point to the various Cab files. The files would automatically download to the local device and then the user could initiate the installation. This is definitely the most scalable way to get a lot of devices updated.

Conclusion

This chapter has touched on elements of SQL Server CE 2.0, the .NET Compact Framework, security, and deployment. Its main goal, though, is to make sure that you're comfortable enough with the Smart Device Extensions that you'll be able to understand and work through the examples presented to you throughout the rest of the book. It's not meant to be an exhaustive look at SDE by any means, just enough to get you going. Now that you're up and running, it's time for ADO.NET.

ADO.NET

NOW THAT YOU KNOW the basics of building and deploying .NET Compact
Framework applications utilizing the Smart Device Extensions, it's time to learn
about the technology used to connect those applications to SQL Server CE 2.0.
ADO.NET is the latest generation of Microsoft data access technology in a family
tree that extends back to ODBC from the Precambrian period. If you did any Visual
Basic and MS Access programming in the early to mid '90s, you probably
remember using Data Access Objects (DAO) to communicate with the Jet engine. A
little later on, Microsoft released a collection of hierarchical objects, called Remote
Data Objects (RDO), that wrapped around ODBC to make life a little easier for
those needing to communicate with enterprise databases. ActiveX Data Objects
(ADO) finally made it onto the scene with the release of the first version of Active
Server Pages (Denali). Because it provided an easy-to-use flat layer of objects on
top of the OLE DB technology for universal database access, ADO was a huge hit.

Now if you were thinking that ADO.NET is just a new version of ADO, you'd be
both wrong and right at the same time. In the purest sense, ADO.NET is nothing
more than a marketing term to describe the namespaces and classes found in the
System.Data namespace in the .NET Framework and is an entirely new data access
technology. Luckily, ADO.NET comes with providers that support both OLE DB
and ODBC data sources just in case your database doesn't come with native
ADO.NET drivers. Probably the most notable thing about ADO.NET is that it provides the best support yet for a completely disconnected model of database
access. The ability to connect to a database at the last possible moment, execute a
query, return data and metadata in an XML format called a DataSet, and then
immediately disconnect from that database provides incredible scalability to mul-
tiuser applications.

In the narrow context of this book, ADO.NET's support for a single connection
to SQL Server CE 2.0 means that scalability isn't as important. Luckily, ADO.NET
also comes armed with a faster, more traditional connected model for working
with databases that you'll find makes more sense when building applications that
use a local database on the Pocket PC. In order to get an initial sense of its capabilities, let's take a look at the ADO.NET namespaces supported by the .NET Compact
Framework.

Namespaces

As I mentioned previously, *ADO.NET* is a term used to generically convey a collection of namespaces and classes that provide data access. Different data capabilities can be added to your application by referencing one or more of the following namespaces.

System.Data

The System.Data namespace is the most of important of all ADO.NET namespaces and provides the foundation for all data access functionality found in the .NET Compact Framework. This namespace is always referenced by default when creating a WinForm-based Smart Device Application. Additionally, this namespace is home to the DataSet class as well as the DataTable, DataColumn, DataRow, and DataView classes.

System.Data.Common

The System.Data.Common namespace is home to the important DataAdapter object, which is used to fill DataSets with data. It also contains classes that help you to create custom table and column mappings between a source database table and a DataTable that gets created inside a DataSet by the DataAdapter. These classes are shared by data providers, thus the .Common distinction.

System.Data.SqlClient

The System.Data.SqlClient namespace is where all the SQL Server Data Provider objects are found. Because this provider is not in the scope of this book, I won't be discussing it in detail. However, you may be interested to know that this provider is the same as the SQL Server provider you may have used on the desktop. The same code you've used in the big .NET Framework will have your .NET Compact Framework application communicating with SQL Server 7 or later directly from your Pocket PC in a two-tier fashion. You can even call stored procedures and use unnamed (?) parameters. Interestingly enough, this data provider supports Windows authentication as long as you pass in the domain, user ID, and password in the connection string. On the other hand, things like connection pooling and distributed transactions are not supported from the Pocket PC.

System.Data.SqlServerCe

The System.Data.SqlServerCe namespace is where the focus of this book lies. This namespace contains all the objects associated with the SQL Server CE 2.0 Data Provider such as SqlCeConnection, SqlCeCommand, SqlCeDataAdapter, and Sql-CeDataReader. This data provider also supports classes that aren't seen elsewhere with other databases, such as the SqlCeEngine class to create and compact databases and the SqlCeReplication and SqlCeRemoteDataAccess classes to perform data synchronization with SQL Server. Like the SqlClient data provider, it supports unnamed (?) parameterized queries, but it doesn't support stored procedures. No surprise there, since SQL Server CE 2.0 doesn't support stored procedures either. It also supports SQL Server CE's database encryption and password protection. Without further ado, let's take a look at the "Big 4" objects that make up ADO.NET in the .NET Compact Framework.

The SqlCeConnection Class

It goes without saying that you've got to be connected to a database if you want your queries to run, so it should come as no surprise that Microsoft has provided a connection class to handle getting you connected to a data source. Creating a Sql-CeConnection object will give you a single connection to SQL Server CE 2.0. Back at the beginning of this chapter, I mentioned that scalability isn't really an issue when developing locally on the handheld against SQL Server CE, because you're dealing with a single-user scenario. Therefore, rather than creating scalable code, I recommend creating a single, global connection variable that remains in scope for the lifetime of your application. To ensure that your code works properly, above your class declaration insert

```
using System.Data.SqlServerCe;
```

for C# or

```
Imports System.Data.SqlServerCe
```

for Visual Basic .NET. At the class level, your connection variable would be declared as described by the following code:

Visual Basic .NET

```
Dim cn as SqlCeConnection
```

C#

```
SqlCeConnection cn = null;
```

Now it's just a matter of calling the SqlCeConnection constructor in order to create the object and thus the connection. You can choose to do this either when your application loads or perhaps just before you need to execute your first query. The constructor can be called either with a connection string . . .

Visual Basic .NET

```
cn = New SqlCeConnection("Data Source=\My Documents\NorthwindDemo.sdf;Password=")
```

C#

```
cn = new SqlCeConnection("Data Source=\\My Documents\\NorthwindDemo.sdf;" +
Password=");
```

. . . or without one if you plan to use the ConnectionString property later on.

Visual Basic .NET

```
cn = New SqlCeConnection()
```

C#

```
cn = new SqlCeConnection();
```

Speaking of properties, take a look at Tables 2-1 and 2-2 to get a quick rundown of the most widely used properties and methods of the SqlCeConnection class.

Table 2-1. SqlCeConnection Properties

PROPERTY	DESCRIPTION
ConnectionString	String used to open a SQL Server CE database
ConnectionTimeout	Amount of time to wait while attempting to create a connection before generating an error
Database	Name of the current database
DataSource	Full path and filename of the database
State	Current state of the database connection

Table 2-2. SqlCeConnection Methods

METHOD	DESCRIPTION
BeginTransaction	Begins a transaction in conjunction with the SqlCeTransaction object
Close	Closes an open connection to a data source
CreateCommand	Creates and returns a SqlCeCommand object
Open	Opens a database connection

Taking a look at the SqlCeConnection properties, you'll notice that you have the opportunity to use the same connection string that I previously demonstrated with the SqlCeConnection constructor. You'll choose to use this property if you decide not to pass a parameter to the constructor. Moving along, you'll be disappointed to know that the ConnectionTimeout property is essentially useless in that it doesn't allow you to set a user-defined timeout. It's actually a read-only property, and the timeout value for SQL Server CE is always zero. Both the Database and the DataSource properties are also read-only and return the path and filename of the database. The bottom line is that before you call the Open method, the only choice you'll need to concern yourself with is either passing the connection string to the constructor or assigning it in conjunction with the ConnectionString property.

Visual Basic .NET

```
cn = New SqlCeConnection()
cn.ConnectionString = "Data Source=\\My Documents\\NorthwindDemo.sdf;Password="
cn.Open()
```

C#

```
cn = new SqlCeConnection();
cn.ConnectionString = "Data Source=\\My Documents\\NorthwindDemo.sdf;Password=";
cn.Open();
```

Last but not least, the State property provides useful information regarding the current state of your database connection as listed in Table 2-3.

Table 2-3. ConnectionState Enum Values

MEMBER NAME	DESCRIPTION	VALUE
Broken	An open connection to a data source has been broken.	16
Closed	Connection is closed.	0
Connecting	Currently connecting to a data source.	2
Executing	Executing a command.	4
Fetching	Retrieving data.	8
Open	Connection is open.	1

Typically, you'll use the State property in conjunction with the Close method.

Visual Basic .NET

```
If cn.State <> ConnectionState.Closed Then
    cn.Close()
End If
```

C#

```
if(cn.State != ConnectionState.Closed)
{
    cn.Close();
}
```

Error Handling

Anyone who's connected to a database before knows that this operation is nothing like sinking a 3-foot putt. There's no guarantee that it's going to work. The network may be down, the database may be in suspect mode, or your connection string might be pointing you in the wrong direction. This is why it's important to use an effective error handling strategy every time you work with a database, and SQL Server CE is no exception.

Luckily for you, the .NET Compact Framework gives you powerful structured error handling in the form of Try-Catch-Finally blocks. You might think that this is all you need, and the Exception object will accurately tell you what kind of error has occurred. Unfortunately, the Exception object will only give you a minimal amount of error data and is therefore not suitable for use as the primary error handler for database operations. Keep in mind that you will still use it as a backup error handler to catch any non-SQL errors. The class that you'll want to use is the SqlCeException class. When catching exceptions with this class, you're provided with a collection of one or more SqlCeErrors that you can iterate through. This way, no stone is left unturned when it comes to figuring out what's wrong with your code or computing environment. I recommend using the following template for all your database error handling needs:

Visual Basic .NET

```
Dim cn As SqlCeConnection
Try
cn = New SqlCeConnection("Data Source=\My Documents\NorthwindDemo.sdf;Password=")
cn.Open()
'Perform your database operation here

'Catch your database errors
Catch sqlex As SqlCeException
    'Declare your SqlCeError object
Dim sqlError As SqlCeError
'Iterate through the collection of database errors
For Each sqlError In sqlex.Errors
    MessageBox.Show(sqlError.Message)
Next

'Catch nondatabase errors
Catch ex As Exception
MessageBox.Show(ex.Message)

'Ensure that the database connection gets closed no matter what errors occur
Finally
If cn.State <> ConnectionState.Closed Then
    cn.Close()
End If
End Try
```

C#

```
SqlCeConnection cn = null;
try
{
cn = new SqlCeConnection("Data Source=\\My Documents\\NorthwindDemo.sdf;" +
```

```
"Password=");
cn.Open();
//Perform your database operation here
}
//Catch your database errors
catch(SqlCeException sqlex)
{
//Iterate through the collection of database errors
foreach(SqlCeError sqlError in sqlex.Errors)
{
    MessageBox.Show(sqlError.Message);
}
}
//Catch nondatabase errors
catch(Exception ex)
{
MessageBox.Show(ex.Message);
}
//Ensure that the database connection gets closed no matter what errors occur
finally
{
if(cn.State != ConnectionState.Closed)
{
    cn.Close();
}
}
}
```

You probably noticed that I haven't touched on the CreateCommand or Begin-Transaction methods of the SqlCeConnection class. Because both of them require elements of the SqlCeCommand class, I'll discuss them with you in the next section.

The SqlCeCommand Class

Now that you know how to connect to SQL Server CE, you'd probably like to get down to business and execute some queries. The SqlCeCommand class allows you to do this and much more. In the last section, I left you hanging just after you called the Open() method of the SqlCeConnection class. Well, now you're going to create a new SqlCeCommand object based on that connection, and you'll utilize the CreateCommand method of the SqlCeConnection class to do so.

Visual Basic .NET

```
Dim cmd As SqlCeCommand = cn.CreateCommand
```

C#

```
SqlCeCommand cmd = cn.CreateCommand();
```

With both your connection open and your command created, you have a number of SqlCeCommand properties and methods at your disposal, and these are listed in Tables 2-4 and 2-5.

Table 2-4. SqlCeCommand Properties

PROPERTY	DESCRIPTION
CommandText	Gets or sets the SQL statement that's executed against the data source
CommandType	Gets or sets a value that determines how the CommandText property is interpreted
Connection	Gets or sets the SqlCeConnection used by this instance of SqlCeCommand
Parameters	Gets the SqlCeParameterCollection
Transaction	Gets or sets the transaction where the SqlCeCommand executes

Table 2-5. SqlCeCommand Methods

METHOD	DESCRIPTION
ExecuteNonQuery	Executes a SQL command and returns the number of rows affected
ExecuteReader	Executes a SQL command and returns a SqlCeDataReader
ExecuteScalar	Executes a SQL command and returns the first column of the first row from the query results
Prepare	Creates a compiled version of the SQL command on the data source

So to clarify things a bit, the CommandText property is what you set equal to your SELECT, INSERT, UPDATE, or DELETE statement. The CommandType property can either be set to Text if you're passing in a query, or it can be set to

TableDirect if you want to return all the columns and rows of data found in a given table. TableDirect works just like a SELECT * statement but is much faster. If you wish to use this feature, you must set the CommandText property equal to the name of the table you wish to query. If you create your SqlCeCommand object in conjunction with the CreateCommand() method of the SqlCeConnection object, then you won't need to use the Connection property for anything.

Parameterized Queries

When it comes to squeezing as much performance as possible out of SQL Server CE, the use of the Parameters property and the Prepare method are invaluable. The majority of your queries will involve the use of values of varying data types that will be passed to the query at runtime. Each time you run this kind of SQL statement, SQL Server CE has to create a new query plan. Even when you're passing in the identical query multiple times, the database slaps you with a performance hit by creating a new plan each time. This performance hit can be avoided by adding your dynamic runtime values to the SqlCeParameterCollection and then calling the Prepare method before executing the query. Performance improvements of 30 percent or more have been reported when following this plan of attack, due to the query plan being created once and then compiled and saved in the database for reuse by subsequent queries. The first step in using parameters is to insert question marks (?) in your command text wherever a dynamic value is needed.

Visual Basic .NET

```
cmd.CommandText = "INSERT INTO Products (" & _
                            "ProductName, " & _
                            "SupplierID, " & _
                            "CategoryID, " & _
                            "UnitPrice, " & _
                            "UnitsInStock, " & _
                            "Discontinued) " & _
                            "VALUES " & _
                            "(?, ?, ?, ?, ?, ?)"
```

C#

```
cmd.CommandText = "INSERT INTO Products (" +
                                "ProductName, " +
                                "SupplierID, " +
                                "CategoryID, " +
                                "UnitPrice, " +
                                "UnitsInStock, " +
                                "Discontinued) " +
                                "VALUES " +
                                "(?, ?, ?, ?, ?, ?)";
```

The next thing you need to do is add all the values represented by question marks to the SqlCeParameterCollection. This is accomplished by calling the Add method of the Parameters property and then passing in a name for the specific parameter and the actual value in literal or variable form. Since SQL Server CE doesn't support named parameters, it doesn't actually matter what name you use for each parameter. All that matters is that you add your parameters in the same order as the question marks in your command text or you may get some errors.

Visual Basic .NET

```
cmd.Parameters.Add("@ProductName", "Axim")
cmd.Parameters.Add("@SupplierID", 1)
cmd.Parameters.Add("@CategoryID", 1)
cmd.Parameters.Add("@UnitPrice", 350)
cmd.Parameters.Add("@UnitsInStock", 20)
cmd.Parameters.Add("@Discontinued", 1)
```

C#

```
cmd.Parameters.Add("@ProductName", "Axim");
cmd.Parameters.Add("@SupplierID", 1);
cmd.Parameters.Add("@CategoryID", 1);
cmd.Parameters.Add("@UnitPrice", 350);
cmd.Parameters.Add("@UnitsInStock", 20);
cmd.Parameters.Add("@Discontinued", 1);
```

The last thing you have to do after setting the command text and parameters is call the Prepare method and then execute the query. If the Prepare method finds a problem with one of your data types due to a variable length issue, it will throw an error. Additionally, keep in mind that Prepare will not work if you set your CommandType to TableDirect. I strongly recommend you take advantage of the Parameter-Prepare combo in all your database applications.

Visual Basic .NET

```
cmd.Prepare()
cmd.ExecuteNonQuery()
```

C#

```
cmd.Prepare();
cmd.ExecuteNonQuery();
```

Transactions

Whenever you run a single query, it commits itself automatically once the query has been executed. In some cases, you may have two or more queries that you'd like to run as a single unit of work, and you don't want to commit their changes to the database until all the queries have been successful. You may want to return the database to its original state in the event that one of your queries fails.

This is precisely how things work at your bank when you want to transfer some money, say $10, from your checking account to your savings account. An UPDATE query is run against your checking account in order to reduce your balance by $10. Then another UPDATE query is run against your savings account to increase your balance by $10. What if the UPDATE query executed against your savings account failed? Without the power to run multiple queries as a single unit of work, you would've lost $10.

ADO.NET provides you with a Transaction object that works in conjunction with both the SqlCeConnection and SqlCeCommand objects. This object gives you the power to wrap multiple SQL statements in a single transaction that only commits if all the queries execute successfully. The first thing you have to do is declare a SqlCeTransaction variable and then instantiate the object by a setting the variable equal to the BeginTransaction method of the SqlCeConnection object. Once you set the Transaction property of the SqlCeCommand object equal to your new transaction object, you can begin executing your queries as a single unit. After the last query has executed, call the Commit method of your transaction object. On the other hand, if the execution of one of your queries causes an exception to be thrown, make sure that you call the Rollback method of your transaction object inside the Catch block to ensure that none of your database changes are committed.

Visual Basic .NET

```
Dim cn As SqlCeConnection
Dim trans as SqlCeTransaction

Try
cn = New SqlCeConnection("Data Source=\My Documents\NorthwindDemo.sdf;Password=")
cn.Open()
Dim cmd As SqlCeCommand = cn.CreateCommand

'Declare your SqlCeTransaction object
 'Start your transaction by calling the BeginTransaction method
trans = cn.BeginTransaction()
'Assign SqlCeTransaction object to the command
cmd.Transaction = trans

 'Perform your transactional database operations here

    'If all goes well
    trans.Commit()
Catch sqlex As SqlCeException
    'If things don't go so well
    trans.Rollback()
Dim sqlError As SqlCeError
For Each sqlError In sqlex.Errors
    MessageBox.Show(sqlError.Message)
Next
Catch ex As Exception
MessageBox.Show(ex.Message)
Finally
If cn.State <> ConnectionState.Closed Then
    cn.Close()
End If
End Try
```

C#

```csharp
SqlCeConnection cn = null;
SqlCeTransaction trans = null;

try
{
cn = new SqlCeConnection("Data Source=\\My Documents\\NorthwindDemo.sdf;" +
                                        "Password=");
cn.Open();
SqlCeCommand cmd = cn.CreateCommand();

//Declare your SqlCeTransaction object
//Start your transaction by calling the BeginTransaction method
trans = cn.BeginTransaction();
//Assign SqlCeTransaction object to the command
cmd.Transaction = trans;

 //Perform your transactional database operations here

    //If all goes well
    trans.Commit();
}
catch(SqlCeException sqlex)
{
    //If things don't go so well
    trans.Rollback();
foreach(SqlCeError sqlError in sqlex.Errors)
{
    MessageBox.Show(sqlError.Message);
}
}
catch(Exception ex)
{
MessageBox.Show(ex.Message);
}
finally
{
if(cn.State != ConnectionState.Closed)
{
    cn.Close();
}
}
```

The SqlCeDataReader Class

The most notable SqlCeCommand method that I left out of the last section was ExecuteReader. Since the SqlCeDataReader object that this method returns is so important to .NET Compact Framework database development, I figured that it deserved a section of its own. Most of the talk about ADO.NET centers on its glamorous, XML-based, disconnected features. What doesn't get much press for some reason is its connected, high-speed, forward-only SqlCeDataReader class. In the single-user, locally connected world of the Pocket PC, this method of database traversal shines as the true star of ADO.NET on the .NET Compact Framework. Because SqlCeDataReader acts like the firehose cursors that you've worked with in the past with ADO, RDO, and DAO, nothing gets data displayed on your form faster than this class. Tables 2-6 and 2-7 list the most widely used properties and methods found in the SqlCeDataReader class.

Table 2-6. SqlCeDataReader Properties

PROPERTY	DESCRIPTION
FieldCount	Returns the number of columns in the current row
IsClosed	Indicates whether the data reader is closed
Item	Gets the value of a column in its native format
RecordsAffected	Returns the number of rows updated, inserted, or deleted as a result of a SQL statement being executed

Table 2-7. SqlCeDataReader Methods

METHOD	DESCRIPTION
Close	Closes the SqlCeDataReader object
GetBoolean	Returns the value of a column as a Boolean
GetByte	Returns the value of a column as a byte
GetBytes	Reads a stream of bytes from a column
GetChars	Reads a stream of characters from a column
GetDateTime	Returns the value of a column as a DateTime object
GetDecimal	Returns the value of a column as a Decimal object
GetDouble	Returns the value of a column as a double-precision floating-point number
GetFieldType	Returns the data type of a column

Table 2-7. SqlCeDataReader Methods (Continued)

METHOD	DESCRIPTION
GetFloat	Returns the value of a column as a single-precision floating-point number
GetGuid	Returns the value of a column as a globally unique identifier
GetInt16	Returns the value of a column as a 16-bit signed integer
GetInt32	Returns the value of a column as a 32-bit signed integer
GetInt64	Returns the value of a column as a 64-bit signed integer
GetName	Returns the name of a column
GetOrdinal	Returns the column ordinal based on the name of that column
GetString	Returns the value of a column as a string
GetValue	Returns the value of a column at the specified ordinal
GetValues	Returns all the attribute columns in the current row
IsDBNull	Returns a value indicating whether the column contains nonexistent or missing values
Read	Advances SqlCeDataReader to the next record
Seek	Places the SqlCeDataReader on the record with indexed values that match the specified parameters
ToString	Returns a string that represents the current object

Putting the SqlCeDataReader to work for you is extremely simple. First you just declare a SqlCeDataReader variable, and then you instantiate it by setting it equal to the ExecuteReader method of the SqlCeCommand object. Retrieving rows of data is just a matter of utilizing the Read method in conjunction with a While loop. Each time you loop through another row, you retrieve the data in the columns via either the column ordinal or the column name. The following example describes all this and also manages to fill a combo box while utilizing the TableDirect CommandType against the Products table in the NorthwindDemo.sdf database.

Visual Basic .NET

```vb.net
Dim cn As SqlCeConnection
Try
    cn = New SqlCeConnection("Data Source=\My Documents\NorthwindDemo.sdf;" & _
    "Password=")
    cn.Open()
    Dim cmd As SqlCeCommand = cn.CreateCommand
    'Declare the SqlCeDataReader variable
    Dim dr As SqlCeDataReader
    cmd.CommandText = "Products"
    cmd.CommandType = CommandType.TableDirect
    'Instantiate the SqlCeDataReader
    dr = cmd.ExecuteReader()
    'Loop through the rows and fill a combo box
    While dr.Read()
        ComboBox1.Items.Add(dr.GetValue(0))
    End While
    'Close the SqlCeDataReader
    dr.Close()
Catch sqlex As SqlCeException
    Dim sqlError As SqlCeError
    For Each sqlError In sqlex.Errors
        MessageBox.Show(sqlError.Message)
    Next
Catch ex As Exception
    MessageBox.Show(ex.Message)
Finally
    If cn.State <> ConnectionState.Closed Then
        cn.Close()
    End If
End Try
```

C#

```csharp
SqlCeConnection cn = null;
try
{
    cn = new SqlCeConnection("Data Source=\\My Documents\\NorthwindDemo.sdf;" +
                                    "Password=");
    cn.Open();
    SqlCeCommand cmd = cn.CreateCommand();
    //Declare the SqlCeDataReader variable
```

```
        SqlCeDataReader dr;
        cmd.CommandText = "Products";
        cmd.CommandType = CommandType.TableDirect;
        //Instantiate the SqlCeDataReader
        dr = cmd.ExecuteReader();
        //Loop through the rows and fill a combo box
        while (dr.Read()) {
            comboBox1.Items.Add(dr.GetValue(0));
        }
        //Close the SqlCeDataReader
        dr.Close();
    }
    catch(SqlCeException sqlex)
    {
        foreach(SqlCeError sqlError in sqlex.Errors)
        {
            MessageBox.Show(sqlError.Message);
        }
    }
    catch(Exception ex)
    {
        MessageBox.Show(ex.Message);
    }
    finally
    {
        if(cn.State != ConnectionState.Closed)
        {
            cn.Close();
        }
    }
```

The SqlCeDataAdapter Class

A disconnected alternative to the SqlCeDataReader class is the SqlCeDataAdapter class. This class provides a gateway between SQL Server CE and a DataSet object. Rather than looping through a stream of incoming rows to populate the contents of graphical controls as you would with a SqlCeDataReader, the SqlCeDataAdapter automatically fills a DataSet with data based on the query you're executing. The resulting DataSet contains one or more DataTables that can have their contents bound to many of the controls provided by the .NET Compact Framework. In most cases, this data binding is accomplished with only one line of code. The following example pulls back all the rows and columns from the Products table using TableDirect, just like the example in the previous section. This time around, you create both a SqlCeDataAdapter object and a DataSet object. Next, you call the Fill method of your SqlCeDataAdapter object in order to load up the DataSet with the information returned from the TableDirect query. Finally, you set the DataSource property of a DataGrid equal to the first DataTable found inside the DataSet in order to populate the DataGrid with data. Pretty easy, I'd say.

Visual Basic .NET

```vbnet
Dim cn As SqlCeConnection
Try
    cn = New SqlCeConnection("Data Source=\My Documents\NorthwindDemo.sdf;" & _
    "Password=")
    cn.Open()
    Dim cmd As SqlCeCommand = cn.CreateCommand
    cmd.CommandText = "Products"
    cmd.CommandType = CommandType.TableDirect
    'Create a SqlCeDataAdapter object
    Dim da As New SqlCeDataAdapter(cmd)
    'Create a DataSet object
    Dim ds As New DataSet
    'Fill the DataSet
    da.Fill(ds)
    'Bind the DataGrid to the DataTable contained in the DataSet
    DataGrid1.DataSource = ds.Tables(0)
Catch sqlex As SqlCeException
    Dim sqlError As SqlCeError
    For Each sqlError In sqlex.Errors
        MessageBox.Show(sqlError.Message)
    Next
Catch ex As Exception
    MessageBox.Show(ex.Message)
Finally
    If cn.State <> ConnectionState.Closed Then
        cn.Close()
    End If
End Try
```

C#

```csharp
SqlCeConnection cn = null;
try
{
    cn = new SqlCeConnection("Data Source=\\My Documents\\NorthwindDemo.sdf;" +
                                            "Password=");
    cn.Open();
    SqlCeCommand cmd = cn.CreateCommand();
    cmd.CommandText = "Products";
    cmd.CommandType = CommandType.TableDirect;
    //Create a SqlCeDataAdapter object
    SqlCeDataAdapter da = new SqlCeDataAdapter(cmd);
    //Create a DataSet object
    DataSet ds = new DataSet();
    //Fill the DataSet
    da.Fill(ds);
    //Bind the DataGrid to the DataTable contained in the DataSet
    dataGrid1.DataSource = ds.Tables[0];
}
catch(SqlCeException sqlex)
{
    foreach(SqlCeError sqlError in sqlex.Errors)
    {
        MessageBox.Show(sqlError.Message);
    }
}
catch(Exception ex)
{
    MessageBox.Show(ex.Message);
}
finally
{
    if(cn.State != ConnectionState.Closed)
    {
        cn.Close();
    }
}
```

Despite the ease with which you can bind both simple and complex data structures to .NET Compact Framework controls, there are a few caveats. In this current version of the .NET Compact Framework (1.0), the process of using SqlCeDataAdapters to fill DataSets and then bind those DataSets to controls is dramatically slower than using SqlCeDataReaders to programmatically populate controls with data. Furthermore, the use of DataSets when working with SQL Server CE seems very redundant to me. The purpose of the DataSet is to help make server applications more scalable and to allow both Web servers and remotely connected smart clients to cache information locally. In the case of a Pocket PC that calls distant Web services in order to retrieve data, the use of a cached DataSet to serve as a local data source would be appropriate. On the other hand, if this same Pocket PC is instead just accessing data locally from a SQL Server CE database, it's fair to say that a high-performance local data source already exists, and creating another one won't serve any purpose other than to waste memory and slow your application down. I don't have anything against the DataSet object, and it's great that Microsoft has included it in the .NET Compact Framework in order to remain on par with ADO.NET on the desktop and server. From a sound software architectural standpoint, it just doesn't make sense to use it if you're already using SQL Server CE as a local data source.

Conclusion

The purpose of this chapter has been to give you a small glimpse of ADO.NET if you aren't already familiar with this data access technology. If you're a desktop and or server ADO.NET expert, you probably just skimmed through. The fact that such experts could do so is a testament to what a good job Microsoft has done making a miniature version of ADO.NET work just like the full-sized version.

In this chapter, I've covered everything you need to know in order to comprehend the concepts and examples provided throughout the rest of this book. You should now have no problems connecting to SQL Server CE, executing SQL commands against it, and returning data for display in your Windows Forms and associated controls. Hopefully along the way you've picked up an understanding of what will make your SQL Server CE applications run slower, and tips on what you can do to make them run faster. Now it's time for you to learn more about what's possible with SQL Server CE via Query Analyzer.

CHAPTER 3

Query Analyzer

BEFORE THE ARRIVAL OF **SQL SERVER CE,** the only Pocket PC database you really had to work with was Pocket Access. Without a graphical utility to build and manipulate database objects, programmers had to do all this work in code. Anyone who read my last book, *Pocket PC Database Development with eMbedded Visual Basic,* learned how to build their own GUI tool to do this work. Luckily, SQL Server CE comes with a slimmed down version of Query Analyzer that you'll find familiar if you've worked with the SQL Server Query Analyzer over the years. As you might imagine, Query Analyzer allows you to view and work with SQL Server CE databases located on your Pocket PC. Not only will you be able to create, view, and manipulate every conceivable database object, but you'll also be able to create, execute, and save SQL queries and view the results of those queries in a grid.

Installation

Since you can't use Query Analyzer until it's installed, I'll run you through the installation details. By virtue of having Visual Studio .NET installed on your computer, you automatically have the Cab files necessary to get Query Analyzer deployed to your Pocket PC. Query Analyzer is installed on your device or emulator the first time you deploy a .NET Compact Framework application that references the System.Data.SqlServerCe namespace. Deployment can occur by selecting either Deploy Solution from the Build menu or by selecting Start from the Debug menu.

You also have the option of performing a manual installation. The files you need to accomplish this can be found in C:\Program Files\Microsoft Visual Studio .NET 2003\CompactFrameworkSDK\v1.0.5000\Windows CE directory. After that, it's just a matter of selecting the subdirectory that matches your operating system version, either WCE300 or WCE400 for Windows CE 3.0 or 4.0, respectively. Then you need to select the appropriate subdirectory that matches the correct processor for your device. For instance, if you're running a Pocket PC with an ARM or XScale processor, then copy the following files to the root or My Device directory of your device:

- sqlce.pp3.arm.cab to install SQL Server CE 2.0

- sqlce.dev.pp3.arm.cab to install Query Analyzer

A single tap on any of the Cab files will uncompress their contents and get them installed. Query Analyzer is called Isqlw20.exe and will install itself in the \Windows\SQLCE 2.0 directory. Additionally, a shortcut to Query Analyzer called SQLCE Query will be added to the Start menu on your device or emulator. On Pocket PC 2003 devices, the Query Analyzer shortcut will appear on the Program Files menu instead.

Overview

Upon launching Query Analyzer, you'll notice that it's comprised of a Tools menu on the bottom and four tabs on the top, Objects, SQL, Grid, and Notes, as shown in Figure 3-1.

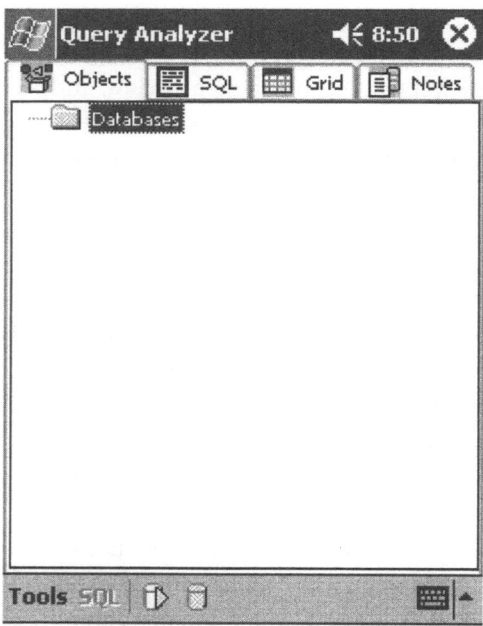

Figure 3-1. Tools menu and Objects, SQL, Grid, and Notes tabs

Before tackling the tabs across the top, I'll briefly describe the Tools menu at the bottom of Query Analyzer. The Refresh menu item refreshes the tree view of all the database objects in the Objects tab. The Logging menu item provides a truly interesting way to learn SQL. Whenever you use one of the visual tools in the Objects tab that performs a DDL or DML statement behind the scenes, that statement is displayed in the SQL tab. The Fonts menu item globally changes the fonts throughout the application. The About menu item displays the version numbers for both Query Analyzer and SQL Server CE. Lastly, the Exit menu item allows you to truly exit the application, whereas the X in the upper-right corner only minimizes Query Analyzer.

Moving on to tabs, the leftmost tab on top of Query Analyzer is the Objects tab. In this tab you can manage connections to databases and their respective objects. Database objects such as tables, columns, and indexes can be viewed and manipulated once a connection is established. The next tab to the right is the SQL tab. Here you're provided with a text editor that allows you to type SQL statements in a free-form manner for execution against the SQL Server CE database. You're also able to save and reuse your SQL statements in this tab. The Grid tab, which comes next, gives you an easy way to view the results of your queries. Last but probably least is the Notes tab. When one of your SQL statements executes successfully, the Notes tab displays how long your query took to run and how many rows may have been affected. Alternatively, if your query crashes and burns, the Notes tab will display an error message and hopefully tell you where you went wrong.

The Objects Tab

As discussed previously, the Objects tab is used to manage databases, their objects, and their connections. In order to better visualize how things work in this tab, you'll utilize the NorthwindDemo.sdf database that you uploaded to your device or emulator back in Chapter 1.

Connecting to an Unmanaged Database

The first time you use Query Analyzer, it's in a state where it isn't managing any databases and therefore looks like Figure 3-1. In other words, the Objects tab is showing the Databases folder and nothing else. In order to connect to the NorthwindDemo.sdf database in this unmanaged state, you must tap the database connection button found on the toolbar as shown in Figure 3-2.

 Figure 3-2. Database connection button with green arrow

The database connection button must be showing a green arrow in order to successfully connect to a database. Once you've tapped the button, a Connect to SQL Server CE dialog box pops up as shown in Figure 3-3.

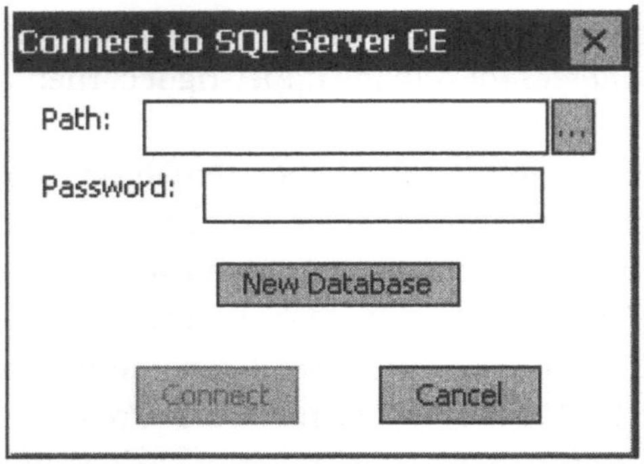

Connect to SQL Server CE ✕

Path: [   ] [...]

Password: [   ]

[New Database]

[Connect]   [Cancel]

Figure 3-3. Connect to SQL Server CE dialog box

In this dialog box, you can either type the path to the database in the Path text box, or you can tap the ellipsis (...) button to browse your Pocket PC or emulator for the database. Once you've found the database you're looking for, you can optionally type in a password if one is needed and then tap the Connect button to make the database connection. In the case of the NorthwindDemo.sdf database, no password is required. If you expand the Databases folder, you'll see what an active database connection looks like as shown in Figure 3-4.

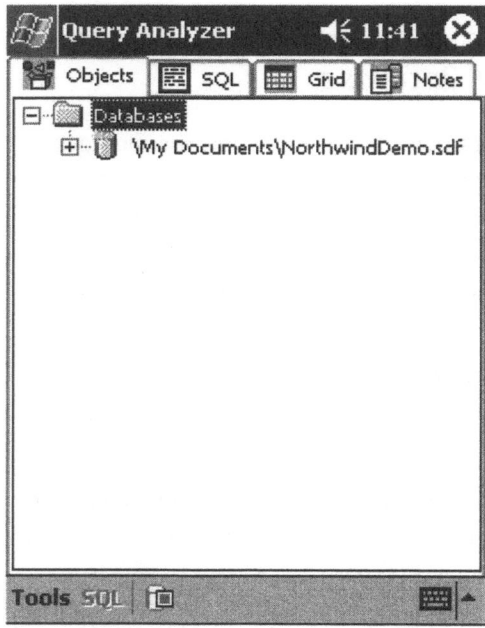

Figure 3-4. An active database connection

Disconnecting from a Database

In order to disconnect from a database, you'll need to select the active database that you wish to disconnect from and then tap the database connection button found on the toolbar. This time around, the button must be showing a red square, indicating that you have a connection as shown in Figure 3-5, in order for this to work properly. If the button is showing a green arrow, you're already disconnected and you'll be out of luck.

 Figure 3-5. Database connection button with red square

Compacting a Database

Now that you're disconnected from the NorthwindDemo.sdf database, it's time to take a look at one of the things you can do with a managed database that you're *not* connected to. Compacting your SQL Server CE database is an important function of database maintenance because, over time, your database will grow in size, become fragmented, and begin to waste valuable disk space. Additionally, this fragmentation can adversely impact the performance of your database and potentially put it into a suspect state. To take care of these issues in Query Analyzer, select the disconnected database you wish to compact, and then tap the compact and repair button on the toolbar as shown in Figure 3-6. The compact and repair operation does not put any results into the Notes tab. It just runs and stops when finished. Compacting not only creates a new database, it puts each table in the database in both logical and physical order. Additionally, if a primary or unique key is used on a given table, it sorts that table's rows by that index.

 Figure 3-6. Compact and repair button

Deleting Databases

The other thing you can do with a managed but disconnected database is delete it. You can perform this task by selecting the disconnected database you want to delete, and then tapping the delete button on the toolbar as shown in Figure 3-7. Don't actually delete NorthwindDemo.sdf since you'll continue to use it throughout this book.

 Figure 3-7. Delete button

Connecting to a Managed Database

When your database is managed by Query Analyzer, it shows up in a tree view beneath the Databases folder. Connecting to that database is as easy as selecting it and then tapping the database connection button with the green arrow. If the database requires a password, Query Analyzer will prompt you for one.

Showing and Hiding System Tables

Now that you're connected, yet again, to the NorthwindDemo.sdf database, you can make some choices as to which tables you'd like to see. If you wish to see all of SQL Server CE's system tables, select the Tables folder and then tap the blue-and-red system table button as shown in Figure 3-8.

 Figure 3-8. Tap this button when it's blue and red to show system tables.

On the other hand, if you're staring at the system tables and you find that they're cluttering your screen, select the Tables folder and then tap the blue-and-gray system table button as shown in Figure 3-9.

 Figure 3-9. Tap this button when it's blue and gray to hide system tables.

Retrieving Table Data

While you're looking at the NorthwindDemo.sdf databases tables, let me show you an easy way to retrieve the complete contents of any table without having to type and execute a SQL statement. All you have to do is expand the Tables folder, select the desired table, and then tap the green execute button on the toolbar as shown in Figure 3-10. Cool, isn't it?

 Figure 3-10. Execute button

You will automatically be taken to the Grid tab where the results will be displayed. I think you'll find this to be a real time-saver when trying to browse the contents of your database tables.

Removing Managed Databases

With all the talk of managed databases, you may find that you no longer want Query Analyzer to manage one or more of your SQL Server CE databases. In the case of the NorthwindDemo.sdf database you've been working with, the first step is to make sure that you're disconnected from it. Next, select the database and then tap the database management button as shown in Figure 3-11 to remove it from Query Analyzer.

Figure 3-11. Database management button

There may be times when you're managing several databases and you want to stop managing all of them. To accomplish this, first make sure that they're all disconnected. Next, select the Databases folder, and then tap the database management button.

Creating Databases

Creating a new database in Query Analyzer is similar to connecting to an unmanaged database in that it all starts out with you selecting the Databases folder and then tapping the database connection button with the green arrow. The same Connect to SQL Server CE dialog box pops up, except this time you type in the path and name of the database you wish to create. You optionally create a password and then tap New Database. At this point, the dialog box changes a little bit to look like Figure 3-12.

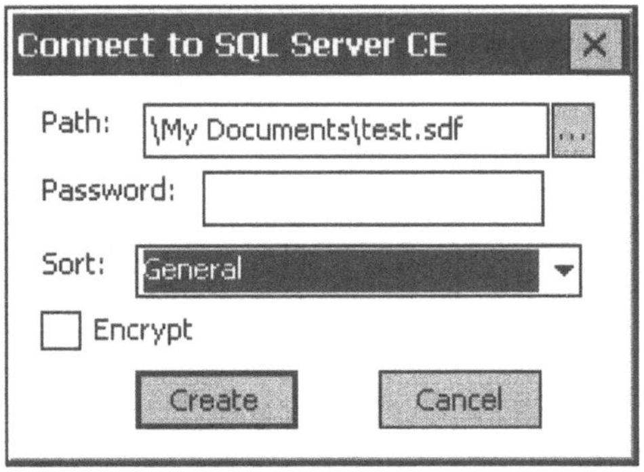

Figure 3-12. Creating a database

You're now presented with a combo box that allows you to specify the database collation. You're also given the option of encrypting the database as long as your Pocket PC supports 128-bit encryption. Obviously, that won't work with the emulator or Pocket PCs with the Pocket PC 2000 operating system without the High Encryption Pack. If you need to download the High Encryption Pack, you can find it at `http://www.microsoft.com/mobile/pocketpc/downloads/ssl128.asp`. When everything is set to your liking, tap the Create button. The new database will show up as both managed and active beneath the Databases folder in Query Analyzer. I created a database called test.sdf in the \My Documents folder.

Creating Tables

With a database built, it's now time to get down to business by creating some tables. The first step you take is to select your active database or its Tables folder and then tap the create table button on the toolbar as shown in Figure 3-13.

Figure 3-13. Create table button

Tapping the create table button will launch the Table Definition dialog box as shown in Figure 3-14. In this dialog box you start out by typing in a name for your table.

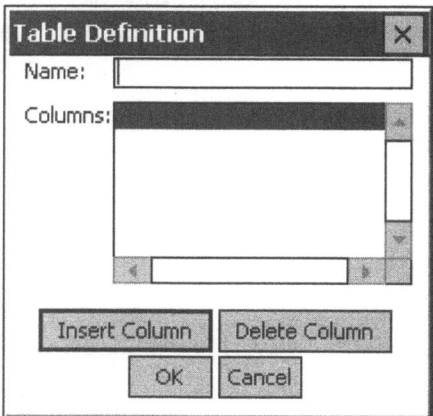

Figure 3-14. Table Definition dialog box

Once you've entered a name for your table, you then have to add at least one column. You do this by tapping the Insert Column button, which pops up the Column Definition dialog box as shown in Figure 3-15.

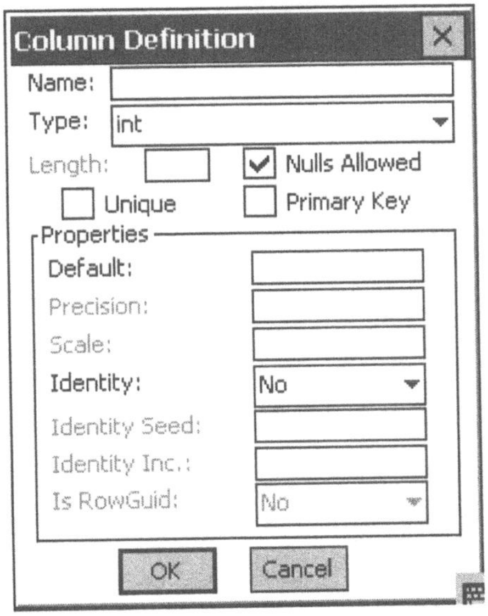

Figure 3-15. Column Definition dialog box

In the Column Definition dialog box you get to detail all the properties and constraints of the column you're about to create. The first things you need to specify are the column name in the Name text box and the data type in the Type combo box. Depending on the data type you choose, you will then be able to specify such things as length for character-based data and whether or not Nulls are permitted. You can also enforce Unique and Primary Key constraints. Additional properties listed in this dialog box include Default values, Precision, Scale, Identity, Seed, Increment value, and Is RowGUID. When you're done with your column, just tap OK to return to the Table Definition dialog box. The new column you created will show up in the Columns multiline text box. If you wish to add more columns, just repeat the process I described. Otherwise, tap OK to complete the creation of your table. I created a table called TestTable with an integer column called Col1. I made my column an identity primary key with a seed value of 1 and an increment value of 1, which automatically created a unique index for me. Figure 3-16 displays the results of my table and column creation.

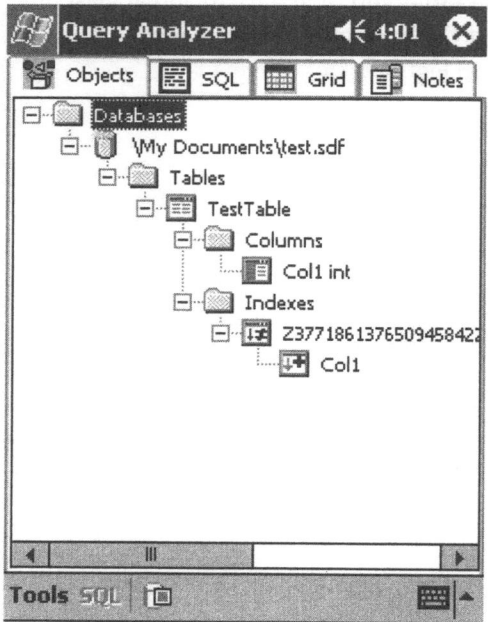

Figure 3-16. A new table, column, and index

Adding Columns

In order to add additional columns to an existing table, you need to first expand the Tables folder to find the table in question. You then must expand that table to reveal the Columns folder. At this point, just select the Columns folder and tap the add column button on the toolbar as shown in Figure 3-17.

 Figure 3-17. Add column button

Tapping this button reveals the familiar Column Definition dialog box. Since I already covered how this works in the previous section, I'll spare you from rehashing it. Needless to say, this process only creates one column at a time and therefore requires you to tap the add column button repeatedly to add multiple columns to a given table.

Creating Indexes

You've already seen how SQL Server CE automatically creates unique indexes whenever you create a table with a UNIQUE or PRIMARY KEY constraint. When you're ready to create your own indexes, just select the table you wish to index and then tap the create index button as shown in Figure 3-18.

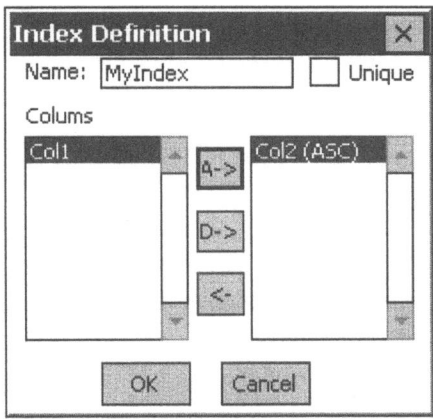 *Figure 3-18. Create index button*

As you'll see, tapping the create index button brings up the Index Definition dialog box as shown in Figure 3-19.

Figure 3-19. Index Definition dialog box

In this dialog box, you get to start out by entering a name for your index and then optionally selecting Unique for your index. Below that is the Columns list box where you get to select which column or columns you want to base your index on. Select a column and then tap A-> if you want that index sorted in ascending order or D-> if you want to sort it in descending order. Tapping either of these buttons moves the desired column to the list box on the right where the components of the index are displayed. If you wish to remove a column from this list, select that column and tap the <- button. When you're done creating your index, tap OK. Notice that the index I created and sorted in ascending order looks like Figure 3-20.

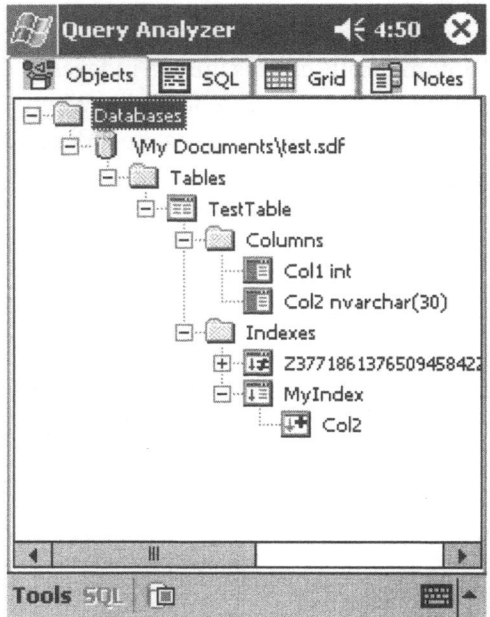

Figure 3-20. MyIndex

If I want to reverse the sort order of a column in MyIndex, I just expand the index I created, select the column whose sort order I wish to reverse, and then tap the reverse sort button on the toolbar as shown in Figure 3-21.

Figure 3-21. Reverse sort button

After tapping that button, the database tree view will be collapsed, so you'll have to reexpand it to see that the sort order of your column has in fact been changed.

Deleting Database Objects

Any object in your database can be deleted whether it's a table, a column, an index, or a column component of an index. Just select the object you wish to delete and then tap the delete button on the toolbar as shown in Figure 3-22.

 Figure 3-22. Delete button

The SQL Tab

Where the Objects tab lets you perform tasks with point-and-tap graphical tools, the SQL tab is designed for the manual creation and execution of SQL code against a SQL Server CE database. With its ability to create, save, and reuse SQL statements and script files, the SQL tab is an extremely useful part of Query Analyzer.

Creating a New SQL Script File

Tapping the New menu item on the SQL menu provides you with a clean slate so you can start creating SQL statements. Assuming that you either are or can get connected to the NorthwindDemo.sdf database, type in a simple SELECT * FROM Customers query in the text editor as shown in Figure 3-23.

Tapping the execute button on the toolbar as shown in Figure 3-24 will do two things. First, you'll be taken to the Notes tab where you'll be informed on both the time elapsed on running the query and how many rows were affected. Then a tap on the Grid tab will reveal the results of the query in a tabular format.

The text editor also allows you to type in multiple SQL statements as long as they're separated by a semicolon. If you have multiple SQL statements but you only want to execute one of them, highlight the statement you wish to execute and then tap the execute button. If you want all your statements executed as a single batch, don't highlight any of them and tap the execute button. It goes without saying (and yet here I am saying it) that selecting the Word Wrap menu item from the SQL menu will cause your SQL code to wrap so that it all fits in the visible part of the text editor. Otherwise, your text will go off the right side of the screen. You also have the ability to cut, copy, and paste your SQL code by tapping the appropriate buttons on the toolbar as shown in Figure 3-25.

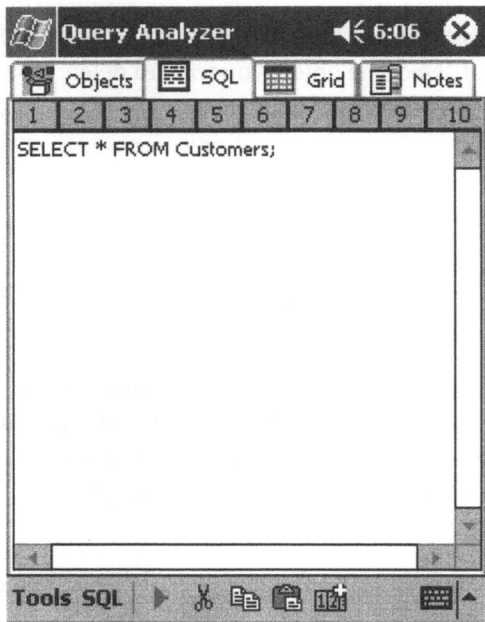

Figure 3-23. A simple query

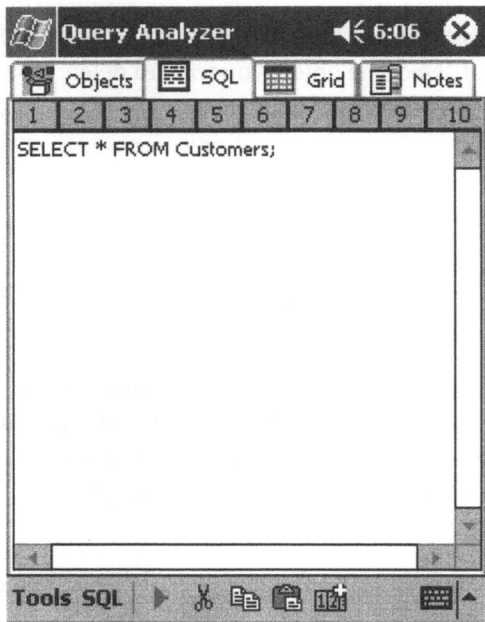 *Figure 3-24. Execute button*

Figure 3-25. Cut, copy, and paste buttons

Saving a SQL Script File

Once you have a SQL script with one or more SQL statements that you'd like to save as a file, it's just a simple matter of selecting the Save menu item from the SQL menu to get the ball rolling. The first time you save a SQL script, a Save As dialog box comes up, prompting you for a name, a folder, a script type, and a memory location as shown in Figure 3-26.

Once you've saved a SQL script, subsequent calls to the Save menu item will automatically save the updates to the current script file without any dialog boxes prompting you for information.

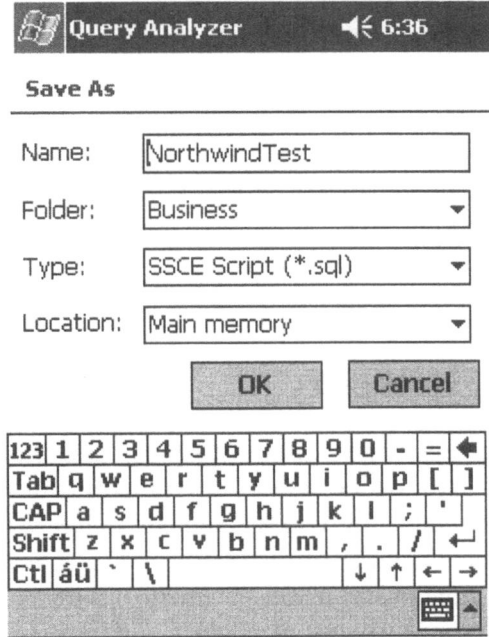

Figure 3-26. Saving a SQL script

Opening a SQL Script File

Once you've saved a SQL script file, you may want to open it again in the future. This is accomplished by selecting the Open menu item of the SQL menu and then choosing the appropriate SQL script file as shown in Figure 3-27.

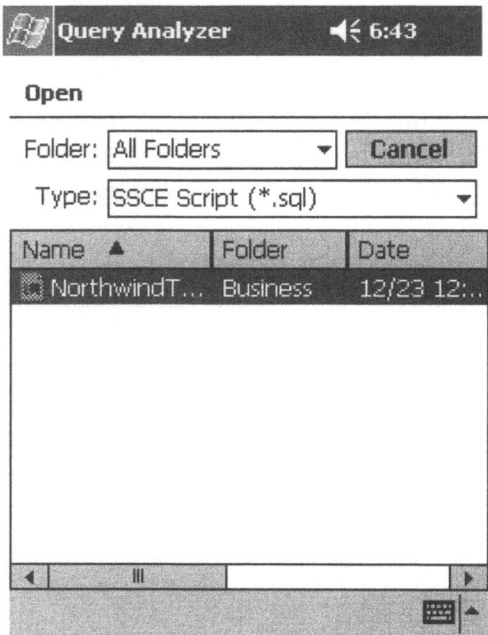

Figure 3-27. Opening a SQL script

Saving Frequently Used SQL Statements

You may have noticed the numbers 1 through 10 going across the top of the SQL tab's text editor and wondered what in the world they were for. As it turns out, they play a role in allowing you to save up to 10 frequently used SQL statements directly inside Query Analyzer. These SQL statements continue to persist even when Query Analyzer is shut down and restarted. In order to save a SQL statement, like the simple SELECT statement you executed previously, just highlight it, and then tap the preset button on the toolbar as shown in Figure 3-28.

   Figure 3-28. Preset button

When you tap the preset button, the Button Presets dialog box pops up, displaying ten preset button numbers as shown in Figure 3-29. Tapping one of the ten preset buttons will cause the first line of the SQL statement you highlighted to show up in the text box adjacent to the preset button you selected. Previously added SQL statements will have the first line of their statement appear next to their assigned button numbers. Adding a new SQL statement to a preset button number that already has a SQL statement assigned to it will cause the older statement to be overwritten.

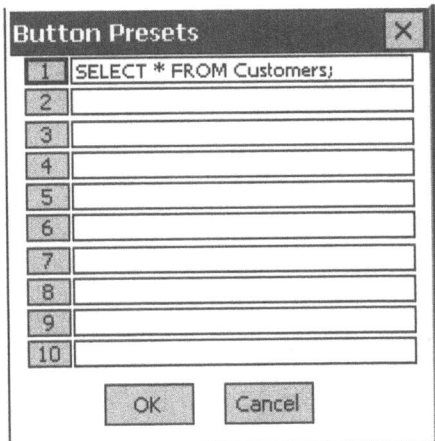

Figure 3-29. Button Presets dialog box

Opening a Saved SQL Statement

Now you finally get to use those numbers found running across the top of the text editor. A tap on any one of them will open the SQL statement that you had saved with a button preset that corresponds to the number you're tapping.

Conclusion

I'm sure it's fair to say that you've learned a lot more than you probably cared to about SQL Server CE's Query Analyzer. At least now you know how to use a tool that allows you to create and work with both the objects that make up a database and the data that fills it up. I should also mention that the easy part is over. From now on, you're doing everything in code, starting with the next chapter where you get to create and modify database objects the hard way. Don't worry, it builds character. Yes, pun intended.

SQL Server CE Data Definition Language

THE SQL DATA DEFINITION LANGUAGE (DDL) specifies how to create, modify, and delete various database objects, including tables, views, privileges, indexes, triggers, and stored procedures. This specification generally assumes that all the functions performed by DDL are written in pure SQL. In the case of SQL Server CE, you'll use a combination of pure SQL and ADO.NET method calls to perform all of your DDL tasks. Before attempting to work with SQL Server CE, you must set a reference to System.Data.SqlServerCe in Visual Studio. Even though you can use Query Analyzer to perform all your DDL tasks, this chapter will focus on doing these things programmatically. Throughout this chapter, I'll provide examples in the form of fully functional code snippets along with the necessary Imports to make the code work properly. Feel free to create a Smart Device Application and type these code snippets into the click events of button controls if you like.

Creating a Database

In order to create a SQL Server CE database on your handheld device, you use the SqlCeEngine class. This class has a method called CreateDatabase that does just what its name says. Before you can execute this method, however, you must first provide a path and filename for your new database, a password, and a Boolean determination as to whether or not you want to encrypt the database. When it comes to the 128-bit encryption option, if you're running the Pocket PC 2000 operating system, you must have the High Encryption Pack installed on your Pocket PC for it to work. If you try to encrypt a database without it, you'll end up throwing a SQL error. Please note that the emulator won't work in encrypted mode either. With that taken care of, you can either pass all these connection string items into the SqlCeEngine constructor or set them equal to the LocalConnectionString property. A call to the Dispose method in the Finally block of your error handling code will release the resources being used by the SqlCeEngine class.

NOTE *If you're running the older Pocket PC 2000 operating system, you can download the High Encryption Pack used to make your device 128-bit enabled from* http://www.microsoft.com/mobile/pocketpc/downloads/ssl128.asp.

Example

In this example, you'll create a SQL Server CE database called **dbvb.sdf** in the \My Documents directory of your Pocket PC or emulator. Attempting to create a duplicate database file where one already exists will cause an error, so you need to first check for the existence of the file you're trying to create and delete it if a duplicate file is found. Once this "defensive code" is executed, you can then instantiate the SqlCeEngine class, set its connection string, create the database, and then release its resources.

Visual Basic .NET

```
'insert at the top of your class
Imports System.Data.SqlServerCe
Imports System.IO

'insert in a function or click event
Dim sqlEngine As SqlCeEngine
Try
    If File.Exists("\My Documents\dbvb.sdf") Then
    File.Delete("\My Documents\dbvb.sdf")
End If
sqlEngine = New SqlServerCe.SqlCeEngine
sqlEngine.LocalConnectionString = "Data Source=\My
Documents\dbvb.sdf;Password=apress;Encrypt Database=False"
sqlEngine.CreateDatabase()
Catch sqlex As SqlCeException
Dim sqlError As SqlCeError
For Each sqlError In sqlex.Errors
    MessageBox.Show(sqlError.Message)
```

```
Next
Catch ex As Exception
MessageBox.Show(ex.Message)
Finally
sqlEngine.Dispose()
End Try
```

C#

```
//insert at the top of your class
using System.Data.SqlServerCe;
using System.IO;

//insert in a function or click event
SqlCeEngine sqlEngine = null;
try
{
if (File.Exists("\\My Documents\\dbcs.sdf"))
{
    File.Delete("\\My Documents\\dbcs.sdf");
}
sqlEngine = new SqlCeEngine();
sqlEngine.LocalConnectionString = "Data Source=\\My
Documents\\dbcs.sdf;Password=apress;Encrypt Database=False";
sqlEngine.CreateDatabase();
}
catch(SqlCeException sqlex)
{
foreach(SqlCeError sqlError in sqlex.Errors)
{
    MessageBox.Show(sqlError.Message);
    }
}
catch(Exception ex)
{
MessageBox.Show(ex.Message);
}
finally
{
sqlEngine.Dispose();
}
```

After executing the preceding code samples, verify that everything worked as expected by viewing the new database files in the File Explorer or, better yet, connecting to your empty databases using Query Analyzer. You won't be able to issue any queries, though, since you haven't populated the database with any data.

Compacting a Database

As you use your SQL Server CE database, it grows over time. It makes sense that a database would grow as more and more data is inserted, but what about when you delete data? You would think that a database would shrink in size when data is deleted, but that's not the case with SQL Server CE. As data is removed from the database, the newfound space isn't reclaimed. Luckily, the SqlCeEngine class has a method called Compact that lets you deal with this problem. Other features of the Compact method include the ability to change the database's password or its encryption.

When a SQL Server CE database is compacted, the existing database file isn't actually the file that gets shrunk. Instead, SQL Server CE creates a new, smaller database file. To get the ball rolling, when you instantiate the SqlCeEngine class, you must pass in a data source to its constructor that includes the path to the existing SQL Server CE database that you wish to compact. Additionally, if your database has a password, you need to include that in the constructor string as well. You'll find that this constructor string looks similar to the connection string you used to create the database.

Now you can call the Compact method with a parameter that includes a data source that points to a new database file. It's important that this new file has a different name than the source database file or you'll get an error. Additionally, if you want this new database to have a different password or encryption level, you can modify this parameter accordingly. Finally, you'll need to delete the source database file and rename the new database file to match the recently deleted source file and/or move the new file to the location of the source file. Keep in mind that none of this will work if you have an application with an open connection to the database you're looking to compact.

Example

In this example, you'll create both source and destination string variables that point to the existing and new database files, respectively. You'll also put in some defensive code to check and see if the source database even exists before going to a lot of trouble. When you instantiate the SqlCeEngine class, you'll pass in both a data source path and a password since you're dealing with the database you created in the last example. Because you're not turning on encryption and don't wish to change the password, you can call the Compact method with only a data source for a parameter.

After that, it's just a matter of tapping into the IO namespace to delete the original database file and then move the new file to the source file's location. Just in case you're wondering, you can use the Move method of the File object to rename the new file using the old file's name. In the case of this example, that's exactly what you're doing since you're not actually moving the new file to another directory. As you experiment with alternate SqlCeEngine constructor and Compact method parameter strings, you'll be glad you included your extensive SqlCeException handling code to give you insight into where your code might be in error. I know I'm glad when I do this, because this seemingly simple Compact method is very tricky.

Visual Basic .NET

```
'insert at the top of your class
Imports System.Data.SqlServerCe
Imports System.IO

'insert in a function or click event
Dim Source As String = "\My Documents\dbvb.sdf"
Dim Destination As String = "\My Documents\new.sdf"
Dim sqlEngine As SqlCeEngine
Try
    If File.Exists(Source) Then
    sqlEngine = New SqlCeEngine("Data Source=" & Source & ";Password=apress;")
    sqlEngine.Compact("Data Source=" & Destination)
    File.Delete(Source)
    File.Move(Destination, Source)
    End If
Catch sqlex As SqlCeException
Dim sqlError As SqlCeError
For Each sqlError In sqlex.Errors
    MessageBox.Show(sqlError.Message)
Next
Catch ex As Exception
    MessageBox.Show(ex.Message)
Finally
sqlEngine.Dispose()
End Try
```

C#

```
//insert at the top of your class
using System.Data.SqlServerCe;
using System.IO;

//insert in a function or click event
String source = "\\My Documents\\dbcs.sdf";
String destination = "\\My Documents\\newcs.sdf";
SqlCeEngine sqlEngine = null;
try
{
if (File.Exists(source))
{
    sqlEngine = new SqlCeEngine("Data Source=" + source + ";Password=apress;");
    sqlEngine.Compact("Data Source=" + destination);
    File.Delete(source);
    File.Move(destination, source);
}
}
catch(SqlCeException sqlex)
{
foreach(SqlCeError sqlError in sqlex.Errors)
{
    MessageBox.Show(sqlError.Message);
}
}
catch(Exception ex)
{
MessageBox.Show(ex.Message);
}
finally
{
sqlEngine.Dispose();
}
```

A great way to see this code in action is to step through the code in the debugger. Stop after the line of code that deletes the source database file and then switch to the File Explorer to see your newly compacted database file before it gets moved and/or renamed.

Deleting a Database

I'm almost embarrassed to discuss what it takes to delete a SQL Server CE database. For the sake of completeness, I'll share the "complex coding techniques" required to eliminate a database from your Pocket PC. Actually, you've already seen the code in the previous examples. As long as there isn't an active connection to the database, just execute the Delete method of the File object in the IO namespace.

Example

In this example, you'll start out with a little defensive code to determine if the database file you're looking to delete exists where you think it does. If so, you call the Delete method of the File object.

Visual Basic .NET

```
'insert at the top of your class
Imports System.IO

'insert in a function or click event
Try
If File.Exists("\My Documents\dbvb.sdf") Then
    File.Delete("\My Documents\dbvb.sdf")
End If
Catch ex As Exception
MessageBox.Show(ex.Message)
End Try
```

C#

```
//insert at the top of your class
using System.IO;

//insert in a function or click event
try
{
if (File.Exists("\\My Documents\\dbcs.sdf"))
{
    File.Delete("\\My Documents\\dbcs.sdf");
}
```

```
}
catch(Exception ex)
{
MessageBox.Show(ex.Message);
}
```

A quick look at the File Explorer should reveal that your databases are gone.

Creating a Table

Now that you know how to build, compact, and delete databases, it's time that you add something useful to them, like tables and columns, so that you can get some actual work done. Creating a table can be simple or complex depending on which options you choose to use. Actually, creating the table itself is easy. It's the addition of columns and their seemingly infinite combination of constraints that can make things difficult. In its simplest form, here's the syntax to create a table:

```
CREATE TABLE TableName (ColumnName DataType [,…n])
```

This doesn't look so hard to understand. The CREATE TABLE part always stays the same. You get to choose the TableName and the ColumnName as long as they don't exceed 128 characters. The DataType part is where you get to plug in some kind of text, binary, or numeric value. The [,…n] part means that you can optionally place a comma after your ColumnName and DataType and add yet another ColumnName and DataType. In fact, you can continue to add commas and as many ColumnName/DataType pairs as you like until you hit the 255-column limit. Though the ColumnName and DataType are the most important parts of the column, many other optional constraints are available out there that add tremendous value to a column. To get more functionality from your tables, you're going to have to go the extra mile with these constraints, and things will start getting a little more complicated as a result. Before you jump off that bridge, take a look at Table 4-1 so that you'll be well equipped to plug in the appropriate values in the DataType part of your CREATE TABLE syntax.

Table 4-1. SQL Server CE Data Types

DATA TYPE	DESCRIPTION
bigint	64-bit integer that ranges from –9,223,372,036,854,775,808 to 9,223,372,036,854,775,807 and requires 8 bytes of storage.
integer	32-bit integer that ranges from –2,147,483,648 to 2,147,483,647 and requires 4 bytes of storage.

Table 4-1. SQL Server CE Data Types (Continued)

DATA TYPE	DESCRIPTION
smallint	16-bit integer that ranges from –32,768 to 32,767 and requires 2 bytes of storage.
tinyint	8-bit integer that ranges from 0 to 255 and requires 1 byte of storage.
bit	1-bit integer with a value of either 1 or 0 that should be used in Boolean situations.
numeric (p, s)	Fixed-precision and scale-numeric data that ranges from -10^{38} to $10^{38}-1$. The p specifies precision and can range from 1 to 38. The s specifies scale and can range from 0 to p.
money	Monetary data that ranges from –922,337,203,685,477.5808 to 922,337,203,685,477.5807 with accuracy to a ten-thousandth of a monetary unit and requires 8 bytes of storage.
float	Floating-point number that ranges from –1.79E+308 to 1.79E+308 and requires 8 bytes of storage.
real	Floating-precision number that ranges from –3.40E+38 to 3.40E+38.
datetime	Date and time data that ranges from January 1, 1753, to December 31, 9999, with an accuracy of 3.33 milliseconds. All values are rounded to increments of .000, .003, or .007 milliseconds. The data is stored as two 4-byte integers. The first 4 bytes store the number of days before or after the system reference date of January 1, 1900. The second 4 bytes store the time of day represented as the number of milliseconds after midnight. Seconds range from 0 to 59.
nchar (n)	Fixed-length Unicode data with a default length of 1 and a maximum length of 255 characters. The required bytes of storage are twice the number of characters entered.
nvarchar (n)	Variable-length Unicode data with a default length of 1 and a maximum length of 255 characters. The required bytes of storage are twice the number of characters entered.
ntext	Variable-length Unicode data with a maximum length of 536,870,911 characters. The required bytes of storage are twice the number of characters entered.
binary (n)	Fixed-length binary data with a default length of 1 and a maximum length of 510 bytes.

Table 4-1. SQL Server CE Data Types (Continued)

DATA TYPE	DESCRIPTION
varbinary (n)	Variable-length binary data with a default length of 1 and a maximum length of 510 bytes.
image	Variable-length binary data with a maximum length of 1,073,741,823 bytes.
uniqueidentifier	A globally unique identifier (GUID) with a storage size of 16 bytes.

Now you can take what you've learned from the simplified CREATE TABLE syntax and the various column data type options presented to you in Table 4-1 and build your first SQL Server CE table. This will give you a good feel for both the ADO.NET and SQL code needed to create a table as well as serve as a foundation to build on.

Example 1

In this example, you'll connect to your SQL Server CE database using the SqlCe-Connection object and then use the SqlCeCommand object to both formulate and execute your SQL code. The most notable thing about this simple example is that all of the 17 different data types supported by SQL Server CE are represented as columns in the new table you're creating. Yes, I realize that most databases have more than one table, and that it's smart to define columns with "meaningful" names, and I suspect you do too. This is just an example.

Visual Basic .NET

```
'insert at the top of your class
Imports System.Data.SqlServerCe

'insert in a function or click event
Dim cn As SqlCeConnection
Try
cn = New SqlCeConnection("Data Source=\My Documents\dbvb.sdf;Password=apress")
cn.Open()
Dim cmd As SqlCeCommand = cn.CreateCommand
cmd.CommandText = "CREATE TABLE TableOne (" & _
                            "ColumnOne bigint, " & _
                            "ColumnTwo integer, " & _
                            "ColumnThree smallint, " & _
```

```
                                       "ColumnFour tinyint, " & _
                                       "ColumnFive bit, " & _
                                       "ColumnSix numeric(2,2), " & _
                                       "ColumnSeven money, " & _
                                       "ColumnEight float, " & _
                                       "ColumnNine real, " & _
                                       "ColumnTen datetime, " & _
                                       "ColumnEleven nchar(20), " & _
                                       "ColumnTwelve nvarchar(20), " & _
                                       "ColumnThirteen ntext, " & _
                                       "ColumnFourteen binary(20), " & _
                                       "ColumnFifteen varbinary(20), " & _
                                       "ColumnSixteen image, " & _
                                       "ColumnSeventeen uniqueidentifier)"
cmd.ExecuteNonQuery()
Catch sqlex As SqlCeException
Dim sqlError As SqlCeError
For Each sqlError In sqlex.Errors
    MessageBox.Show(sqlError.Message)
Next
Catch ex As Exception
MessageBox.Show(ex.Message)
Finally
If cn.State <> ConnectionState.Closed Then
    cn.Close()
End If
End Try
```

C#

```
//insert at the top of your class
using System.Data.SqlServerCe;

//insert in a function or click event
SqlCeConnection cn = null;
try
{
cn = new SqlCeConnection("Data Source=\\My Documents\\dbcs.sdf;Password=apress");
cn.Open();
SqlCeCommand cmd = cn.CreateCommand();
cmd.CommandText = "CREATE TABLE TableOne (" +
                              "ColumnOne bigint, " +
                              "ColumnTwo integer, " +
```

```
                                        "ColumnThree smallint, " +
                                        "ColumnFour tinyint, " +
                                        "ColumnFive bit, " +
                                        "ColumnSix numeric(2,2), " +
                                        "ColumnSeven money, " +
                                        "ColumnEight float, " +
                                        "ColumnNine real, " +
                                        "ColumnTen datetime, " +
                                        "ColumnEleven nchar(20), " +
                                        "ColumnTwelve nvarchar(20), " +
                                        "ColumnThirteen ntext, " +
                                        "ColumnFourteen binary(20), " +
                                        "ColumnFifteen varbinary(20), " +
                                        "ColumnSixteen image, " +
                                        "ColumnSeventeen uniqueidentifier)";
    cmd.ExecuteNonQuery();
    }
    catch(SqlCeException sqlex)
    {
    foreach(SqlCeError sqlError in sqlex.Errors)
    {
        MessageBox.Show(sqlError.Message);
    }
    }
    catch(Exception ex)
    {
    MessageBox.Show(ex.Message);
    }
    finally
    {
    if(cn.State != ConnectionState.Closed)
    {
        cn.Close();
    }
    }
```

A quick glance at the Query Analyzer will confirm that the table and 17 columns have been created as shown in Figure 4-1.

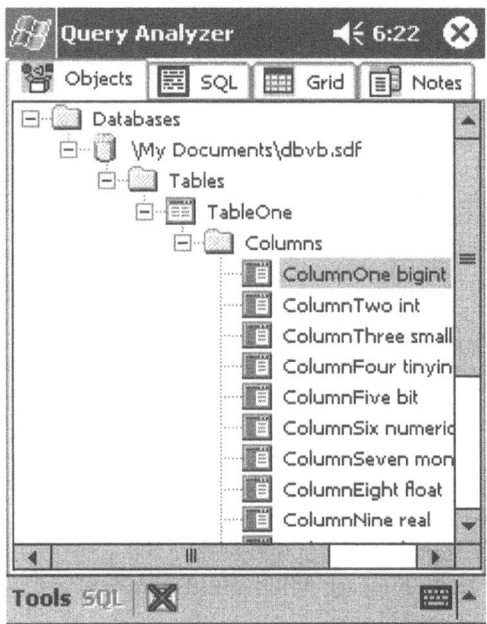

Figure 4-1. Query Analyzer displaying the results of Example 1

CREATE TABLE Syntax

Assuming it's a safe bet that you understand all aspects of the ColumnName and DataType parts of the column, it's time to move on. Let's start off by looking at the complete syntax for the CREATE TABLE statement. Afterward, I'll describe the important constraints and such and throw in a few more examples for your programming pleasure.

```
CREATE TABLE TableName
    ( { < ColumnDefinition > | < TableConstraint > } [ ,...n ] )

< ColumnDefinition > ::=
    { ColumnName DataType }
    [ { DEFAULT Value | [ IDENTITY [(Seed,Increment)]] } ]
    [ ROWGUIDCOL ]
    [ < ColumnConstraint > [ ...n ] ]

< ColumnConstraint > ::=
    [ CONSTRAINT Name ]
    { [ NULL | NOT NULL ]
        | [ PRIMARY KEY | UNIQUE ]
```

```
        | REFERENCES ReferenceTable [(ReferenceColumn)]
        [ ON DELETE { CASCADE | NO ACTION } ]
        [ ON UPDATE { CASCADE | NO ACTION } ] }


< TableConstraint > ::=
    [ CONSTRAINT Name ]
    { [ { PRIMARY KEY | UNIQUE }
      { (Column [ ,...n ] ) }]
    | FOREIGN KEY
      [ (Column [ ,...n ] ) ]
    REFERENCES ReferenceTable (ReferenceColumn [ ,...n ] )
      [ ON DELETE { CASCADE | NO ACTION } ]
      [ ON UPDATE { CASCADE | NO ACTION } ] }
```

With all the possible permutations available in the CREATE TABLE statement, it's no wonder most developers prefer the easy-to-use tools in SQL Server Enterprise Manager over writing the code themselves. I'm going do a play-by-play of all these permutations from top to bottom so you'll have a better understanding of what they mean.

Column Definition

At the top, after you've included the obligatory CREATE TABLE TableName line, you get to decide if you're going to define a normal column with associated constraints or if you're going to create a table constraint. Assuming you're going to create a normal column, you move down to the ColumnDefinition section. You're most certainly going to add a ColumnName and a DataType as you've done previously. After that, you can optionally give your column a DEFAULT value, or you can make it an auto-incrementing IDENTITY column with a seed value to start out with and a value to increment the number by each time a new row is inserted. With a DEFAULT column, if you don't provide a value by the start of the INSERT operation, one will be provided for you. Alternatively, with an IDENTITY column, a value is always provided for you at INSERT time.

Moving down, if you have a column that's using a uniqueidentifier data type, you can designate that column to be the row global unique identifier column with the optional ROWGUIDCOL. This means a new GUID will be automatically generated for this column whenever you insert a new row into the table. That sounds a lot like an IDENTITY column, except it gives you 128-bit unique identifiers at INSERT time instead of ever-increasing integers.

Example 2

In this example, you'll create a table designed to reinforce what you've just learned about putting together a column definition with a few column constraints thrown in for good measure. The first column you'll create in this new table will be an integer that's not null, and includes a PRIMARY KEY constraint and an IDENTITY constraint with a seed of 1 and an increment of 1. The second column will be nothing special, just an nvarchar to hold any string you might want to store in it. For the third column you'll specify a uniqueidentifier data type and place a ROWGUIDCOL constraint upon it. You'll give the last column a data type of datetime that has a DEFAULT value that happens to be a built-in function called GETDATE. When you perform an INSERT operation on this table, ColumnOne will create an auto-incrementing number for you, ColumnThree will create a new GUID for you, and ColumnFour will use the GETDATE function to add the current date and time for you. ColumnTwo requires a string (and you may provide a value for ColumnFour), so this is the only column that you have to actually name and provide a value for in your INSERT statement.

Visual Basic .NET

```
'insert at the top of your class
Imports System.Data.SqlServerCe

'insert in a function or click event
Dim cn As SqlCeConnection
Try
cn = New SqlCeConnection("Data Source=\My Documents\dbvb.sdf;Password=apress")
cn.Open()
Dim cmd As SqlCeCommand = cn.CreateCommand
cmd.CommandText = "CREATE TABLE ColumnDefinition (" & _
                "ColumnOne integer IDENTITY(1, 1) NOT NULL PRIMARY KEY, " & _
                "ColumnTwo nvarchar(20), " & _
                "ColumnThree uniqueidentifier ROWGUIDCOL, " & _
                "ColumnFour datetime DEFAULT GETDATE())"
    cmd.ExecuteNonQuery()
Catch sqlex As SqlCeException
Dim sqlError As SqlCeError
For Each sqlError In sqlex.Errors
    MessageBox.Show(sqlError.Message)
Next
Catch ex As Exception
MessageBox.Show(ex.Message)
Finally
```

```
If cn.State <> ConnectionState.Closed Then
    cn.Close()
End If
End Try
```

C#

```
//insert at the top of your class
using System.Data.SqlServerCe;

//insert in a function or click event
SqlCeConnection cn = null;
try
{
cn = new SqlCeConnection("Data Source=\\My Documents\\dbcs.sdf;Password=apress");
cn.Open();
SqlCeCommand cmd = cn.CreateCommand();
cmd.CommandText = "CREATE TABLE ColumnDefinition (" +
                    "ColumnOne integer IDENTITY(1, 1) NOT NULL PRIMARY KEY, " +
                    "ColumnTwo nvarchar(20), " +
                    "ColumnThree uniqueidentifier ROWGUIDCOL, " +
                    "ColumnFour datetime DEFAULT GETDATE())";
cmd.ExecuteNonQuery();
}
catch(SqlCeException sqlex)
{
foreach(SqlCeError sqlError in sqlex.Errors)
{
    MessageBox.Show(sqlError.Message);
}
}
catch(Exception ex)
{
MessageBox.Show(ex.Message);
}
finally
{
if(cn.State != ConnectionState.Closed)
    {
    cn.Close();
    }
}
```

Column Constraints

Now you've arrived at the ColumnConstraint section, which, as you saw earlier in the CREATE TABLE Syntax section, is a completely optional choice. If you want to add constraints (business rules) to your column, you have the option of using the CONSTRAINT keyword and giving your constraint a name if you so desire.

Next, you can optionally decide if you want to allow null values to be inserted in your column's rows. Choose NOT NULL if you intend on selecting either PRIMARY KEY or UNIQUE at the next level down. These two constraints are the same in that they use a unique index to provide entity integrity to a column or group of columns. The difference is that there can only be one PRIMARY KEY constraint per table, whereas a table can have multiple UNIQUE constraints.

If your column isn't UNIQUE nor a PRIMARY KEY, it could be the FOREIGN KEY to a parent table's PRIMARY KEY. In that case, you have the option to add the REFERENCES constraint, which cements that parent-child relationship. You must also include the table name and column name of the parent table that your new FOREIGN KEY column is referencing. If you put referential integrity in place by including the REFERENCES constraint, you also get to decide what happens to the rows of your child table when a DELETE statement is executed on a row in the parent table that you've set a reference to. That was a mouthful.

Anyway, if you choose to add the ON DELETE CASCADE constraint, whenever you delete a row in the parent table, SQL Server CE deletes the corresponding rows in the child table that references it. On the other hand, if you choose the ON DELETE NO ACTION constraint, whenever you delete a row in the parent table, SQL Server CE will raise an error and roll back that deletion as long as there is at least one row in the child table that references it. This referential integrity ripple effect also works with UPDATE statements. If you choose to add the ON UPDATE CASCADE constraint, whenever you update a row in the parent table, SQL Server CE updates the corresponding rows in the child table that references it. Should you choose the ON UPDATE NO ACTION constraint, whenever you update a row in the parent table, SQL Server CE will raise an error and roll back that update as long as there is at least one row in the child table that references it.

Example 3

In Example 2, you used up almost all the column constraints you had at your disposal. Luckily, I've saved the all-important creation of a FOREIGN KEY relationship for this example. ColumnOne will have the same syntax as in Example 2. ColumnTwo, on the other hand, will be an integer that makes a reference back to the ColumnDefinition table and ColumnOne column you created in Example 2. Additionally, you'll add the syntax to enable cascading deletes.

After you've created this table, you can test to check that the referential integrity works in Query Analyzer by first adding a bunch of rows to the Column-Definition table and then adding a few rows to the ColumnConstraints table. Keep in mind that you need to use a value from ColumnOne of the ColumnDefinition table for the integer value in ColumnTwo of the ColumnConstraints table. Now delete a row in the ColumnDefinition table that contains the value you just selected. A quick glance at the ColumnConstraints table will reveal that all the rows that had a FOREIGN KEY constraint based on the value you selected are now gone.

Visual Basic .NET

```
'insert at the top of your class
Imports System.Data.SqlServerCe

'insert in a function or click event
Dim cn As SqlCeConnection
Try
cn = New SqlCeConnection("Data Source=\My Documents\dbvb.sdf;Password=apress")
cn.Open()
Dim cmd As SqlCeCommand = cn.CreateCommand
cmd.CommandText = "CREATE TABLE ColumnConstraints (" & _
"ColumnOne integer IDENTITY(1, 1) NOT NULL PRIMARY KEY, " & _
"ColumnTwo integer REFERENCES ColumnDefinition(ColumnOne) ON DELETE CASCADE)"
cmd.ExecuteNonQuery()
Catch sqlex As SqlCeException
Dim sqlError As SqlCeError
For Each sqlError In sqlex.Errors
    MessageBox.Show(sqlError.Message)
Next
Catch ex As Exception
MessageBox.Show(ex.Message)
Finally
If cn.State <> ConnectionState.Closed Then
    cn.Close()
End If
End Try
```

C#

```csharp
//insert at the top of your class
using System.Data.SqlServerCe;

//insert in a function or click event
SqlCeConnection cn = null;
try
{
cn = new SqlCeConnection("Data Source=\\My Documents\\dbcs.sdf;Password=apress");
cn.Open();
SqlCeCommand cmd = cn.CreateCommand();
cmd.CommandText = "CREATE TABLE ColumnConstraints (" +
"ColumnOne integer IDENTITY(1, 1) NOT NULL PRIMARY KEY, " +
"ColumnTwo integer REFERENCES ColumnDefinition(ColumnOne) ON DELETE CASCADE)";
cmd.ExecuteNonQuery();
}
catch(SqlCeException sqlex)
{
foreach(SqlCeError sqlError in sqlex.Errors)
{
    MessageBox.Show(sqlError.Message);
}
}
catch(Exception ex)
{
MessageBox.Show(ex.Message);
}
finally
{
if(cn.State != ConnectionState.Closed)
{
    cn.Close();
}
}
```

Table Constraints

If you've made it down to the TableConstraint part of this elaborate CREATE TABLE syntax, it's because you're finished defining columns. Table constraints look remarkably similar to column constraints except that they're all about the use of multiple columns. In other words, when more than one column is used in a table to define a PRIMARY KEY, a UNIQUE constraint, or a FOREIGN KEY, table constraints will be used instead of column constraints. SQL Server CE doesn't allow you to use these constraint keywords multiple times next to multiple columns in a CREATE TABLE statement. Therefore, you'll create all of your column definitions without constraints of any kind, since you'll be taking care of this later on with your table constraints.

You start out with the optional use of the CONSTRAINT keyword along with a name of your choosing. Now, just as with column constraints, you're faced with the PRIMARY KEY, UNIQUE, or FOREIGN KEY constraint decision. If you want to pick what's behind door number one, you use the PRIMARY KEY keyword and then enclose the names of the columns that make up the constraint, separated by commas, inside parenthesis. You follow the exact same steps, with a different keyword, of course, when defining multiple columns as a UNIQUE or FOREIGN KEY constraint. Right after the list of columns in a FOREIGN KEY constraint, you add the REFERENCES keyword, along with the parent table you're referencing, and enclose the names of the reference columns, separated by commas, inside parenthesis. After creating referential integrity, the rules for ON DELETE and ON UPDATE are the same as described in the "Column Constraints" section.

Example 4

In this example, you'll create a table whose PRIMARY KEY is comprised of three different columns. You'll create three integer columns without any column constraints, and then you'll create a table constraint to group the three columns together to make a PRIMARY KEY. Additionally, you'll use the CONSTRAINT keyword and name the constraint PK.

Visual Basic .NET

```
'insert at the top of your class
Imports System.Data.SqlServerCe

'insert in a function or click event
Dim cn As SqlCeConnection
Try
cn = New SqlCeConnection("Data Source=\My Documents\dbvb.sdf;Password=apress")
cn.Open()
Dim cmd As SqlCeCommand = cn.CreateCommand
cmd.CommandText = "CREATE TABLE TableConstraints (" & _
            "ColumnOne integer, " & _
```

```
                    "ColumnTwo integer, " & _
                    "ColumnThree integer, " & _
                    "CONSTRAINT PK PRIMARY KEY (ColumnOne, ColumnTwo, ColumnThree))"
cmd.ExecuteNonQuery()
Catch sqlex As SqlCeException
Dim sqlError As SqlCeError
For Each sqlError In sqlex.Errors
    MessageBox.Show(sqlError.Message)
Next
Catch ex As Exception
MessageBox.Show(ex.Message)
Finally
If cn.State <> ConnectionState.Closed Then
    cn.Close()
End If
End Try
```

C#

```
//insert at the top of your class
using System.Data.SqlServerCe;

//insert in a function or click event
SqlCeConnection cn = null;
try
{
cn = new SqlCeConnection("Data Source=\\My Documents\\dbcs.sdf;Password=apress");
cn.Open();
SqlCeCommand cmd = cn.CreateCommand();
cmd.CommandText = "CREATE TABLE TableConstraints (" +
        "ColumnOne integer, " +
        "ColumnTwo integer, " +
        "ColumnThree integer, " +
        "CONSTRAINT PK PRIMARY KEY (ColumnOne, ColumnTwo, ColumnThree))";
cmd.ExecuteNonQuery();
}
catch(SqlCeException sqlex)
{
foreach(SqlCeError sqlError in sqlex.Errors)
{
    MessageBox.Show(sqlError.Message);
}
}
```

```
catch(Exception ex)
{
MessageBox.Show(ex.Message);
}
finally
{
if(cn.State != ConnectionState.Closed)
{
    cn.Close();
}
}
```

If you bring up the TableConstraints table in Query Analyzer and look inside its Indexes folder, you'll see an index called PK that is made up of ColumnOne, ColumnTwo, and ColumnThree as shown in Figure 4-2.

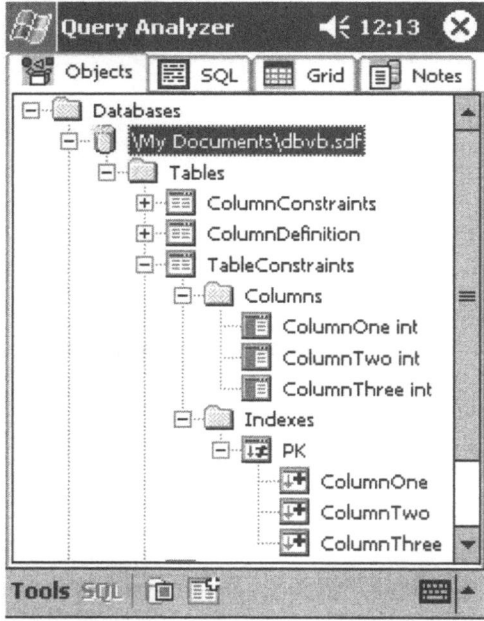

Figure 4-2. Query Analyzer displaying a multicolumn PRIMARY KEY

Modifying a Table

In the event that you didn't get things right when you created your table, you can use the ALTER TABLE statement to modify it to your liking. This statement allows you to modify, add, or delete columns and constraints for a given table. Use this statement carefully, since you can lose data when you delete columns. I'll start off by showing you the complete syntax of the ALTER TABLE statement.

```
ALTER TABLE TableName

{ [ ALTER COLUMN ColumnName
{DROP DEFAULT | SET DEFAULT value | IDENTITY [ (seed , increment) ]}
| ADD { < ColumnDefinition > | < TableConstraint > } [ ,...n ]
| DROP { [ CONSTRAINT ] name | COLUMN column }] }

< ColumnDefinition > ::=
   { ColumnName DataType }
   [ [ DEFAULT value ] | IDENTITY [ (seed , increment) ] ]
   [ROWGUIDCOL]
   [ < ColumnConstraint > ] [ ...n ] ]

< ColumnConstraint > ::=
   [ NULL | NOT NULL ]
   [ CONSTRAINT name ]
   {
      | { PRIMARY KEY | UNIQUE }
      | REFERENCES ReferenceTable [ ( ReferenceColumn ) ]
      [ ON DELETE { CASCADE | NO ACTION } ]
      [ ON UPDATE { CASCADE | NO ACTION } ] }

< TableConstraint > ::=
   [ CONSTRAINT name ]
   { [ { PRIMARY KEY | UNIQUE }
      { ( column [ ,...n ] ) } }
      | FOREIGN KEY
      [ ( column [ ,...n ] ) ]
      REFERENCES ReferenceTable [ ( ReferenceColumn [ ,...n ] ) ]
      [ ON DELETE { CASCADE | NO ACTION } ]
      [ ON UPDATE { CASCADE | NO ACTION } ] }
```

As you can see, most of this syntax looks identical to the syntax found in the CREATE TABLE statement, so I'm not going to give you the same exhaustive play-by-play on what this all means. At the very top, you're always going to include the ALTER TABLE line and provide a TableName. As you may have noticed, there is no mechanism to change the name of the table. Next on the list, you get to make one of three choices: to modify, to add to, or to delete from the table.

Modify

If your intent is to modify an existing column, then you'll use the ALTER COLUMN syntax along with the name of the column you wish to modify. You're then faced with three modifications you can make to that column. If your column has a DEFAULT value in place, you can get rid of it with DROP DEFAULT. If your column doesn't have a DEFAULT value, you can add one by using SET DEFAULT along with a value. You can also use SET DEFAULT to change an existing DEFAULT value. Finally, you can add the IDENTITY constraint along with the appropriate seed and increment values to a column. If you already have an IDENTITY column, you can modify that column's existing seed and increment values.

Example 1

In this example, you'll make a modification to the ColumnDefinition table you created back in the "Creating a Table" section of this chapter. ColumnOne of that table has an IDENTITY constraint with a seed of 1 and an increment of 1. You're going to use the ALTER COLUMN statement against that column to change the seed value to 100 and the increment value to 10. To test the outcome of this ALTER TABLE operation, bring up Query Analyzer, run an INSERT statement against the ColumnDefinition table, and then view the results. You should see the value of ColumnOne jump to 100, and then go to 110, and so on.

Visual Basic .NET

```
'insert at the top of your class
Imports System.Data.SqlServerCe

'insert in a function or click event
Dim cn As SqlCeConnection
Try
cn = New SqlCeConnection("Data Source=\My Documents\dbvb.sdf;Password=apress")
cn.Open()
Dim cmd As SqlCeCommand = cn.CreateCommand
cmd.CommandText = "ALTER TABLE ColumnDefinition " & _
                                "ALTER COLUMN ColumnOne IDENTITY(100, 10)"
cmd.ExecuteNonQuery()
Catch sqlex As SqlCeException
Dim sqlError As SqlCeError
For Each sqlError In sqlex.Errors
    MessageBox.Show(sqlError.Message)
Next
```

```vb
Catch ex As Exception
MessageBox.Show(ex.Message)
Finally
If cn.State <> ConnectionState.Closed Then
    cn.Close()
End If
End Try
```

C#

```csharp
//insert at the top of your class
using System.Data.SqlServerCe;

//insert in a function or click event
SqlCeConnection cn = null;
try
{
cn = new SqlCeConnection("Data Source=\\My Documents\\dbcs.sdf;Password=apress");
cn.Open();
SqlCeCommand cmd = cn.CreateCommand();
cmd.CommandText = "ALTER TABLE ColumnDefinition " +
"ALTER COLUMN ColumnOne IDENTITY(100, 10)";
cmd.ExecuteNonQuery();
}
catch(SqlCeException sqlex)
{
foreach(SqlCeError sqlError in sqlex.Errors)
{
    MessageBox.Show(sqlError.Message);
}
}
catch(Exception ex)
{
MessageBox.Show(ex.Message);
}
finally
{
if(cn.State != ConnectionState.Closed)
{
    cn.Close();
}
}
```

Add

If you don't want to modify an existing column, you have the option of adding either a new table constraint or a column definition to the end of your table. The ALTER TABLE syntax is the same as before except that you use the ADD keyword instead of ALTER COLUMN. All the other code possibilities for both the column definitions and table constraints are the same as they were with CREATE TABLE, so there's no need to rehash all their complexities. Since you can add new columns to a table that already contains data, keep in mind that the new column values will be NULL.

Example 2

In this example, you'll add a new column, called NewColumn, to the ColumnDefinition table with a bit data type.

Visual Basic .NET

```
'insert at the top of your class
Imports System.Data.SqlServerCe

'insert in a function or click event
Dim cn As SqlCeConnection
Try
cn = New SqlCeConnection("Data Source=\My Documents\dbvb.sdf;Password=apress")
cn.Open()
Dim cmd As SqlCeCommand = cn.CreateCommand
cmd.CommandText = "ALTER TABLE ColumnDefinition " & _
                                "ADD NewColumn bit"
cmd.ExecuteNonQuery()
Catch sqlex As SqlCeException
Dim sqlError As SqlCeError
For Each sqlError In sqlex.Errors
    MessageBox.Show(sqlError.Message)
Next
Catch ex As Exception
MessageBox.Show(ex.Message)
Finally
If cn.State <> ConnectionState.Closed Then
    cn.Close()
End If
End Try
```

C#

```
//insert at the top of your class
using System.Data.SqlServerCe;

//insert in a function or click event
SqlCeConnection cn = null;
try
{
cn = new SqlCeConnection("Data Source=\\My Documents\\dbcs.sdf;Password=apress");
cn.Open();
SqlCeCommand cmd = cn.CreateCommand();
cmd.CommandText = "ALTER TABLE ColumnDefinition " +
                                "ADD NewColumn bit";
cmd.ExecuteNonQuery();
}
catch(SqlCeException sqlex)
{
foreach(SqlCeError sqlError in sqlex.Errors)
{
    MessageBox.Show(sqlError.Message);
}
}
catch(Exception ex)
{
MessageBox.Show(ex.Message);
}
finally
{
if(cn.State != ConnectionState.Closed)
    {
    cn.Close();
}
}
```

Delete

Your final table-altering option is to delete existing table constraints and columns. You'll use the DROP COLUMN keywords along with the desired column name to delete a column. To delete a table constraint, you'll use the DROP keyword and optionally use the CONSTRAINT keyword along with the name of the constraint. You might think this could present a problem if you didn't name your constraint when you created your table. However, SQL Server CE gives your table constraints a name whether you choose to name them or not.

Example 3

In this example, you'll delete the PRIMARY KEY constraint you created earlier for the TableConstraints table. With the DROP CONSTRAINT keywords and the PK constraint name, you'll eliminate the three-column PRIMARY KEY. A look at the Query Analyzer afterward will reveal that there is no longer an index named PK.

Visual Basic .NET

```vbnet
'insert at the top of your class
Imports System.Data.SqlServerCe

'insert in a function or click event
Dim cn As SqlCeConnection
Try
cn = New SqlCeConnection("Data Source=\My Documents\dbvb.sdf;Password=apress")
cn.Open()
Dim cmd As SqlCeCommand = cn.CreateCommand
cmd.CommandText = "ALTER TABLE TableConstraints " & _
                                  "DROP CONSTRAINT PK"
    cmd.ExecuteNonQuery()
Catch sqlex As SqlCeException
Dim sqlError As SqlCeError
For Each sqlError In sqlex.Errors
    MessageBox.Show(sqlError.Message)
Next
Catch ex As Exception
MessageBox.Show(ex.Message)
Finally
If cn.State <> ConnectionState.Closed Then
    cn.Close()
End If
End Try
```

C#

```
//insert at the top of your class
using System.Data.SqlServerCe;

//insert in a function or click event
SqlCeConnection cn = null;
try
{
cn = new SqlCeConnection("Data Source=\\My Documents\\dbcs.sdf;Password=apress");
cn.Open();
SqlCeCommand cmd = cn.CreateCommand();
cmd.CommandText = "ALTER TABLE TableConstraints " +
                                "DROP CONSTRAINT PK";
cmd.ExecuteNonQuery();
}
catch(SqlCeException sqlex)
{
foreach(SqlCeError sqlError in sqlex.Errors)
{
    MessageBox.Show(sqlError.Message);
}
}
catch(Exception ex)
{
MessageBox.Show(ex.Message);
}
finally
{
if(cn.State != ConnectionState.Closed)
{
    cn.Close();
}
}
```

Deleting a Table

Removing a table from your SQL Server CE database is a very simple and straight-forward matter. Using the DROP TABLE keywords along with the table name is all it takes to get the job done. That being said, if the table you want to delete is refer-enced by a FOREIGN KEY constraint from a child table, you have to delete that child table before SQL Server CE will let you delete the parent table. The last thing to remember about deleting a table is that you can't use the DROP TABLE statement to delete a system table.

Example

In this example, you'll use the DROP TABLE keywords along with the ColumnConstraints table name to remove that table from your database.

Visual Basic .NET

```
'insert at the top of your class
Imports System.Data.SqlServerCe

'insert in a function or click event
Dim cn As SqlCeConnection
Try
cn = New SqlCeConnection("Data Source=\My Documents\dbvb.sdf;Password=apress")
cn.Open()
Dim cmd As SqlCeCommand = cn.CreateCommand
cmd.CommandText = "DROP TABLE ColumnConstraints"
cmd.ExecuteNonQuery()
Catch sqlex As SqlCeException
Dim sqlError As SqlCeError
For Each sqlError In sqlex.Errors
    MessageBox.Show(sqlError.Message)
Next
Catch ex As Exception
MessageBox.Show(ex.Message)
Finally
If cn.State <> ConnectionState.Closed Then
    cn.Close()
End If
End Try
```

C#

```
//insert at the top of your class
using System.Data.SqlServerCe;

//insert in a function or click event
SqlCeConnection cn = null;
try
```

```
{
cn = new SqlCeConnection("Data Source=\\My Documents\\dbcs.sdf;Password=apress");
cn.Open();
SqlCeCommand cmd = cn.CreateCommand();
cmd.CommandText = "DROP TABLE ColumnConstraints";
cmd.ExecuteNonQuery();
}
catch(SqlCeException sqlex)
{
foreach(SqlCeError sqlError in sqlex.Errors)
{
    MessageBox.Show(sqlError.Message);
}
}
catch(Exception ex)
{
MessageBox.Show(ex.Message);
}
finally
{
if(cn.State != ConnectionState.Closed)
{
    cn.Close();
}
}
}
```

Creating an Index

Nothing provides more of a performance boost to a relational database than an index, and SQL Server CE is no exception. Why spend minutes or hours searching for a word in a book by performing a page-by-page search, when you can look it up in the index and find it in seconds? This same principle applies to databases as well.

If you search for a value from a column using a WHERE clause in an unindexed table, the query processor will have to perform a table scan that involves looking at every row in order to find a match. On the other hand, if you index that same column and you rerun your SELECT statement with the same WHERE clause, the query processor will quickly find you a match by looking up the value in the index. It goes without saying that columns that you frequently include in WHERE clauses are great candidates for indexing to improve performance. The use of indexes on your tables is so important that the folks at Microsoft allow you to have as many as 249 indexes per table. Not bad for an embedded database that only takes up 1MB of space on your Pocket PC.

Here's the syntax to create an index on a table:

```
CREATE [UNIQUE] INDEX IndexName
ON TableName (ColumnName [ASC | DESC] [,…n])
```

A quick look at the first line of this syntax reveals that you start things off with the CREATE INDEX keywords and an IndexName of your choosing. Squeezed in between CREATE and INDEX is the optional UNIQUE keyword. What this does is create a unique index in which no two rows in a given column can have the same value. Once a unique index is in place, any UPDATE or INSERT statements that might generate a duplicate value in the indexed column are rolled back and an error returned. SQL Server CE automatically creates UNIQUE indexes when you add a UNIQUE or PRIMARY KEY constraint in a CREATE TABLE statement. It's important to have PRIMARY KEYS and FOREIGN KEYS indexed to improve the performance of queries where a JOIN is involved.

Now moving down to the second line, you get to specify the TableName and one or more ColumnNames to index. Now why might you want to create a composite index by including two or more columns in a single index? In some cases, SQL Server CE does that for you when you create a multicolumn PRIMARY KEY constraint. You might also want to do this if you find yourself frequently including two or more columns in your WHERE clauses.

The last thing to note in this syntax is the optional choice of including ascending (ASC) or descending (DESC) order for your indexed columns. If you do nothing, your indexed data is automatically stored in ascending order, so there's really no need to ever use the ASC keyword. If for some reason you find yourself wanting to view some data in reverse order, then the DESC keyword is for you. You should note that indexes do a great job of speeding up sorting. Columns that are frequently acted upon by the ORDER BY clause should be indexed to reap the benefits of faster sorting.

The Dark Side

After all the raving I've done about indexes, using them all over the place sounds like a slam dunk. Unfortunately, there are some negative issues to contend with when using indexes. If you're running short on hard drive space, you should remember that indexes store copies of data from the columns you've indexed. Depending on how many indexes you place on each of your tables, you can find yourself using twice the amount of disk space that unindexed tables would take up. Personally, I don't think that wasting disk space is a good enough reason not to use indexes.

Performance can be hampered in highly indexed transactional databases where indexes have to be constantly updated due to the frequent execution of INSERT and DELETE statements. Every time you add a new row to an indexed table, you incur a performance hit because SQL Server CE must update that table's indexes. The same thing goes for the removal of a row from an indexed table. If you find that your Pocket PC database application spends more time inserting data than retrieving it, you might consider reducing the number of indexes you use.

Example

In this example, you'll create a single column index called idxColumnTwo on the nvarchar ColumnTwo in the ColumnDefinition table.

Visual Basic .NET

```
'insert at the top of your class
Imports System.Data.SqlServerCe

'insert in a function or click event
Dim cn As SqlCeConnection
Try
cn = New SqlCeConnection("Data Source=\My Documents\dbvb.sdf;Password=apress")
cn.Open()
Dim cmd As SqlCeCommand = cn.CreateCommand
cmd.CommandText = "CREATE INDEX idxColumnTwo ON ColumnDefinition (ColumnTwo)"
cmd.ExecuteNonQuery()
Catch sqlex As SqlCeException
Dim sqlError As SqlCeError
For Each sqlError In sqlex.Errors
    MessageBox.Show(sqlError.Message)
Next
Catch ex As Exception
MessageBox.Show(ex.Message)
Finally
If cn.State <> ConnectionState.Closed Then
    cn.Close()
End If
End Try
```

C#

```csharp
//insert at the top of your class
using System.Data.SqlServerCe;

//insert in a function or click event
SqlCeConnection cn = null;
try
{
cn = new SqlCeConnection("Data Source=\\My Documents\\dbcs.sdf;Password=apress");
cn.Open();
SqlCeCommand cmd = cn.CreateCommand();
cmd.CommandText = "CREATE INDEX idxColumnTwo ON ColumnDefinition (ColumnTwo)";
cmd.ExecuteNonQuery();
}
catch(SqlCeException sqlex)
{
foreach(SqlCeError sqlError in sqlex.Errors)
{
    MessageBox.Show(sqlError.Message);
}
}
catch(Exception ex)
{
MessageBox.Show(ex.Message);
}
finally
{
if(cn.State != ConnectionState.Closed)
    {
    cn.Close();
}
}
```

If you bring up the ColumnDefinition table in Query Analyzer and look inside its Indexes folder, you'll see an index called idxColumnTwo that consists of ColumnTwo as shown in Figure 4-3.

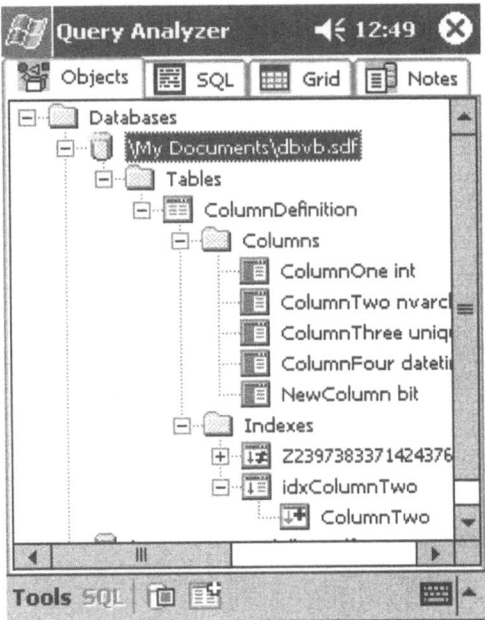

Figure 4-3. Query Analyzer displaying the idxColumnTwo index

Deleting an Index

Removing an index from a table in a SQL Server CE database is accomplished through the use of the DROP INDEX statement. The arguments required by this statement include the name of the table and the name of the index, separated by a dot. Keep in mind that the DROP INDEX statement won't work on indexes found in system tables, nor will it work with indexes created by either the PRIMARY KEY or UNIQUE constraints.

Example

In this example, you'll delete the idxColumnTwo index that you previously created in the CREATE INDEX example.

Visual Basic .NET

```
'insert at the top of your class
Imports System.Data.SqlServerCe

'insert in a function or click event
Dim cn As SqlCeConnection
Try
cn = New SqlCeConnection("Data Source=\My Documents\dbvb.sdf;Password=apress")
cn.Open()
Dim cmd As SqlCeCommand = cn.CreateCommand
cmd.CommandText = "DROP INDEX ColumnDefinition.idxColumnTwo"
cmd.ExecuteNonQuery()
Catch sqlex As SqlCeException
Dim sqlError As SqlCeError
For Each sqlError In sqlex.Errors
    MessageBox.Show(sqlError.Message)
Next
Catch ex As Exception
MessageBox.Show(ex.Message)
Finally
If cn.State <> ConnectionState.Closed Then
    cn.Close()
End If
End Try
```

C#

```
//insert at the top of your class
using System.Data.SqlServerCe;

//insert in a function or click event
SqlCeConnection cn = null;
try
{
cn = new SqlCeConnection("Data Source=\\My Documents\\dbcs.sdf;Password=apress");
cn.Open();
SqlCeCommand cmd = cn.CreateCommand();
cmd.CommandText = "DROP INDEX ColumnDefinition.idxColumnTwo";
cmd.ExecuteNonQuery();
}
catch(SqlCeException sqlex)
{
```

```
foreach(SqlCeError sqlError in sqlex.Errors)
{
    MessageBox.Show(sqlError.Message);
}
}
catch(Exception ex)
{
MessageBox.Show(ex.Message);
}
finally
{
if(cn.State != ConnectionState.Closed)
{
    cn.Close();
}
}
```

Conclusion

First you created, compacted, and deleted databases in this chapter. Next you created, modified, and deleted tables. Lastly, you created and deleted indexes. At this point, you can say that you've mastered the Data Definition Language of SQL Server CE. You now know why most database developers use graphical, automated tools to perform the tasks that you've just performed in code. That being said, you now possess the skills you need to create your own graphical, automated tools for SQL Server CE that could compete with the Query Analyzer. Of course, you still need a way to view all the various database objects and metadata, and I'll cover this in the next chapter.

CHAPTER 5
Metadata

As a professional developer, you probably spend a portion of your time building database applications that allow users to both enter and retrieve some kind of data. Data makes up the content of a given database and is generally what's most important to the users of a database system. This person needs a data acquisition program, and that person wants a business intelligence reporting application. With all the focus on data, why should anyone care too much about metadata? For starters, metadata is data about data. Without it, you'd have an awfully hard time figuring out where to put data and how to get it back out. Metadata describes things like column names, data types, indexes, and most other database objects and structures. As you might imagine, creating database queries would be impossible without prior knowledge of database metadata. You've actually spent a lot of time working with metadata during the last two chapters. When you created tables and columns visually with Query Analyzer or with Data Definition Language code, you were creating database metadata. While Query Analyzer made it easy to view that metadata, I'm sure you'd like the option of discovering and viewing this information programmatically.

Information Schema

Buried deep inside SQL Server CE are a number of Information Schema views that reveal the metadata contained in the database you're working with. Table 5-1 gives you a rundown of the views available to you along with their description.

Table 5-1. Information Schema Views

VIEW	DESCRIPTION
COLUMNS	Returns information about available columns in the current database
INDEXES	Returns data about the indexes in the current database
KEY_COLUMN_USAGE	Lists the keys in the current database
PROVIDER_TYPES	Displays the data types supported by SQL Server CE

Table 5-1. Information Schema Views (Continued)

VIEW	DESCRIPTION
TABLES	Returns information about available tables in the current database
TABLE_CONSTRAINTS	Lists the table constraints in the current database

Desired metadata is returned from these views through the use of SQL statements executed against INFORMATION_SCHEMA. For instance, in order to retrieve information about the data types supported by SQL Server CE, you would execute the following query:

```
SELECT * FROM INFORMATION_SCHEMA.PROVIDER_TYPES
```

Running this statement in Query Analyzer would return a number of columns and rows listing information about SQL Server CE data types. With the exception of this particular view, running these queries in Query Analyzer seems pretty redundant, as it already provides you with a visual description of all metadata found in a given database. Since I know that you enjoy writing lots of code as much as I do, I figured it would be fun to show you how to re-create the visual metadata portion of Query Analyzer. I'll take you through each of the six views so that you'll have a complete, and visual, understanding of how to discover metadata in your database.

Building a Metadata Viewer

I don't expect you to build something quite as slick as Query Analyzer, but I promise that the example metadata viewer will be a close approximation. This will be a simple, single-form application, with a TreeView control, a Connect button, and six other buttons for each of the six views that are available to be called. In this application, you'll be using the NorthwindDemo.sdf database for all the examples. Now it's time to fire up Visual Studio and create a Smart Device Application. As usual, I'm going to be bilingual, so it doesn't matter if you choose to work with C# or VB .NET. When the IDE comes up, you might want to go to the Project Properties window and set the device's Output File Folder option to \Windows\Start Menu\Programs if you so desire for easy access to your application long after you've developed it. You could also throw in an application icon for good measure as well, even though your only choices are the same icons you've been forced to use since Visual Basic 3.0.

Building the Form

Before you get to the excitement of writing code, you've got to take care of the visual elements of the application first. You'll be dragging and dropping some controls from the Toolbox onto your form. In the forthcoming tables, I'll specify several properties for each of the controls so that the form will look and act properly with the underlying code that you'll be adding shortly. Table 5-2 has just a few form properties for you to set to get you started.

Table 5-2. Form Properties

PROPERTY	VALUE
Name	Form1
Text	Meta Data Viewer
MinimizeBox	False

TreeView Control

A TreeView control will be used to display your database metadata in a hierarchical manner, so drag a TreeView control onto the form. Table 5-3 lists the TreeView properties that you need to set.

Table 5-3. TreeView Control Properties

PROPERTY	VALUE
Name	TreeView1 (VB .NET)/treeView1 (C#)
X	0
Y	0
Width	240
Height	160

Connect Button

A Connect button will be used to connect and disconnect from the North-windDemo.sdf database, so add a Button control to the form. Table 5-4 lists the properties that you need to set for the Connect button.

Table 5-4. Connect Button Properties

PROPERTY	VALUE
Name	btnConnect
Text	Connect
X	8
Y	168
Width	224
Height	20

Tables Button

You'll add another button, the Tables button, to return a list of tables found in the NorthwindDemo.sdf database, so drag another Button control onto the form. Table 5-5 lists the properties that you need to set for this Button control.

Table 5-5. Tables Button Properties

PROPERTY	VALUE
Name	btnTables
Text	Tables
X	8
Y	192
Width	104
Height	20

Columns Button

Next, you'll add a Columns button to display a list of columns based on a table that's been selected in the TreeView control, so drop another Button control onto the form. The properties that you need to set for this Button control are shown in Table 5-6.

Table 5-6. Columns Button Properties

PROPERTY	VALUE
Name	btnColumns
Text	Columns
X	8
Y	216
Width	104
Height	20

Key Columns Button

The next button you'll add is the Key Columns button, which is used to return the list of column(s) that make up the key of the table that's been selected in the TreeView control, so drag a Button control onto the form. Table 5-7 lists the properties that you need to set for this Button control.

Table 5-7. Key Columns Button

PROPERTY	VALUE
Name	btnKeyColumns
Text	Key Columns
X	8
Y	240
Width	104
Height	20

Table Constraints Button

Next up is a Table Constraints button, which you'll use to retrieve a list of table constraints based on the table selected in the TreeView control. Drag another Button control onto the form and set its properties as shown in Table 5-8.

Table 5-8. Table Constraints Button Properties

PROPERTY	VALUE
Name	btnTableConstraints
Text	Table Constraints
X	120
Y	192
Width	112
Height	20

Indexes Button

You'll use an Indexes button to display a given table's indexes based on a table that's been selected in the TreeView control. Drop a Button control onto the form and set the properties listed in Table 5-9.

Table 5-9. Indexes Button Properties

PROPERTY	VALUE
Name	btnIndexes
Text	Indexes
X	120
Y	216
Width	112
Height	20

Provider Types Button

The last button you'll add is a Provider Types button used to return the list of data types supported by SQL Server CE, so drop one more Button control onto the form. Table 5-10 lists the properties that you need to set for this Button control.

Table 5-10. Provider Types Button Properties

PROPERTY	VALUE
Name	btnProviderTypes
Text	Provider Types
X	120
Y	240
Width	112
Height	20

Now that all the controls are properly placed on the form and their properties are correctly set, your form should appear as shown in Figure 5-1.

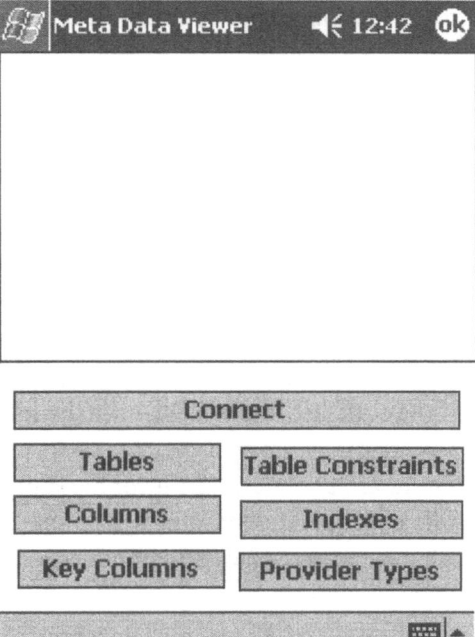

Figure 5-1. Meta Data Viewer

Connection

Normally, I would provide you with self-contained code snippets that include their own database connection management. Since I'm having you build a small application this time around, I thought it would be important to show you how SQL Server CE connections should be maintained. Because SQL Server CE only supports one connection, and your application is the only user of that single connection, it makes more sense to create that connection up front and only destroy it when it's no longer needed. In other words, take the performance hit of connecting to a database just once instead of every time you need to access it. Your application will be noticeably faster. One of the first things you need to do is set a reference to the System.Data.SqlServerCe assembly. Additionally, you should add an Imports (VB .NET) or using statement (C#) for the System.Data.SqlServerCe namespace at the top of your Form class. Now since you're going to be using a single, global connection throughout your application, you need to declare a SqlCeConnection variable at the form's class level so it can be seen by all the form's event handlers. This code looks like the following:

```
SqlCeConnection cn = null;    //C#
Private cn as SqlCeConnection    'VB .NET
```

This code can be placed before or after, but not inside, the class constructor. With that done, all that's needed now is to wire up the proper connection code in the Connect button's event handler.

Example

In this example, you'll create a case statement that allows you to alternate between a connected and disconnected state each time you tap the button. If the button text reads Connect, then tapping it will cause your application to open a connection to the NorthwindDemo.sdf database and then switch the button text to Disconnect. If, on the other hand, the button text reads Disconnect, tapping it will cause your application to disconnect from the database. Disable the button while the code is executing in order to prevent any errors occurring if the user clicks the button again before you've finished. Both standard and ADO.NET error handling code is included as well. Keep in mind that none of the other buttons will be able to perform their functions unless the application is connected to the database via the Connect button.

Visual Basic .NET

```vbnet
Private Sub btnConnect_Click(ByVal sender As System.Object, _
    ByVal e As System.EventArgs) Handles btnConnect.Click

    Try
    btnConnect.Enabled = False
    Select Case btnConnect.Text
        Case "Connect"
            cn = New SqlCeConnection( _
                "Data Source=\My Documents\NorthwindDemo.sdf;Password=")
            cn.Open()
            btnConnect.Text = "Disconnect"
        Case "Disconnect"
            If cn.State <> ConnectionState.Closed Then
                cn.Close()
            End If
            btnConnect.Text = "Connect"
    End Select
Catch sqlex As SqlCeException
    Dim sqlError As SqlCeError
    For Each sqlError In sqlex.Errors
        MessageBox.Show(sqlError.Message)
    Next
Catch ex As Exception
    MessageBox.Show(ex.Message)
Finally
    btnConnect.Enabled = True
End Try
End Sub
```

C#

```csharp
private void btnConnect_Click(object sender, System.EventArgs e)
{
try
{
    btnConnect.Enabled = false;
    switch (btnConnect.Text)
    {
        case "Connect":
            cn = new SqlCeConnection(
                "Data Source=\\My Documents\\NorthwindDemo.sdf;Password=");
```

```
                cn.Open();
                btnConnect.Text = "Disconnect";
                break;
            case "Disconnect":
                if(cn.State != ConnectionState.Closed)
                {
                        cn.Close();
                }
                btnConnect.Text = "Connect";
                break;
        }
    }
    catch(SqlCeException sqlex)
    {
        foreach(SqlCeError sqlError in sqlex.Errors)
        {
            MessageBox.Show(sqlError.Message);
        }
    }
    catch(Exception ex)
    {
        MessageBox.Show(ex.Message);
    }
    finally
    {
        btnConnect.Enabled = true;
    }
}
```

Tables

The TABLES view provides you with a list of all the tables, including system tables, found in the database you're connected to. Columns returned from this query include TABLE_CATALOG, TABLE_SCHEMA, TABLE_NAME, and TABLE_TYPE.

Example

In this example, you'll create a Command object from a valid SQL connection that queries the INFORMATION_SCHEMA.TABLES view to return a list of user tables from the NorthwindDemo.sdf database. In this case, you're only looking to return data from the TABLE_NAME column. Additionally, you'll specify a TABLE_TYPE of TABLE so that the system tables aren't returned along with the user tables. Since your goal is to populate the TreeView control with a list of tables, there are a few things you'll need to do. For starters, calling the TreeView's BeginUpdate method locks the visual elements of the control while you're adding things to it. This helps speed up both the real and perceived performance of the TreeView control. You'll also need to clear any nodes that may already be in the TreeView control so that your new data doesn't get appended to existing data. After that, you'll create the root node, which you'll name Tables. Next, you'll create a variable to handle the child nodes beneath the Tables root node. It's then time to retrieve the data, so you'll need to create a DataReader object that loops through the data and inserts it into the child nodes of the TreeView. Afterwards, you'll tell the TreeView control to expand all its nodes and then unlock the TreeView's visual display by calling the EndUpdate method. When it's all done, you should have a TreeView control with a Tables root node, and a bunch of Table Name child nodes.

Visual Basic .NET

```
Private Sub btnTables_Click(ByVal sender As System.Object, _
    ByVal e As System.EventArgs) Handles btnTables.Click

    Try
    btnTables.Enabled = False
    Dim cmd As SqlCeCommand = cn.CreateCommand
    cmd.CommandText = "SELECT TABLE_NAME " & _
                    "FROM INFORMATION_SCHEMA.TABLES " & _
                    "WHERE TABLE_TYPE = 'TABLE'"

    TreeView1.BeginUpdate()
    TreeView1.Nodes.Clear()
    TreeView1.Nodes.Add(New TreeNode("Tables"))
    Dim childNode As TreeNode = TreeView1.Nodes(0)
    Dim childCount As Integer = 0
    Dim dr As SqlCeDataReader = cmd.ExecuteReader
    While dr.Read()
        childNode.Nodes.Insert(childCount, New TreeNode(dr(0)))
        childCount += 1
    End While
    dr.Close()
    TreeView1.ExpandAll()
    TreeView1.EndUpdate()
    Catch sqlex As SqlCeException
        Dim sqlError As SqlCeError
    For Each sqlError In sqlex.Errors
        MessageBox.Show(sqlError.Message)
```

```
        Next
Catch ex As Exception
    MessageBox.Show(ex.Message)
    Finally
    btnTables.Enabled = True
    End Try
End Sub
```

C#

```csharp
private void btnTables_Click(object sender, System.EventArgs e)
{
try
{
    btnTables.Enabled = false;
    SqlCeCommand cmd = cn.CreateCommand();
    cmd.CommandText = "SELECT TABLE_NAME " +
                      "FROM INFORMATION_SCHEMA.TABLES " +
                      "WHERE TABLE_TYPE = 'TABLE'";
    treeView1.BeginUpdate();
    treeView1.Nodes.Clear();
    treeView1.Nodes.Add(new TreeNode("Tables"));
    TreeNode childNode = treeView1.Nodes[0];
    int childCount = 0;
    SqlCeDataReader dr = cmd.ExecuteReader();
    while(dr.Read())
    {
        childNode.Nodes.Insert(childCount, new TreeNode(dr[0].ToString()));
        childCount++;
    }
    dr.Close();
    treeView1.ExpandAll();
    treeView1.EndUpdate();
}
catch(SqlCeException sqlex)
{
    foreach(SqlCeError sqlError in sqlex.Errors)
    {
        MessageBox.Show(sqlError.Message);
    }
}
catch(Exception ex)
{
```

```
        MessageBox.Show(ex.Message);
    }
    finally
    {
        btnTables.Enabled = true;
    }
}
```

If all went well with your coding, the tables should be displayed in the TreeView control as shown in Figure 5-2.

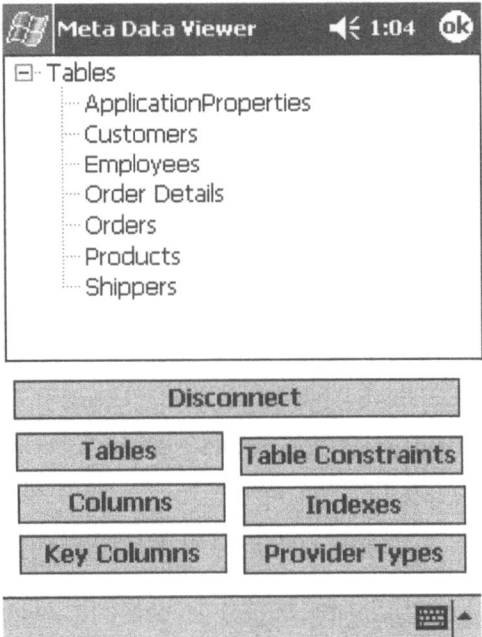

Figure 5-2. Tables displayed in TreeView

Table Constraints

The TABLE_CONSTRAINTS view provides you with a list of all the table constraints that exist in the database you're connected to. Columns returned from this query include CONSTRAINT_CATALOG, CONSTRAINT_SCHEMA, CONSTRAINT_NAME, TABLE_CATALOG, TABLE_SCHEMA, TABLE_NAME, CONSTRAINT_TYPE, IS_DEFERRABLE, INITIALLY_DEFERRED, and DESCRIPTION.

Example

In this example, your goal is to list all the table constraints found in a given table. This time around, you require a table name to be selected in the TreeView before clicking the Table Constraints button to pull this off. So first of all, you need to set the TreeView's SelectedNode.Text property equal to a local string variable. You'll then use that variable in the WHERE clause of your query against the INFORMATION_SCHEMA.TABLE_CONSTRAINTS view. After doing the usual stuff to the TreeView control, you'll use the DataReader to loop through the data and fill the TreeView control with both the name of the constraint as well as the constraint type.

Visual Basic .NET

```vbnet
Private Sub btnTableConstraints_Click(ByVal sender As System.Object, _
    ByVal e As System.EventArgs) Handles btnTableConstraints.Click

    Try
    btnTableConstraints.Enabled = False
    Dim selectedTable As String = TreeView1.SelectedNode.Text
    Dim cmd As SqlCeCommand = cn.CreateCommand
    cmd.CommandText = "SELECT CONSTRAINT_NAME, " & _
                      "CONSTRAINT_TYPE " & _
                      "FROM INFORMATION_SCHEMA.TABLE_CONSTRAINTS " & _
                      "WHERE TABLE_NAME = '" & selectedTable & "'"

    TreeView1.BeginUpdate()
    TreeView1.Nodes.Clear()
    TreeView1.Nodes.Add(New TreeNode(selectedTable))
    Dim childNode As TreeNode = TreeView1.Nodes(0)
    Dim childCount As Integer = 0
    Dim dr As SqlCeDataReader = cmd.ExecuteReader
    While dr.Read()
        childNode.Nodes.Insert(childCount, New TreeNode(dr(0) & " " & dr(1)))
        childCount += 1
    End While
    dr.Close()
    TreeView1.ExpandAll()
    TreeView1.EndUpdate()
Catch sqlex As SqlCeException
    Dim sqlError As SqlCeError
    For Each sqlError In sqlex.Errors
        MessageBox.Show(sqlError.Message)
```

```
    Next
Catch ex As Exception
    MessageBox.Show(ex.Message)
Finally
    btnTableConstraints.Enabled = True
End Try
End Sub
```

C#

```csharp
private void btnTableConstraints_Click(object sender, System.EventArgs e)
{
try
{
    btnTableConstraints.Enabled = false;
    string selectedTable = treeView1.SelectedNode.Text;
    SqlCeCommand cmd = cn.CreateCommand();
    cmd.CommandText = "SELECT CONSTRAINT_NAME, " +
                      "CONSTRAINT_TYPE " +
                      "FROM INFORMATION_SCHEMA.TABLE_CONSTRAINTS " +
                      "WHERE TABLE_NAME = '" + selectedTable + "'";

    treeView1.BeginUpdate();
    treeView1.Nodes.Clear();
    treeView1.Nodes.Add(new TreeNode(selectedTable));
    TreeNode childNode = treeView1.Nodes[0];
    int childCount = 0;
    SqlCeDataReader dr = cmd.ExecuteReader();
    while(dr.Read())
    {
        childNode.Nodes.Insert(childCount, new TreeNode(dr[0].ToString() +
        " (" + dr[1].ToString() + ")"));
        childCount++;
    }
    dr.Close();
    treeView1.ExpandAll();
    treeView1.EndUpdate();
}
catch(SqlCeException sqlex)
{
    foreach(SqlCeError sqlError in sqlex.Errors)
    {
        MessageBox.Show(sqlError.Message);
```

```
    }
}
catch(Exception ex)
{
    MessageBox.Show(ex.Message);
}
finally
{
    btnTableConstraints.Enabled = true;
}
}
```

Assuming that your code works properly, all the table constraints should appear in the TreeView control as shown in Figure 5-3.

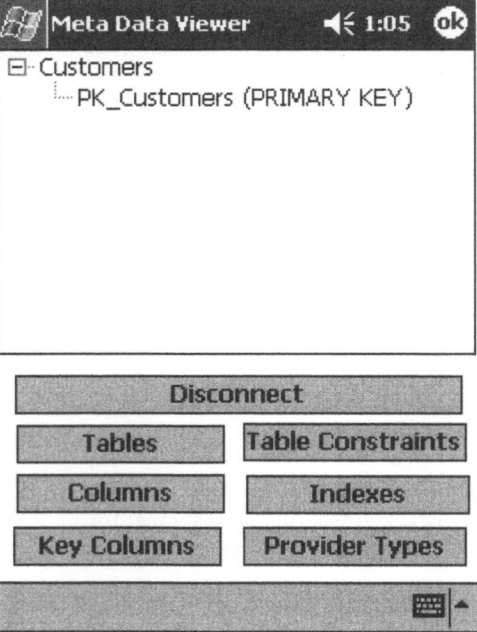

Figure 5-3. Table constraints in TreeView

Columns

The COLUMNS view shows you all the columns found in the database you're connected to. Columns returned from this query include TABLE_CATALOG, TABLE_SCHEMA, TABLE_NAME, COLUMN_NAME, COLUMN_GUID,

COLUMN_PROPID, ORDINAL_POSITION, COLUMN_HASDEFAULT, COLUMN_DEFAULT, COLUMN_FLAGS, IS_NULLABLE, DATA_TYPE, TYPE_GUID, CHARACTER_MAXIMUM_LENGTH, CHARACTER_OCTET_LENGTH, NUMERIC_PRECISION, NUMERIC_SCALE, DATETIME_PRECISION, CHARACTER_SET_CATALOG, CHARACTER_SET_SCHEMA, COLLATION_CATALOG, COLLATION_NAME, DOMAIN_CATALOG, DOMAIN_SCHEMA, and DOMAIN_NAME.

Example

In this example, you need to fill the TreeView control with column names, associated data types, and optionally the maximum length for the given column data type. As with the last example, you need to have code that allows you to capture a selected table name for use in the WHERE clause in the query against the INFORMATION_SCHEMA.COLUMNS view. When it's time to use the DataReader to loop through the data stream, you'll need to run the information from the DATA_TYPE column through a case statement in order to translate integers into meaningful data type names. Additionally, you'll have to check for null values in the CHARACTER_MAXIMUM_LENGTH column to decide whether or not to display that data in the TreeView control.

Visual Basic .NET

```vbnet
Private Sub btnColumns_Click(ByVal sender As System.Object, _
    ByVal e As System.EventArgs) Handles btnColumns.Click

    Try
    btnColumns.Enabled = False
    Dim selectedTable As String = TreeView1.SelectedNode.Text
    Dim cmd As SqlCeCommand = cn.CreateCommand
    cmd.CommandText = "SELECT COLUMN_NAME, " & _
                    "DATA_TYPE, " & _
                    "CHARACTER_MAXIMUM_LENGTH " & _
                    "FROM INFORMATION_SCHEMA.COLUMNS " & _
                    "WHERE TABLE_NAME = '" & selectedTable & "'"

    TreeView1.BeginUpdate()
    TreeView1.Nodes.Clear()
    TreeView1.Nodes.Add(New TreeNode(selectedTable))
    Dim childNode As TreeNode = TreeView1.Nodes(0)
```

```
Dim childCount As Integer = 0
Dim dataType As String
Dim dataLength As String
Dim dr As SqlCeDataReader = cmd.ExecuteReader
While dr.Read()
    Select Case dr(1)
        Case 2
            dataType = "smallint"
        Case 3
            dataType = "int"
        Case 4
            dataType = "real"
        Case 5
            dataType = "float"
        Case 6
            dataType = "money"
        Case 11
            dataType = "bit"
        Case 17
            dataType = "tinyint"
        Case 20
            dataType = "bigint"
        Case 72
            dataType = "uniqueidentifier"
        Case 128
            dataType = "binary"
        Case 130
            dataType = "nvarchar"
        Case 131
            dataType = "numeric"
        Case 135
            dataType = "datetime"
        Case Else
            dataType = "unknown"
    End Select
    If Not IsDBNull(dr(2)) Then
        dataLength = "(" & dr(2) & ")"
    Else
        dataLength = ""
    End If
```

```
            childNode.Nodes.Insert(childCount, New TreeNode(dr(0) & _
                " (" & dataType & ") " & dataLength))
            childCount += 1
        End While
        dr.Close()
        TreeView1.ExpandAll()
        TreeView1.EndUpdate()
Catch sqlex As SqlCeException
    Dim sqlError As SqlCeError
    For Each sqlError In sqlex.Errors
        MessageBox.Show(sqlError.Message)
    Next
Catch ex As Exception
    MessageBox.Show(ex.Message)
Finally
    btnColumns.Enabled = True
End Try
End Sub
```

C#

```
private void btnColumns_Click(object sender, System.EventArgs e)
{
try
{
    btnColumns.Enabled = false;
    string selectedTable = treeView1.SelectedNode.Text;
    SqlCeCommand cmd = cn.CreateCommand();
    cmd.CommandText = "SELECT COLUMN_NAME, " +
                      "DATA_TYPE, " +
                      "CHARACTER_MAXIMUM_LENGTH " +
                      "FROM INFORMATION_SCHEMA.COLUMNS " +
                      "WHERE TABLE_NAME = '" + selectedTable + "'";

    treeView1.BeginUpdate();
    treeView1.Nodes.Clear();
    treeView1.Nodes.Add(new TreeNode(selectedTable));
    TreeNode childNode = treeView1.Nodes[0];
    int childCount = 0;
    string dataType = "";
```

```
string dataLength = "";
SqlCeDataReader dr = cmd.ExecuteReader();
while(dr.Read())
{
    switch (dr[1].ToString())
    {
        case "2":
            dataType = "smallint";
            break;
        case "3":
            dataType = "int";
            break;
        case "4":
                dataType = "real";
            break;
        case "5":
                dataType = "float";
            break;
        case "6":
            dataType = "money";
            break;
        case "11":
            dataType = "bit";
            break;
        case "17":
            dataType = "tinyint";
            break;
        case "20":
            dataType = "bigint";
            break;
        case "72":
            dataType = "uniqueidentifier";
            break;
        case "128":
            dataType = "binary";
            break;
        case "130":
            dataType = "nvarchar";
            break;
        case "131":
            dataType = "numeric";
            break;
```

```
                case "135":
                    dataType = "datetime";
                    break;
                default:
                    dataType = "unknown";
                    break;
            }
            if(!dr.IsDBNull(2))
            {
                dataLength = "(" + dr[2] + ")";
            }
            else
            {
                dataLength = "";
            }
            childNode.Nodes.Insert(childCount, new TreeNode(dr[0].ToString() +
                " (" + dataType + ") " + dataLength));
            childCount++;
        }
        dr.Close();
        treeView1.ExpandAll();
        treeView1.EndUpdate();
    }
    catch(SqlCeException sqlex)
    {
        foreach(SqlCeError sqlError in sqlex.Errors)
        {
            MessageBox.Show(sqlError.Message);
        }
    }
    catch(Exception ex)
    {
        MessageBox.Show(ex.Message);
    }
    finally
    {
        btnColumns.Enabled = true;
    }
}
```

If your code executes as planned, all the columns should be visible in the
TreeView control as shown in Figure 5-4.

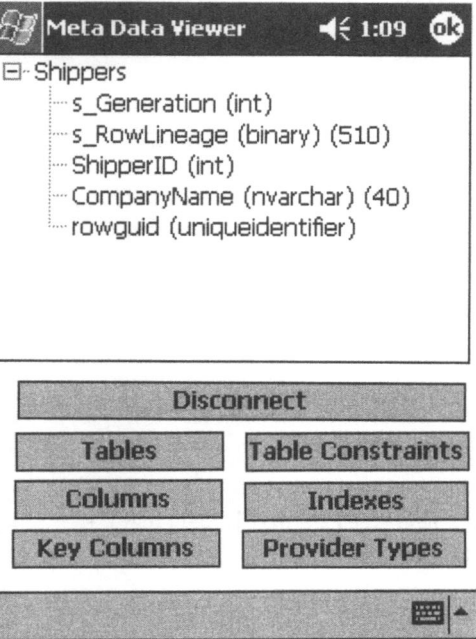

Figure 5-4. Columns in TreeView

Indexes

The INDEXES view returns a list of all indexes found in the database you're connected to. Columns returned from this query include TABLE_CATALOG, TABLE_SCHEMA, TABLE_NAME, INDEX_CATALOG, INDEX_SCHEMA, INDEX_NAME, PRIMARY_KEY, UNIQUE, CLUSTERED, TYPE, FILL_FACTOR, INITIAL_SIZE, NULLS, SORT_BOOKMARKS, AUTO_UPDATE, NULL_COLLATION, ORDINAL_POSITION, COLUMN_NAME, COLUMN_GUID, COLUMN_PROPID, COLLATION, CARDINALITY, PAGES, FILTER_CONDITION, and INTEGRATED.

Example

In this example, you'll be filling the TreeView control with a list of index names, column names, and indications as to whether an index is UNIQUE or a PRIMARY KEY. As usual, you need to have code that allows you to capture a selected table name for use in the WHERE clause in the query against the INFORMATION_SCHEMA.INDEXES view. As you loop through the data with the DataReader, you'll have to run the UNIQUE column against an If/Then statement to translate all values of True to UNIQUE. You'll have to do the same thing with the PRIMARY KEY column as well. The values of these two columns will only be shown in the TreeView control if they exist.

Visual Basic .NET

```vbnet
Private Sub btnIndexes_Click(ByVal sender As System.Object, _
    ByVal e As System.EventArgs) Handles btnIndexes.Click

    Try
    btnIndexes.Enabled = False
    Dim selectedTable As String = TreeView1.SelectedNode.Text
    Dim cmd As SqlCeCommand = cn.CreateCommand
    cmd.CommandText = "SELECT INDEX_NAME, " & _
                    "COLUMN_NAME, " & _
                    """UNIQUE"", " & _
                    "PRIMARY_KEY " & _
                    "FROM INFORMATION_SCHEMA.INDEXES " & _
                    "WHERE TABLE_NAME = '" & selectedTable & "'"

    TreeView1.BeginUpdate()
    TreeView1.Nodes.Clear()
    TreeView1.Nodes.Add(New TreeNode(selectedTable))
    Dim childNode As TreeNode = TreeView1.Nodes(0)
    Dim childCount As Integer = 0
    Dim indexUnique As String
    Dim indexPrimaryKey As String
    Dim dr As SqlCeDataReader = cmd.ExecuteReader
    While dr.Read()
        If dr(2) = "True" Then
            indexUnique = "(UNIQUE)"
        Else
            indexUnique = ""
        End If
        If dr(3) = "True" Then
            indexPrimaryKey = "(PRIMARY KEY)"
        Else
            indexPrimaryKey = ""
        End If
        childNode.Nodes.Insert(childCount, New TreeNode( _
            dr(0) & " (" & dr(1) & ") " & indexUnique & " " & indexPrimaryKey))
        childCount += 1
    End While
    dr.Close()
```

```
        TreeView1.ExpandAll()
        TreeView1.EndUpdate()
Catch sqlex As SqlCeException
    Dim sqlError As SqlCeError
    For Each sqlError In sqlex.Errors
        MessageBox.Show(sqlError.Message)
    Next
Catch ex As Exception
    MessageBox.Show(ex.Message)
Finally
    btnIndexes.Enabled = True
End Try
End Sub
```

C#

```
private void btnIndexes_Click(object sender, System.EventArgs e)
{
try
{
    btnIndexes.Enabled = false;
    string selectedTable = treeView1.SelectedNode.Text;
    SqlCeCommand cmd = cn.CreateCommand();
    cmd.CommandText = "SELECT INDEX_NAME, " +
                      "COLUMN_NAME, " +
                      "\"UNIQUE\", " +
                      "PRIMARY_KEY " +
                      "FROM INFORMATION_SCHEMA.INDEXES " +
                      "WHERE TABLE_NAME = '" + selectedTable + "'";

    treeView1.BeginUpdate();
    treeView1.Nodes.Clear();
    treeView1.Nodes.Add(new TreeNode(selectedTable));
    TreeNode childNode = treeView1.Nodes[0];
    int childCount = 0;
    string indexUnique = "";
    string indexPrimaryKey = "";
    SqlCeDataReader dr = cmd.ExecuteReader();
    while(dr.Read())
    {
        if(dr[2].ToString() == "True")
        {
            indexUnique = "(UNIQUE)";
```

```
        }
        else
        {
            indexUnique = "";
        }
        if(dr[3].ToString() == "True")
        {
            indexPrimaryKey = "(PRIMARY KEY)";
        }
        else
        {
            indexPrimaryKey = "";
        }
            childNode.Nodes.Insert(childCount, new TreeNode(dr[0].ToString() +
                " (" + dr[1].ToString() + ") " + indexUnique + " " +
                indexPrimaryKey));
        childCount++;
    }
    dr.Close();
    treeView1.ExpandAll();
    treeView1.EndUpdate();
}
catch(SqlCeException sqlex)
{
    foreach(SqlCeError sqlError in sqlex.Errors)
    {
        MessageBox.Show(sqlError.Message);
    }
}
catch(Exception ex)
{
    MessageBox.Show(ex.Message);
}
finally
{
    btnIndexes.Enabled = true;
}
}
```

If everything worked out with your code, then all the indexes should be visible in the TreeView control as shown in Figure 5-5.

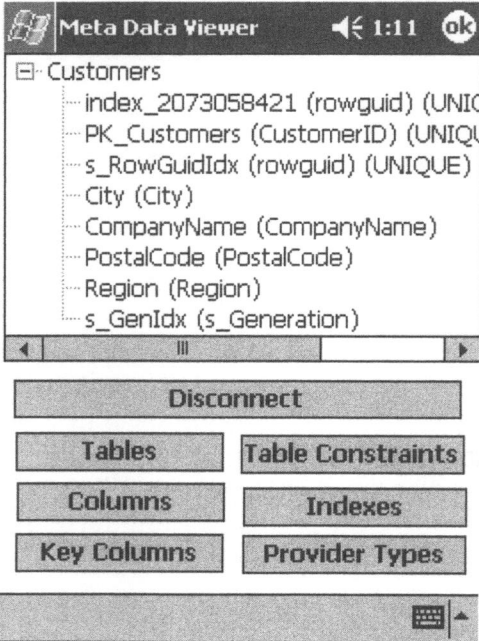

Figure 5-5. Indexes in TreeView

Key Column Usage

The KEY_COLUMN_USAGE view returns all the keys and columns that make up those keys in the database you're connected to. Columns returned from this query include CONSTRAINT_CATALOG, CONSTRAINT_SCHEMA, CONSTRAINT_NAME, TABLE_CATALOG, TABLE_SCHEMA, TABLE_NAME, COLUMN_NAME, COLUMN_GUID, COLUMN_PROPID, and ORDINAL_POSITION.

Example

In this example, you'll fill the TreeView control with the columns that make up a PRIMARY or FOREIGN KEY in a given table. You'll know the name of that given table up front by retrieving the Text property of the selected node in the TreeView control. This table name can then be used in the WHERE clause in the query against the INFORMATION_SCHEMA.KEY_COLUMN_USAGE view. After that, you'll just loop through the data to display the appropriate Key columns in the TreeView control.

Visual Basic .NET

```
Private Sub btnKeyColumns_Click(ByVal sender As System.Object, _
    ByVal e As System.EventArgs) Handles btnKeyColumns.Click

    Try
    btnKeyColumns.Enabled = False
    Dim selectedTable As String = TreeView1.SelectedNode.Text
    Dim cmd As SqlCeCommand = cn.CreateCommand
    cmd.CommandText = "SELECT CONSTRAINT_NAME, " & _
                    "COLUMN_NAME " & _
                    "FROM INFORMATION_SCHEMA.KEY_COLUMN_USAGE " & _
                    "WHERE TABLE_NAME = '" & selectedTable & "'"

    TreeView1.BeginUpdate()
    TreeView1.Nodes.Clear()
    TreeView1.Nodes.Add(New TreeNode(selectedTable))
    Dim childNode As TreeNode = TreeView1.Nodes(0)
    Dim childCount As Integer = 0
    Dim dr As SqlCeDataReader = cmd.ExecuteReader
    While dr.Read()
        childNode.Nodes.Insert(childCount, New TreeNode( _
            dr(0) & " (" & dr(1) & ")"))
        childCount += 1
    End While
    dr.Close()
    TreeView1.ExpandAll()
    TreeView1.EndUpdate()
Catch sqlex As SqlCeException
    Dim sqlError As SqlCeError
    For Each sqlError In sqlex.Errors
        MessageBox.Show(sqlError.Message)
    Next
Catch ex As Exception
    MessageBox.Show(ex.Message)
Finally
    btnKeyColumns.Enabled = True
End Try
End Sub
```

C#

```csharp
private void btnKeyColumns_Click(object sender, System.EventArgs e)
{
try
{
    btnKeyColumns.Enabled = false;
    string selectedTable = treeView1.SelectedNode.Text;
    SqlCeCommand cmd = cn.CreateCommand();
    cmd.CommandText = "SELECT CONSTRAINT_NAME, " +
                      "COLUMN_NAME " +
                      "FROM INFORMATION_SCHEMA.KEY_COLUMN_USAGE " +
                      "WHERE TABLE_NAME = '" + selectedTable + "'";

    treeView1.BeginUpdate();
    treeView1.Nodes.Clear();
    treeView1.Nodes.Add(new TreeNode(selectedTable));
    TreeNode childNode = treeView1.Nodes[0];
    int childCount = 0;
    SqlCeDataReader dr = cmd.ExecuteReader();
    while(dr.Read())
    {
        childNode.Nodes.Insert(childCount, new TreeNode(
            dr[0].ToString() + " (" + dr[1].ToString() + ")"));
        childCount++;
    }
    dr.Close();
    treeView1.ExpandAll();
    treeView1.EndUpdate();
}
catch(SqlCeException sqlex)
{
    foreach(SqlCeError sqlError in sqlex.Errors)
    {
        MessageBox.Show(sqlError.Message);
    }
}
catch(Exception ex)
{
    MessageBox.Show(ex.Message);
}
```

```
finally
{
    btnKeyColumns.Enabled = true;
}
}
```

As long as your code works properly, then all the key columns should be visible in the TreeView control as shown in Figure 5-6.

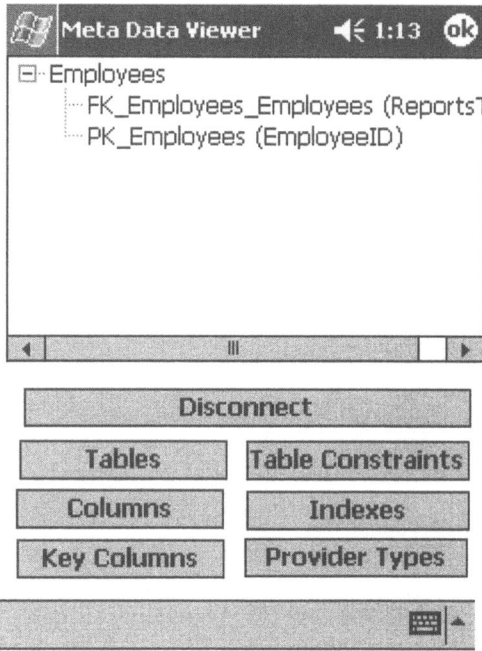

Figure 5-6. Key column usage

Provider Types

The PROVIDER_TYPES view gives you a list of all the data types supported by SQL Server CE. Columns returned from this query include TYPE_NAME, DATA_TYPE, COLUMN_SIZE, LITERAL_PREFIX, LITERAL_SUFFIX, CREATE_PARAMS, IS_NULLABLE, and CASE_SENSITIVE.

Example

In this example, you're going to display a list of all the data types available in SQL Server CE. This time around, your query doesn't depend on capturing a table name from the TreeView control in order to run properly. A quick loop through the data with the DataReader gives you a complete list of data types and sizes.

Visual Basic .NET

```
Private Sub btnProviderTypes_Click(ByVal sender As System.Object, _
    ByVal e As System.EventArgs) Handles btnProviderTypes.Click

Try
    btnProviderTypes.Enabled = False
    Dim cmd As SqlCeCommand = cn.CreateCommand
    cmd.CommandText = "SELECT TYPE_NAME, " & _
                    "COLUMN_SIZE " & _
                    "FROM INFORMATION_SCHEMA.PROVIDER_TYPES"

    TreeView1.BeginUpdate()
    TreeView1.Nodes.Clear()
    TreeView1.Nodes.Add(New TreeNode("Data Types"))
    Dim childNode As TreeNode = TreeView1.Nodes(0)
    Dim childCount As Integer = 0
    Dim dr As SqlCeDataReader = cmd.ExecuteReader
    While dr.Read
        childNode.Nodes.Insert(childCount, New TreeNode( _
            dr(0) & " (" & dr(1) & ")"))
        childCount += 1
    End While
    dr.Close()
    TreeView1.ExpandAll()
    TreeView1.EndUpdate()
Catch sqlex As SqlCeException
    Dim sqlError As SqlCeError
    For Each sqlError In sqlex.Errors
        MessageBox.Show(sqlError.Message)
    Next
Catch ex As Exception
    MessageBox.Show(ex.Message)
Finally
    btnProviderTypes.Enabled = True
End Try
End Sub
```

C#

```csharp
private void btnProviderTypes_Click(object sender, System.EventArgs e)
{
try
{
    btnProviderTypes.Enabled = false;
    SqlCeCommand cmd = cn.CreateCommand();
    cmd.CommandText = "SELECT TYPE_NAME, " +
                        "COLUMN_SIZE " +
                        "FROM INFORMATION_SCHEMA.PROVIDER_TYPES";

    treeView1.BeginUpdate();
    treeView1.Nodes.Clear();
    treeView1.Nodes.Add(new TreeNode("Data Types"));
    TreeNode childNode = treeView1.Nodes[0];
    int childCount = 0;
    SqlCeDataReader dr = cmd.ExecuteReader();
    while(dr.Read())
    {
        childNode.Nodes.Insert(childCount, new TreeNode(
            dr[0].ToString() + " (" + dr[1].ToString() + ")"));
        childCount++;
    }
    dr.Close();
    treeView1.ExpandAll();
    treeView1.EndUpdate();
}
catch(SqlCeException sqlex)
{
    foreach(SqlCeError sqlError in sqlex.Errors)
    {
        MessageBox.Show(sqlError.Message);
    }
}
catch(Exception ex)
{
    MessageBox.Show(ex.Message);
}
finally
{
    btnProviderTypes.Enabled = true;
}
}
```

If all goes well with your code, then all the SQL Server CE data types should be visible in the TreeView control as shown in Figure 5-7.

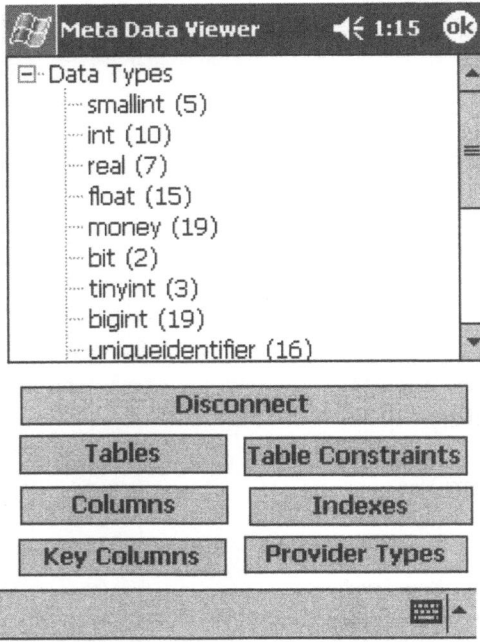

Figure 5-7. Provider types in TreeView

Conclusion

You're now the proud owner of the first .NET Compact Framework–based SQL Server CE metadata viewer on your block. While not meant to compete with Query Analyzer in the number of features or robustness of code, it does teach you how to view all the database objects yourself. I hope that you've found this exercise in metadata discovery useful and can incorporate these techniques into future projects. Now it's time to leave the world of database object construction and metadata discovery behind and enter the realm of actual data manipulation.

Data Manipulation Language

THE SQL DATA MANIPULATION LANGUAGE (DML) specifies how data is inserted, updated, retrieved, and deleted in the objects defined using the Data Definition Language (DDL). Considering that you're now an expert at creating, manipulating, and viewing SQL Server CE database objects and metadata thanks to Chapters 4 and 5, it's time to shift gears and start working with actual data. In this chapter, you'll utilize the NorthwindDemo.sdf database when working with examples that help to illustrate a variety of DML concepts. In order to work with the examples found in the chapter, you'll need to create a new Pocket PC Smart Device Application and place both a DataGrid and a Button control on the form. This way, you'll be able to type the example code into the click event of the button and then see the results via DataSets bound to the DataGrid. Because you'll be working with DataSets and SQL Server CE, you'll need to add a reference to both System.Data.SqlServerCe and System.Data.Common. Additionally, all my code examples will include a reminder to insert the appropriate Imports or using statement at the top of your class. If a particular topic in this chapter requires more than one example in order to explain everything, only the first example will include the full source code. Subsequent examples within a topic will only display the information that's different. It's time to start inserting, selecting, updating, and deleting, so let's get to it.

Inserting Data

It's hard to work with data when you have a database full of empty tables. That's where the handy INSERT statement comes into play with its ability to add complete or partial rows of data to a given table. The following syntax and parameter descriptions will provide you with the structure needed to use the INSERT statement effectively.

Syntax

INSERT [INTO] TableName [(ColumnName, ...n)]

VALUES ({DEFAULT | NULL | expression} [, ...n])

Parameters

[INTO]

This is an optional keyword that may be used after INSERT.

TableName

This is the name of the table in which the data will be inserted.

[(ColumnName, ...n)]

This is an optional list of the specific columns, enclosed by parentheses and separated by commas, that data is to be inserted into. If you choose not to include a list of column names, then SQL Server CE assumes that you're providing a value for every column. If you choose to leave out a column name, then it must be nullable, have a default value, or be an IDENTITY or ROWGUID column. Otherwise, SQL Server CE will return an error.

VALUES

This keyword comes before the list of data values to be inserted. If a list of column names is used, then there must be one data value for each column name, and those values must be in the same order as the columns. If no column list is specified, the values must be in the order in which the columns are stored in the database. The data values must be enclosed by parentheses and separated by commas.

DEFAULT

This keyword specifies that the default value for a column should be used instead of a new data value.

NULL

This keyword indicates that the data value for a given column is unknown and should not be confused with a zero (0) or an empty string ("").

expression

This represents data values such as characters, numbers, expressions, variables, or constants.

Example

In this example, you'll be inserting information about a Pocket PC into the Products table. You'll probably notice that several of the column names aren't mentioned in the INSERT statement. This is because these columns are IDENTITY columns, have default values, or are ROWGUID columns with an auto-generated uniqueidentifier. After you insert the data, you'll set the Command object's CommandType equal to TableDirect. This allows you to name the table you want to look at and have all its data returned. It works just like SELECT * FROM TableName, but you'll learn more about that later. Your results should look the same as those displayed in Figure 6-1.

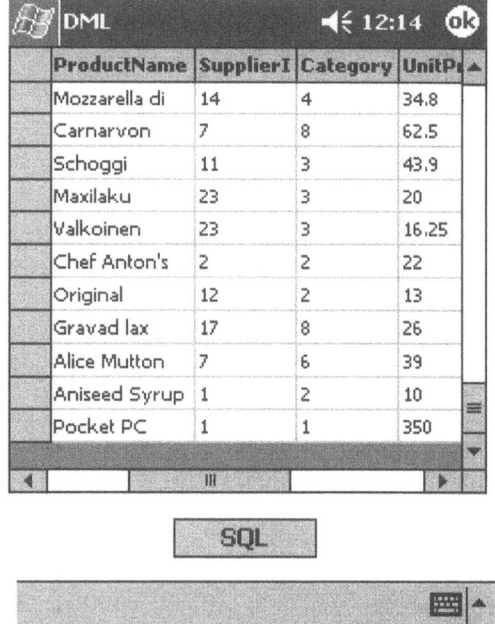

Figure 6-1. A newly inserted product, Pocket PC, is displayed in the Products table.

Visual Basic .NET

```
'insert at the top of your class
Imports System.Data.SqlServerCe

'insert in a function or click event
Dim cn As SqlCeConnection
Try
cn = New SqlCeConnection("Data Source=\My Documents\NorthwindDemo.sdf;Password="")
```

```
cn.Open()
Dim cmd As SqlCeCommand = cn.CreateCommand
cmd.CommandText = "INSERT INTO Products (" & _
                                "ProductName, " & _
                                "SupplierID, " & _
                                "CategoryID, " & _
                                "UnitPrice, " & _
                                "UnitsInStock, " & _
                                "Discontinued) " & _
                                "VALUES " & _
                                "(?, ?, ?, ?, ?, ?)"
cmd.Parameters.Add("ProductName", "Pocket PC")
cmd.Parameters.Add("SupplierID", 1)
cmd.Parameters.Add("CategoryID", 1)
cmd.Parameters.Add("UnitPrice", 350)
cmd.Parameters.Add("UnitsInStock", 20)
cmd.Parameters.Add("Discontinued", 1)
cmd.ExecuteNonQuery()
"Display results of the Insert
cmd.CommandType = CommandType.TableDirect
cmd.CommandText = "Products"
Dim da As New SqlCeDataAdapter(cmd)
Dim ds As New DataSet
da.Fill(ds)
DataGrid1.Enabled = False
DataGrid1.DataSource = ds.Tables(0)
Catch sqlex As SqlCeException
Dim sqlError As SqlCeError
For Each sqlError In sqlex.Errors
    MessageBox.Show(sqlError.Message)
Next
Catch ex As Exception
MessageBox.Show(ex.Message)
Finally
DataGrid1.Enabled = True
If cn.State <> ConnectionState.Closed Then
    cn.Close()
End If
End Try
```

C#

```
//insert at the top of your class
using System.Data.SqlServerCe;

//insert in a function or click event
SqlCeConnection cn = null;
try
{
cn = new SqlCeConnection("Data Source=\\My Documents\\NorthwindDemo.sdf;" +
                                        "Password=");
cn.Open();
SqlCeCommand cmd = cn.CreateCommand();
cmd.CommandText = "INSERT INTO Products (" +
                                "ProductName, " +
                                "SupplierID, " +
                                "CategoryID, " +
                                "UnitPrice, " +
                                "UnitsInStock, " +
                                "Discontinued) " +
                                "VALUES " +
                                "(?, ?, ?, ?, ?, ?)";
cmd.Parameters.Add("ProductName", "Pocket PC");
cmd.Parameters.Add("SupplierID", 1);
cmd.Parameters.Add("CategoryID", 1);
cmd.Parameters.Add("UnitPrice", 350);
cmd.Parameters.Add("UnitsInStock", 20);
cmd.Parameters.Add("Discontinued", 1);
cmd.ExecuteNonQuery();
//Display results of the Insert
cmd.CommandType = CommandType.TableDirect;
cmd.CommandText = "Products";
SqlCeDataAdapter da = new SqlCeDataAdapter(cmd);
DataSet ds = new DataSet();
da.Fill(ds);
dataGrid1.Enabled = false;
dataGrid1.DataSource = ds.Tables[0];
}
catch(SqlCeException sqlex)
{
foreach(SqlCeError sqlError in sqlex.Errors)
{
    MessageBox.Show(sqlError.Message);
}
```

```
}
catch(Exception ex)
{
MessageBox.Show(ex.Message);
}
finally
{
dataGrid1.Enabled = true;
if(cn.State != ConnectionState.Closed)
{
    cn.Close();
}
}
```

Retrieving Data

The retrieval of information from a database table or tables is accomplished through what's generally called a SELECT statement. This statement is very powerful and encompasses not only data retrieval, but also the filtering, sorting, grouping, and joining of data from one or more tables. There's no question that your use of the SELECT statement will easily outstrip your use of any other SQL operation. Since that SELECT statement is a very broad subject to cover, I'll break it up into logical pieces. Therefore, you'll start out by just looking at the combination of the SELECT and FROM clauses for now. You really can't run even a basic query without the participation of those two clauses. To keep things simple, you'll just utilize the most minimal features of the FROM clause needed to make things work. The following syntax and parameter descriptions will provide you with the structure needed to use the SELECT and FROM clauses effectively.

Syntax

SELECT [ALL | DISTINCT]

* | {TableName.* | TableAlias.*} | {ColumnName | expression} [[AS] ColumnAlias] [, …n]

FROM TableName [[AS] TableAlias] [, …n]

Parameters

ALL

This keyword means that duplicate rows can show up in a given result set of data. Since ALL is the default, it's not necessary to use it.

DISTINCT

This keyword means that only unique rows can show up in a given result set of data.

*

This symbol means that all columns from all the tables specified in the FROM clause should be returned. That being said, if you don't need to return all the columns, don't ever use this symbol in a production application, as your program will suffer a performance hit.

TableName.* | TableAlias.*

This reduces the scope of the * symbol to only returning rows from the table specified by TableName. TableAlias is used in situations where a table is given an alias in the FROM clause.

ColumnName

ColumnName is what you'll be using most often to specify the names of one or more columns of data to return. In the event that two tables you've joined together both contain a column by the same name, you must append the appropriate table name along with a dot (.) in front of ColumnName in order to distinguish the two.

expression

This may be either a function, constant, or any combination of column names that are connected by one or more operators.

ColumnAlias

This is used in conjunction with the AS keyword to replace an actual column name in the result set of data. More often, it's used to create a column name for the results of a function or operator.

TableName

This is used to specify the table(s) or view(s) to pull data from.

TableAlias

This is used in concert with the AS keyword to give a replacement name to an existing table name. Keep in mind that once you create a table alias in the FROM clause, you must use only the alias anywhere in your query where you would normally use the actual table name.

Example 1

In this example, you'll execute the most commonly used SELECT statement, the one that includes the * symbol, against the Shippers table in order to return everything in the table. Your results should look the same as those displayed in Figure 6-2.

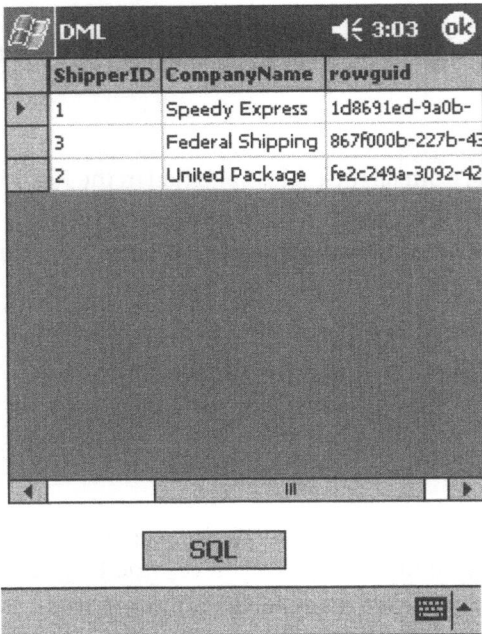

Figure 6-2. All shippers are displayed.

Visual Basic .NET

```
'insert at the top of your class
Imports System.Data.SqlServerCe

'insert in a function or click event
Dim cn As SqlCeConnection
Try
cn = New SqlCeConnection("Data Source=\My Documents\NorthwindDemo.sdf;Password=")
cn.Open()
Dim cmd As SqlCeCommand = cn.CreateCommand
cmd.CommandText = "SELECT * FROM Shippers"
Dim da As New SqlCeDataAdapter(cmd)
Dim ds As New DataSet
da.Fill(ds)
DataGrid1.Enabled = False
DataGrid1.DataSource = ds.Tables(0)
Catch sqlex As SqlCeException
Dim sqlError As SqlCeError
For Each sqlError In sqlex.Errors
    MessageBox.Show(sqlError.Message)
```

```
Next
Catch ex As Exception
MessageBox.Show(ex.Message)
Finally
DataGrid1.Enabled = True
If cn.State <> ConnectionState.Closed Then
    cn.Close()
End If
End Try
```

C#

```csharp
//insert at the top of your class
using System.Data.SqlServerCe;

//insert in a function or click event
SqlCeConnection cn = null;
try
{
cn = new SqlCeConnection("Data Source=\\My Documents\\NorthwindDemo.sdf;" +
                                        "Password=");
cn.Open();
SqlCeCommand cmd = cn.CreateCommand();
cmd.CommandText = "SELECT * FROM Shippers";
SqlCeDataAdapter da = new SqlCeDataAdapter(cmd);
DataSet ds = new DataSet();
da.Fill(ds);
dataGrid1.Enabled = false;
dataGrid1.DataSource = ds.Tables[0];
}
catch(SqlCeException sqlex)
{
foreach(SqlCeError sqlError in sqlex.Errors)
{
    MessageBox.Show(sqlError.Message);
}
}
catch(Exception ex)
{
MessageBox.Show(ex.Message);
}
finally
{
```

```
dataGrid1.Enabled = true;
if(cn.State != ConnectionState.Closed)
{
    cn.Close();
}
}
```

Example 2

In this example, you use the DISTINCT keyword in order to remove redundant data and display only unique CategoryID values from the Products table. Your results should look the same as those displayed in Figure 6-3.

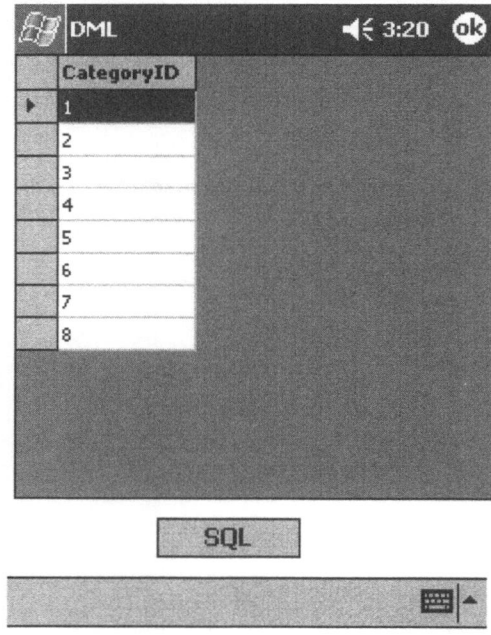

Figure 6-3. Only unique CategoryID values are displayed.

Visual Basic .NET

```
'insert at the top of your class
Imports System.Data.SqlServerCe

'insert in a function or click event
cmd.CommandText = "SELECT DISTINCT CategoryID FROM Products"
```

C#

```
//insert at the top of your class
using System.Data.SqlServerCe;

//insert in a function or click event
cmd.CommandText = "SELECT DISTINCT CategoryID FROM Products";
```

Example 3

In this example, you'll knock out two birds with two stones in the alias department. You'll create an alias for the Products table called P, and you'll create an alias for the column ProductName called WidgetName. You'll display both the WidgetName and UnitPrice columns. Your results should look the same as those displayed in Figure 6-4.

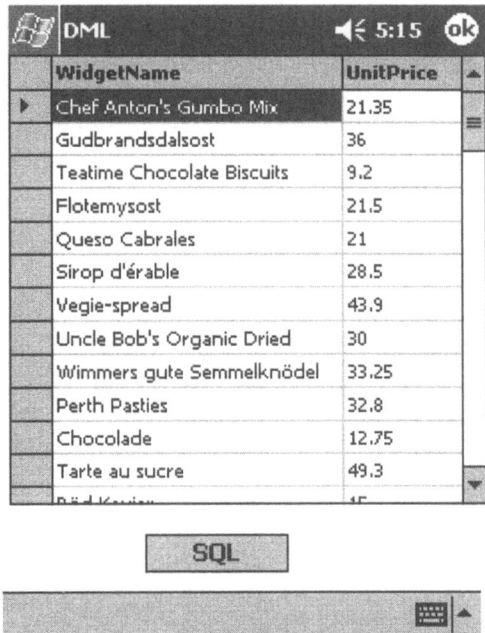

Figure 6-4. WidgetNames and UnitPrices

Visual Basic .NET

```
'insert at the top of your class
Imports System.Data.SqlServerCe

'insert in a function or click event
cmd.CommandText = "SELECT P.ProductName AS WidgetName, P.UnitPrice " & _
                                "FROM Products P"
```

C#

```
//insert at the top of your class
using System.Data.SqlServerCe;

//insert in a function or click event
cmd.CommandText = "SELECT P.ProductName AS WidgetName, P.UnitPrice " +
                                "FROM Products P";
```

Joining Tables

Whenever you need to return data from two or more tables, you'll find yourself using one of SQL Server CE's supported joins in the FROM clause of your query. The following syntax and parameter descriptions will provide you with the structure needed to use the various join options you have in the FROM clause effectively.

Syntax

FROM TableName [[AS] TableAlias]

[INNER | {LEFT | RIGHT} [OUTER]] JOIN

TableName [[AS] TableAlias]

ON JoinExpression

Parameters

INNER

This keyword dictates that all matching rows from both tables are returned while all unmatched rows are discarded.

LEFT [OUTER]

This keyword specifies that all matching rows from both tables are returned as well as all rows from the left table, whether they matched or not. The left table refers to the first table after the FROM keyword.

RIGHT [OUTER]

This keyword dictates that all matching rows from both tables are returned as well as all rows from the right table, whether they matched or not. The right table refers to the second table after the FROM keyword.

JOIN

This keyword points out that the given tables should be joined.

ON JoinExpression

This specifies the condition by which the join can occur. This expression works in a similar fashion as the WHERE clause.

Example 1

In this example, you'll perform an INNER JOIN on the Orders and Order Details tables. You'll display the OrderDate, UnitPrice, and Quantity values for items with equivalent OrderIDs. Only matching rows from both tables will be returned. Your results should look the same as those displayed in Figure 6-5.

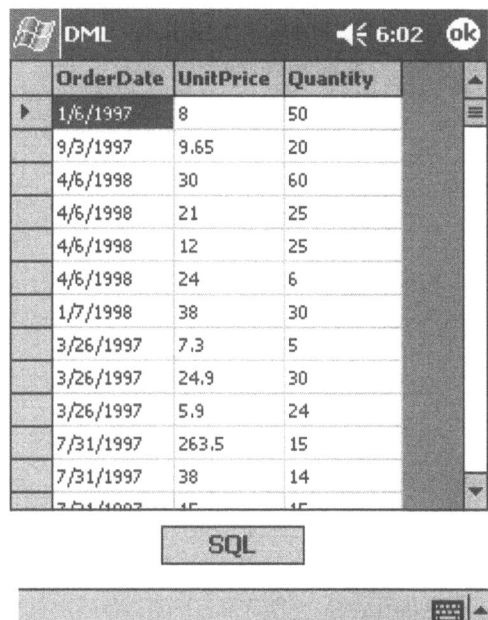

Figure 6-5. OrderDates, UnitPrices, and Quantities for rows matching in both tables

Visual Basic .NET

```vbnet
'insert at the top of your class
Imports System.Data.SqlServerCe

'insert in a function or click event
Dim cn As SqlCeConnection
Try
cn = New SqlCeConnection("Data Source=\My Documents\NorthwindDemo.sdf;Password=")
cn.Open()
Dim cmd As SqlCeCommand = cn.CreateCommand
cmd.CommandText = "SELECT OrderDate, OD.UnitPrice, OD.Quantity " & _
                            "FROM Orders INNER JOIN ""Order Details"" OD " & _
                            "ON Orders.OrderID = OD.OrderID"
Dim da As New SqlCeDataAdapter(cmd)
Dim ds As New DataSet
da.Fill(ds)
DataGrid1.Enabled = False
DataGrid1.DataSource = ds.Tables(0)
Catch sqlex As SqlCeException
Dim sqlError As SqlCeError
For Each sqlError In sqlex.Errors
    MessageBox.Show(sqlError.Message)
Next
Catch ex As Exception
MessageBox.Show(ex.Message)
Finally
DataGrid1.Enabled = True
If cn.State <> ConnectionState.Closed Then
    cn.Close()
End If
End Try
```

C#

```csharp
//insert at the top of your class
using System.Data.SqlServerCe;

//insert in a function or click event
SqlCeConnection cn = null;
try
{
cn = new SqlCeConnection("Data Source=\\My Documents\\NorthwindDemo.sdf;" +
                                        "Password=");
cn.Open();
SqlCeCommand cmd = cn.CreateCommand();
cmd.CommandText = "SELECT OrderDate, OD.UnitPrice, OD.Quantity " +
                                "FROM Orders INNER JOIN \"Order Details\" OD " +
                                "ON Orders.OrderID = OD.OrderID";
SqlCeDataAdapter da = new SqlCeDataAdapter(cmd);
DataSet ds = new DataSet();
da.Fill(ds);
dataGrid1.Enabled = false;
dataGrid1.DataSource = ds.Tables[0];
}
catch(SqlCeException sqlex)
{
foreach(SqlCeError sqlError in sqlex.Errors)
{
    MessageBox.Show(sqlError.Message);
}
}
catch(Exception ex)
{
MessageBox.Show(ex.Message);
}
finally
{
dataGrid1.Enabled = true;
if(cn.State != ConnectionState.Closed)
{
    cn.Close();
}
}
```

Example 2

In this example, you'll perform a LEFT OUTER JOIN on the Orders and Order Details tables. You'll display the OrderDate, UnitPrice, and Quantity values for items with equivalent OrderIDs. Matching rows from both tables as well as all the rows from the Orders table will be returned.

Visual Basic .NET

```
'insert at the top of your class
Imports System.Data.SqlServerCe

'insert in a function or click event
cmd.CommandText = "SELECT OrderDate, OD.UnitPrice, OD.Quantity " & _
                  "FROM Orders LEFT OUTER JOIN ""Order Details"" OD " & _
                  "ON Orders.OrderID = OD.OrderID"
```

C#

```
//insert at the top of your class
using System.Data.SqlServerCe;

//insert in a function or click event
cmd.CommandText = "SELECT OrderDate, OD.UnitPrice, OD.Quantity " +
                  "FROM Orders LEFT OUTER JOIN \"Order Details\" OD " +
                  "ON Orders.OrderID = OD.OrderID";
```

Example 3

In this example, you'll perform a RIGHT OUTER JOIN on the Orders and Order Details tables. You'll display the OrderDate, UnitPrice, and Quantity values for items with equivalent OrderIDs. Matching rows from both tables as well as all the rows from the Order Details table will be returned.

Visual Basic .NET

```
'insert at the top of your class
Imports System.Data.SqlServerCe
```

```
'insert in a function or click event
cmd.CommandText = "SELECT OrderDate, OD.UnitPrice, OD.Quantity " & _
                  "FROM Orders RIGHT OUTER JOIN ""Order Details"" OD " & _
                  "ON Orders.OrderID = OD.OrderID"
```

C#

```
//insert at the top of your class
using System.Data.SqlServerCe;

//insert in a function or click event
cmd.CommandText = "SELECT OrderDate, OD.UnitPrice, OD.Quantity " +
                  "FROM Orders RIGHT OUTER JOIN \"Order Details\" OD " +
                  "ON Orders.OrderID = OD.OrderID";
```

Filtering Data

Without some kind of filtering mechanism, every query you'd run would return all the data contained in the designated tables. This leads to data overload and the inability to find what you're looking for very quickly. Luckily, you're provided with the WHERE clause, which lets you specify all kinds of search conditions that help you to narrow down your result set of data. The following syntax and parameter descriptions will provide you with the structure needed to use the WHERE clause effectively.

Syntax

[WHERE WhereExpression]

Parameters

WhereExpression

This expression can reduce the rows returned in the result set through the use of an unlimited number of operators and functions.

Example

In this example, you'll display the ProductName, UnitPrice, and CategoryID values for items that have a UnitPrice of greater than $200 and a CategoryID equal to 1. Your results should look the same as those displayed in Figure 6-6.

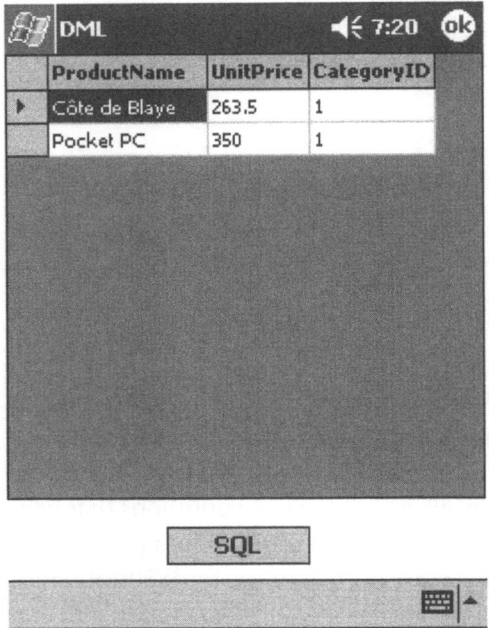

Figure 6-6. ProductNames, UnitPrice, and CategoryID of items that cost over $200

Visual Basic .NET

```
'insert at the top of your class
Imports System.Data.SqlServerCe

'insert in a function or click event
Dim cn As SqlCeConnection
Try
cn = New SqlCeConnection("Data Source=\My Documents\NorthwindDemo.sdf;Password=")
cn.Open()
Dim cmd As SqlCeCommand = cn.CreateCommand
cmd.CommandText = "SELECT ProductName, UnitPrice, CategoryID " & _
                            "FROM Products " & _
                            "WHERE CategoryID = 1 " & _
                            "AND UnitPrice > 200"
```

```
Dim da As New SqlCeDataAdapter(cmd)
Dim ds As New DataSet
da.Fill(ds)
DataGrid1.Enabled = False
DataGrid1.DataSource = ds.Tables(0)
Catch sqlex As SqlCeException
Dim sqlError As SqlCeError
For Each sqlError In sqlex.Errors
    MessageBox.Show(sqlError.Message)
Next
Catch ex As Exception
MessageBox.Show(ex.Message)
Finally
DataGrid1.Enabled = True
If cn.State <> ConnectionState.Closed Then
    cn.Close()
End If
End Try
```

C#

```
//insert at the top of your class
using System.Data.SqlServerCe;

//insert in a function or click event
SqlCeConnection cn = null;
try
{
cn = new SqlCeConnection("Data Source=\\My Documents\\NorthwindDemo.sdf;" +
                                        "Password=");
cn.Open();
SqlCeCommand cmd = cn.CreateCommand();
cmd.CommandText = "SELECT ProductName, UnitPrice, CategoryID " +
                            "FROM Products " +
                            "WHERE CategoryID = 1 " +
                            "AND UnitPrice > 200";
SqlCeDataAdapter da = new SqlCeDataAdapter(cmd);
DataSet ds = new DataSet();
da.Fill(ds);
dataGrid1.Enabled = false;
dataGrid1.DataSource = ds.Tables[0];
}
catch(SqlCeException sqlex)
```

```
{
foreach(SqlCeError sqlError in sqlex.Errors)
{
    MessageBox.Show(sqlError.Message);
}
}
catch(Exception ex)
{
MessageBox.Show(ex.Message);
}
finally
{
dataGrid1.Enabled = true;
if(cn.State != ConnectionState.Closed)
{
    cn.Close();
}
}
}
```

Joining Query Results

If instead of joining two tables, you'd rather join two or more SELECT statements, the UNION operator will help you in accomplishing that task. It combines the results of one or more queries, removes the duplicates, and returns a single result set of data. The following syntax and parameter descriptions will provide you with the structure needed to use the UNION operator effectively.

Syntax

query UNION [ALL] query

[UNION [ALL] query [...n]]

Parameters

query

The first query will return data that will be combined with one or more other queries. While the column definitions of the various queries combined by the UNION operator don't have to be the same, they must be capable of implicit conversion.

UNION

This operator specifies that one or more result sets be combined as a single result set of data.

ALL

This keyword specifies that all rows be included in the result set of data.

Example

In this example, you'll build two queries and connect them together with the UNION operator. The end result will be the display of ProductName, UnitPrice, and CategoryID values for items with a CategoryID equal to both 1 and 2. Your results should look the same as those displayed in Figure 6-7.

Figure 6-7. The union of two queries

Visual Basic .NET

```
'insert at the top of your class
Imports System.Data.SqlServerCe
```

```vb
'insert in a function or click event
Dim cn As SqlCeConnection
Try
cn = New SqlCeConnection("Data Source=\My Documents\NorthwindDemo.sdf;Password=")
cn.Open()
Dim cmd As SqlCeCommand = cn.CreateCommand
cmd.CommandText = "SELECT ProductName, UnitPrice, CategoryID " & _
                            "FROM Products " & _
                            "WHERE CategoryID = 1 " & _
                            "UNION " & _
                          "SELECT ProductName, UnitPrice, CategoryID " & _
                            "FROM Products " & _
                            "WHERE CategoryID = 2"
Dim da As New SqlCeDataAdapter(cmd)
Dim ds As New DataSet
da.Fill(ds)
DataGrid1.Enabled = False
DataGrid1.DataSource = ds.Tables(0)
Catch sqlex As SqlCeException
Dim sqlError As SqlCeError
For Each sqlError In sqlex.Errors
    MessageBox.Show(sqlError.Message)
Next
Catch ex As Exception
MessageBox.Show(ex.Message)
Finally
DataGrid1.Enabled = True
If cn.State <> ConnectionState.Closed Then
    cn.Close()
End If
End Try
```

C#

```csharp
//insert at the top of your class
using System.Data.SqlServerCe;

//insert in a function or click event
SqlCeConnection cn = null;
try
{
cn = new SqlCeConnection("Data Source=\\My Documents\\NorthwindDemo.sdf;" +
                                "Password=");
```

```
cn.Open();
SqlCeCommand cmd = cn.CreateCommand();
cmd.CommandText = "SELECT ProductName, UnitPrice, CategoryID " +
                                "FROM Products " +
                                "WHERE CategoryID = 1 " +
                                "UNION " +
                                "SELECT ProductName, UnitPrice, CategoryID " +
                                "FROM Products " +
                                "WHERE CategoryID = 2";
SqlCeDataAdapter da = new SqlCeDataAdapter(cmd);
DataSet ds = new DataSet();
da.Fill(ds);
dataGrid1.Enabled = false;
dataGrid1.DataSource = ds.Tables[0];
}
catch(SqlCeException sqlex)
{
foreach(SqlCeError sqlError in sqlex.Errors)
{
    MessageBox.Show(sqlError.Message);
}
}
catch(Exception ex)
{
MessageBox.Show(ex.Message);
}
finally
{
dataGrid1.Enabled = true;
if(cn.State != ConnectionState.Closed)
{
    cn.Close();
}
}
```

Grouping Data

If you're looking to divide a table into groups based on column names or computed columns, the GROUP BY clause can get you where you want to go. In practical terms, if you're tasked with creating reports for your company that contain aggregate data, you have no alternative to the GROUP BY clause. The following syntax and parameter descriptions will provide you with the structure needed to use the GROUP BY clause effectively.

Syntax

[GROUP BY GroupByExpression [, ...n]]

Parameters

GroupByExpression

This expression is usually either a column name or a nonaggregate expression that references a column.

Example

In this example, you'll display the name of each city in the Customers table, and the number of times that city shows up in the table. This is possible through the combination of grouping rows by city and using the COUNT(*) function. Your results should look the same as those displayed in the scrolled-down view shown in Figure 6-8.

Figure 6-8. The number of times a city shows up in the Customers table

Visual Basic .NET

```vbnet
'insert at the top of your class
Imports System.Data.SqlServerCe

'insert in a function or click event
Dim cn As SqlCeConnection
Try
cn = New SqlCeConnection("Data Source=\My Documents\NorthwindDemo.sdf;Password=")
cn.Open()
Dim cmd As SqlCeCommand = cn.CreateCommand
'Since Count is a reserved word in SQL, you must enclose it in quotes
cmd.CommandText = "SELECT City, COUNT(*) AS ""Count"" " & _
                                "FROM Customers " & _
                                "GROUP BY City"
Dim da As New SqlCeDataAdapter(cmd)
Dim ds As New DataSet
da.Fill(ds)
DataGrid1.Enabled = False
DataGrid1.DataSource = ds.Tables(0)
Catch sqlex As SqlCeException
Dim sqlError As SqlCeError
For Each sqlError In sqlex.Errors
    MessageBox.Show(sqlError.Message)
Next
Catch ex As Exception
MessageBox.Show(ex.Message)
Finally
DataGrid1.Enabled = True
If cn.State <> ConnectionState.Closed Then
    cn.Close()
End If
End Try
```

C#

```csharp
//insert at the top of your class
using System.Data.SqlServerCe;

//insert in a function or click event
SqlCeConnection cn = null;
try
{
```

```csharp
cn = new SqlCeConnection("Data Source=\\My Documents\\NorthwindDemo.sdf;" +
                                        "Password=");
cn.Open();
SqlCeCommand cmd = cn.CreateCommand();
//Since Count is a reserved word in SQL, you must enclose it in quotes
cmd.CommandText = "SELECT City, COUNT(*) AS \"Count\" " +
                                "FROM Customers " +
                                "GROUP BY City";
SqlCeDataAdapter da = new SqlCeDataAdapter(cmd);
DataSet ds = new DataSet();
da.Fill(ds);
dataGrid1.Enabled = false;
dataGrid1.DataSource = ds.Tables[0];
}
catch(SqlCeException sqlex)
{
foreach(SqlCeError sqlError in sqlex.Errors)
{
    MessageBox.Show(sqlError.Message);
}
}
catch(Exception ex)
{
MessageBox.Show(ex.Message);
}
finally
{
dataGrid1.Enabled = true;
if(cn.State != ConnectionState.Closed)
{
    cn.Close();
}
}
}
```

Filtering Grouped Data

Another way to filter data is through the use of the HAVING clause. A HAVING clause is like a WHERE clause except that it acts on groups, whereas the WHERE clause acts on individual rows. This time around, you're using a filter designed to eliminate unwanted groups from your result set when using the GROUP BY clause. It should be noted that the HAVING clause must always follow the GROUP BY clause. The following syntax and parameter descriptions will provide you with the structure needed to use the HAVING clause effectively.

Syntax

[HAVING HavingExpression]

Parameters

HavingExpression

This works similarly to the WHERE clause in that it can use aggregate and non-aggregate expressions. Columns specified in the GROUP BY clause can be used in nonaggregate expressions.

Example

In this example, just like the last one, you'll display the city and the number of times that city shows up in the Customers table. This time around, only cities that show up more than three times will be displayed. Your results should look the same as those displayed in Figure 6-9.

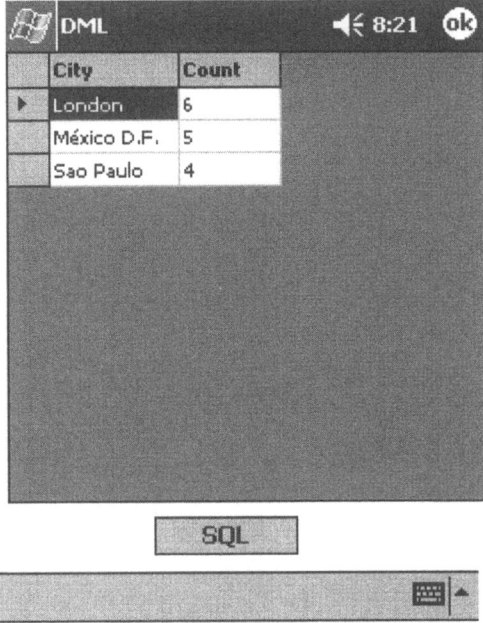

Figure 6-9. Cities that show up more than three times

Visual Basic .NET

```vb
'insert at the top of your class
Imports System.Data.SqlServerCe

'insert in a function or click event
Dim cn As SqlCeConnection
Try
cn = New SqlCeConnection("Data Source=\My Documents\NorthwindDemo.sdf;Password=")
cn.Open()
Dim cmd As SqlCeCommand = cn.CreateCommand
cmd.CommandText = "SELECT City, COUNT(*) AS ""Count"" " & _
                                "FROM Customers " & _
                                "GROUP BY City " & _
                                "HAVING COUNT(*) > 3"
Dim da As New SqlCeDataAdapter(cmd)
Dim ds As New DataSet
da.Fill(ds)
DataGrid1.Enabled = False
DataGrid1.DataSource = ds.Tables(0)
Catch sqlex As SqlCeException
Dim sqlError As SqlCeError
For Each sqlError In sqlex.Errors
    MessageBox.Show(sqlError.Message)
Next
Catch ex As Exception
MessageBox.Show(ex.Message)
Finally
DataGrid1.Enabled = True
If cn.State <> ConnectionState.Closed Then
    cn.Close()
End If
End Try
```

C#

```csharp
//insert at the top of your class
using System.Data.SqlServerCe;

//insert in a function or click event
SqlCeConnection cn = null;
try
{
```

```
cn = new SqlCeConnection("Data Source=\\My Documents\\NorthwindDemo.sdf;" +
                                    "Password=");
cn.Open();
SqlCeCommand cmd = cn.CreateCommand();
cmd.CommandText = "SELECT City, COUNT(*) AS \"Count\" " +
                            "FROM Customers " +
                            "GROUP BY City " +
                            "HAVING COUNT(*) > 3";
SqlCeDataAdapter da = new SqlCeDataAdapter(cmd);
DataSet ds = new DataSet();
da.Fill(ds);
dataGrid1.Enabled = false;
dataGrid1.DataSource = ds.Tables[0];
}
catch(SqlCeException sqlex)
{
foreach(SqlCeError sqlError in sqlex.Errors)
{
    MessageBox.Show(sqlError.Message);
}
}
catch(Exception ex)
{
MessageBox.Show(ex.Message);
}
finally
{
dataGrid1.Enabled = true;
if(cn.State != ConnectionState.Closed)
{
    cn.Close();
}
}
}
```

Sorting Data

When you retrieve data from a table, it may appear that the data is returned in no particular order. Data is actually retrieved in the order in which it appears in the table. Despite the fact that you can filter and group your data, you may also want to sort the rows in your result sets. This task is easily accomplished through the use of the ORDER BY clause. The following syntax and parameter descriptions will provide you with the structure needed to use the ORDER BY clause effectively.

Syntax

[ORDER BY OrderByExpression [ASC | DESC] [, ...n]]

Parameters

OrderByExpression

This expression specifies either the name or alias of the column on which you wish to sort. You can also sort more than one column. Which columns take sort precedence is dependent upon the sequence in which they appear in the ORDER BY clause.

ASC

This keyword dictates that the values in the specified column be sorted in ascending order (lower values first). This is the default sort order.

DESC

This keyword dictates that the values in the specified column be sorted in descending order, which is from the highest to the lowest value.

Example 1

In this example, you'll display the CompanyName and City values found in the Customers table. Most importantly, you'll use the default ORDER BY syntax to sort your data by city. Your results should look the same as those displayed in Figure 6-10.

Visual Basic .NET

```
'insert at the top of your class
Imports System.Data.SqlServerCe

'insert in a function or click event
Dim cn As SqlCeConnection
Try
cn = New SqlCeConnection("Data Source=\My Documents\NorthwindDemo.sdf;Password=")
cn.Open()
Dim cmd As SqlCeCommand = cn.CreateCommand
cmd.CommandText = "SELECT CompanyName, City " & _
                            "FROM Customers " & _
                            "ORDER BY City"
```

```
Dim da As New SqlCeDataAdapter(cmd)
Dim ds As New DataSet
da.Fill(ds)
DataGrid1.Enabled = False
DataGrid1.DataSource = ds.Tables(0)
Catch sqlex As SqlCeException
Dim sqlError As SqlCeError
For Each sqlError In sqlex.Errors
    MessageBox.Show(sqlError.Message)
Next
Catch ex As Exception
MessageBox.Show(ex.Message)
Finally
DataGrid1.Enabled = True
If cn.State <> ConnectionState.Closed Then
    cn.Close()
End If
End Try
```

C#

```
//insert at the top of your class
using System.Data.SqlServerCe;

//insert in a function or click event
SqlCeConnection cn = null;
try
{
cn = new SqlCeConnection("Data Source=\\My Documents\\NorthwindDemo.sdf;" +
                                        "Password=");
cn.Open();
SqlCeCommand cmd = cn.CreateCommand();
cmd.CommandText = "SELECT CompanyName, City " +
                                "FROM Customers " +
                                "ORDER BY City";
SqlCeDataAdapter da = new SqlCeDataAdapter(cmd);
DataSet ds = new DataSet();
da.Fill(ds);
dataGrid1.Enabled = false;
dataGrid1.DataSource = ds.Tables[0];
}
catch(SqlCeException sqlex)
{
```

```csharp
foreach(SqlCeError sqlError in sqlex.Errors)
{
    MessageBox.Show(sqlError.Message);
}
}
catch(Exception ex)
{
MessageBox.Show(ex.Message);
}
finally
{
dataGrid1.Enabled = true;
if(cn.State != ConnectionState.Closed)
{
    cn.Close();
}
}
```

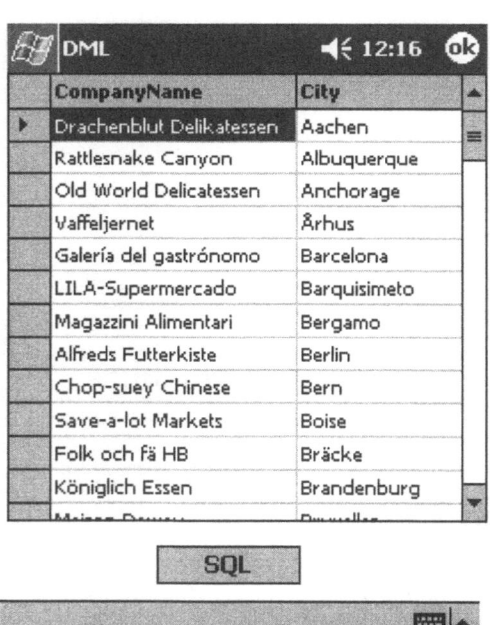

Figure 6-10. CompanyNames and City values sorted in ascending order by city

Example 2

In this example, you'll display the CompanyName and City values found in the Customers table again. This time around, you'll use the ORDER BY syntax with the DESC keyword to sort your data by city in descending order. Your results should look the same as those displayed in Figure 6-11.

Figure 6-11. CompanyName and City values sorted in descending order by city

Visual Basic .NET

```
'insert at the top of your class
Imports System.Data.SqlServerCe

'insert in a function or click event
cmd.CommandText = "SELECT CompanyName, City " & _
                       "FROM Customers " & _
                       "ORDER BY City DESC"
```

C#

```
//insert at the top of your class
using System.Data.SqlServerCe;

//insert in a function or click event
cmd.CommandText = "SELECT CompanyName, City " +
                            "FROM Customers " +
                            "ORDER BY City DESC";
```

Updating Data

When you have data in your table, and you're just looking to change that existing data, you use the UPDATE statement. The following syntax and parameter descriptions will provide you with the structure needed to use the UPDATE statement effectively.

Syntax

UPDATE TableName

SET ColumnName = {expression | NULL | DEFAULT} [, ...n]

[WHERE WhereExpression]

Parameters

TableName

This is the name of the table in which data will be updated.

SET

This keyword specifies the column names to be updated.

ColumnName

This is the name of the column whose data is set to be modified. Ensure that you don't specify any IDENTITY columns, because they can't be updated.

expression

This can be a character or numeric value or even a variable or expression that returns a value. Either way, the value of this expression is used to replace the current value in the designated column name.

DEFAULT

Using this keyword means that you want the default value of the specified column to replace its current value. If the column doesn't have a default value but is nullable, using this keyword will change the column to NULL.

NULL

If the column in question is nullable, this keyword can be used to replace the current value of the column with that of NULL.

WHERE

The use of the WHERE clause is designed to filter and thereby limit the rows that get updated. Keep in mind that if you choose not to include a WHERE clause, all rows in the specified table will be updated.

WhereExpression

Anything you can use in a WHERE clause is fair game here in helping to create the necessary condition for the rows to be updated. Each row in the table gets evaluated before any rows in the table are updated.

Example

In this example, you'll use the UPDATE statement against the Customers table to change the value of Region to UNKNOWN whenever it's equal to NULL. You'll then display the results of this change using the TableDirect CommandType. Your results should look the same as those displayed in the scrolled-down view shown in Figure 6-12.

Visual Basic .NET

```
'insert at the top of your class
Imports System.Data.SqlServerCe

'insert in a function or click event
Dim cn As SqlCeConnection
Try
cn = New SqlCeConnection("Data Source=\My Documents\NorthwindDemo.sdf;Password=")
cn.Open()
Dim cmd As SqlCeCommand = cn.CreateCommand
cmd.CommandText = "UPDATE Customers " & _
                             "SET Region = 'UNKNOWN' " & _
                             "WHERE Region IS NULL"

cmd.ExecuteNonQuery()
```

```
cmd.CommandType = CommandType.TableDirect
cmd.CommandText = "Customers"
Dim da As New SqlCeDataAdapter(cmd)
Dim ds As New DataSet
da.Fill(ds)
DataGrid1.Enabled = False
DataGrid1.DataSource = ds.Tables(0)
Catch sqlex As SqlCeException
Dim sqlError As SqlCeError
For Each sqlError In sqlex.Errors
    MessageBox.Show(sqlError.Message)
Next
Catch ex As Exception
MessageBox.Show(ex.Message)
Finally
DataGrid1.Enabled = True
If cn.State <> ConnectionState.Closed Then
    cn.Close()
End If
End Try
```

C#

```
//insert at the top of your class
using System.Data.SqlServerCe;

//insert in a function or click event
SqlCeConnection cn = null;
try
{
cn = new SqlCeConnection("Data Source=\\My Documents\\NorthwindDemo.sdf;" +
                                        "Password=");
cn.Open();
SqlCeCommand cmd = cn.CreateCommand();
cmd.CommandText = "UPDATE Customers " +
                                    "SET Region = 'UNKNOWN' " +
                                    "WHERE Region IS NULL";
cmd.ExecuteNonQuery();
cmd.CommandType = CommandType.TableDirect;
cmd.CommandText = "Customers";
SqlCeDataAdapter da = new SqlCeDataAdapter(cmd);
DataSet ds = new DataSet();
da.Fill(ds);
```

```
dataGrid1.Enabled = false;
dataGrid1.DataSource = ds.Tables[0];
}
catch(SqlCeException sqlex)
{
foreach(SqlCeError sqlError in sqlex.Errors)
{
    MessageBox.Show(sqlError.Message);
}
}
catch(Exception ex)
{
MessageBox.Show(ex.Message);
}
finally
{
dataGrid1.Enabled = true;
if(cn.State != ConnectionState.Closed)
{
    cn.Close();
}
}
```

Figure 6-12. Null Region values turn into UNKNOWN Region values

Deleting Data

If you're looking to remove one or more rows of data from a table, look no further than the DELETE statement to do the job for you. The following syntax and parameter descriptions will provide you with the necessary blueprints to use the DELETE statement effectively.

Syntax

DELETE [FROM] TableName [WHERE WhereExpression]

Parameters

[FROM]

This is an optional keyword that you may use after the DELETE keyword.

TableName

This is the name of the table whose rows are being deleted.

WHERE

The use of the WHERE clause is designed to filter and thereby limit the rows that get deleted. Keep in mind that if you choose not to include a WHERE clause, all rows in the specified table will be deleted, so be careful.

WhereExpression

Anything you can use in a WHERE clause is fair game here in helping to create the necessary condition for the rows to be deleted. Each row in the table gets evaluated before any rows in the table are deleted.

Example

In this example, you'll come full circle by deleting the very first item you inserted at the beginning of this chapter. Occupying the last row of the Products table is the result of your INSERT statement, with which you added a ProductName of Pocket PC. You'll now delete that row and then display to the whole world that it is in fact gone. Your results should look the same as those displayed in the scrolled-down view shown in Figure 6-13.

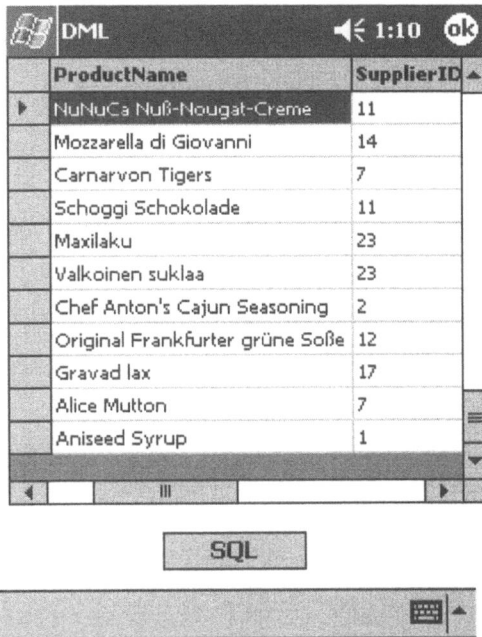

Figure 6-13. The Pocket PC ProductName has been deleted.

Visual Basic .NET

```
'insert at the top of your class
Imports System.Data.SqlServerCe

'insert in a function or click event
Dim cn As SqlCeConnection
Try
cn = New SqlCeConnection("Data Source=\My Documents\NorthwindDemo.sdf;Password=")
cn.Open()
Dim cmd As SqlCeCommand = cn.CreateCommand
cmd.CommandText = "DELETE Products " & _
                                "WHERE ProductName = 'Pocket PC'"
cmd.ExecuteNonQuery()
cmd.CommandType = CommandType.TableDirect
cmd.CommandText = "Products"
Dim da As New SqlCeDataAdapter(cmd)
Dim ds As New DataSet
da.Fill(ds)
DataGrid1.Enabled = False
DataGrid1.DataSource = ds.Tables(0)
```

```
Catch sqlex As SqlCeException
Dim sqlError As SqlCeError
For Each sqlError In sqlex.Errors
    MessageBox.Show(sqlError.Message)
Next
Catch ex As Exception
MessageBox.Show(ex.Message)
Finally
DataGrid1.Enabled = True
If cn.State <> ConnectionState.Closed Then
    cn.Close()
End If
End Try
```

C#

```
//insert at the top of your class
using System.Data.SqlServerCe;

//insert in a function or click event
SqlCeConnection cn = null;
try
{
cn = new SqlCeConnection("Data Source=\\My Documents\\NorthwindDemo.sdf;" +
                                    "Password=");
cn.Open();
SqlCeCommand cmd = cn.CreateCommand();
cmd.CommandText = "DELETE Products " +
                                "WHERE ProductName = 'Pocket PC'";
cmd.ExecuteNonQuery();
cmd.CommandType = CommandType.TableDirect;
cmd.CommandText = "Products";
SqlCeDataAdapter da = new SqlCeDataAdapter(cmd);
DataSet ds = new DataSet();
da.Fill(ds);
dataGrid1.Enabled = false;
dataGrid1.DataSource = ds.Tables[0];
}
catch(SqlCeException sqlex)
{
foreach(SqlCeError sqlError in sqlex.Errors)
{
    MessageBox.Show(sqlError.Message);
```

```
}
}
catch(Exception ex)
{
MessageBox.Show(ex.Message);
}
finally
{
dataGrid1.Enabled = true;
if(cn.State != ConnectionState.Closed)
{
    cn.Close();
}
}
```

Conclusion

Well, this wraps up an exhaustive and example-filled look at what you can do with the Data Manipulation Language supported by SQL Server CE. You've been given a small taste of what you can do with WHERE, GROUP BY, and HAVING clauses. In the next two chapters, you'll learn about the SQL Server CE built-in operators and functions that make these three clauses infinitely more powerful. If you want to learn more about optimizing your DML statements, check out http://www.microsoft.com/technet/treeview/default.asp?url=/technet/prodtechnol/sql/maintain/Optimize/SSCEQPOP.asp.

Operator Reference

THE ABILITY TO MANIPULATE and filter the data you're retrieving is one of the most important features of a database. SQL Server CE 2.0 provides you with an array of operators designed to help you accomplish that goal. Technically speaking, an operator is just a symbol that specifies an action to be performed on one or more expressions. Whether you need to perform a mathematical operation against the values in two different columns or you just want insight into their equality, SQL Server CE has 30 different operators to help meet your needs. While the intent of this chapter is to serve you as a reference, I thought it would be helpful to provide you with an example for each of the operators.

Furthermore, I want you to run these examples, see the results, and compare them to my results just to make sure you're doing everything properly. To do this, I'll need you to create a new Pocket PC Smart Device Application and then drag and drop a Button and a DataGrid onto the form. You can then type my code examples into the click event of the button, execute them, and see the results in the DataGrid. To make sure your ADO.NET code can communicate with SQL Server CE and utilize DataSets, add a reference to both System.Data.SqlServerCe and System.Data.Common.

As I mentioned before, this will be an example-filled reference in which the C# and Visual Basic .NET code will look the same each time as it connects to the NorthwindDemo.sdf database, creates a query utilizing a given operator, uses a DataAdapter to fill a DataSet, binds the result to a DataGrid, and then catches any errors that may be thrown. Therefore, I will only show the complete code in this chapter's first example so as to limit the number of trees killed in the creation of this book. All subsequent examples will just display the unique queries assigned to the CommandText property of the Command object. It's time to learn about operators and see how they can add value to your Pocket PC database application.

Arithmetic

Arithmetic operators are used to perform mathematical computations like adding, subtracting, multiplying, and dividing. These operations may be performed on any two expressions whose data type is in the numeric category.

+ (Add)

The addition arithmetic operator adds two numeric expressions together. Additionally, no pun intended, the addition operator can be used to add a number, in days, to a given date.

Syntax

expression + expression

Example

In this example, you'll display the UnitPrice column and then you'll display the results of adding 1 to the value of UnitPrice in the New Unit Price column. Your results should look the same as those shown in Figure 7-1.

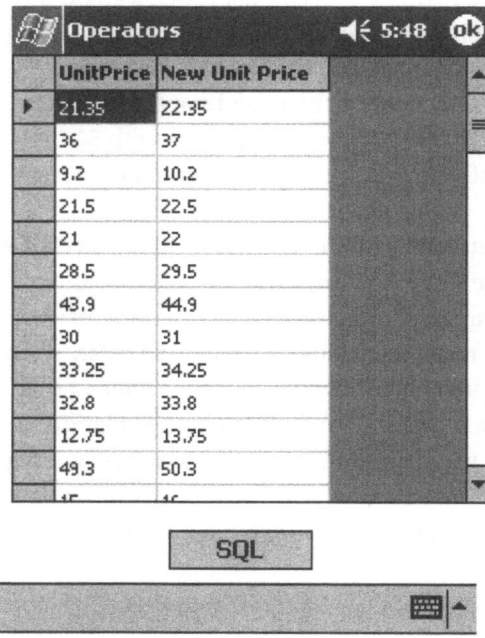

Figure 7-1. New Unit Price value is one higher than UnitPrice value

Visual Basic .NET

```vbnet
'insert at the top of your class
Imports System.Data.SqlServerCe


'insert in a function or click event
Dim cn As SqlCeConnection
Try
cn = New SqlCeConnection("Data Source=\My Documents\NorthwindDemo.sdf;Password=")
cn.Open()
Dim cmd As SqlCeCommand = cn.CreateCommand
cmd.CommandText = "SELECT UnitPrice, (UnitPrice + 1) " & _
                                  "AS ""New Unit Price"" FROM Products"
Dim da As New SqlCeDataAdapter(cmd)
Dim ds As New DataSet
da.Fill(ds)
DataGrid1.Enabled = False
DataGrid1.DataSource = ds.Tables(0)
Catch sqlex As SqlCeException
Dim sqlError As SqlCeError
For Each sqlError In sqlex.Errors
    MessageBox.Show(sqlError.Message)
Next
Catch ex As Exception
MessageBox.Show(ex.Message)
Finally
DataGrid1.Enabled = True
If cn.State <> ConnectionState.Closed Then
    cn.Close()
End If
End Try
```

C#

```csharp
//insert at the top of your class
using System.Data.SqlServerCe;

//insert in a function or click event
SqlCeConnection cn = null;
try
{
cn = new SqlCeConnection("Data Source=\\My Documents\\NorthwindDemo.sdf;" +
                                  "Password=");
```

```
cn.Open();
SqlCeCommand cmd = cn.CreateCommand();
cmd.CommandText = "SELECT UnitPrice, (UnitPrice + 1) " +
                                "AS \"New Unit Price\" FROM Products";
SqlCeDataAdapter da = new SqlCeDataAdapter(cmd);
DataSet ds = new DataSet();
da.Fill(ds);
dataGrid1.Enabled = false;
dataGrid1.DataSource = ds.Tables[0];
}
catch(SqlCeException sqlex)
{
foreach(SqlCeError sqlError in sqlex.Errors)
{
    MessageBox.Show(sqlError.Message);
}
}
catch(Exception ex)
{
MessageBox.Show(ex.Message);
}
finally
{
dataGrid1.Enabled = true;
if(cn.State != ConnectionState.Closed)
{
    cn.Close();
}
}
}
```

- (Subtract)

The subtraction arithmetic operator subtracts one numeric expression from another. The subtraction operator can also subtract a number, in days, from a given date.

Syntax

expression - expression

Example

In this example, you'll display the UnitPrice column and then you'll display the result of subtracting 1 from the value of UnitPrice in the New Unit Price column. Your results should look the same as those displayed in Figure 7-2.

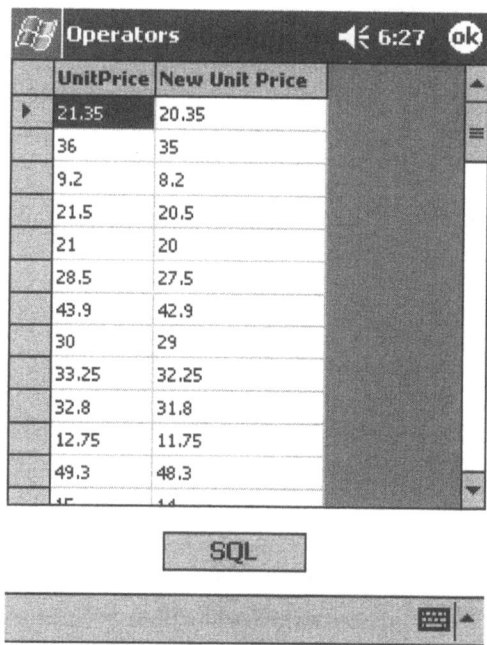

Figure 7-2. New Unit Price value is one less than UnitPrice value

Visual Basic .NET

```
'insert at the top of your class
Imports System.Data.SqlServerCe

'insert in a function or click event
cmd.CommandText = "SELECT UnitPrice, (UnitPrice - 1) " & _
                            "AS ""New Unit Price"" FROM Products"
```

C#

```
//insert at the top of your class
using System.Data.SqlServerCe;

//insert in a function or click event
cmd.CommandText = "SELECT UnitPrice, (UnitPrice - 1) " +
                                "AS \"New Unit Price\" FROM Products";
```

* (Multiply)

The multiplication arithmetic operator multiplies two numeric expressions together. It can't be used with the datetime data type.

Syntax

expression * expression

Example

In this example, you'll display the UnitPrice column and then you'll display the result of multiplying 2 against the value of UnitPrice in the New Unit Price column. Your results should look the same as those displayed in Figure 7-3.

Visual Basic .NET

```
'insert at the top of your class
Imports System.Data.SqlServerCe

'insert in a function or click event
cmd.CommandText = "SELECT UnitPrice, (UnitPrice * 2) " & _
                                "AS ""New Unit Price"" FROM Products"
```

C#

```
//insert at the top of your class
using System.Data.SqlServerCe;

//insert in a function or click event
cmd.CommandText = "SELECT UnitPrice, (UnitPrice * 2) " +
                                "AS \"New Unit Price\" FROM Products";
```

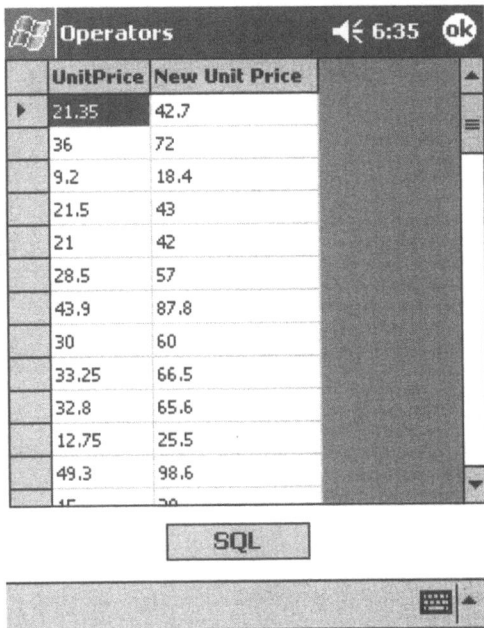

Figure 7-3. New Unit Price value is twice as much as UnitPrice value

/ (Divide)

The division arithmetic operator divides one numeric expression by another. The numeric expression to be divided is called the *dividend* and it comes first. The numeric expression that's used to divide the dividend is called the *divisor* and it comes second. It can't be used with the datetime data type.

Syntax

dividend / divisor

Example

In this example, you'll display the UnitPrice column and then you'll display the result of dividing the value of UnitPrice by 2 in the New Unit Price column. Your results should look the same as those displayed in Figure 7-4.

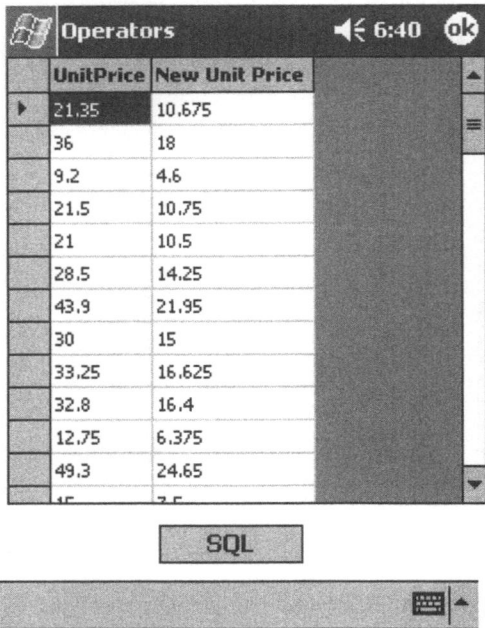

Figure 7-4. New Unit Price value is half as much as UnitPrice value

Visual Basic .NET

```
'insert at the top of your class
Imports System.Data.SqlServerCe

'insert in a function or click event
cmd.CommandText = "SELECT UnitPrice, (UnitPrice / 2) " & _
                              "AS ""New Unit Price"" FROM Products"
```

C#

```
//insert at the top of your class
using System.Data.SqlServerCe;

//insert in a function or click event
cmd.CommandText = "SELECT UnitPrice, (UnitPrice / 2) " +
                              "AS \"New Unit Price\" FROM Products";
```

% (Modulo)

The modulo arithmetic operator provides the remainder of one numeric expression divided by another. I remember using the modulo operator along with an integer counter variable to give even rows in a grid a different background color than odd rows.

Syntax

dividend % divisor

Example

In this example, you'll use the modulo operator to return the UnitPrice and UnitsInStock only where the UnitsInStock equals an even number. Your results should look the same as those displayed in Figure 7-5.

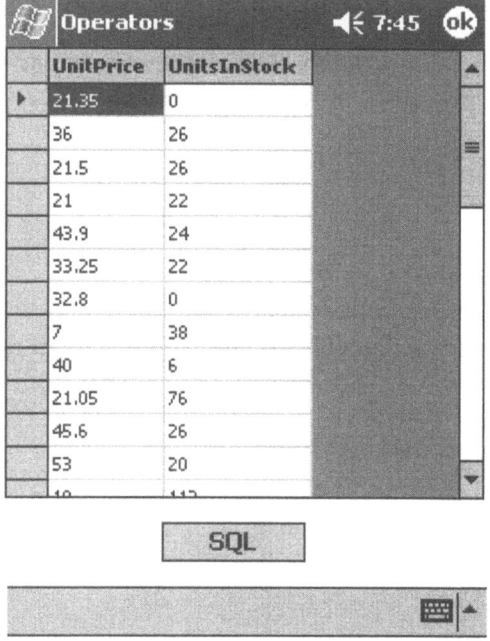

Figure 7-5. Only even UnitsInStock values are displayed

Visual Basic .NET

```vb
'insert at the top of your class
Imports System.Data.SqlServerCe

'insert in a function or click event
cmd.CommandText = "SELECT UnitPrice, UnitsInStock FROM Products " & _
                            "WHERE UnitsInStock % 2 = '0'"
```

C#

```csharp
//insert at the top of your class
using System.Data.SqlServerCe;

//insert in a function or click event
cmd.CommandText = "SELECT UnitPrice, UnitsInStock FROM Products " +
                            "WHERE UnitsInStock % 2 = '0'";
```

Bitwise

Bitwise operators are used to perform bit manipulations. These bit manipulations may be performed between any two expressions whose data types are in the integer category.

& (AND)

The bitwise AND operator is used to perform a bitwise logical AND operation between two numeric expressions of the integer data type category. In comparing the bits in both numeric expressions, the result bits are set to 1 if the bits in both expressions are also 1. Otherwise, the bits are set to 0.

Syntax

expression & expression

Example

In this example, you'll run a bitwise AND against the SupplierID and CategoryID columns and display the decimal results in the Bitwise And column. Your results should look the same as those displayed in Figure 7-6.

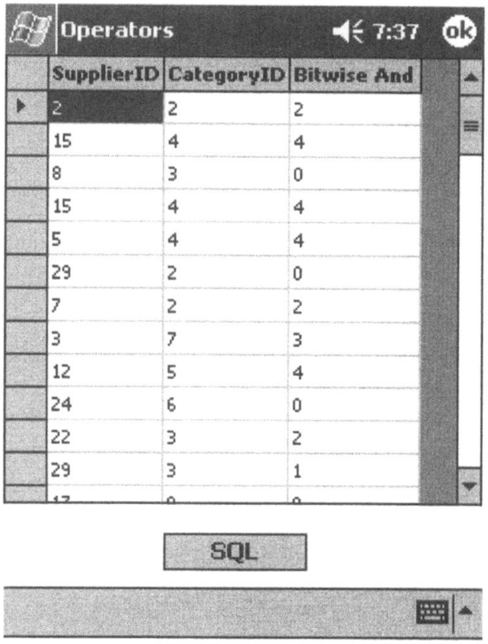

Figure 7-6. SupplierID, CategoryID, and the Bitewise AND result

Visual Basic .NET

```
'insert at the top of your class
Imports System.Data.SqlServerCe

'insert in a function or click event
cmd.CommandText = "SELECT SupplierID, CategoryID, (SupplierID & CategoryID) " & _
                            "AS ""Bitwise And"" FROM Products"
```

C#

```
//insert at the top of your class
using System.Data.SqlServerCe;

//insert in a function or click event
cmd.CommandText = "SELECT SupplierID, CategoryID, (SupplierID & CategoryID) " +
                            "AS \"Bitwise And\" FROM Products";
```

| (OR)

The bitwise OR operator performs a bitwise logical OR operation between two numeric expressions in the integer data type category. In comparing the bits in both numeric expressions, the result bits are set to 1 if either or both bits have a value of 1. If neither bit in the expressions is 1, then the bits are set to 0.

Syntax

expression | expression

Example

In this example, you'll run a bitwise OR against the SupplierID and CategoryID columns and display the decimal results in the Bitwise OR column. Your results should look the same as those displayed in Figure 7-7.

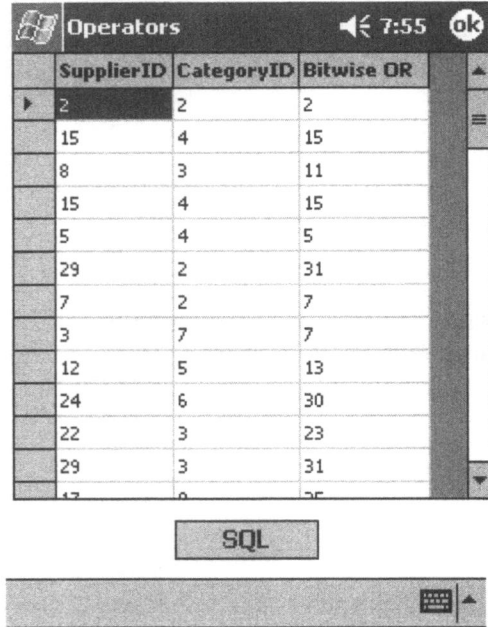

Figure 7-7. SupplierID, CategoryID, and the Bitwise OR result

Visual Basic .NET

```
'insert at the top of your class
Imports System.Data.SqlServerCe

'insert in a function or click event
cmd.CommandText = "SELECT SupplierID, CategoryID, (SupplierID | CategoryID) " & _
                          "AS ""Bitwise OR"" FROM Products"
```

C#

```
//insert at the top of your class
using System.Data.SqlServerCe;

//insert in a function or click event
cmd.CommandText = "SELECT SupplierID, CategoryID, (SupplierID | CategoryID) " +
                          "AS \"Bitwise OR\" FROM Products";
```

^ (Exclusive OR)

The bitwise exclusive OR operator performs a bitwise exclusive OR operation between two numeric expressions that are in the integer data type category. In comparing the bits in both numeric expressions, the result bits are set to 1 if either bit, but not both, have a value of 1. If both bits in the expressions are 0 or 1, then the bits are set to 0.

Syntax

expression ^ expression

Example

In this example, you'll run an exclusive OR against the SupplierID and CategoryID columns and display the decimal results in the Exclusive OR column. Your results should look the same as those displayed in Figure 7-8.

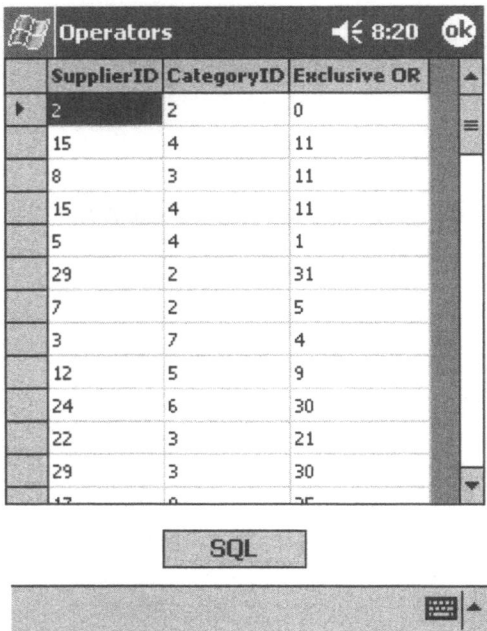

Figure 7-8. SupplierID, CategoryID, and the exclusive OR result

Visual Basic .NET

```
'insert at the top of your class
Imports System.Data.SqlServerCe

'insert in a function or click event
cmd.CommandText = "SELECT SupplierID, CategoryID, (SupplierID ^ CategoryID) " & _
                            "AS ""Exclusive OR"" FROM Products"
```

C#

```
//insert at the top of your class
using System.Data.SqlServerCe;

//insert in a function or click event
cmd.CommandText = "SELECT SupplierID, CategoryID, (SupplierID ^ CategoryID) " +
                            "AS \"Exclusive OR\" FROM Products";
```

~ (NOT)

The bitwise NOT operator performs a bitwise logical NOT operation against just one numeric expression in the integer data type category.

Syntax

~ expression

Example

In this example, you'll perform a bitwise logical NOT operation against the integers found in SupplierID column and display the results in the Bitwise Not column. Your results should look the same as those displayed in Figure 7-9.

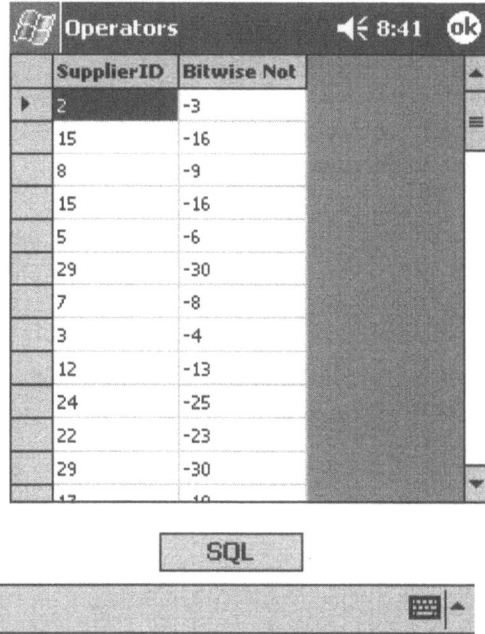

Figure 7-9. SupplierID and the Bitwise NOT result

Visual Basic .NET

```
'insert at the top of your class
Imports System.Data.SqlServerCe

'insert in a function or click event
cmd.CommandText = "SELECT SupplierID, (~ SupplierID) " & _
                              "AS ""Bitwise Not"" FROM Products"
```

C#

```
//insert at the top of your class
using System.Data.SqlServerCe;

//insert in a function or click event
cmd.CommandText = "SELECT SupplierID, (~ SupplierID) " +
                              "AS \"Bitwise Not\" FROM Products";
```

Comparison

Comparison operators are used to test whether or not two expressions are the same. The result of a comparison operator is a bit data type that gives you the Boolean TRUE or FALSE answer.

= (Equals)

The equals comparison operator compares two expressions. When comparing nonnull expressions, the result is TRUE if they're equal, otherwise it's FALSE.

Syntax

expression = expression

Example

In this example, you'll display both the ProductName and CategoryID for items with a CategoryID equal to 2. Your results should look the same as those displayed in Figure 7-10.

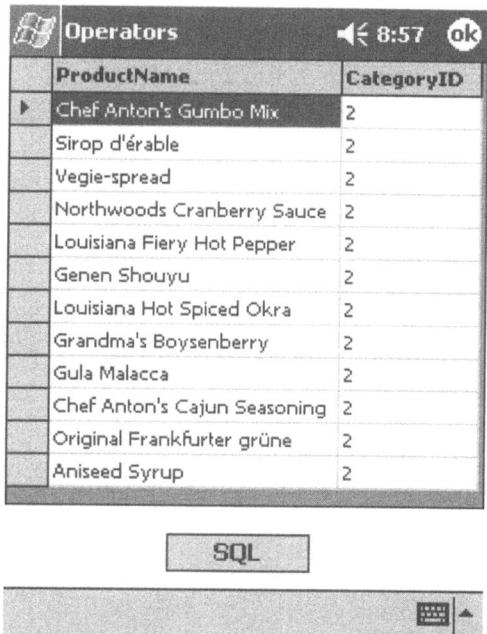

Figure 7-10. The ProductName items with CategoryID value equal to 2

Visual Basic .NET

```
'insert at the top of your class
Imports System.Data.SqlServerCe

'insert in a function or click event
cmd.CommandText = "SELECT ProductName, CategoryID FROM Products " & _
                              "WHERE CategoryID = 2"
```

C#

```
//insert at the top of your class
using System.Data.SqlServerCe;

//insert in a function or click event
cmd.CommandText = "SELECT ProductName, CategoryID FROM Products " +
                              "WHERE CategoryID = 2";
```

> (Greater Than)

The greater-than comparison operator compares two expressions. When comparing nonnull expressions, the result is TRUE when the expression on the left has a higher value than the one on the right.

Syntax

expression > expression

Example

In this example, you display both the ProductName and UnitsInStock for items with a UnitsInStock value greater than 20. Your results should look the same as those displayed in Figure 7-11.

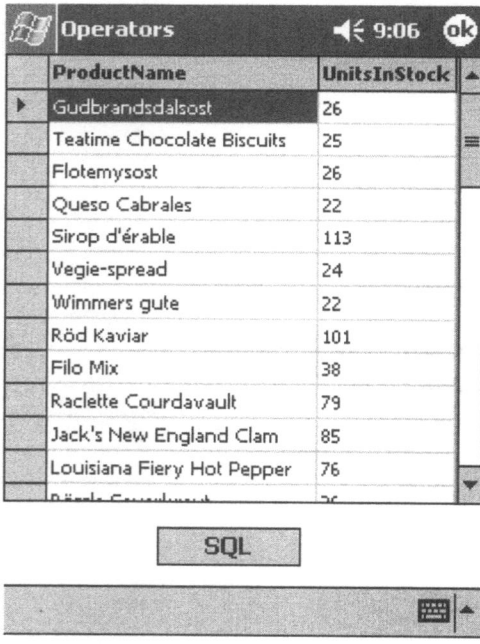

Figure 7-11. The ProductName items with UnitsInStock value greater than 20

Visual Basic .NET

```vbnet
'insert at the top of your class
Imports System.Data.SqlServerCe

'insert in a function or click event
cmd.CommandText = "SELECT ProductName, UnitsInStock FROM Products " & _
                                "WHERE UnitsInStock > 20"
```

C#

```csharp
//insert at the top of your class
using System.Data.SqlServerCe;

//insert in a function or click event
cmd.CommandText = "SELECT ProductName, UnitsInStock FROM Products " +
                                "WHERE UnitsInStock > 20";
```

< (Less Than)

The less-than comparison operator compares two expressions. When comparing nonnull expressions, the result is TRUE when the expression on the left has a lower value than the one on the right.

Syntax

expression < expression

Example

In this example, you'll display the ProductName and UnitPrice for items with a UnitPrice value less than 20. Your results should look the same as those displayed in Figure 7-12.

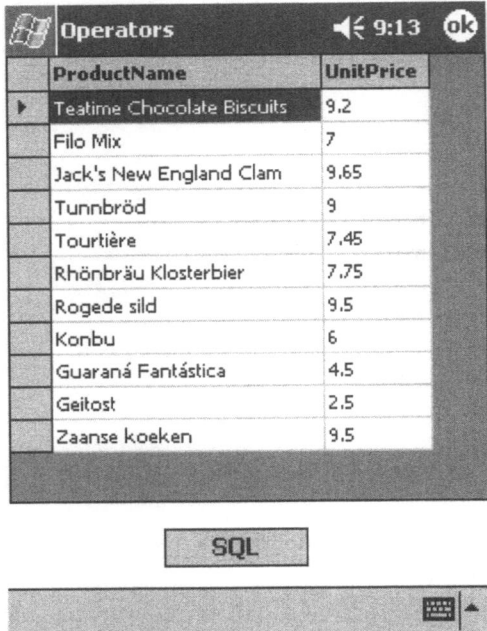

Figure 7-12. The ProductName items with UnitPrice value less than 10

Visual Basic .NET

```
'insert at the top of your class
Imports System.Data.SqlServerCe

'insert in a function or click event
cmd.CommandText = "SELECT ProductName, UnitPrice FROM Products " & _
                                "WHERE UnitPrice < 10"
```

C#

```
//insert at the top of your class
using System.Data.SqlServerCe;

//insert in a function or click event
cmd.CommandText = "SELECT ProductName, UnitPrice FROM Products " +
                                "WHERE UnitPrice < 10";
```

>= (Greater Than or Equal To)

The greater-than-or-equal-to comparison operator compares two expressions. When comparing nonnull expressions, the result is TRUE when the expression on the left has a higher value than or is equal to the one on the right.

Syntax

expression >= expression

Example

In this example, you'll display both the ProductName and UnitsInStock columns for items with a UnitPrice value greater than or equal to 30. Your results should look the same as those displayed in Figure 7-13.

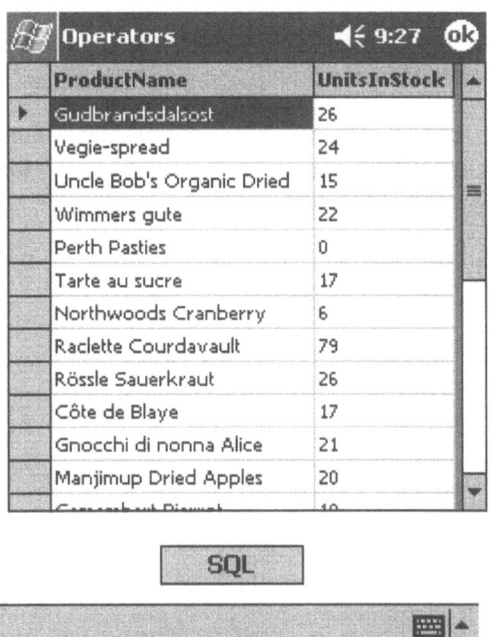

Figure 7-13. The ProductName items with UnitPrice value greater than or equal to 30

Visual Basic .NET

```
'insert at the top of your class
Imports System.Data.SqlServerCe

'insert in a function or click event
cmd.CommandText = "SELECT ProductName, UnitsInStock FROM Products " & _
                            "WHERE UnitPrice >= 30"
```

C#

```
//insert at the top of your class
using System.Data.SqlServerCe;

//insert in a function or click event
cmd.CommandText = "SELECT ProductName, UnitsInStock FROM Products " +
                            "WHERE UnitPrice >= 30";
```

<= (Less Than or Equal To)

The less-than-or-equal-to comparison operator compares two expressions. When comparing nonnull expressions, the result is TRUE when the expression on the left has a lower value than or is equal to the one on the right.

Syntax

expression <= expression

Example

In this example, you'll display the FirstName, LastName, and HireDate of employees who were hired on or before 10/17/1993. Your results should look the same as those displayed in Figure 7-14.

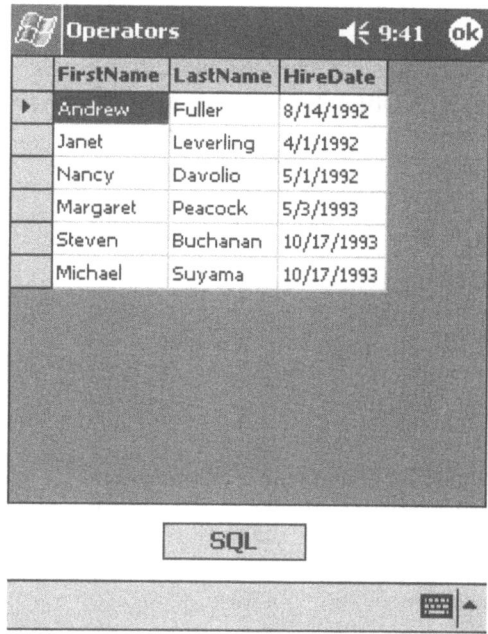

Figure 7-14. Employees who were hired on or before 10/17/1993

Visual Basic .NET

```
'insert at the top of your class
Imports System.Data.SqlServerCe

'insert in a function or click event
cmd.CommandText = "SELECT FirstName, LastName, HireDate FROM Employees " & _
                            "WHERE HireDate <= '1993-10-17'"
```

C#

```
//insert at the top of your class
using System.Data.SqlServerCe;

//insert in a function or click event
cmd.CommandText = "SELECT FirstName, LastName, HireDate FROM Employees " +
                            "WHERE HireDate <= '1993-10-17'";
```

<> (Not Equal To)

The not-equal-to comparison operator compares two expressions. When comparing nonnull expressions, the result is TRUE when the expression on the left is not equal to the one on the right.

Syntax

expression <> expression

Example

In this example, you'll display the FirstName, LastName, and Title values of employees whose title isn't Sales Representative. Your results should look the same as those displayed in Figure 7-15.

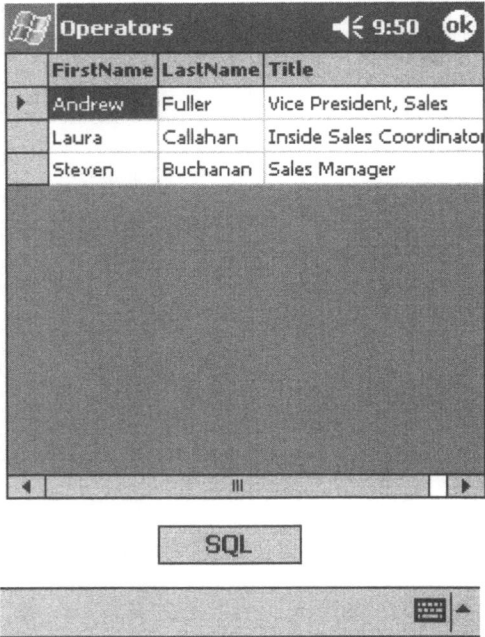

Figure 7-15. Employees who aren't sales representatives

Visual Basic .NET

```
'insert at the top of your class
Imports System.Data.SqlServerCe

'insert in a function or click event
cmd.CommandText = "SELECT FirstName, LastName, Title FROM Employees " & _
                             "WHERE Title <> 'Sales Representative'"
```

C#

```
//insert at the top of your class
using System.Data.SqlServerCe;

//insert in a function or click event
cmd.CommandText = "SELECT FirstName, LastName, Title FROM Employees " +
                             "WHERE Title <> 'Sales Representative'";
```

!= (Not Equal To)

The not-equal-to comparison operator compares two expressions. When comparing nonnull expressions, the result is TRUE when the expression on the left is not equal to the one on the right.

Syntax

expression != expression

Example

In this example, you'll display the FirstName, LastName, and City values of the employees who don't live in London. Your results should look the same as those displayed in Figure 7-16.

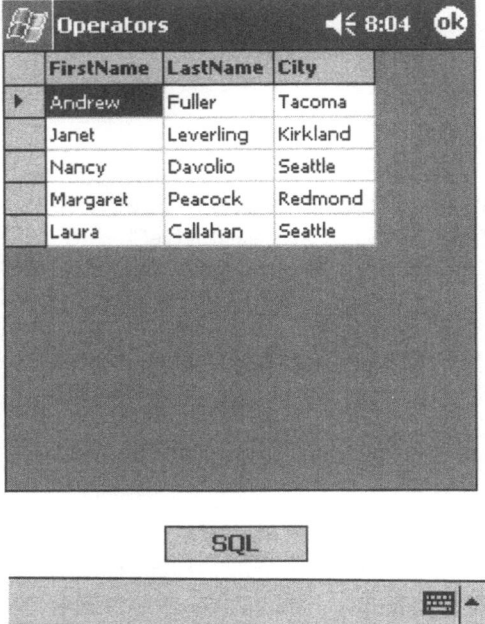

Figure 7-16. Employees who don't live in London

Visual Basic .NET

```
'insert at the top of your class
Imports System.Data.SqlServerCe

'insert in a function or click event
cmd.CommandText = "SELECT FirstName, LastName, City FROM Employees " & _
                              "WHERE City != 'London'"
```

C#

```
//insert at the top of your class
using System.Data.SqlServerCe;

//insert in a function or click event
cmd.CommandText = "SELECT FirstName, LastName, City FROM Employees " +
                              "WHERE City != 'London'";
```

!< (Not Less Than)

The not-less-than comparison operator compares two expressions. When comparing nonnull expressions, the result is TRUE when the expression on the left has a value that is not less than the one on the right.

Syntax

expression !< expression

Example

In this example, you'll display the ProductName and UnitsInStock columns for items with a UnitsInStock value not less than 100. Your results should look the same as those displayed in Figure 7-17.

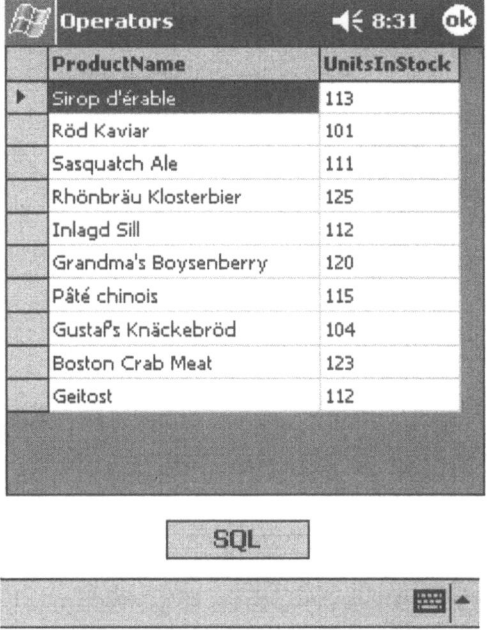

Figure 7-17. Products whose UnitsInStock values aren't less than 100

Visual Basic .NET

```
'insert at the top of your class
Imports System.Data.SqlServerCe

'insert in a function or click event
cmd.CommandText = "SELECT ProductName, UnitsInStock FROM Products " & _
                            "WHERE UnitsInStock !< 100"
```

C#

```
//insert at the top of your class
using System.Data.SqlServerCe;

//insert in a function or click event
cmd.CommandText = "SELECT ProductName, UnitsInStock FROM Products " +
                            "WHERE UnitsInStock !< 100";
```

!> (Not Greater Than)

The not-greater-than comparison operator compares two expressions. When comparing nonnull expressions, the result is TRUE when the expression on the left has a value that is not greater than the one on the right.

Syntax

expression !> expression

Example

In this example, you'll do the opposite of the previous example and display the ProductName and UnitsInStock columns for items with a UnitsInStock value not greater than 100. Your results should look the same as those displayed in Figure 7-18.

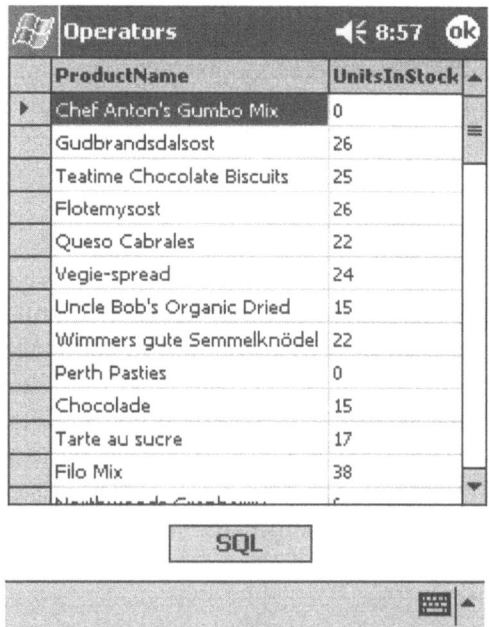

Figure 7-18. Products whose UnitsInStock values aren't greater than 100

Visual Basic .NET

```
'insert at the top of your class
Imports System.Data.SqlServerCe

'insert in a function or click event
cmd.CommandText = "SELECT ProductName, UnitsInStock FROM Products " & _
                            "WHERE UnitsInStock !> 100"
```

C#

```
//insert at the top of your class
using System.Data.SqlServerCe;

//insert in a function or click event
cmd.CommandText = "SELECT ProductName, UnitsInStock FROM Products " +
                            "WHERE UnitsInStock !> 100";
```

Logical

Logical operators are similar to conditional operators in that they're testing for a condition's truth. Therefore, it should come as no surprise that the result of any logical operation is a bit data type giving you a Boolean TRUE or FALSE answer.

ALL

The ALL logical operator is used to compare a scalar value with a single-column set of values. In the WHERE clause, a single value from a given column is compared to the results of a subquery. Any of the comparison operators listed previously can be used and the results of the subquery must be of the same data type as the scalar value. The subquery must be a SELECT statement that doesn't include an ORDER BY clause, the COMPUTE clause, or the INTO keyword. The result is TRUE when the comparison specified is TRUE for the scalar value and all the values returned by the subquery.

Syntax

Scalar expression {=|<>|!=|>|>=|!>|<|<=|!<} ALL (subquery)

Example

In this example, things get a little more complicated due to the introduction of a subquery whose integer result is 24. Now it's a matter of displaying the ProductName and UnitsInStock columns for items with a UnitsInStock value less than the result of the subquery. Your results should look the same as those displayed in Figure 7-19.

Visual Basic .NET

```
'insert at the top of your class
Imports System.Data.SqlServerCe

'insert in a function or click event
cmd.CommandText = "SELECT ProductName, UnitsInStock FROM Products " & _
                  "WHERE UnitsInStock < ALL " & _
                  "(SELECT ProductID FROM Products " & _
                  "WHERE SupplierID = 10)"
```

C#

```
//insert at the top of your class
using System.Data.SqlServerCe;

//insert in a function or click event
cmd.CommandText = "SELECT ProductName, UnitsInStock FROM Products " +
                  "WHERE UnitsInStock < ALL " +
                  "(SELECT ProductID FROM Products " +
                  "WHERE SupplierID = 10)";
```

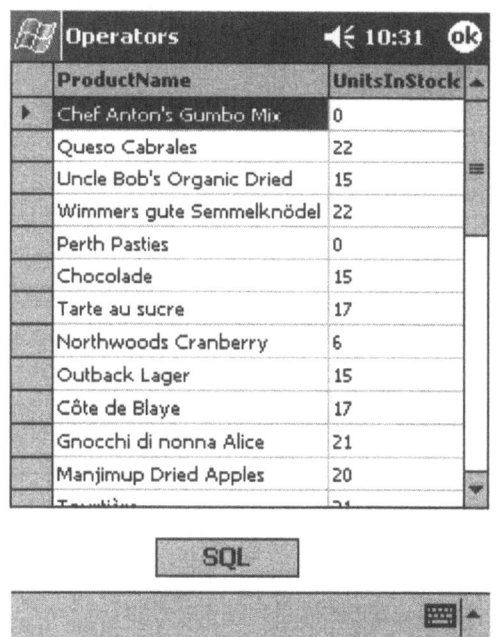

Figure 7-19. Products whose UnitsInStock values are less than 24

AND

The AND logical operator combines two Boolean expressions and returns TRUE when both expressions are TRUE.

Syntax

Boolean expression AND Boolean expression

Example

In this example, you'll display the ProductName and UnitsInStock columns for items with a UnitsInStock value less than 100 and a CategoryID value equal 2. Your results should look the same as those displayed in Figure 7-20.

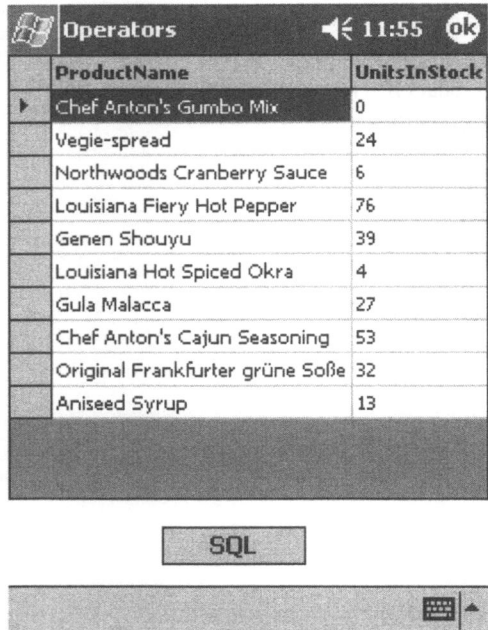

Figure 7-20. Products whose UnitsInStock value is less than 100 and CategoryID value is equal to 2

Visual Basic .NET

```
'insert at the top of your class
Imports System.Data.SqlServerCe

'insert in a function or click event
cmd.CommandText = "SELECT ProductName, UnitsInStock FROM Products " & _
                     "WHERE UnitsInStock < 100 " & _
                     "AND CategoryID = 2"
```

C#

```
//insert at the top of your class
using System.Data.SqlServerCe;

//insert in a function or click event
cmd.CommandText = "SELECT ProductName, UnitsInStock FROM Products " +
                      "WHERE UnitsInStock < 100 " +
                      "AND CategoryID = 2";
```

SOME/ANY

The SOME/ANY logical operators are used to compare a scalar value with a single column set of values. In the WHERE clause, a single value from a given column is compared to the results of a subquery. Any of the comparison operators listed previously can be used and the results of the subquery must be of the same data type as the scalar value. The subquery must be a SELECT statement that doesn't include an ORDER BY clause, the COMPUTE clause, or the INTO keyword. The result is TRUE when the comparison specified is TRUE for the scalar value and any of the values returned by the subquery.

Syntax

Scalar expression {=|<>|!=|>|>=|!>|<|<=|!<} SOME|ANY (subquery)

Example

In this example, you'll display the ProductName and UnitsInStock columns for items with a UnitsInStock value equal to some or any of the values returned from the subquery. In this case, ProductID's 5, 65, 66, and 4 exist when the SupplierID value equals 2 in the subquery. Your results should look the same as those displayed in Figure 7-21.

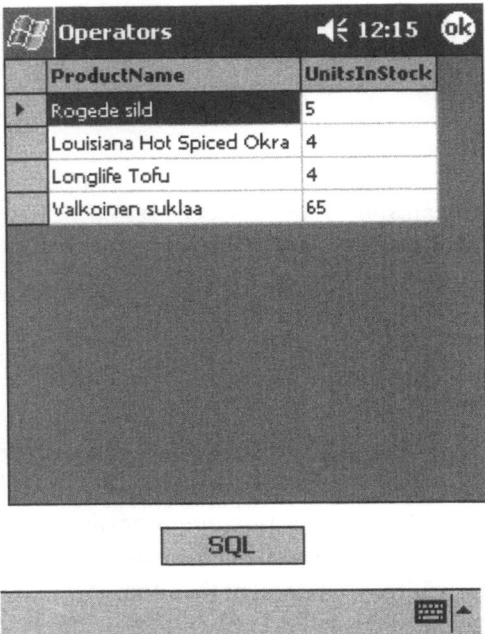

Figure 7-21. Products whose UnitsInStock value is equal to either 5, 65, 66, or 4

Visual Basic .NET

```vb
'insert at the top of your class
Imports System.Data.SqlServerCe

'insert in a function or click event
cmd.CommandText = "SELECT ProductName, UnitsInStock FROM Products " & _
                    "WHERE UnitsInStock = ANY " & _
                    "(SELECT ProductID FROM Products " & _
                    "WHERE SupplierID = 2)"
```

C#

```csharp
//insert at the top of your classusing System.Data.SqlServerCe;

//insert in a function or click event
cmd.CommandText = "SELECT ProductName, UnitsInStock FROM Products " +
                    "WHERE UnitsInStock = ANY " +
                    "(SELECT ProductID FROM Products " +
                    "WHERE SupplierID = 2)";
```

BETWEEN

The BETWEEN logical operator allows you to test an expression between a range of a beginning expression and an ending expression of the same data type. A Boolean value of TRUE is returned if the value of the test expression is greater than or equal to the value of the beginning expression and less than or equal to the value of the ending expression. If you want to make everything a little bit backwards, you can throw in the NOT argument so that a value of TRUE is returned if the value of the test expression is less than the value of the beginning expression or greater than the value of the ending expression.

Syntax

Test expression [NOT] BETWEEN beginning expression AND ending expression

Example

In this example, you'll display the ProductName and UnitsInStock columns for items with a UnitsInStock value between 60 and 70. Your results should look the same as those displayed in Figure 7-22.

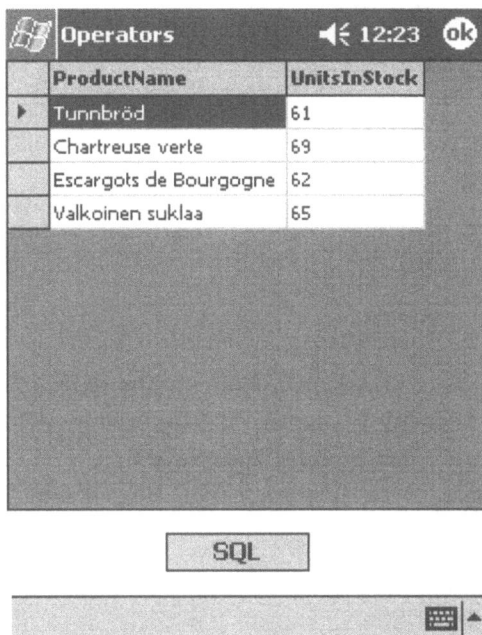

Figure 7-22. Products whose UnitsInStock value is between 60 and 70

Visual Basic .NET

```
'insert at the top of your class
Imports System.Data.SqlServerCe

'insert in a function or click event
cmd.CommandText = "SELECT ProductName, UnitsInStock FROM Products " & _
                           "WHERE UnitsInStock BETWEEN 60 AND 70"
```

C#

```
//insert at the top of your class
using System.Data.SqlServerCe;

//insert in a function or click event
cmd.CommandText = "SELECT ProductName, UnitsInStock FROM Products " +
                           "WHERE UnitsInStock BETWEEN 60 AND 70";
```

EXISTS

The EXISTS logical operator allows you to test a subquery for the existence of a row. Both the COMPUTE clause and the INTO keyword are not allowed in the subquery SELECT statement. EXISTS returns a value of TRUE if the subquery contains one or more rows.

Syntax

EXISTS subquery

Example

In this example, you'll utilize a subquery that tests for the existence of rows of data where the CustomerID column in the Orders table is equivalent to the CustomerID column in the Customers table. If rows exist, your query will display the CompanyName and ContactName columns of the Customers table. Your results should look the same as those displayed in Figure 7-23.

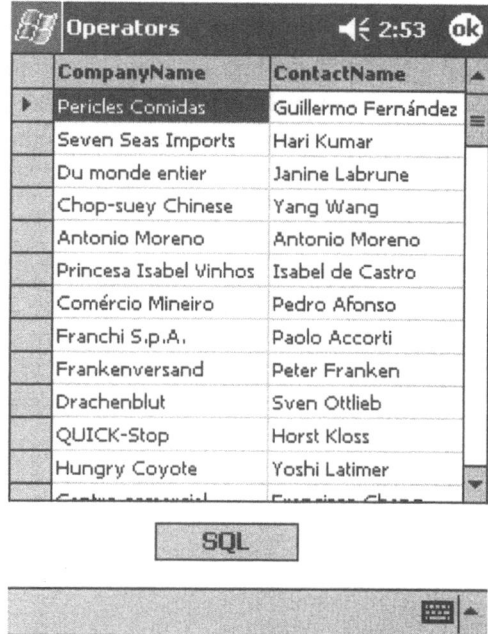

Figure 7-23. CompanyName and ContactName values when rows exist

Visual Basic .NET

```
'insert at the top of your class
Imports System.Data.SqlServerCe

'insert in a function or click event
cmd.CommandText = "SELECT CompanyName, ContactName FROM Customers " & _
                  "WHERE EXISTS " & _
                  "(SELECT CustomerID FROM Orders " & _
                  "WHERE Orders.CustomerID = Customers.CustomerID)"
```

C#

```
//insert at the top of your class
using System.Data.SqlServerCe;

//insert in a function or click event
cmd.CommandText = "SELECT CompanyName, ContactName FROM Customers " +
                  "WHERE EXISTS " +
                  "(SELECT CustomerID FROM Orders " +
                  "WHERE Orders.CustomerID = Customers.CustomerID)";
```

IN

The IN logical operator takes an expression and tests it against any value found in a subquery or list to see if there's a match, and if so returns a result of TRUE. The NOT argument can be used in front of the IN operator to reverse the criteria for the test.

Syntax

Test expression [NOT] IN (subquery | expression [, ...n])

Example

In this example, you'll display the CompanyName and Region columns for those items with a Region value of OR, WA, or BC. Your results should look the same as those displayed in Figure 7-24.

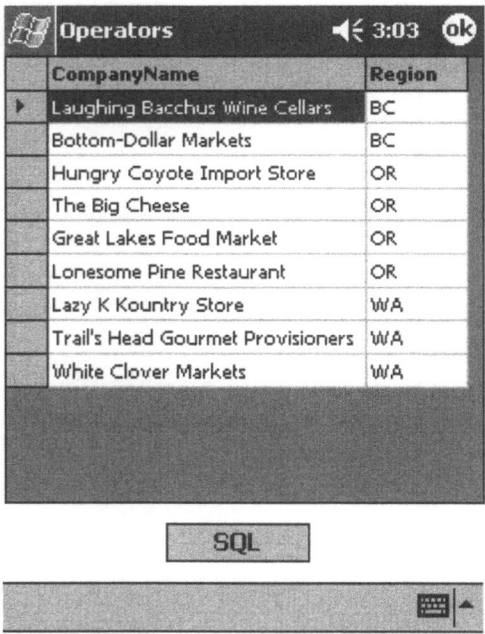

Figure 7-24. CompanyName items with a Region value containing OR, WA, or BC

Visual Basic .NET

```
'insert at the top of your class
Imports System.Data.SqlServerCe

'insert in a function or click event
cmd.CommandText = "SELECT CompanyName, Region FROM Customers " & _
                        "WHERE Region IN ('OR', 'WA', 'BC')"
```

C#

```
//insert at the top of your class
using System.Data.SqlServerCe;

//insert in a function or click event
cmd.CommandText = "SELECT CompanyName, Region FROM Customers " +
                        "WHERE Region IN ('OR', 'WA', 'BC')";
```

LIKE

The LIKE logical operator searches a given character string and returns TRUE when it finds a match to a specified pattern. Such a pattern can include both regular and wildcard characters. When using regular characters, an exact match must be found in order to return TRUE. On the other hand, the use of wildcard characters makes it much more easy to find a match. Also note that the NOT argument can be introduced to reverse the outcome of a pattern-matching operation. The commonly used % wildcard character allows you to specify a string of zero or more characters to search against. Surrounding a string with % wildcard characters will return a match if the string is found anywhere inside a column's data. You can use a % wildcard in front of a string if you're looking for a match where the data ends with the value of your string. Likewise, placing a % wildcard at the end of your string indicates that you're looking for a match where the data begins with the value of your string. You can also use the _ wildcard character in your searches to specify a single character rather than a variable-length string like the % wildcard.

Syntax

Match expression [NOT] LIKE pattern [ESCAPE escape character]

Example

In this example, you'll display the ShipName and ShipCountry columns for items with a ShipCountry value that contains the letters *us*. Your results should look the same as those displayed in Figure 7-25.

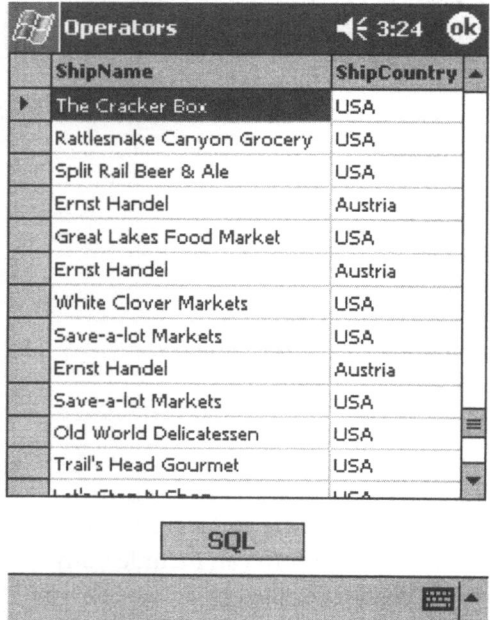

Figure 7-25. ShipName items with a ShipCountry value containing us

Visual Basic .NET

```
'insert at the top of your class
Imports System.Data.SqlServerCe

'insert in a function or click event
cmd.CommandText = "SELECT ShipName, ShipCountry FROM Orders " & _
                            "WHERE ShipCountry LIKE '%us%'"
```

C#

```
//insert at the top of your class
using System.Data.SqlServerCe;
```

```
//insert in a function or click event
cmd.CommandText = "SELECT ShipName, ShipCountry FROM Orders " +
                            "WHERE ShipCountry LIKE '%us%'";
```

NOT

The NOT logical operator is used to reverse the value of any Boolean expression.

Syntax

[NOT] Boolean expression

Example

In this example, you'll do the opposite of the previous example by displaying the ShipName and ShipCountry columns for items with a ShipCountry value that does *not* contain the letters *us*. Your results should look the same as those displayed in Figure 7-26.

Figure 7-26. ShipName items with a ShipCountry value that does not contain us

Visual Basic .NET

```
'insert at the top of your class
Imports System.Data.SqlServerCe

'insert in a function or click event
cmd.CommandText = "SELECT ShipName, ShipCountry FROM Orders " & _
                                "WHERE ShipCountry NOT LIKE '%us%'"
```

C#

```
//insert at the top of your class
using System.Data.SqlServerCe;

//insert in a function or click event
cmd.CommandText = "SELECT ShipName, ShipCountry FROM Orders " +
                                "WHERE ShipCountry NOT LIKE '%us%'";
```

OR

The OR logical operator combines two Boolean expressions and returns TRUE when either of the expressions are TRUE.

Syntax

Boolean expression OR Boolean expression

Example

In this example, you'll display the ShipName and ShipCountry columns for items with a ShipCountry value of either Italy or Ireland. Your results should look the same as those displayed in Figure 7-27.

Figure 7-27. ShipName items with a ShipCountry value of Ireland or Italy

Visual Basic .NET

```
'insert at the top of your class
Imports System.Data.SqlServerCe

'insert in a function or click event
cmd.CommandText = "SELECT ShipName, ShipCountry FROM Orders " & _
                        "WHERE ShipCountry = 'Ireland' " & _
                        "OR ShipCountry = 'Italy'"
```

C#

```
//insert at the top of your class
using System.Data.SqlServerCe;

//insert in a function or click event
cmd.CommandText = "SELECT ShipName, ShipCountry FROM Orders " +
                        "WHERE ShipCountry = 'Ireland' " +
                        "OR ShipCountry = 'Italy'";
```

Unary

Unlike all the previous operators, unary operators perform an operation only on a single expression. With the exception of the datetime data type, unary operators can be used with any data types in the numeric category.

+ (Positive)

The positive unary operator returns the positive value of a numeric expression.

Syntax

+ numeric expression

Example

In this example, you display the result of the value of Freight (34.82) minus 50. With or without the positive unary operator in front of the numeric expression, the result is –15.18 as shown in Figure 7-28.

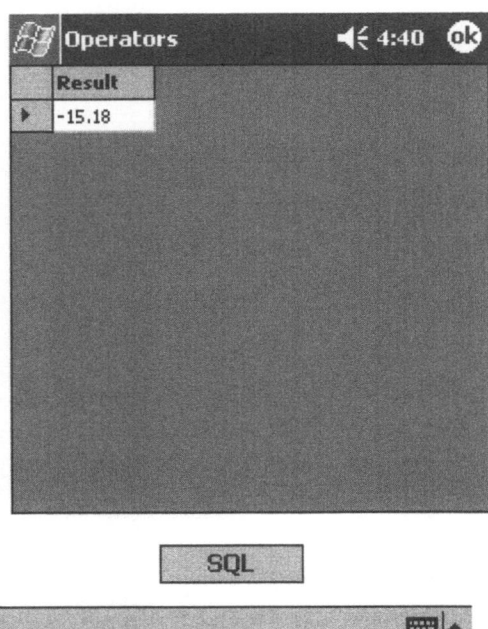

Figure 7-28. The result of the value of freight minus 50 with the positive unary operator

Visual Basic .NET

```
'insert at the top of your class
Imports System.Data.SqlServerCe

'insert in a function or click event
cmd.CommandText = "SELECT +(Freight - 50) AS ""Result"" FROM Orders " & _
                              "WHERE OrderID = 10405"
```

C#

```
//insert at the top of your classusing System.Data.SqlServerCe;

//insert in a function or click event
cmd.CommandText = "SELECT +(Freight - 50) AS \"Result\" FROM Orders " +
                              "WHERE OrderID = 10405";
```

- (Negative)

The negative unary operator returns the negative value of a numeric expression.

Syntax

- numeric expression

Example

In this example, you display the result of the value of Freight (34.82) minus 50. This time you include the negative unary operator in front of the numeric expression with a result of 15.18 instead of –15.18 as shown in Figure 7-29.

Visual Basic .NET

```
'insert at the top of your class
Imports System.Data.SqlServerCe

'insert in a function or click event
cmd.CommandText = "SELECT -(Freight - 50) AS ""Result"" FROM Orders " & _
                              "WHERE OrderID = 10405"
```

C#

```
//insert at the top of your class
using System.Data.SqlServerCe;

//insert in a function or click event
cmd.CommandText = "SELECT -(Freight - 50) AS \"Result\" FROM Orders " +
                              "WHERE OrderID = 10405";
```

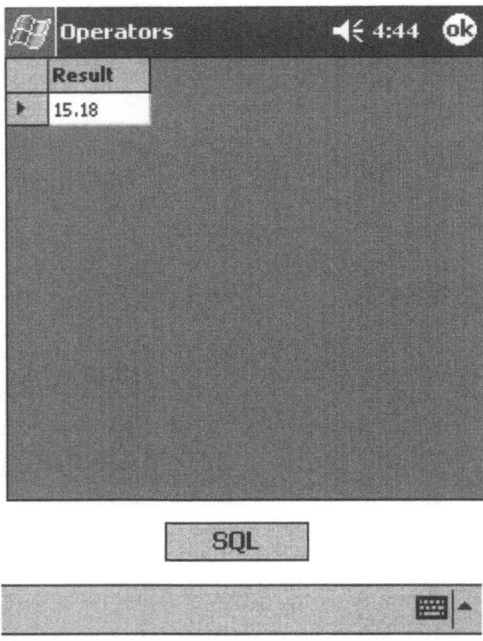

Figure 7-29. The result of the value of freight minus 50 with the negative unary operator

Conclusion

If you can't get it done with SQL Server CE's thirty different operators, then there's no pleasing you. Luckily, Chapter 8 is on deck with a enough functions to rival any server database on the market.

CHAPTER 8

Function Reference

NOT TO BE OUTDONE by the 30 operators in the last chapter, this chapter gives you an in-depth look at SQL Server CE's 53 powerful, built-in functions. SQL Server CE does a good job of holding its own against big brother SQL Server 2000 in this department. You're provided with functions that help you with mathematics, string manipulation, and date arithmetic among other things. This chapter serves as a reference guide to all these functions and includes complete descriptions, proper usage syntax, and a working example for each. It's important that you run these examples and compare your results with mine to ensure that you're on the right track. Just as in Chapter 7, you'll need to create a Pocket PC Smart Device Application and place both a DataGrid control and a Button control on the form. You'll need to reference System.Data.Common and System.Data.SqlServerCe in order to query SQL Server CE and produce DataSets from the data found in the NorthwindDemo.sdf database. The function code examples can be typed into the click event of the button with the results displayed in the DataGrid whenever the button is tapped. A full code example will be provided with the first function description and then only the unique SQL will be displayed in the function examples thereafter.

Aggregate Functions

Aggregate functions run calculations against a set of values and return a single value. These functions ignore null values with the exception of the COUNT function. They are most frequently used with the GROUP BY clause.

AVG

The AVG aggregate function returns the average of the values in a group. The group of expressions must either be of the exact or approximate numeric data type categories.

Syntax

AVG ([ALL] expression)

Example

In this example, you'll display the results of averaging all the Freight prices together from the Orders table in the Freight Average column. Your results should look the same as those displayed in Figure 8-1.

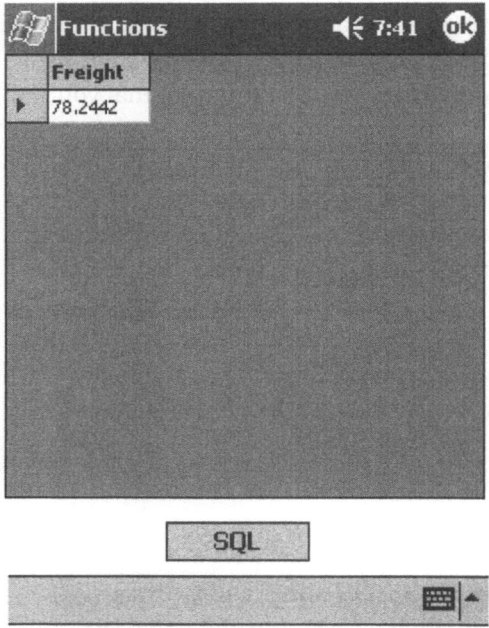

Figure 8-1. The average freight price

Visual Basic .NET

```
'insert at the top of your class
Imports System.Data.SqlServerCe

'insert in a function or click event
Dim cn As SqlCeConnection
Try
    cn = New SqlCeConnection("Data Source=\My Documents\NorthwindDemo.sdf; " & _
                                          "Password=")
```

```
        cn.Open()
        Dim cmd As SqlCeCommand = cn.CreateCommand
        cmd.CommandText = "SELECT AVG(Freight) AS ""Freight Average"" FROM Orders"
        Dim da As New SqlCeDataAdapter(cmd)
        Dim ds As New DataSet
        da.Fill(ds)
        DataGrid1.Enabled = False
        DataGrid1.DataSource = ds.Tables(0)
Catch sqlex As SqlCeException
        Dim sqlError As SqlCeError
        For Each sqlError In sqlex.Errors
            MessageBox.Show(sqlError.Message)
        Next
Catch ex As Exception
        MessageBox.Show(ex.Message)
Finally
        DataGrid1.Enabled = True
        If cn.State <> ConnectionState.Closed Then
            cn.Close()
        End If
End Try
```

C#

```
//insert at the top of your class
using System.Data.SqlServerCe;

//insert in a function or click event
SqlCeConnection cn = null;
try
{
    cn = new SqlCeConnection("Data Source=\\My Documents\\NorthwindDemo.sdf; " +
                             "Password=");
    cn.Open();
    SqlCeCommand cmd = cn.CreateCommand();
    cmd.CommandText = "SELECT AVG(Freight) AS \"Freight Average\" FROM Orders";
    SqlCeDataAdapter da = new SqlCeDataAdapter(cmd);
    DataSet ds = new DataSet();
    da.Fill(ds);
    dataGrid1.Enabled = false;
    dataGrid1.DataSource = ds.Tables[0];
}
catch(SqlCeException sqlex)
```

```
{
    foreach(SqlCeError sqlError in sqlex.Errors)
    {
        MessageBox.Show(sqlError.Message);
    }
}
catch(Exception ex)
{
    MessageBox.Show(ex.Message);
}
finally
{
    dataGrid1.Enabled = true;
    if (cn.State != ConnectionState.Closed)
    {
        cn.Close();
    }
}
```

COUNT

The COUNT aggregate function returns the number of items in a group. This function can't be used with uniqueidentifier, ntext, or image data types. If an asterisk is used without any other parameters, the total number of rows in the table is returned.

Syntax

COUNT ({[ALL] expression *})

Example

In this example, you'll display the total number of rows found in the Orders table in the Number of Rows column. Your results should look the same as those displayed in Figure 8-2.

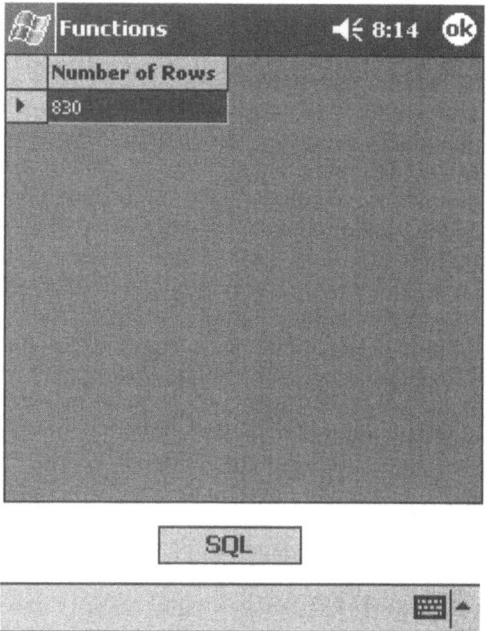

Figure 8-2. The number of rows

Visual Basic .NET

```
'insert at the top of your class
Imports System.Data.SqlServerCe

'insert in a function or click event
cmd.CommandText = "SELECT COUNT(*) AS ""Number of Rows"" FROM Orders"
```

C#

```
//insert at the top of your class
using System.Data.SqlServerCe;

//insert in a function or click event
cmd.CommandText = "SELECT COUNT(*) AS \"Number of Rows\" FROM Orders";
```

MAX

The MAX aggregate function returns the highest value from a set of values. This function can't be used with bit columns, but interestingly enough can be used with character columns. In the case of character columns, MAX returns the highest value in the collating sequence.

Syntax

MAX ([ALL] expression)

Example

In this example, you'll display the highest freight price in the Highest Freight Price column. Your results should look the same as those displayed in Figure 8-3.

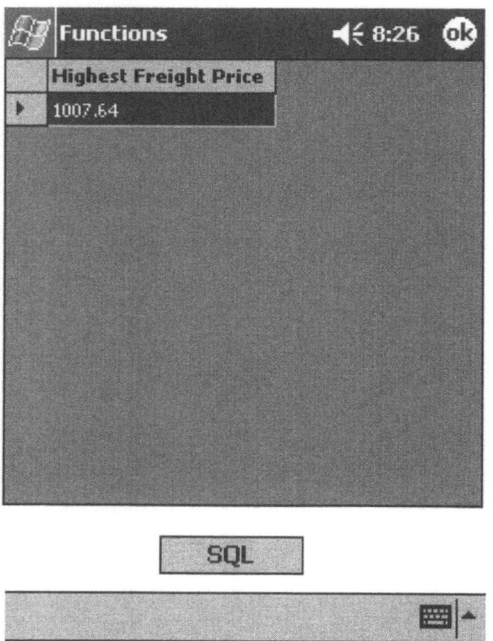

Figure 8-3. The highest freight price

Visual Basic .NET

```
'insert at the top of your class
Imports System.Data.SqlServerCe

'insert in a function or click event
cmd.CommandText = "SELECT MAX(Freight) AS ""Highest Freight Price"" FROM Orders"
```

C#

```
//insert at the top of your class
using System.Data.SqlServerCe;

//insert in a function or click event
cmd.CommandText = "SELECT MAX(Freight) AS \"Highest Freight Price\" FROM Orders";
```

MIN

The MIN aggregate function returns the lowest value from a set of values. This function can't be used with bit columns. In the case of character columns, MIN returns the lowest value in the collating sequence.

Syntax

MIN ([ALL] expression)

Example

In this example, you'll display the lowest freight price in the Lowest Freight Price column. Your results should look the same as those displayed in Figure 8-4.

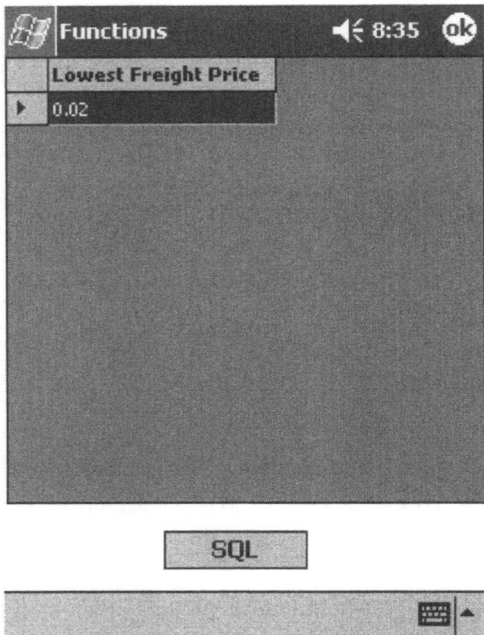

Figure 8-4. The lowest freight price

Visual Basic .NET

```
'insert at the top of your class
Imports System.Data.SqlServerCe

'insert in a function or click event
cmd.CommandText = "SELECT MIN(Freight) AS ""Lowest Freight Price"" FROM Orders"
```

C#

```
//insert at the top of your class
using System.Data.SqlServerCe;

//insert in a function or click event
cmd.CommandText = "SELECT MIN(Freight) AS \"Lowest Freight Price\" FROM Orders";
```

SUM

The SUM aggregate function returns the sum of the set of values in the expression. Bit columns can't be used.

Syntax

SUM ([ALL] expression)

Example

In this example, you add all the freight prices together and display them in The Sum of All Freight Prices column. Your results should look the same as those displayed in Figure 8-5.

Figure 8-5. Adding all the freight prices together

Visual Basic .NET

```
'insert at the top of your class
Imports System.Data.SqlServerCe

'insert in a function or click event
cmd.CommandText = "SELECT SUM(Freight) AS ""The Sum of all Freight Prices"" " & _
                  "FROM Orders"
```

C#

```
//insert at the top of your class
using System.Data.SqlServerCe;

//insert in a function or click event
cmd.CommandText = "SELECT SUM(Freight) AS \"The Sum of all Freight Prices\" " +
                  "FROM Orders";
```

Date/Time Manipulation

Date and time functions perform operations on date and time values to return numeric, date, time, or string values.

DATEADD

The DATEADD date/time function adds an interval to a given date to return a new datetime value. The first parameter could be a year, day, or any other part of a date that you'd like to add. The second parameter is a number that specifies how many of the first parameters you would like to add. The last parameter is the source date in question that will have a number of date parts added to it.

Syntax

DATEADD (datepart, number, date)

Table 8-1 lists the valid date parts you can use in this syntax.

Table 8-1. Valid Dateparts to Choose From

DATEPART	ABBREVIATIONS
year	yy, yyyy
quarter	qq, q
month	mm, m
dayofyear	dy, y
day	dd, d
week	wk, ww
hour	hh
minute	mi, n
second	ss, s
millisecond	ms

Example

In this example, you'll add one month to the OrderDate value and then you'll display that result in the OrderDate + 1 Month column along with the OrderDate column. Your results should look the same as those displayed in Figure 8-6.

Visual Basic .NET

```
'insert at the top of your class
Imports System.Data.SqlServerCe

'insert in a function or click event
cmd.CommandText = "SELECT OrderDate, DATEADD(m, 1, OrderDate) " & _
                "AS ""OrderDate + 1 Month"" FROM Orders"
```

C#

```
//insert at the top of your class
using System.Data.SqlServerCe;

//insert in a function or click event
cmd.CommandText = "SELECT OrderDate, DATEADD(m, 1, OrderDate) " +
                "AS \"OrderDate + 1 Month\" FROM Orders";
```

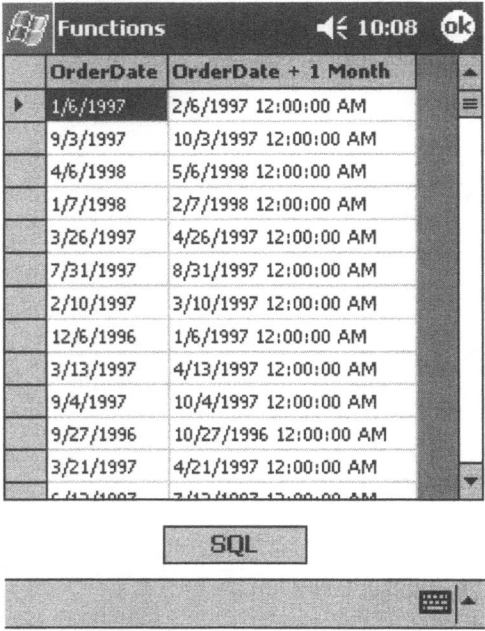

Figure 8-6. Adding one month to the OrderDate value

DATEDIFF

The DATEDIFF date/time function returns the number of dateparts found between a given start date and end date. In other words, it could tell you the number of days found between the beginning and end of December, for instance.

Syntax

DATEDIFF (datepart, startdate, enddate)

Example

In this example, you display both the OrderDate and RequiredDate columns. Additionally, you'll calculate the number of days between those two dates and display them in the Diff column. Your results should look the same as those displayed in Figure 8-7.

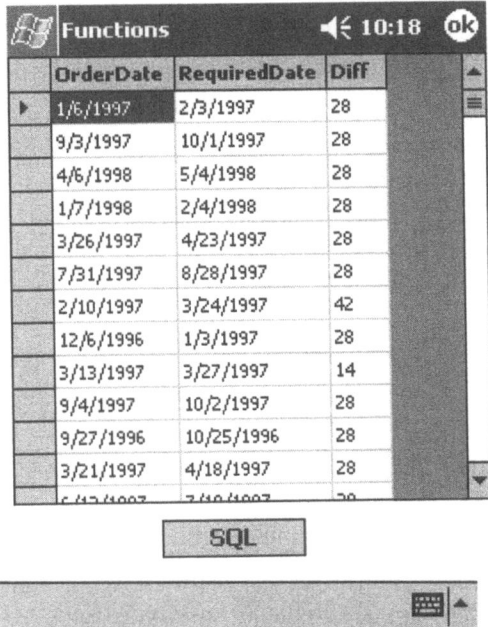

Figure 8-7. The number of days between OrderDate and RequiredDate values

Visual Basic .NET

```
'insert at the top of your class
Imports System.Data.SqlServerCe

'insert in a function or click event
cmd.CommandText = "SELECT OrderDate, RequiredDate, " & _
                "DATEDIFF(d, OrderDate, RequiredDate) AS ""Diff"" FROM Orders"
```

C#

```
//insert at the top of your class
using System.Data.SqlServerCe;

//insert in a function or click event
cmd.CommandText = "SELECT OrderDate, RequiredDate, " +
                "DATEDIFF(d, OrderDate, RequiredDate) AS \"Diff\" FROM Orders";
```

DATENAME

The DATENAME date/time function returns the string representation of the datepart of the specified date. In other words, if your datepart parameter is weekday and your date parameter is February 9, 2003, then your result would be Sunday. I used the weekday example for the datepart parameter since it's a datepart that wasn't included in Table 8-1, but can be used for the DATENAME function. The abbreviation for weekday is dw.

Syntax

DATENAME (datepart, date)

Example

In this example, you'll display the OrderDate column as well as the character representation of its day of the week in the Day of the Week column. Your results should look the same as those displayed in Figure 8-8.

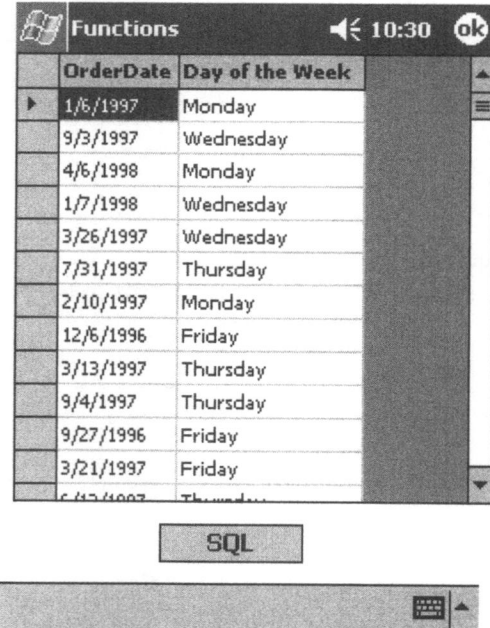

Figure 8-8. The OrderDate's Day of the Week values

Visual Basic .NET

```
'insert at the top of your class
Imports System.Data.SqlServerCe

'insert in a function or click event
cmd.CommandText = "SELECT OrderDate, DATENAME(dw, OrderDate) " & _
                  "AS ""Day of the Week"" FROM Orders"
```

C#

```
//insert at the top of your class
using System.Data.SqlServerCe;

//insert in a function or click event
cmd.CommandText = "SELECT OrderDate, DATENAME(dw, OrderDate) " +
                  "AS \"Day of the Week\" FROM Orders";
```

DATEPART

The DATEPART date/time function returns an integer that represents the datepart argument of the specified date argument. If your date argument is December 14, 1966, and your datepart argument is month, then your result would be 12.

Syntax

DATEPART (datepart, date)

Example

In this example, you'll display the OrderDate column along with the numeric representation of its month in the Month column. Your results should look the same as those displayed in Figure 8-9.

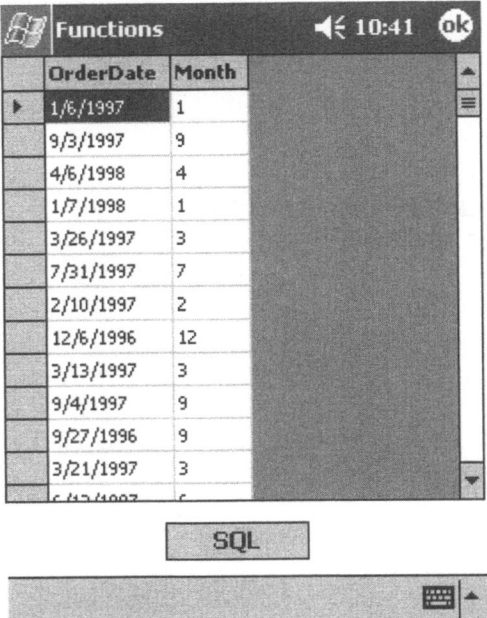

Figure 8-9. The OrderDate's Month values

Visual Basic .NET

```
'insert at the top of your class
Imports System.Data.SqlServerCe

'insert in a function or click event
cmd.CommandText = "SELECT OrderDate, DATEPART(m, OrderDate) " & _
                  "AS ""Month"" FROM Orders"
```

C#

```
//insert at the top of your class
using System.Data.SqlServerCe;

//insert in a function or click event
cmd.CommandText = "SELECT OrderDate, DATEPART(m, OrderDate) " +
                  "AS \"Month\" FROM Orders";
```

GETDATE

The GETDATE date/time function returns the current system date and time.

Syntax

GETDATE ( )

Example

While used almost exclusively to insert today's date into a table, in this example you'll use GETDATE in a SELECT query so that you can see that the function actually works. Unlike SQL Server 2000, SQL Server CE won't just let you execute the function without querying an actual table. Therefore, you'll run a query against the Orders table and display the result in the Today's Date column. You'll use a WHERE clause so that the Today's Date value isn't repeated by the number of rows in the table. Your results should look the same as those displayed in Figure 8-10.

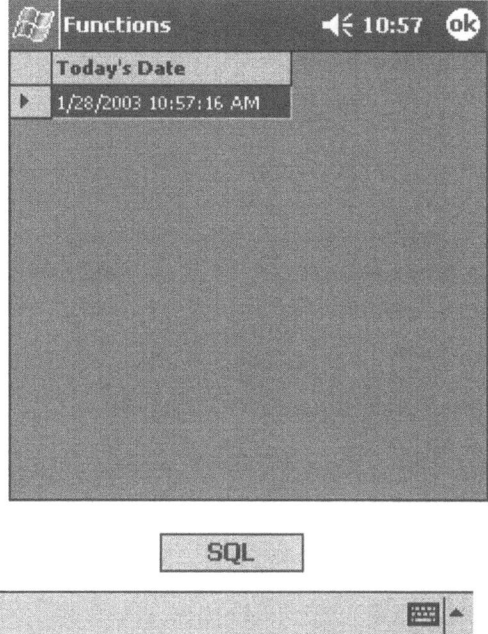

Figure 8-10. Today's Date value

Visual Basic .NET

```
'insert at the top of your class
Imports System.Data.SqlServerCe

'insert in a function or click event
cmd.CommandText = "SELECT GETDATE() AS ""Today's Date"" FROM Orders " & _
                  "WHERE OrderID = 10405"
```

C#

```
//insert at the top of your class
using System.Data.SqlServerCe;

//insert in a function or click event
cmd.CommandText = "SELECT GETDATE() AS \"Today's Date\" FROM Orders " +
                  "WHERE OrderID = 10405";
```

Mathematical Functions

The mathematical functions perform numeric calculations based on a variety of input values and return a single numeric result.

ABS

The ABS mathematical function returns a positive, absolute value for a given expression. Expressions that result in a negative value are turned into positive values when the ABS function is run against those expressions.

Syntax

ABS (numeric expression)

Example

In this example, you display the results of subtracting 100 from the freight price in the Freight – 100 column. Additionally, you'll display the effect of the ABS function on the same equation in the ABS(Freight – 100) column. Your results should look the same as those displayed in Figure 8-11.

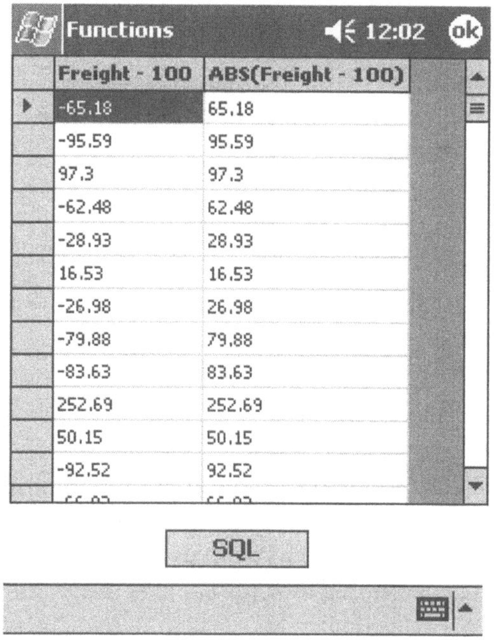

Figure 8-11. Comparing freight calculations with and without ABS

Visual Basic .NET

```
'insert at the top of your class
Imports System.Data.SqlServerCe


'insert in a function or click event
cmd.CommandText = "SELECT (Freight - 100) AS ""Freight - 100"", " & _
                  "ABS(Freight - 100) AS ""ABS(Freight - 100) "" FROM Orders"
```

C#

```
//insert at the top of your class
using System.Data.SqlServerCe;


//insert in a function or click event
cmd.CommandText = "SELECT (Freight - 100) AS \"Freight - 100\", " +
                  "ABS(Freight - 100) AS \"ABS(Freight - 100)\ " FROM Orders";
```

ACOS

Known as the arccosine or inverse cosine, the ACOS mathematical function returns the angle in radians from a given cosine (specified as a float expression). This float expression must range from –1 through 1.

Syntax

ACOS (float expression)

Example

In this example, you'll display the inverse cosine of freight in the Arccosine column for items with a freight price of less than or equal to 1. It should be noted that the Freight column values are being used as float expressions and in no way represent actual trigonometric information. Your results should look the same as those displayed in Figure 8-12.

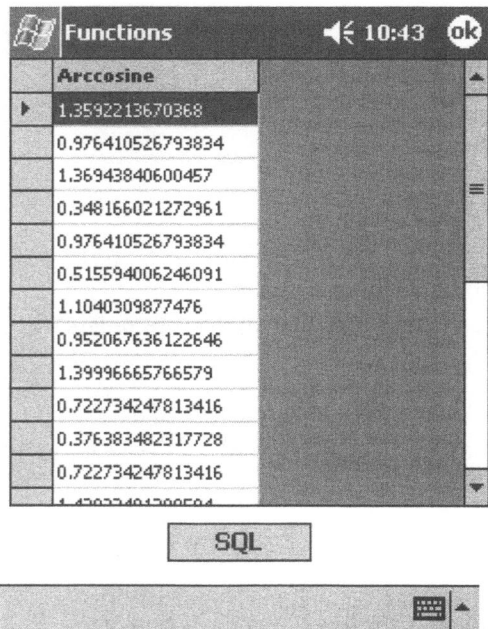

Figure 8-12. *The inverse cosine of freight prices that are less than or equal to 1*

Visual Basic .NET

```
'insert at the top of your class
Imports System.Data.SqlServerCe

'insert in a function or click event
cmd.CommandText = "SELECT ACOS(Freight) AS ""Arccosine"" FROM Orders " & _
                "WHERE Freight <= 1"
```

C#

```
//insert at the top of your class
using System.Data.SqlServerCe;

//insert in a function or click event
cmd.CommandText = "SELECT ACOS(Freight) AS \"Arccosine\" FROM Orders " +
                "WHERE Freight <= 1";
```

ASIN

The arcsine mathematical function returns the angle in radians whose sine is the specified float expression. The float expression must from range from –1 through 1.

Syntax

ASIN (float expression)

Example

In this example, you'll display the arcsine of freight in the Arcsine column for items with a freight price of less than or equal to 1. Again, please note that we're only using the Freight column values as float expressions, and they in no way represent actual trigonometric information. Your results should look the same as those displayed in Figure 8-13.

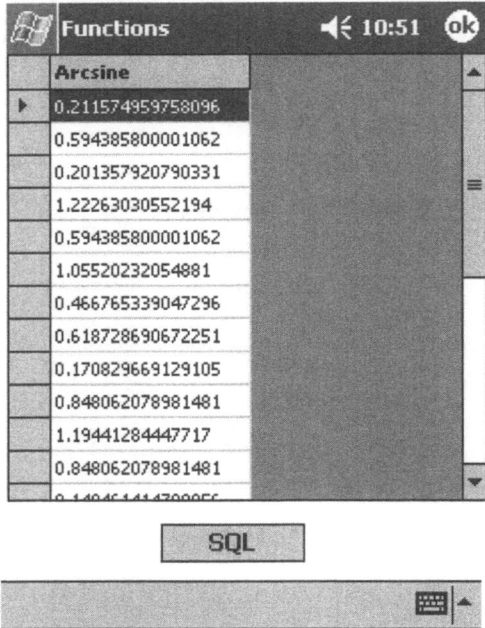

Figure 8-13. The arcsine of freight prices that are less than or equal to 1

Visual Basic .NET

```
'insert at the top of your class
Imports System.Data.SqlServerCe

'insert in a function or click event
cmd.CommandText = "SELECT ASIN(Freight) AS ""Arcsine"" FROM Orders " & _
                "WHERE Freight <= 1"
```

C#

```
//insert at the top of your class
using System.Data.SqlServerCe;

//insert in a function or click event
cmd.CommandText = "SELECT ASIN(Freight) AS \"Arcsine\" FROM Orders " +
                "WHERE Freight <= 1";
```

ATAN

The arctangent mathematical function returns the angle in radians whose tangent is the given float expression.

Syntax

ATAN (float expression)

Example

In this example, you'll display the arctangent of freight in the Arctangent column for items with a freight price of less than or equal to 1. As with ACOS and ASIN, it should be noted that the Freight column values are only being used as float expressions and in no way represent actual trigonometric information. Your results should look the same as those displayed in Figure 8-14.

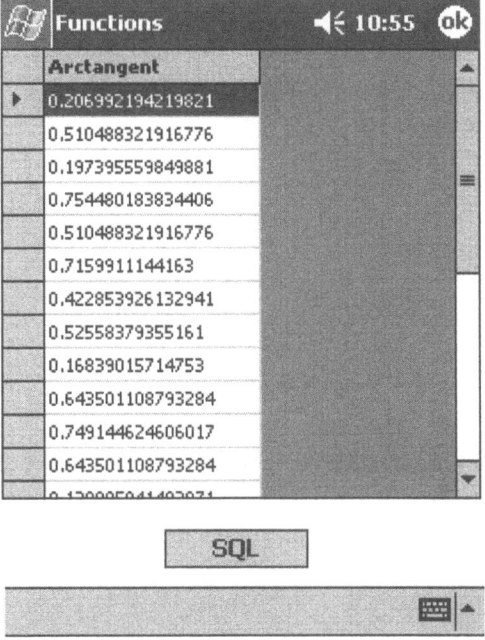

Figure 8-14. The arctangent of freight prices that are less than or equal to 1

Visual Basic .NET

```
'insert at the top of your class
Imports System.Data.SqlServerCe

'insert in a function or click event
cmd.CommandText = "SELECT ATAN(Freight) AS ""Arctangent"" FROM Orders " & _
                  "WHERE Freight <= 1"
```

C#

```
//insert at the top of your class
using System.Data.SqlServerCe;

//insert in a function or click event
cmd.CommandText = "SELECT ATAN(Freight) AS \"Arctangent\" FROM Orders " +
                  "WHERE Freight <= 1";
```

ATN2

The arctangent "2" mathematical function returns the angle in radians whose tangent is the quotient of two float expressions.

Syntax

ATN2 (float expression, float expression)

Example

In this example, you'll display an angle in radians in the ATN2 column based on the quotient of Freight and Freight – 0.3 values. Again, you're only using the Freight column values as convenient float expressions, although these values have no actual relationship to trigonometry. Your results should look the same as those displayed in Figure 8-15.

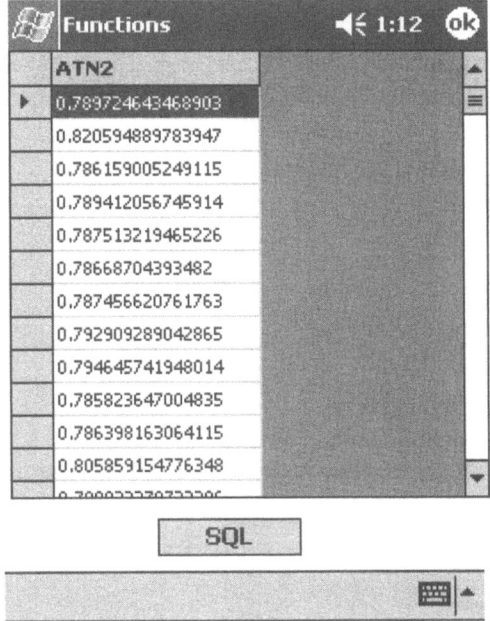

Figure 8-15. The ATN2 result

Visual Basic .NET

```
'insert at the top of your class
Imports System.Data.SqlServerCe

'insert in a function or click event
cmd.CommandText = "SELECT ATN2(Freight, (Freight - .3)) AS ""ATN2"" FROM Orders"
```

C#

```
//insert at the top of your class
using System.Data.SqlServerCe;

//insert in a function or click event
cmd.CommandText = "SELECT ATN2(Freight, (Freight - .3)) AS \"ATN2\" FROM Orders";
```

CEILING

The CEILING mathematical function returns the smallest integer that's greater than or equal to a specified numeric expression. In most cases, it's an easy way to round a floating number upward to the nearest whole number.

Syntax

CEILING (numeric expression)

Example

In this example, you'll display both the Freight column and the rounded-up price of freight in the Freight Ceiling column. Your results should look the same as those displayed in Figure 8-16.

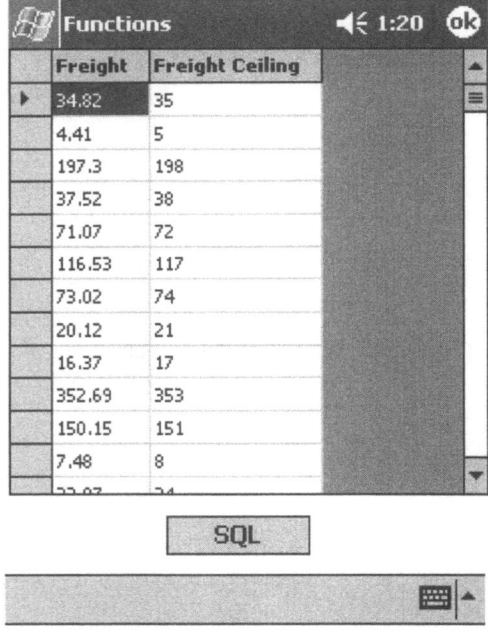

Figure 8-16. Ceiling rounds up the freight prices

Visual Basic .NET

```
'insert at the top of your class
Imports System.Data.SqlServerCe

'insert in a function or click event
cmd.CommandText = "SELECT Freight, CEILING(Freight) " & _
                  "AS ""Freight Ceiling"" FROM Orders"
```

C#

```
//insert at the top of your class
using System.Data.SqlServerCe;

//insert in a function or click event
cmd.CommandText = "SELECT Freight, CEILING(Freight) " +
                  "AS \"Freight Ceiling\" FROM Orders";
```

COS

The COS mathematical function returns the cosine of an angle in radians for a specified expression.

Syntax

COS (float expression)

Example

In this example, you'll display the cosine of freight in the Cosine column. It should be noted that the Freight column values are only being used as float expressions and in no way represent actual trigonometric information. Your results should look the same as those displayed in Figure 8-17.

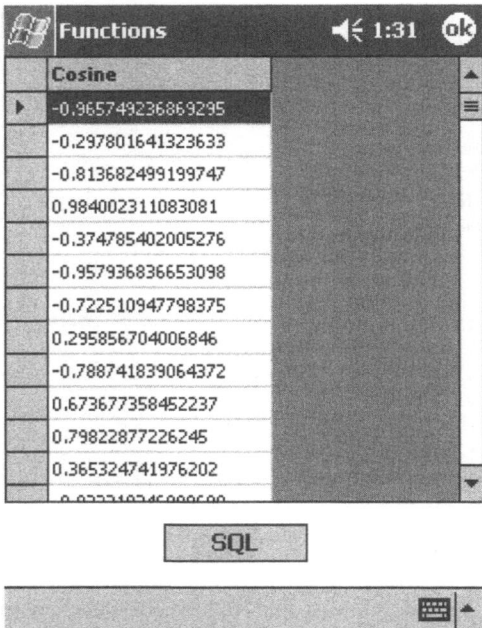

Figure 8-17. The cosine of freight prices

Visual Basic .NET

```
'insert at the top of your class
Imports System.Data.SqlServerCe

'insert in a function or click event
cmd.CommandText = "SELECT COS(Freight) AS ""Cosine"" FROM Orders"
```

C#

```
//insert at the top of your class
using System.Data.SqlServerCe;

//insert in a function or click event
cmd.CommandText = "SELECT COS(Freight) AS \"Cosine\" FROM Orders";
```

COT

The COT mathematical function returns the cotangent of an angle in radians for a given float expression.

Syntax

COT (float expression)

Example

In this example, you'll display the cotangent of the freight prices in the Cotangent column. Again, the Freight column values are only being used as float expressions and in no way represent actual trigonometric information. Your results should look the same as those displayed in Figure 8-18.

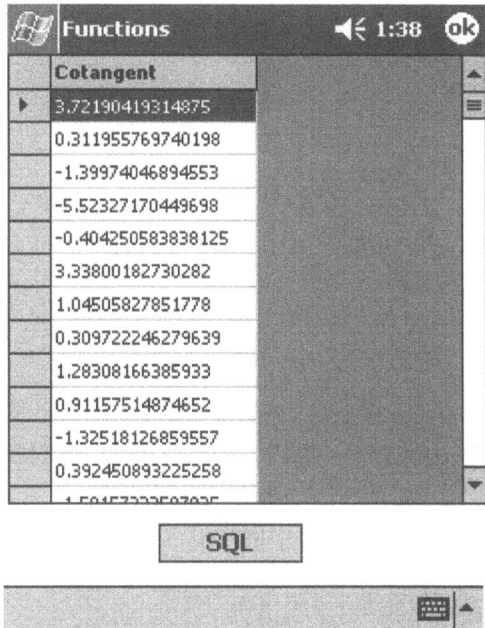

Figure 8-18. The cotangent of freight prices

Visual Basic .NET

```
'insert at the top of your class
Imports System.Data.SqlServerCe

'insert in a function or click event
cmd.CommandText = "SELECT COT(Freight) AS ""Cotangent"" FROM Orders"
```

C#

```
//insert at the top of your class
using System.Data.SqlServerCe;

//insert in a function or click event
cmd.CommandText = "SELECT COT(Freight) AS \"Cotangent\" FROM Orders";
```

DEGREES

The DEGREES mathematical function returns an angle in degrees for a given angle in radians.

Syntax

DEGREES (numeric expression)

Example

In this example, you'll display an angle in degrees returned from the freight price in the Degrees column. It should be noted that the Freight column values are only being used as float expressions and in no way represent actual trigonometric information. Your results should look the same as those displayed in Figure 8-19.

Visual Basic .NET

```
'insert at the top of your class
Imports System.Data.SqlServerCe

'insert in a function or click event
cmd.CommandText = "SELECT DEGREES(Freight) AS ""Degrees"" FROM Orders"
```

C#

```
//insert at the top of your class
using System.Data.SqlServerCe;

//insert in a function or click event
cmd.CommandText = "SELECT DEGREES(Freight) AS \"Degrees\" FROM Orders";
```

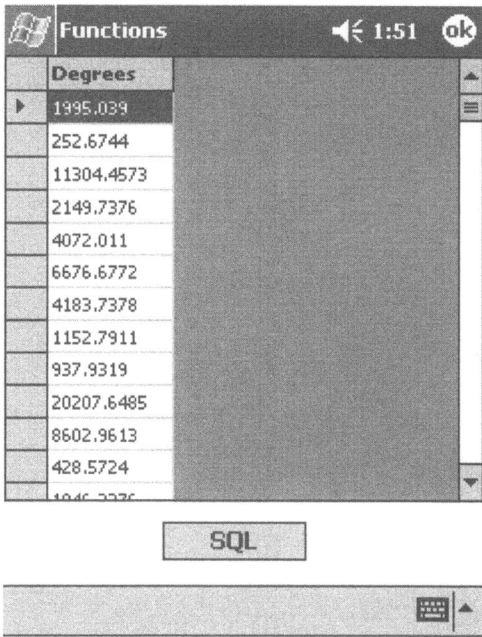

Figure 8-19. Degrees returned from freight prices

EXP

The EXP mathematical function returns the exponential value of a specified float expression.

Syntax

EXP (float expression)

Example

In this example, you'll display the Freight column and the exponent of the freight value in the Exponential Freight column for items with a price of freight that is less than 100. The reason you're filtering the query with the WHERE clause is to prevent numeric overflows caused by freight prices that are already too high. Your results should look the same as those displayed in Figure 8-20.

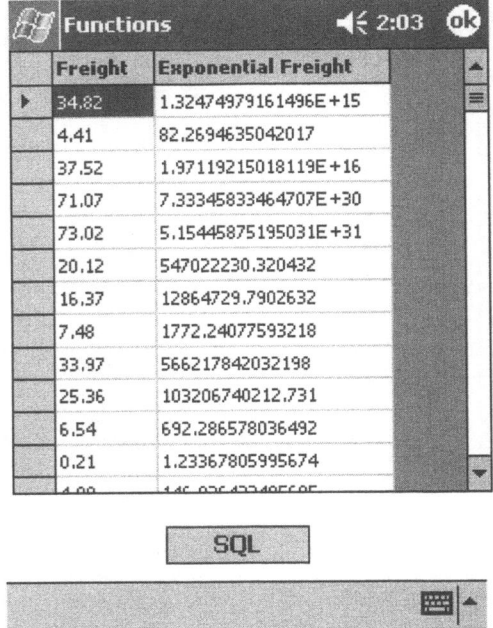

Figure 8-20. The exponential values of freight prices

Visual Basic .NET

```
'insert at the top of your class
Imports System.Data.SqlServerCe

'insert in a function or click event
cmd.CommandText = "SELECT Freight, EXP(Freight) " & _
                "AS ""Exponential Freight"" FROM Orders " & _
                "WHERE Freight < 100"
```

C#

```
//insert at the top of your class
using System.Data.SqlServerCe;

//insert in a function or click event
cmd.CommandText = "SELECT Freight, EXP(Freight) " +
                  "AS \"Exponential Freight\" FROM Orders " +
                  "WHERE Freight < 100";
```

FLOOR

The FLOOR mathematical function returns the largest integer that is less than or equal to a specified numeric expression. The function provides an easy way to round a float down to a whole number.

Syntax

FLOOR (numeric expression)

Example

In this example, you'll display the Freight column and the rounded-down price of freight in the Freight Floor column. Your results should look the same as those displayed in Figure 8-21.

Visual Basic .NET

```
'insert at the top of your class
Imports System.Data.SqlServerCe

'insert in a function or click event
cmd.CommandText = "SELECT Freight, FLOOR(Freight) " & _
                  "AS ""Freight Floor"" FROM Orders"
```

C#

```
//insert at the top of your class
using System.Data.SqlServerCe;

//insert in a function or click event
cmd.CommandText = "SELECT Freight, FLOOR(Freight) " +
                  "AS \"Freight Floor\" FROM Orders";
```

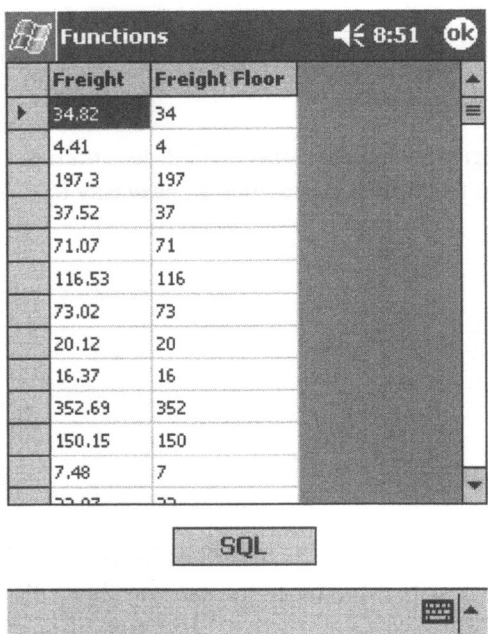

Figure 8-21. Floor rounds down the freight prices

LOG

The LOG mathematical function returns the natural logarithm of a specified float expression.

Syntax

LOG (float expression)

Example

In this example, you'll display the Freight column as well as the natural logarithm of the freight prices in the Freight Logarithm column. Your results should look the same as those displayed in Figure 8-22.

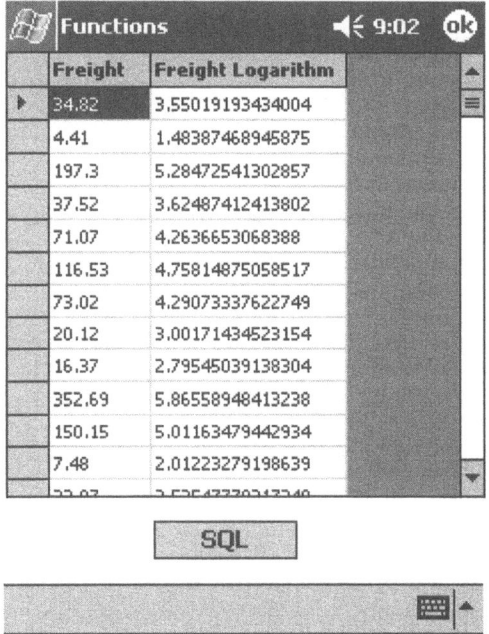

Figure 8-22. The natural logarithm of the freight prices

Visual Basic .NET

```
'insert at the top of your class
Imports System.Data.SqlServerCe

'insert in a function or click event
cmd.CommandText = "SELECT Freight, LOG(Freight) " & _
                "AS ""Freight Logarithm"" FROM Orders"
```

C#

```
//insert at the top of your class
using System.Data.SqlServerCe;

//insert in a function or click event
cmd.CommandText = "SELECT Freight, LOG(Freight) " +
                  "AS \"Freight Logarithm\" FROM Orders";
```

LOG10

The LOG10 mathematical function returns the base-10 logarithm of a specified float expression.

Syntax

LOG10 (float expression)

Example

In this example, you'll display the Freight column as well as the base-10 logarithm of the freight prices in the Freight Base 10 Logarithm column. Your results should look the same as those displayed in Figure 8-23.

Visual Basic .NET

```
'insert at the top of your class
Imports System.Data.SqlServerCe

'insert in a function or click event
cmd.CommandText = "SELECT Freight, LOG10(Freight) " & _
                  "AS ""Freight Base 10 Logarithm"" FROM Orders"
```

C#

```
//insert at the top of your class
using System.Data.SqlServerCe;

//insert in a function or click event
cmd.CommandText = "SELECT Freight, LOG10(Freight) " +
                  "AS \"Freight Base 10 Logarithm\" FROM Orders";
```

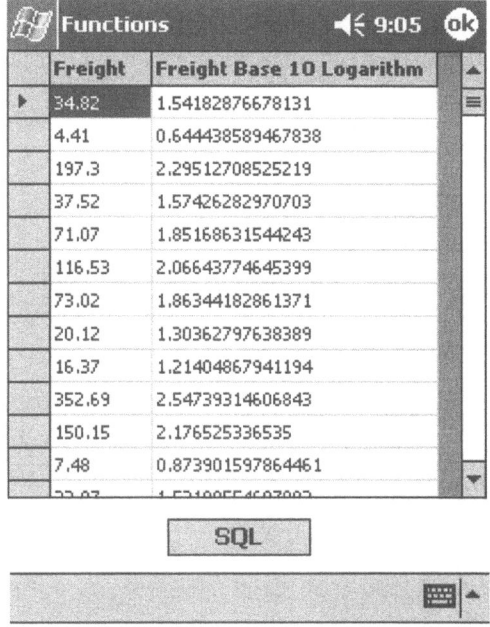

Figure 8-23. The base-10 logarithm of the freight prices

PI

The PI mathematical function returns the constant value of PI.

Syntax

```
PI ()
```

Example

In this example, you'll display the result of the PI function in the PI column. Your results should look the same as those displayed in Figure 8-24.

Visual Basic .NET

```
'insert at the top of your class
Imports System.Data.SqlServerCe

'insert in a function or click event
cmd.CommandText = "SELECT PI() AS ""PI"" FROM Orders"
```

C#

```
//insert at the top of your class
using System.Data.SqlServerCe;

//insert in a function or click event
cmd.CommandText = "SELECT PI() AS \"PI\" FROM Orders";
```

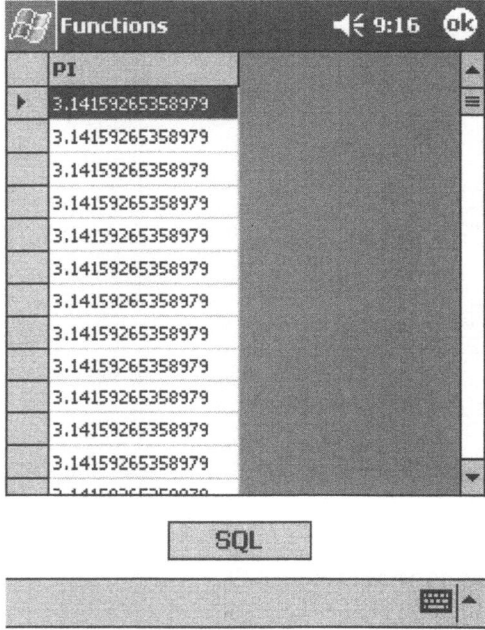

Figure 8-24. PI

POWER

The POWER mathematical function takes a numeric expression and returns its value to the power specified in the second argument.

Syntax

POWER (numeric expression, y)

Example

In this example, you'll display the Freight column as well as the freight prices to the power of 3 in the Freight Cubed column. Your results should look the same as those displayed in Figure 8-25 (once you scroll down the results a bit).

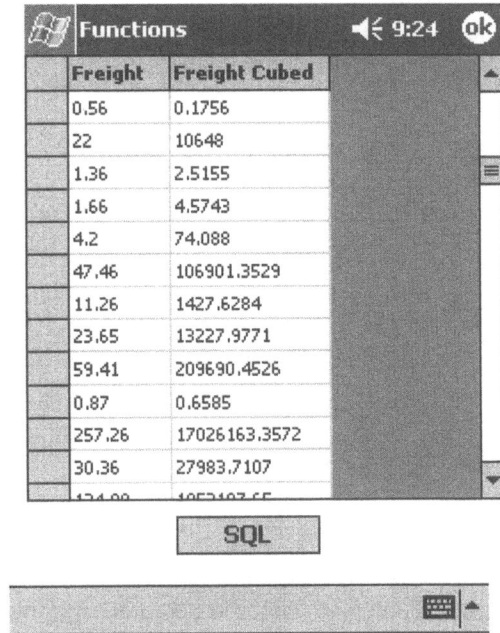

Figure 8-25. The freight prices cubed

Visual Basic .NET

```
'insert at the top of your class
Imports System.Data.SqlServerCe

'insert in a function or click event
cmd.CommandText = "SELECT Freight, POWER(Freight, 3) " & _
                "AS ""Freight Cubed"" FROM Orders"
```

C#

```
//insert at the top of your class
using System.Data.SqlServerCe;

//insert in a function or click event
cmd.CommandText = "SELECT Freight, POWER(Freight, 3) " +
                  "AS \"Freight Cubed\" FROM Orders";
```

RADIANS

The RADIANS mathematical function returns an angle in radians for a given angle in degrees.

Syntax

RADIANS (numeric expression)

Example

In this example, you'll display the Freight column and the angle in radians returned from the freight prices in the Radians column. It should be noted that the Freight column values are only being used as numeric expressions and in no way represent actual trigonometric information. Your results should look the same as those displayed in Figure 8-26.

Visual Basic .NET

```
'insert at the top of your class
Imports System.Data.SqlServerCe

'insert in a function or click event
cmd.CommandText = "SELECT Freight, RADIANS(Freight) " & _
                  "AS ""Radians"" FROM Orders"
```

C#

```
//insert at the top of your class
using System.Data.SqlServerCe;

//insert in a function or click event
cmd.CommandText = "SELECT Freight, RADIANS(Freight) " +
                  "AS \"Radians\" FROM Orders";
```

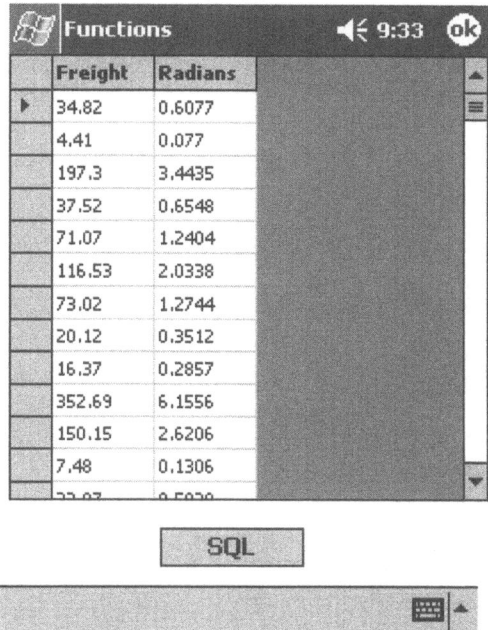

Figure 8-26. Radians of the freight prices

RAND

The RAND mathematical function takes an integer seed value and returns a random float value from 0 through 1. It should be noted that the repeated use of RAND in the same query would return the same value for a very unrandom result.

Syntax

RAND ([seed])

Example

In this example, you'll display the EmployeeID column and a random number that utilizes the EmployeeID value as a seed in the Random Numbers column. Your results should look the same as those displayed in Figure 8-27.

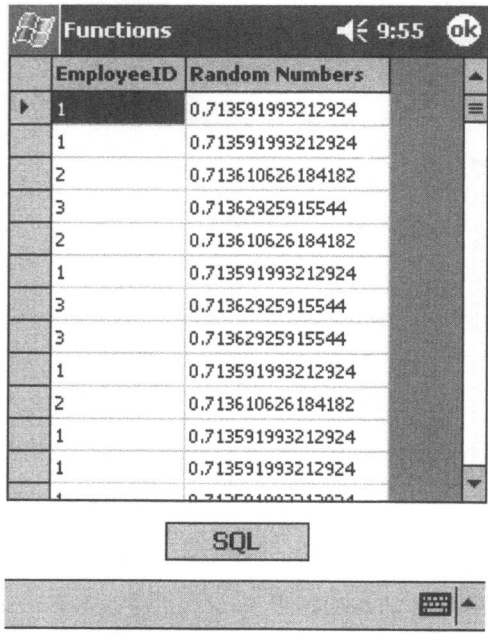

Figure 8-27. EmployeeID values as seeds to generate not-so-random numbers

Visual Basic .NET

```
'insert at the top of your class
Imports System.Data.SqlServerCe

'insert in a function or click event
cmd.CommandText = "SELECT EmployeeID, RAND(EmployeeID) " & _
                "AS ""Random Numbers"" FROM Orders"
```

C#

```
//insert at the top of your class
using System.Data.SqlServerCe;

//insert in a function or click event
cmd.CommandText = "SELECT EmployeeID, RAND(EmployeeID) " +
                  "AS \"Random Numbers\" FROM Orders";
```

ROUND

The ROUND mathematical function returns a numeric expression that's rounded to the specified length. If the length were 3, then the result would only go out to three decimal places.

Syntax

ROUND (numeric expression, length [, function])

Example

In this example, you'll display the Freight column as well as the freight prices rounded to one decimal place in the Rounded column. Your results should look the same as those displayed in Figure 8-28.

Visual Basic .NET

```
'insert at the top of your class
Imports System.Data.SqlServerCe

'insert in a function or click event
cmd.CommandText = "SELECT Freight, ROUND(Freight, 1) " & _
                  "AS ""Rounded"" FROM Orders"
```

C#

```
//insert at the top of your class
using System.Data.SqlServerCe;

//insert in a function or click event
cmd.CommandText = "SELECT Freight, ROUND(Freight, 1) " +
                  "AS \"Rounded\" FROM Orders";
```

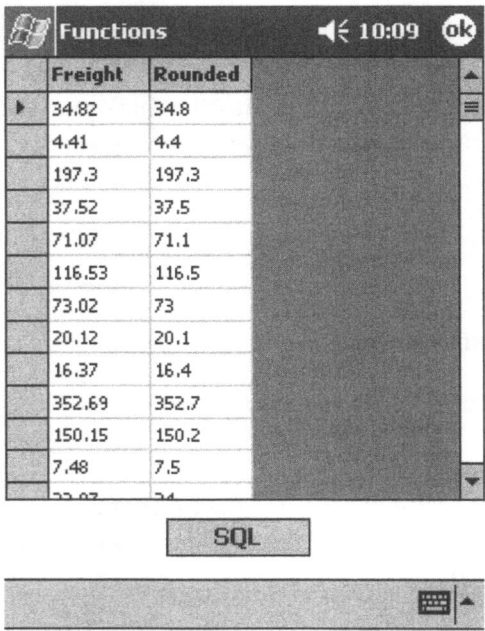

Figure 8-28. Freight prices rounded to one decimal place

SIGN

The SIGN mathematical function returns the positive, zero, or negative sign of a specified expression.

Syntax

SIGN (numeric expression)

Example

In this example, you'll display the result of subtracting 100 from the freight prices in the Freight – 100 column. Additionally, you'll use the SIGN function with the same equation to return the proper sign and display it in the Sign column. Your results should look the same as those displayed in Figure 8-29.

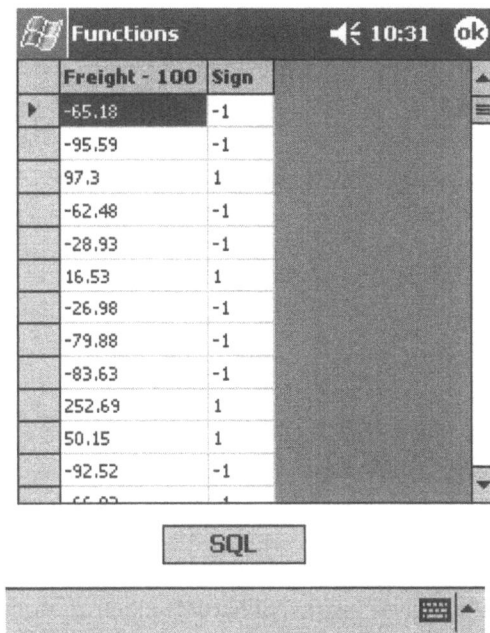

Figure 8-29. The sign of freight prices when 100 is subtracted from them

Visual Basic .NET

```
'insert at the top of your class
Imports System.Data.SqlServerCe

'insert in a function or click event
cmd.CommandText = "SELECT (Freight - 100) AS ""Freight - 100"", " & _
                  "SIGN(Freight - 100) AS ""Sign"" FROM Orders"
```

C#

```
//insert at the top of your class
using System.Data.SqlServerCe;

//insert in a function or click event
cmd.CommandText = "SELECT (Freight - 100) AS ""Freight - 100"", " +
                  "SIGN(Freight - 100) AS \"Sign\" FROM Orders";
```

SIN

The SIN mathematical function returns the sine of an angle in radians of a float expression.

Syntax

SIN (float expression)

Example

In this example, you'll display the Freight column as well as the sine of the freight prices in the SINE column. It should be noted that the Freight column values are only being used as float expressions and in no way represent actual trigonometric information. Your results should look the same as those displayed in Figure 8-30.

Visual Basic .NET

```
'insert at the top of your class
Imports System.Data.SqlServerCe

'insert in a function or click event
cmd.CommandText = "SELECT Freight, SIN(Freight) AS ""SINE"" FROM Orders"
```

C#

```
//insert at the top of your class
using System.Data.SqlServerCe;

//insert in a function or click event
cmd.CommandText = "SELECT Freight, SIN(Freight) AS \"SINE\" FROM Orders";
```

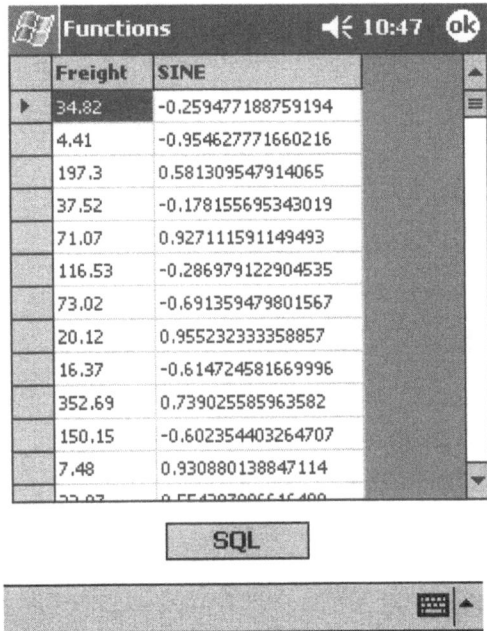

Figure 8-30. The sine of freight prices

SQRT

The SQRT mathematical function returns the square root of a specified expression.

Syntax

SQRT (float expression)

Example

In this example, you'll display the Freight column and the square root of the freight prices in the Square Root column. Your results should look the same as those displayed in Figure 8-31.

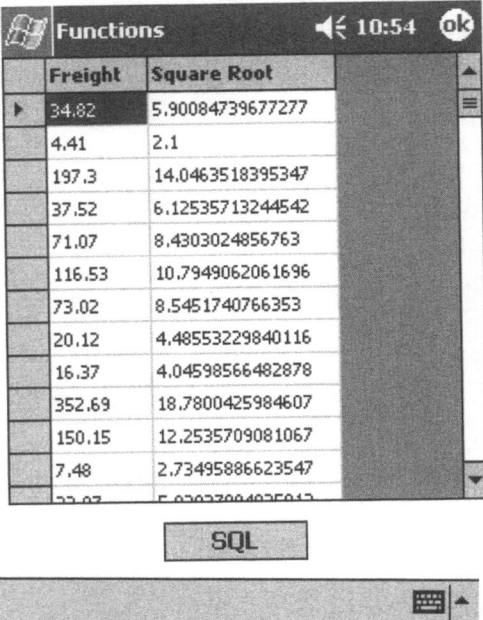

Figure 8-31. Square root of freight prices

Visual Basic .NET

```
'insert at the top of your class
Imports System.Data.SqlServerCe

'insert in a function or click event
cmd.CommandText = "SELECT Freight, SQRT(Freight) AS ""Square Root"" FROM Orders"
```

C#

```
//insert at the top of your class
using System.Data.SqlServerCe;

//insert in a function or click event
cmd.CommandText = "SELECT Freight, SQRT(Freight) AS \"Square Root\" FROM Orders";
```

TAN

The TAN mathematical function returns the tangent of the given expression.

Syntax

TAN (float expression)

Example

In this example, you'll display the Freight column and the tangent of the freight prices in the Tangent column. It should be noted that the Freight column values are only being used as float expressions and in no way represent actual trigonometric information. Your results should look the same as those displayed in Figure 8-32.

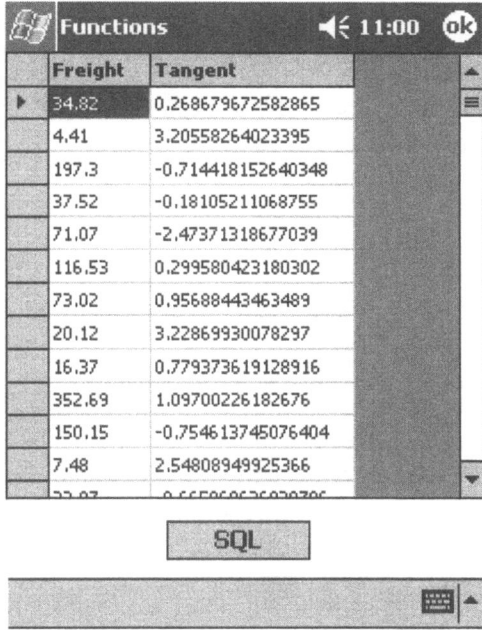

Figure 8-32. The tangent of freight prices

Visual Basic .NET

```
'insert at the top of your class
Imports System.Data.SqlServerCe

'insert in a function or click event
cmd.CommandText = "SELECT Freight, TAN(Freight) AS ""Tangent"" FROM Orders"
```

C#

```
//insert at the top of your class
using System.Data.SqlServerCe;

//insert in a function or click event
cmd.CommandText = "SELECT Freight, TAN(Freight) AS \"Tangent\" FROM Orders";
```

String Manipulation

The string functions perform an operation on a string value and return either a string or numeric value.

NCHAR

The NCHAR string function returns a Unicode character for a specified integer expression. The expression must be a whole number from 0 through 65535.

Syntax

NCHAR (integer expression)

Example

In this example, you'll display the EmployeeID column and the Unicode character representation of the EmployeeID values in the Strange Characters column. Your results should look the same as those displayed in Figure 8-33.

Visual Basic .NET

```
'insert at the top of your class
Imports System.Data.SqlServerCe

'insert in a function or click event
cmd.CommandText = "SELECT EmployeeID, NCHAR(EmployeeID) " & _
                  "AS ""Strange Characters"" FROM Orders"
```

C#

```
//insert at the top of your class
using System.Data.SqlServerCe;

//insert in a function or click event
cmd.CommandText = "SELECT EmployeeID, NCHAR(EmployeeID) " +
                  "AS \"Strange Characters\" FROM Orders";
```

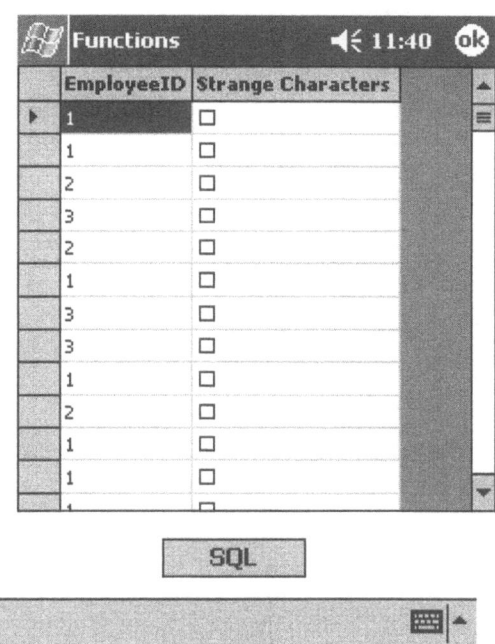

Figure 8-33. Unicode character representations of EmployeeID values

CHARINDEX

The CHARINDEX string function returns the starting position of a given expression in a character string. The first expression is a sequence of one or more characters that you're searching for. The second expression is the name of the column where you wish to search. The optional start location is the character position from which to start searching for the sequence of characters that you're seeking.

Syntax

CHARINDEX (expression1, expression2 [, start location])

Example

In this example, you'll display the ShipCity column and the position of the character "n" in the ShipCity values in the Position of 'n' column. Your results should look the same as those displayed in Figure 8-34.

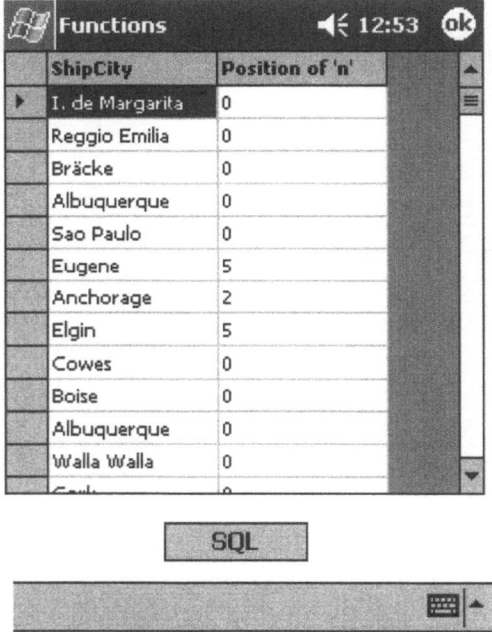

Figure 8-34. The position of "n" in the ShipCity values

Visual Basic .NET

```
'insert at the top of your class
Imports System.Data.SqlServerCe

'insert in a function or click event
cmd.CommandText = "SELECT ShipCity, CHARINDEX('n', ShipCity) " & _
                  "AS ""Position of 'n'"" FROM Orders"
```

C#

```
//insert at the top of your class
using System.Data.SqlServerCe;

//insert in a function or click event
cmd.CommandText = "SELECT ShipCity, CHARINDEX('n', ShipCity) " +
                "AS \"Position of 'n'\" FROM Orders";
```

LEN

The LEN string function returns the number of characters, excluding trailing blanks, in a given string expression.

Syntax

LEN (string expression)

Example

In this example, you'll display the ShipCity column as well as the length of the ShipCity values in the Length column. Your results should look the same as those displayed in Figure 8-35.

Visual Basic .NET

```
'insert at the top of your class
Imports System.Data.SqlServerCe

'insert in a function or click event
cmd.CommandText = "SELECT ShipCity, LEN(ShipCity) " & _
                "AS ""Length"" FROM Orders"
```

C#

```
//insert at the top of your class
using System.Data.SqlServerCe;

//insert in a function or click event
cmd.CommandText = "SELECT ShipCity, LEN(ShipCity) " +
                  "AS \"Length\" FROM Orders";
```

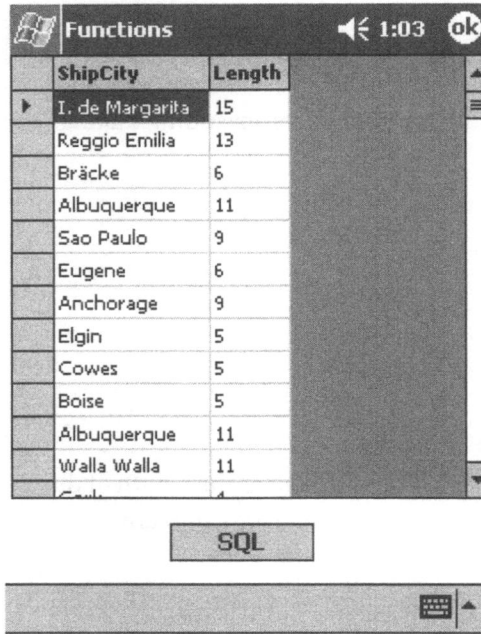

Figure 8-35. The length of ShipCity values

LOWER

The LOWER string function returns a character expression that has had its uppercase characters converted to lowercase equivalents.

Syntax

LOWER (character expression)

Example

In this example, you'll display the ShipCity column and the lowercase representation of the ShipCity values in the Lower Case column. Your results should look the same as those displayed in Figure 8-36.

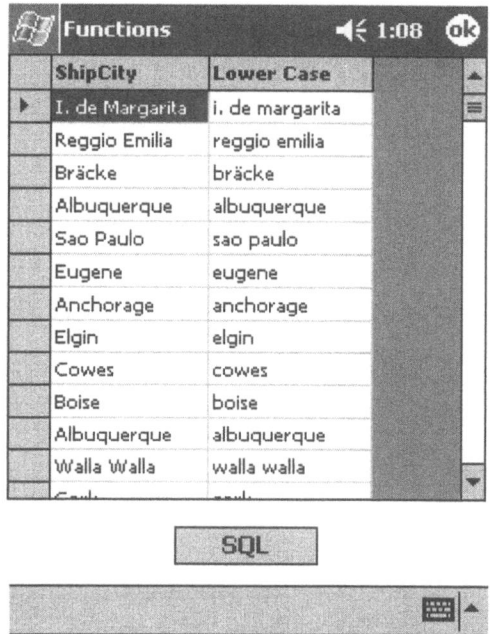

Figure 8-36. Converting ShipCity values to lowercase characters

Visual Basic .NET

```
'insert at the top of your class
Imports System.Data.SqlServerCe

'insert in a function or click event
cmd.CommandText = "SELECT ShipCity, LOWER(ShipCity) " & _
                "AS ""Lower Case"" FROM Orders"
```

C#

```
//insert at the top of your class
using System.Data.SqlServerCe;

//insert in a function or click event
cmd.CommandText = "SELECT ShipCity, LOWER(ShipCity) " +
                  "AS \"Lower Case\" FROM Orders";
```

LTRIM

The LTRIM string function returns a character expression minus any leading blank spaces.

Syntax

> LTRIM (character expression)

Example

In this example, you'll display the ShipCity values with some spaces appended to the front of them in the Spaced ShipCity column. Additionally, you'll use the LTRIM function with the same expression to show how those spaces are removed in the Spaces Removed column. Your results should look the same as those displayed in Figure 8-37.

Visual Basic .NET

```
'insert at the top of your class
Imports System.Data.SqlServerCe

'insert in a function or click event
cmd.CommandText = "SELECT ('    ' + ShipCity) AS ""Spaced ShipCity"", " & _
                  "LTRIM('    ' + ShipCity) AS ""Spaces removed"" FROM Orders"
```

C#

```
//insert at the top of your class
using System.Data.SqlServerCe;

//insert in a function or click event
cmd.CommandText = "SELECT ('    ' + ShipCity) AS \"Spaced ShipCity\", " +
                  "LTRIM('    ' + ShipCity) AS \"Spaces removed\" FROM Orders";
```

Figure 8-37. ShipCity values with and without leading spaces

PATINDEX

The PATINDEX string function returns the starting position of the first occurrence of a pattern in a column containing character data types. Similar to the way you use the LIKE operator, your pattern can include wildcard characters.

Syntax

PATINDEX ('%pattern%', expression)

Example

In this example, you'll display the ShipCity column and all ShipCity values that begin with an "S" in the Cities that start with 'S' column. Your results should look the same as those displayed in Figure 8-38.

Figure 8-38. Finding ShipCity values that start with an "S"

Visual Basic .NET

```
'insert at the top of your class
Imports System.Data.SqlServerCe

'insert in a function or click event
cmd.CommandText = "SELECT ShipCity, PATINDEX('S%', ShipCity) " & _
                  "AS ""Cities that start with 'S'"" FROM Orders"
```

C#

```
//insert at the top of your class
using System.Data.SqlServerCe;

//insert in a function or click event
cmd.CommandText = "SELECT ShipCity, PATINDEX('S%', ShipCity) " +
                  "AS \"Cities that start with 'S'\" FROM Orders";
```

REPLACE

The REPLACE string function searches the first string expression looking for occurrences of the second string expression. Whenever the second string expression is found, it is replaced with the character or binary data found in the third string expression.

Syntax

REPLACE ('string expression1', 'string expression2', 'string expression3')

Example

In this example, you'll display the ShipCity column and you'll replace every instance of Seattle from that column with Silverdale and display the results in the Replaced column. Your results should look the same as those in Figure 8-39 (if you scroll down the results a bit).

Visual Basic .NET

```
'insert at the top of your class
Imports System.Data.SqlServerCe

'insert in a function or click event
cmd.CommandText = "SELECT ShipCity, " & _
REPLACE(ShipCity, 'Seattle', 'Silverdale') AS ""Replaced"" FROM Orders"
```

C#

```
//insert at the top of your class
using System.Data.SqlServerCe;

//insert in a function or click event
cmd.CommandText = "SELECT ShipCity, REPLACE(ShipCity, 'Seattle', 'Silverdale') " +
                  "AS \"Replaced\" FROM Orders";
```

Figure 8-39. Replacing Seattle with Silverdale

REPLICATE

The REPLICATE string function repeats an alphanumeric character expression a given positive number of times.

Syntax

REPLICATE (character expression, integer expression)

Example

In this example, you'll display the ShipCity column and then you'll replicate the values found in ShipCity three times and display the results in the Replicated 3 Times column. Your results should look the same as those displayed in Figure 8-40.

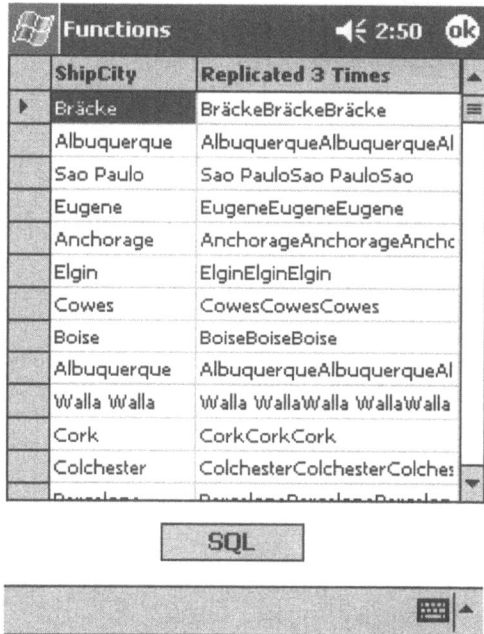

Figure 8-40. Replicating ShipCity values three times

Visual Basic .NET

```
'insert at the top of your class
Imports System.Data.SqlServerCe

'insert in a function or click event
cmd.CommandText = "SELECT ShipCity, REPLICATE(ShipCity, 3) " & _
                "AS ""Replicated 3 Times"" FROM Orders"
```

C#

```
//insert at the top of your class
using System.Data.SqlServerCe;

//insert in a function or click event
cmd.CommandText = "SELECT ShipCity, REPLICATE(ShipCity, 3) " +
                  "AS \"Replicated 3 Times\" FROM Orders";
```

RTRIM

The RTRIM string function returns a character expression minus any trailing blank spaces.

Syntax

RTRIM (character expression)

Example

In this example, you'll append spaces to the values found in ShipCity in the Spaced ShipCity column. Additionally, you'll use the RTRIM function to remove those spaces and display the result in the Spaces removed column. Your results should look the same as those displayed in Figure 8-41.

Visual Basic .NET

```
'insert at the top of your class
Imports System.Data.SqlServerCe

'insert in a function or click event
cmd.CommandText = "SELECT (ShipCity + '    ') AS ""Spaced ShipCity"", " & _
                  "RTRIM(ShipCity + '    ') AS ""Spaces removed"" FROM Orders"
```

C#

```
//insert at the top of your class
using System.Data.SqlServerCe;

//insert in a function or click event
cmd.CommandText = "SELECT (ShipCity + '    ') AS \"Spaced ShipCity\", " +
                  "RTRIM(ShipCity + '    ') AS \"Spaces removed\" FROM Orders";
```

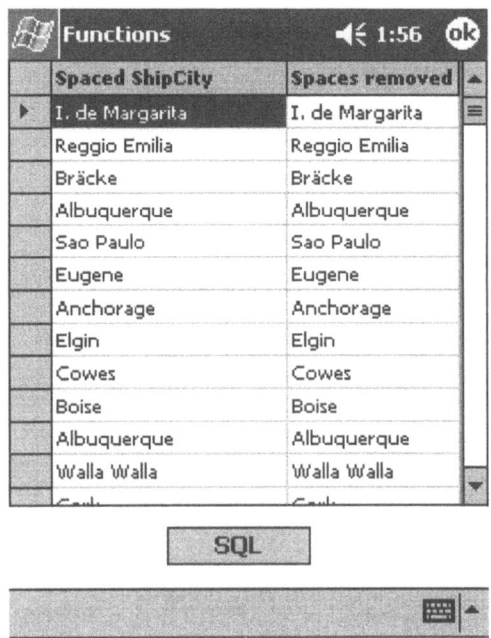

Figure 8-41. ShipCity values with and without trailing spaces

SPACE

The SPACE string function returns a string of repeated spaces equivalent to the positive integer expression argument.

Syntax

SPACE (integer expression)

Example

In this example, you'll display values from the ShipCity column, three spaces, and values from the ShipAddress column all inside the Ship City and Address column. Your results should look the same as those displayed in Figure 8-42.

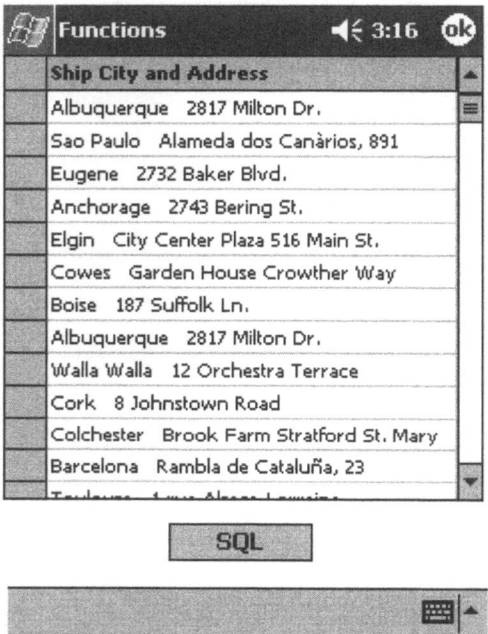

Figure 8-42. ShipCity and ShipAddress values separated by three spaces

Visual Basic .NET

```
'insert at the top of your class
Imports System.Data.SqlServerCe

'insert in a function or click event
cmd.CommandText = "SELECT ShipCity + SPACE(3) + ShipAddress " & _
                  "AS ""Ship City and Address"" FROM Orders"
```

C#

```
//insert at the top of your class
using System.Data.SqlServerCe;

//insert in a function or click event
cmd.CommandText = "SELECT ShipCity + SPACE(3) + ShipAddress " +
                  "AS \"Ship City and Address\" FROM Orders";
```

STR

The STR string function returns character data that's converted from a float expression. The optional length argument specifies the total length, including spaces, signs, digits, and decimal points. The optional decimal argument specifies the number of places to the right of the decimal point.

Syntax

STR (float expression [, length [, decimal]])

Example

In this example, you'll display the Freight column and a character representation of the freight prices out to one decimal place in the STR column. Your results should look the same as those displayed in Figure 8-43.

Visual Basic .NET

```
'insert at the top of your class
Imports System.Data.SqlServerCe

'insert in a function or click event
cmd.CommandText = "SELECT Freight, STR(Freight, 6, 1) " & _
                  "AS ""STR"" FROM Orders"
```

C#

```
//insert at the top of your class
using System.Data.SqlServerCe;

//insert in a function or click event
cmd.CommandText = "SELECT Freight, STR(Freight, 6, 1) " +
                  "AS \"STR\" FROM Orders";
```

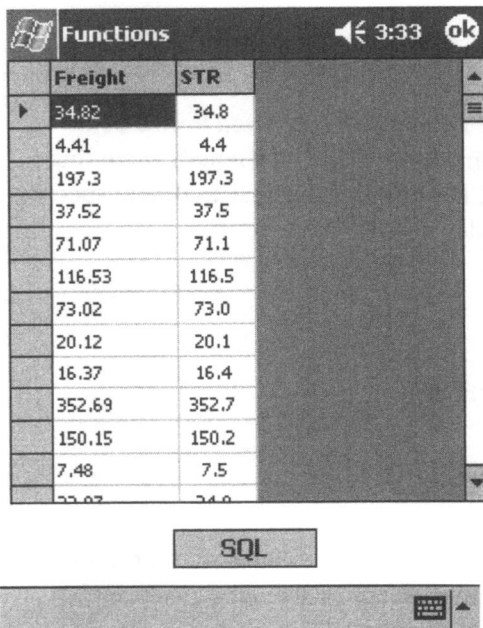

Figure 8-43. Freight prices converted to character data

STUFF

The STUFF string function effectively inserts one string into another string. It does this by moving to the start position in the first string of characters, deleting subsequent characters in that string equal to the specified length, and then inserting the second string in their place.

Syntax

STUFF (character expression, start, length, character expression)

Example

In this example, you'll display the ShipCity column and then you'll use STUFF to insert the characters "SQL" into the ShipCity values starting at the third position and extending for three characters. You'll display those results in the A Stuffed ShipCity column. Your results should look the same as those displayed in Figure 8-44.

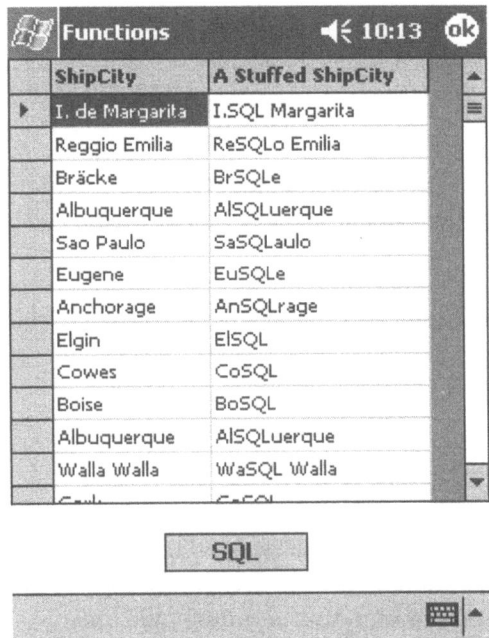

Figure 8-44. ShipCity values with "SQL" inserted

Visual Basic .NET

```
'insert at the top of your class
Imports System.Data.SqlServerCe

'insert in a function or click event
cmd.CommandText = "SELECT ShipCity, STUFF(ShipCity, 3, 3, 'SQL') " & _
                  "AS ""A Stuffed ShipCity"" FROM Orders"
```

C#

```
//insert at the top of your class
using System.Data.SqlServerCe;

//insert in a function or click event
cmd.CommandText = "SELECT ShipCity, STUFF(ShipCity, 3, 3, 'SQL') " +
                    "AS \"A Stuffed ShipCity\" FROM Orders";
```

SUBSTRING

The SUBSTRING string function returns part of a string by first specifying the target string or column name in question, then specifying the starting point in the target string, and finally specifying the length of the string to be returned.

Syntax

SUBSTRING (expression, start, length)

Example

In this example, you'll display the ShipCity column and then you'll use the SUBSTRING function to extract the first three characters from the ShipCity values and display that result in The first 3 characters column. Your results should look the same as those displayed in Figure 8-45.

Visual Basic .NET

```
'insert at the top of your class
Imports System.Data.SqlServerCe

'insert in a function or click event
cmd.CommandText = "SELECT ShipCity, SUBSTRING(ShipCity, 1, 3) " & _
                    "AS ""The first 3 characters"" FROM Orders"
```

C#

```
//insert at the top of your class
using System.Data.SqlServerCe;

//insert in a function or click event
cmd.CommandText = "SELECT ShipCity, SUBSTRING(ShipCity, 1, 3) " +
                  "AS \"The first 3 characters\" FROM Orders";
```

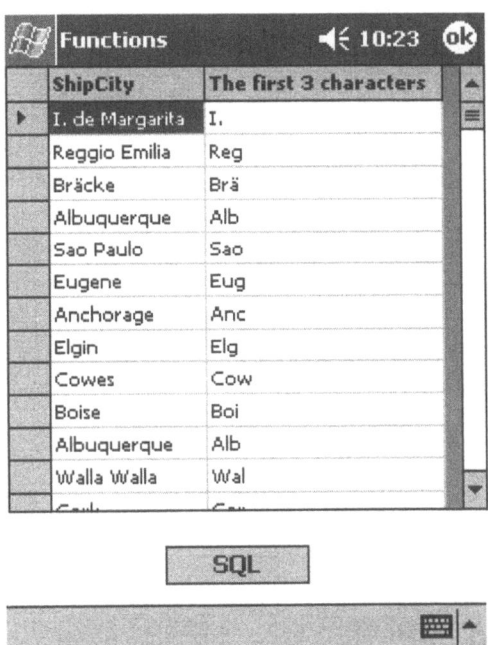

Figure 8-45. Using SUBSTRING to extract the first three characters of ShipCity values

UNICODE

The UNICODE string function returns the integer value, as defined by the Unicode standard, of the first character in the expression.

Syntax

UNICODE ('ncharacter expression')

Example

In this example, you'll display the ShipCity column and then you'll return the Unicode value of the first character found in the ShipCity values and display that result in The UNICODE value column. Your results should look the same as those displayed in Figure 8-46.

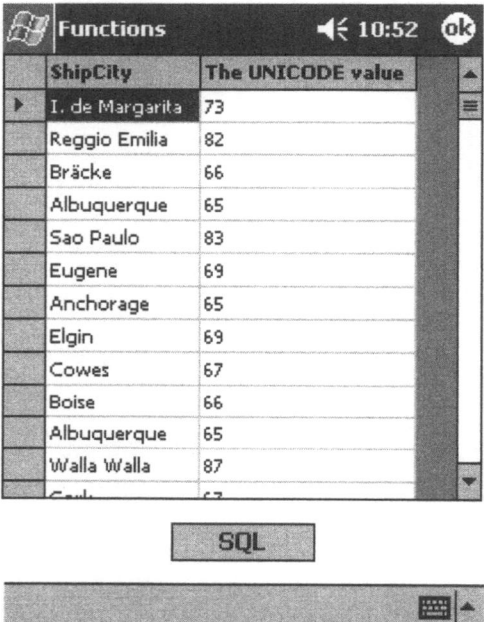

Figure 8-46. The UNICODE value of the first character

Visual Basic .NET

```
'insert at the top of your class
Imports System.Data.SqlServerCe

'insert in a function or click event
cmd.CommandText = "SELECT ShipCity, UNICODE(ShipCity) " & _
                  "AS ""The UNICODE value"" FROM Orders"
```

C#

```
//insert at the top of your class
using System.Data.SqlServerCe;

//insert in a function or click event
cmd.CommandText = "SELECT ShipCity, UNICODE(ShipCity) " +
                  "AS \"The UNICODE value\" FROM Orders";
```

UPPER

The UPPER string function returns a character expression that has had its lowercase characters converted to uppercase equivalents.

Syntax

UPPER (character expression)

Example

In this example, you'll display the ShipCity column as well as an uppercase representation of the values found in ShipCity in the Uppercase ShipCity column. Your results should look the same as those displayed in Figure 8-47.

Visual Basic .NET

```
'insert at the top of your class
Imports System.Data.SqlServerCe

'insert in a function or click event
cmd.CommandText = "SELECT ShipCity, UPPER(ShipCity) " & _
                  "AS ""Uppercase ShipCity"" FROM Orders"
```

C#

```
//insert at the top of your class
using System.Data.SqlServerCe;

//insert in a function or click event
cmd.CommandText = "SELECT ShipCity, UPPER(ShipCity) " +
                  "AS \"Uppercase ShipCity\" FROM Orders";
```

Figure 8-47. Uppercased ShipCity values

System Functions and Variables

The system functions work with and return information related to objects, settings, and values in SQL Server CE.

@@IDENTITY

The @@IDENTITY system function returns the last inserted identity value generated by a given INSERT statement.

Syntax

@@IDENTITY

Example

In this example, you'll first create a table called IdentityTable that contains an identity column as well as an nchar column. Next, you'll insert some data into this new table, which will have the effect of incrementing the value of the identity column. Finally, you'll use the @@IDENTITY function to retrieve the identity column's new value and display it in the @@IDENTITY column. Your results should look the same as those displayed in Figure 8-48.

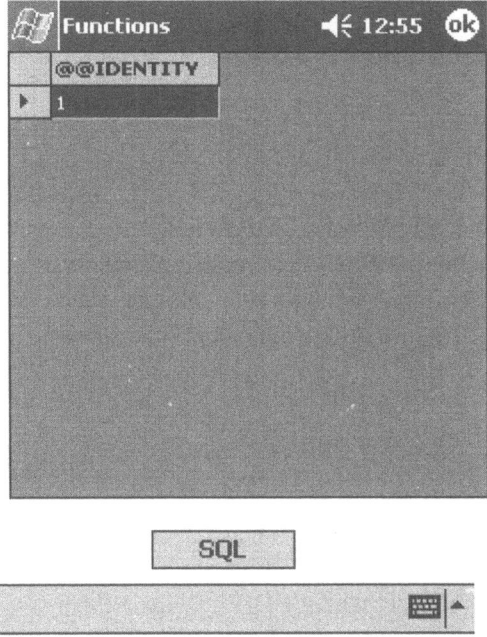

Figure 8-48. Latest value from an identity column

Visual Basic .NET

```
'insert at the top of your class
Imports System.Data.SqlServerCe

'insert in a function or click event
cmd.CommandText = "CREATE TABLE IdentityTable (Col1 int identity, Col2 nchar(20))"
```

```
cmd.ExecuteNonQuery()
cmd.CommandText = "INSERT INTO IdentityTable (Col2) VALUES ('some data')"
cmd.ExecuteNonQuery()
cmd.CommandText = "SELECT @@IDENTITY AS ""@@IDENTITY"" FROM IdentityTable"
```

C#

```
//insert at the top of your class
using System.Data.SqlServerCe;

//insert in a function or click event
cmd.CommandText = "CREATE TABLE IdentityTable (Col1 int identity, Col2 nchar(20))";
cmd.ExecuteNonQuery();
cmd.CommandText = "INSERT INTO IdentityTable (Col2) VALUES ('some data')";
cmd.ExecuteNonQuery();
cmd.CommandText = "SELECT @@IDENTITY AS \"@@IDENTITY\" FROM IdentityTable";
```

CASE

The CASE system function assesses a list of conditions and returns one of many potential result expressions. With two different modes of operation available to it, the simple CASE function compares one expression with a set of expressions to return a result, whereas the searched CASE function evaluates a set of Boolean expressions to return a result.

Syntax

```
CASE input expression
WHEN when expression THEN result expression
    [...n]
[
    ELSE else result expression
]
END

CASE
WHEN Boolean expression THEN result expression
    [...n]
[
    ELSE else result expression
]
END
```

Example

In this example, you'll use the CASE function to look at various ShipCity values. When you find Seattle, you'll display Coffee. When you find Eugene, you'll display Ducks. When you find San Francisco, you'll display Golden Gate. Your results should look the same as those displayed in Figure 8-49.

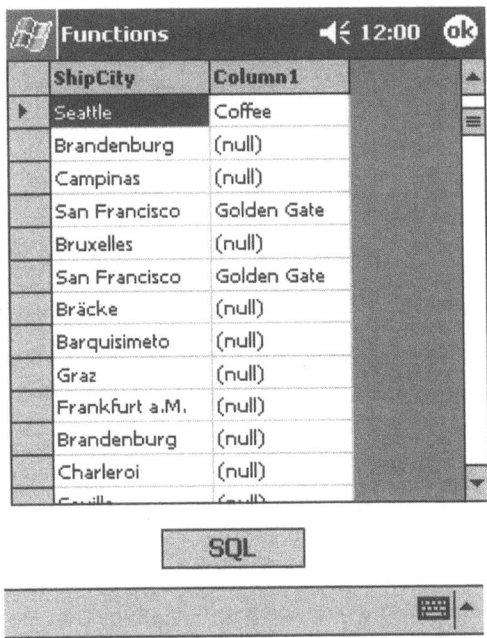

Figure 8-49. Using the CASE function on the Seattle, Eugene, and San Francisco ShipCity values

Visual Basic .NET

```
'insert at the top of your class
Imports System.Data.SqlServerCe

'insert in a function or click event
cmd.CommandText = "SELECT ShipCity, " & _
                "CASE ShipCity " & _
                "WHEN 'Seattle' THEN 'Coffee' " & _
                "WHEN 'Eugene' THEN 'Ducks' " & _
                "WHEN 'San Francisco' THEN 'Golden Gate' " & _
                "END " & _
                "FROM Orders"
```

C#

```
//insert at the top of your class
using System.Data.SqlServerCe;

//insert in a function or click event
cmd.CommandText = "SELECT ShipCity, " +
                  "CASE ShipCity " +
                  "WHEN 'Seattle' THEN 'Coffee' " +
                  "WHEN 'Eugene' THEN 'Ducks' " +
                  "WHEN 'San Francisco' THEN 'Golden Gate' " +
                  "END " +
                  "FROM Orders";
```

COALESCE

The COALESCE system function looks at one or more expressions and returns the first nonnull expression. If all expressions are null, then COALESCE returns null.

Syntax

COALESCE (expression [, ...n])

Example

In this example, you'll display the Region and ReportsTo columns as well as the result of running the COALESCE function against those two columns, which you'll display in the Coalesce column. Your results should look the same as those in Figure 8-50.

Visual Basic .NET

```
'insert at the top of your class
Imports System.Data.SqlServerCe

'insert in a function or click event
cmd.CommandText = "SELECT Region, ReportsTo, COALESCE(Region, ReportsTo) " & _
                  "AS ""Coalesce"" FROM Employees"
```

C#

```
//insert at the top of your class
using System.Data.SqlServerCe;

//insert in a function or click event
cmd.CommandText = "SELECT Region, ReportsTo, COALESCE(Region, ReportsTo) " +
                  "AS \"Coalesce\" FROM Employees";
```

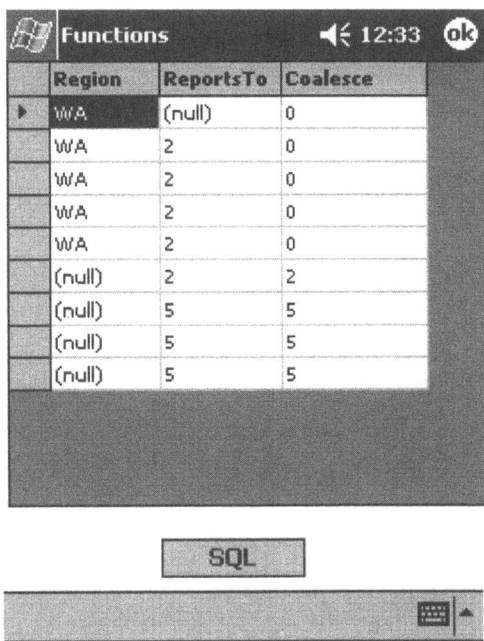

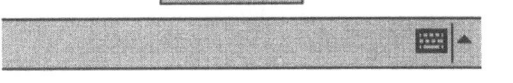

Figure 8-50. Coalescing the Region and ReportsTo columns

CONVERT

The CONVERT system function converts an expression of one data type to another. The data type you want to convert your expression to is the first argument of the function. Next is an optional length parameter that's used with nchar, nvarchar, binary, and varbinary data types. Then follows the actual expression you're looking to convert to something else. You use the final, optional, style parameter to manipulate the style of various data types when converting to character data, as discussed in the next section.

Syntax

CONVERT (data type [(length)], expression [, style])

The style parameter is used to manipulate the style of the date format when you convert datetime data to character data as shown in Table 8-2. Additionally, you can use it to determine the styles of float and real data when converting them to character data as shown in Table 8-3 or the style of money data when converting it to character data as shown in Table 8-4. Whoever thought converting data could get so complex?

Table 8-2. Datetime Styles

WITHOUT CENTURY (YY)	WITH CENTURY (YYYY)	STANDARD	OUTPUT
	0 or 100	Default	mon dd yyyy hh:miAM (or PM)
1	101	USA	mm/dd/yy
2	102	ANSI	yy.mm.dd
3	103	British/French	dd/mm/yy
4	104	German	dd.mm.yy
5	105	Italian	dd-mm-yy
6	106		dd mon yy
7	107		Mon dd, yy
8	108		hh:mm:ss
	9 or 109 1	Default + milliseconds	mon dd yyyy hh:mi:ss:mmmAM (or PM)
10	110	USA	mm-dd-yy
11	111	JAPAN	yy/mm/dd
12	112	ISO	yymmdd
	13 or 113 1	Europe default + milliseconds	dd mon yyyy hh:mm:ss:mmm (24h)
14	114		hh:mi:ss:mmm(24h)
	20 or 120 1	ODBC canonical	yyyy-mm-dd hh:mi:ss (24h)
	21 or 121 1	ODBC canonical (with milliseconds)	yyyy-mm-dd hh:mi:ss.mmm (24h)

Table 8-2. Datetime Styles (Continued)

WITHOUT CENTURY (YY)	WITH CENTURY (YYYY)	STANDARD	OUTPUT
	1263	ISO8601	yyyy-mm-dd Thh:mm:ss.mmm (no spaces)
	1301	Hijri4	dd mon yyyy hh:mi:ss:mmmAM
	1311	Hijri4	dd/mm/yy hh:mi:ss:mmmAM

Table 8-3. Float and Real Styles

VALUE	OUTPUT
0 (default)	Maximum of 6 digits. May be used in scientific notation.
1	8 digits. Use in scientific notation.
2	16 digits. Use in scientific notation.

Table 8-4. Money Styles

VALUE	OUTPUT
0 (default)	No commas every 3 digits to the left of the decimal point and 2 digits to the right of the decimal point (4321.12)
1	Commas every 3 digits to the left of the decimal point and 2 digits to the right of the decimal point (4,321.12)
2	No commas every 3 digits to the left of the decimal point and 4 digits to the right of the decimal point (4321.1234)

Example

In this example, you'll display the OrderDate column and then you'll run the CONVERT function with the ANSI style against the OrderDate values and display those results in the Converted ANSI style column. Your results should look the same as those displayed in Figure 8-51.

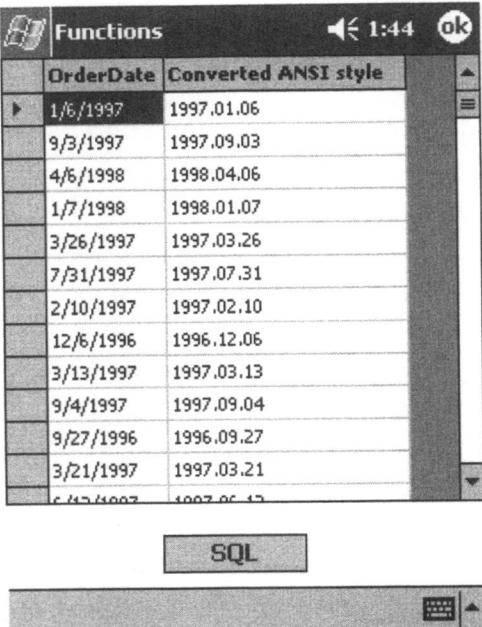

Figure 8-51. Converting the OrderDate values

Visual Basic .NET

```
'insert at the top of your class
Imports System.Data.SqlServerCe

'insert in a function or click event
cmd.CommandText = "SELECT OrderDate, CONVERT(nvarchar(10), OrderDate, 102) " & _
                "AS ""Converted ANSI style"" FROM Orders"
```

C#

```
//insert at the top of your class
using System.Data.SqlServerCe;

//insert in a function or click event
cmd.CommandText = "SELECT OrderDate, CONVERT(nvarchar(10), OrderDate, 102) " +
                "AS \" Converted ANSI style \" FROM Orders";
```

DATALENGTH

The DATALENGTH system function returns the number of bytes used to represent any given expression of any data type.

Syntax

DATALENGTH (expression)

Example

In this example, you'll display the ShipCity column as well as the length of the ShipCity values in the DATALENGTH column. Your results should look the same as those displayed in Figure 8-52.

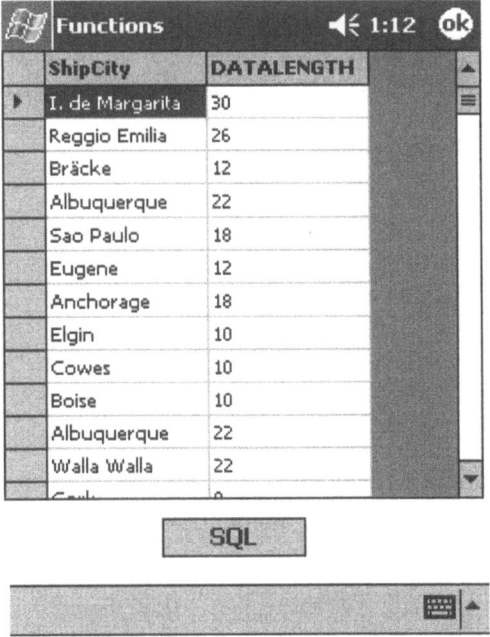

Figure 8-52. The length of the ShipCity values

Visual Basic .NET

```
'insert at the top of your class
Imports System.Data.SqlServerCe

'insert in a function or click event
cmd.CommandText = "SELECT ShipCity, DATALENGTH(ShipCity) " & _
                  "AS ""DATALENGTH"" FROM Orders"
```

C#

```
//insert at the top of your class
using System.Data.SqlServerCe;

//insert in a function or click event
cmd.CommandText = "SELECT ShipCity, DATALENGTH(ShipCity) " +
                  "AS \"DATALENGTH\" FROM Orders";
```

NEWID

The NEWID system function creates a unique value of type uniqueidentifier.

Syntax

NEWID ( )

Example

In this example, you'll use the NEWID function to return a GUID and you'll display that value in the Unique Identifier column. Your results should look similar to those displayed in Figure 8-53.

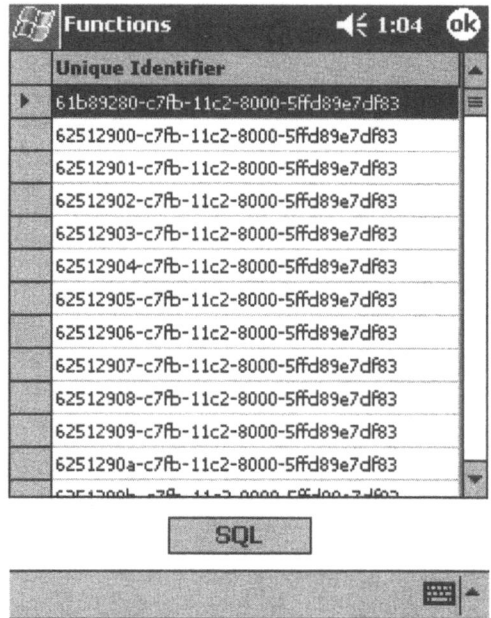

Figure 8-53. Unique identifiers

Visual Basic .NET

```
'insert at the top of your class
Imports System.Data.SqlServerCe

'insert in a function or click event
cmd.CommandText = "SELECT NEWID() AS ""Unique Identifier"" FROM Orders"
```

C#

```
//insert at the top of your class
using System.Data.SqlServerCe;

//insert in a function or click event
cmd.CommandText = "SELECT NEWID() AS \"Unique Identifier\" FROM Orders";
```

Conclusion

Well that was certainly a long chapter. Hopefully, it will serve you well as an exhaustive reference for every date, string, and mathematical function you'll ever need.

CHAPTER 9

Remote Data Access

NOW YOU'RE IN the home stretch. You've learned about the inner workings of SQL
Server CE and how to program against it with ADO.NET. These final two chapters
will take you outside the database and show you how to securely move data back
and forth between SQL Server and SQL Server CE. Not only that, you'll be able to
add new data and change existing data on your Pocket PC and see those changes
and additions reflected on the server. At the beginning of the book, I discussed
some things that you don't usually see in a computer book. Remember those FBI
agents working in Phoenix and Minneapolis who couldn't get their critical field
memos to the right people in Washington, D.C. before 9/11? Well, in this chapter
and the next, you're going to build a system that will facilitate the creation and
movement of simple field memos between a Pocket PC and a SQL Server. I'm not a
business intelligence expert, so I'll leave it to someone more qualified than myself
to implement a data mining system to analyze these memos in order to connect
the dots. In this chapter, I'm going to cover doing this with a technology called
Remote Data Access, or RDA for short. Compared to the next chapter's coverage of
merge replication, RDA is relatively easy to get up and running and works with SQL
Server versions 6.5, 7.0, and 2000.

RDA Architecture

RDA provides a framework of client-side and server-side components that allow
devices running SQL Server CE to communicate with SQL Server 6.5/7.0/2000 via
HTTP and HTTPS. Internet Information Server (IIS) acts as the intermediary in the
transfer of data back and forth between the Pocket PC and the server. Due to the
use of IIS, RDA can take advantage of things like the ability to utilize proxy servers
and communicate through firewalls, and it can make use of various security
mechanisms. RDA is also well suited for wireless or slower-speed networks due to
its use of data compression.

Client Agent

The SQL Server CE Client Agent runs on your Pocket PC and sits in between your .NET Compact Framework application and the SQL Server CE Database Engine. It exposes all the properties and methods that your application will use to control RDA. Based on the methods you call, the Client Agent will manipulate the Database Engine and communicate with the SQL Server CE Server Agent via IIS and HTTP/S. The three methods included in the SqlCeRemoteDataAccess class that do all the work for your RDA application are Pull, Push, and SubmitSQL.

Pull

The Pull method is designed to retrieve tables, indexes, and data from SQL Server and store it locally in a SQL Server CE database. You can optionally choose to have the local inserts, updates, and deletes of this retrieved data tracked by the Database Engine.

Push

The Push method is designed to take any tracked local data and send the changes to the Server Agent, where it will execute the appropriate inserts, updates, or deletes against SQL Server.

SubmitSQL

The SubmitSQL method allows you to submit SQL statements for execution on the remote SQL Server. Only inserts, updates, deletes, and calls to stored procedures are allowed, since this method isn't designed to return rows to the Pocket PC.

Database Engine

The SQL Server CE Database Engine is designed to manage the data store on your Pocket PC. When the Pull method is invoked, the Database Engine will create the appropriate tables and indexes as necessary. The Database Engine even tracks the database records that are inserted, updated, and deleted when the Pull method is called with the tracking option enabled.

Server Agent

The SQL Server CE Server Agent runs as an ISAPI DLL on your IIS server, where it handles HTTP/S requests made by the Client Agent and then makes calls to the SQL Server OLE DB Provider to fulfill those requests. The ISAPI extension is called sscesa20.dll, and it resides in the special IIS virtual directory that you create for your RDA application.

Security Considerations

Normally, you only have to deal with one set of security credentials when working with an application. Both RDA and merge replication require you to work with two different security schemes. IIS provides the gateway to moving your data back and forth across the Internet, so you have to deal with its security first. SQL Server has its own security requirements that you have to meet to access the data you need to get the job done. Both IIS and SQL Server utilize Windows security behind the scenes, so technically you've got three security hurdles to overcome. When you mesh these systems together, you're faced with myriad technical challenges.

IIS Security

IIS supports Anonymous Access, Basic Authentication, and Integrated Windows Authentication for gaining access to its resources. Additionally, IIS provides support for Secure Sockets Layer (SSL) encryption in order to protect your data stream as it flows across the Internet. These different security options are described in Table 9-1.

Table 9-1. IIS Security Options

AUTHENTICATION	DESCRIPTION
Anonymous Access	This basically means that there is no security. Anyone can access the server without being authenticated.
Basic Authentication	Access to server resources requires a valid username and password. These credentials are sent over the wire using Base64 encoding, which is simply a means of encoding binary data as a string, and doesn't involve encrypting the data. Therefore, this form of authentication must be combined with SSL to keep both the security credentials and the data safe.

Table 9-1. IIS Security Options (Continued)

AUTHENTICATION	DESCRIPTION
Integrated Windows Authentication	Server resources are accessed via the use of a Windows Domain account. A hashing algorithm is used to encode the username and password as they're sent over the wire. This method of authentication will only work if the Pocket PC, IIS, and SQL Server are on the same LAN and are all part of the same Windows Domain. Furthermore, this form of authentication won't work through firewalls or proxy servers, nor will it work if your SQL Server is running on a different computer from IIS. These limitations will go away with the release of Pocket PC 2003 due to its support for Kerberos.
Secure Sockets Layer (SSL)	All data sent over the wire is encrypted at levels all the way up to 128-bit. The client and the server establish a trust relationship based on a Certificate Authority like VeriSign.

SQL Server Security

SQL Server supports Integrated Windows Authentication as well as SQL Server Authentication for gaining access to its resources. These two security options are described in Table 9-2.

Table 9-2. SQL Server Security Options

AUTHENTICATION	DESCRIPTION
SQL Server Authentication	This is the same type of database security mechanism used by all major databases, in which an unencrypted username and password are sent over the wire. Therefore, it is recommended that these credentials are passed from server to server on a secure LAN behind a firewall, and not out across the Internet.
Integrated Windows Authentication	This type of authentication requires a trusted Windows Domain username and password that are mapped to a SQL Server username and password.

Conclusions

A number of things are going on here to make all the components of an RDA system come together. As you might imagine, whatever credentials you send to IIS are being used by SQL Server to gain access to the data you need. No matter what type of IIS authentication you choose, the credentials you send could be mapped to a Windows Domain user account that is then utilized by SQL Server, which is using Integrated Windows Authentication. You know for sure that nobody is going to use Anonymous Access because there is zero security, so go ahead and cross that off your list. You also know that Integrated Windows Authentication can't be delegated across multiple servers and won't work with firewalls or proxy servers either. This means that you should only go with this method of authentication if all your assets are on the same LAN and both your SQL Server database and IIS are running on the same box. I imagine that you would only see this configuration in a development or test scenario but not in production.

Clearly, you're going to use SQL Server Authentication on the database side and you're going to use Basic Authentication along with SSL on the Internet Information Server side of things. In your RDA code, you're going to pass along a username and password to satisfy the Basic Authentication requirements of IIS, and you're going to potentially pass along a different username and password to satisfy SQL Server's internal authentication needs. The reason you're going to do this is for flexibility and scalability. If users of an RDA-like system were in the office and on the LAN, they'd definitely use their desktop PC instead of a Pocket PC to get the message across. Obviously, RDA technology is designed for people working out in the field and not in the office. If you're an agent out and about writing a memo about suspicious activity in Houston, Texas, you're probably not on a Windows Domain. When it comes to scalability, the thought of running SQL Server and IIS on the same server is abhorrent. If you have thousands of people working all over the world who need to routinely sync up with the home office, you're going to have to configure your servers to handle that load. You'll need to create highly scalable sync-farms utilizing load-balanced servers running IIS. This gives you the flexibility to scale out when necessary to keep up with the demands of more and more simultaneously connected users. Furthermore, you may want to take advantage of SQL Server's clustering capabilities on the data tier to help beef up throughput there as well. So remember: Basic Authentication, SSL, SQL Server Authentication, and separate SQL Server and IIS servers.

Installing the Server Tools

Before anything can happen with this RDA project, you must first install the SQL Server CE Server Tools. Since you are likely working with SQL Server 2000 by now, it's a sure bet that you've installed Service Pack 3 on your database server in order to protect it from the Slammer worm. You can determine which version of SQL Server you're running by executing @@version in Query Analyzer. Therefore, you'll need to download the latest version of the Server Tools that is designed to work with SQL Server 2000 Service Pack 3 at http://www.microsoft.com/sql/downloads/ ce/sp3.asp. The actual file that you'll be downloading is sqlce20sql2ksp3.exe. Once you've downloaded this file, install the Server Tools on the computer that's running IIS. The requirements for this server are described in Table 9-3.

Table 9-3. Server Tools Server Requirements

OPERATING SYSTEM	WEB SERVER	SERVICE PACK
Windows NT	IIS 4	SP6
Windows 2000	IIS 5	SP3
Windows XP	IIS 5.1	SP1
Windows Server 2003	IIS 6	

I've shown the first screen of the SQL Server CE Server Tools Setup Wizard in Figure 9-1 just so you can make sure you're installing the correct product.

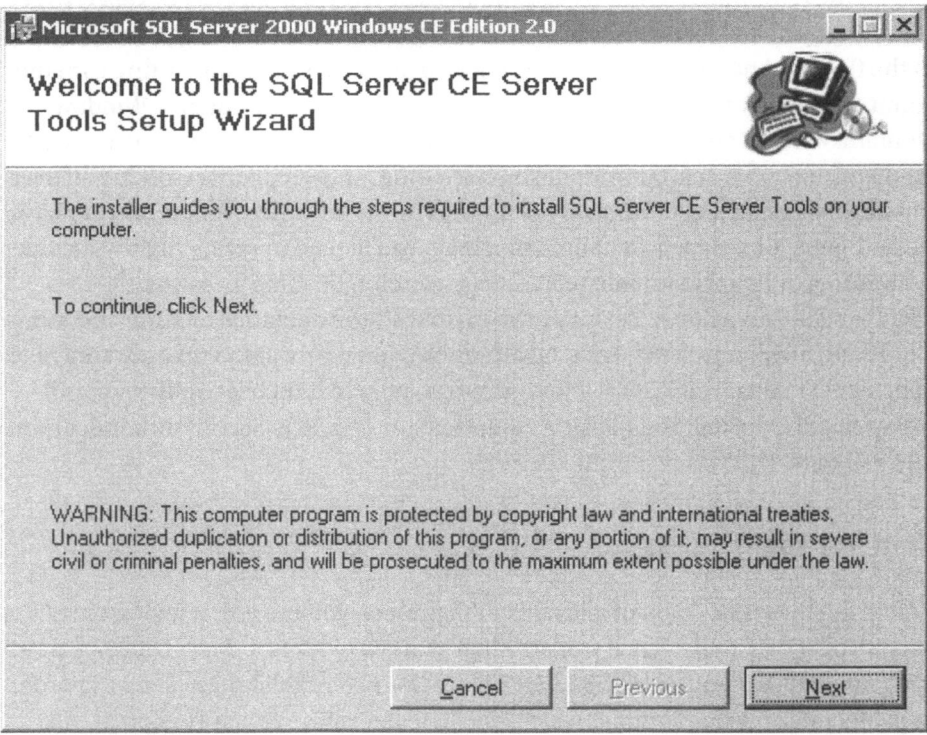

Figure 9-1. SQL Server CE Server Tools Setup Wizard

After you've made it through the setup wizard and you arrive at the final screen as shown in Figure 9-2, make sure that the checkbox to launch the SQL Server CE Virtual Directory Creation Wizard is checked before you click Close.

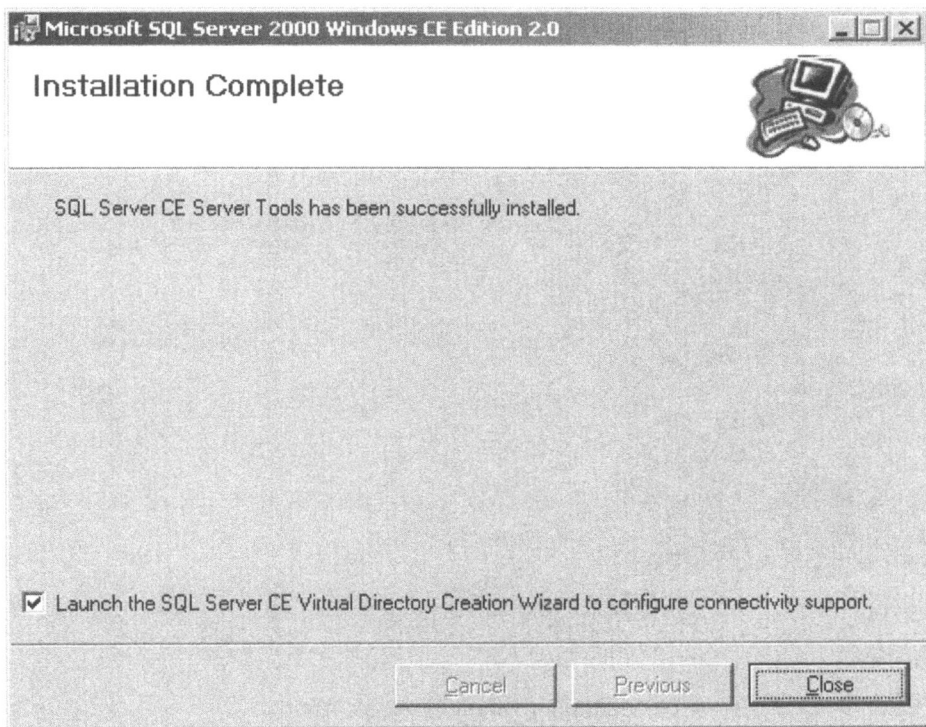

Figure 9-2. Installation complete

When working with the server-side components of SQL Server CE in the past, it was usually up to you to configure the IIS virtual directory and set up the appropriate HTTP and NTFS permissions. All this is now a thing of the past with the advent of the SQL Server CE Virtual Directory Creation Wizard as shown in Figure 9-3.

The first screen after starting this wizard creates a virtual directory as shown in Figure 9-4. You're prompted to enter an alias for this virtual directory, and then you need to associate a new or existing folder with the virtual directory. The folder will contain a log file and a file called sscesa20.dll, which is the SQL Server CE Server Agent. For the purposes of this RDA project, enter FieldAgentRDA for the alias and C:\FieldAgentRDA for the folder, and then click Next.

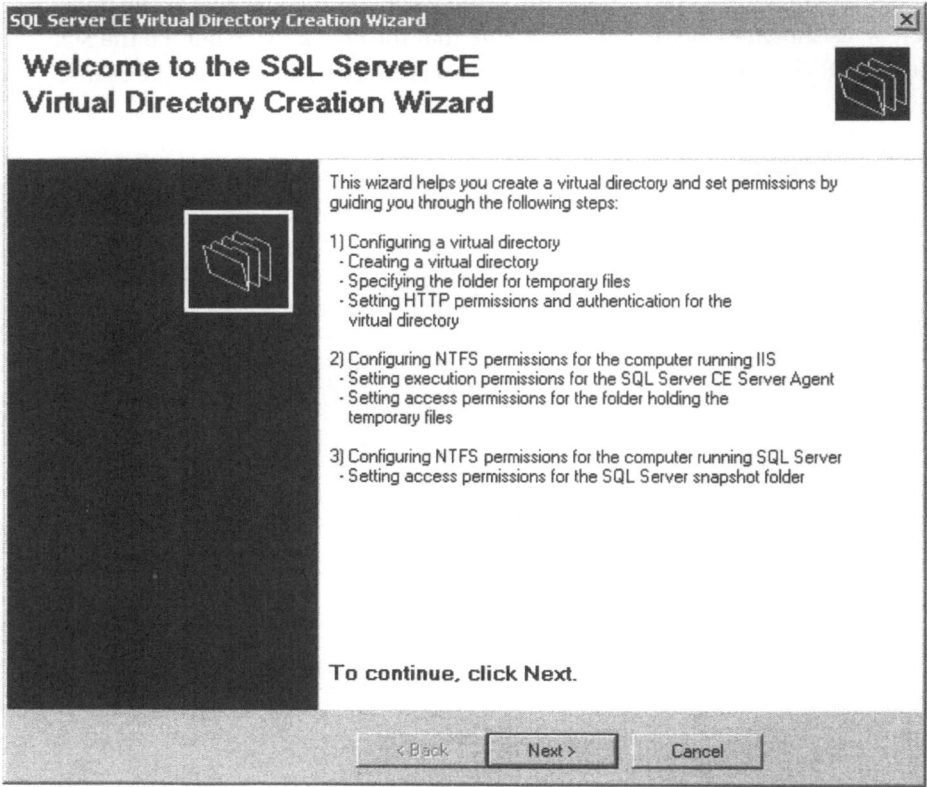

Figure 9-3. SQL Server CE Virtual Directory Creation Wizard

Once you click Next, the dialog box shown in Figure 9-5 will pop up to notify you that the C:\FieldAgentRDA folder you created doesn't contain the SQL Server CE Server Agent. Click Yes and the wizard will automatically copy the Server Agent to your folder and then register it.

The next screen allows you to choose which kind of authentication you want to use for your virtual directory, as shown in Figure 9-6. Your choices are Anonymous Access, Basic Authentication, and Integrated Windows Authentication. You surely don't want to use Anonymous Authentication, because you're building an application that can only be used by valid field agents rather than random people on the Internet. I wouldn't necessarily suggest the use of Integrated Windows Authentication, because it's better suited to an intranet application. Furthermore, Integrated Windows Authentication won't work for you in a multiserver scenario if you decide to use merge replication. The only option is Basic Authentication, through which you'll be sending your credentials over the Internet via clear text. Not to worry, you'll be protecting your data with SSL. You might notice that underneath the Basic authentication checkbox, the screen says Domain: along with either your computer's name or the domain that it's logged into. What this means is that when it's time to pass in your username from your Pocket PC, you won't have to pass in the domain name in front of it, since it already knows which domain you're coming from.

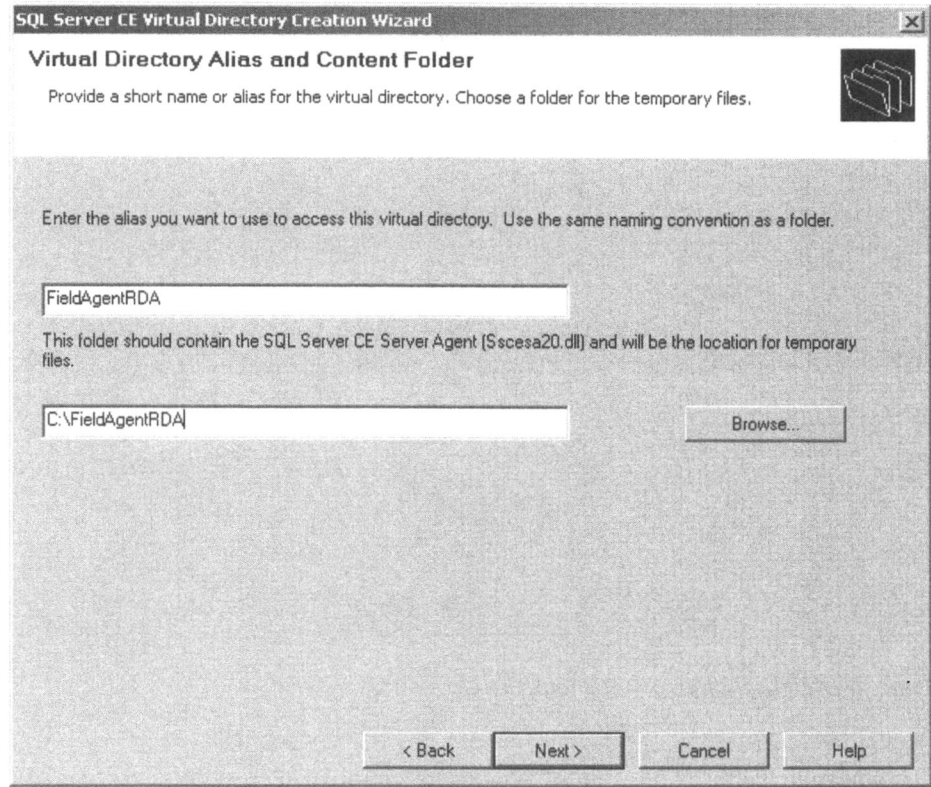

Figure 9-4. Creating a virtual directory alias and content folder

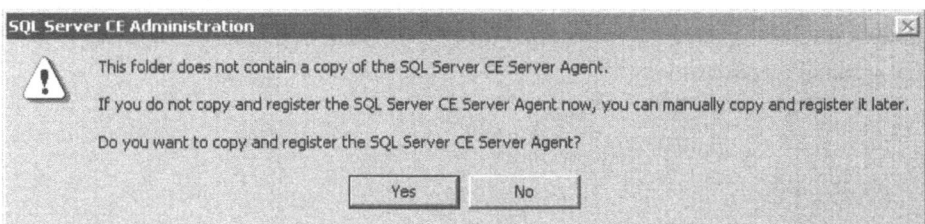

Figure 9-5. Copying and registering the SQL Server CE Server Agent

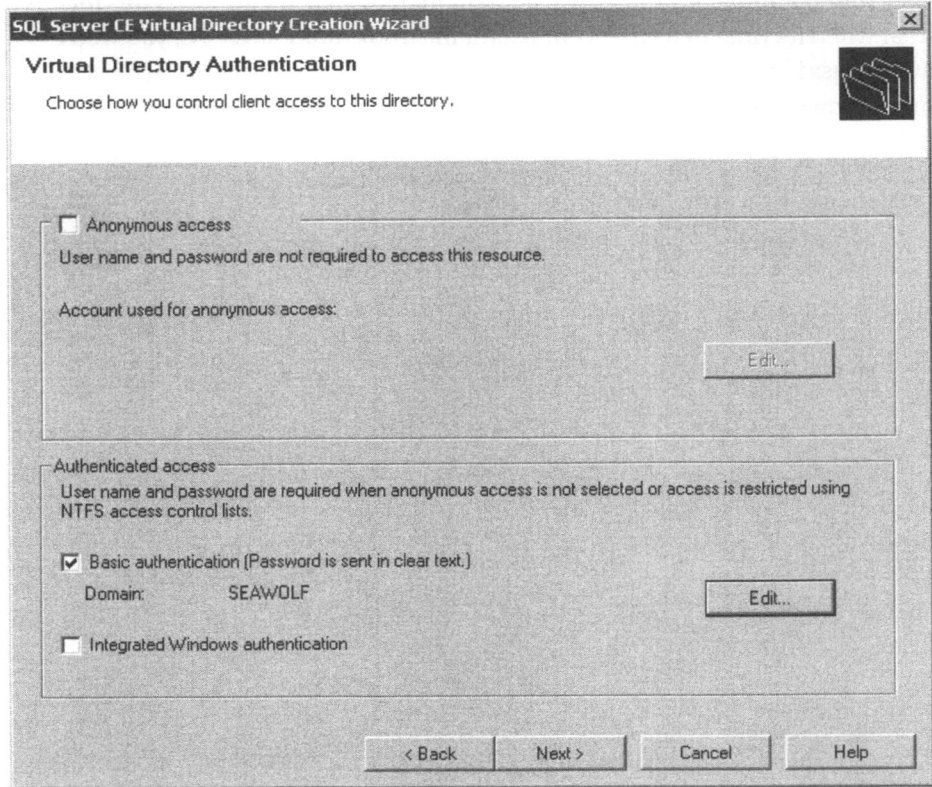

Figure 9-6. Virtual directory authentication

Now that you've set up your HTTP authentication, you must take care of NTFS permission issues on the next screen as shown in Figure 9-7. Despite the fact that the wizard already knows which domain you belong to, on this screen you must enter a valid domain\username. Keep in mind that this username is the same one that each field agent will be passing in as his or her credentials from the field.

You'll disregard the next screen, shown in Figure 9-8, and click Next, as it's designed to set up NTFS permissions for SQL Server snapshot folders when utilizing merge replication.

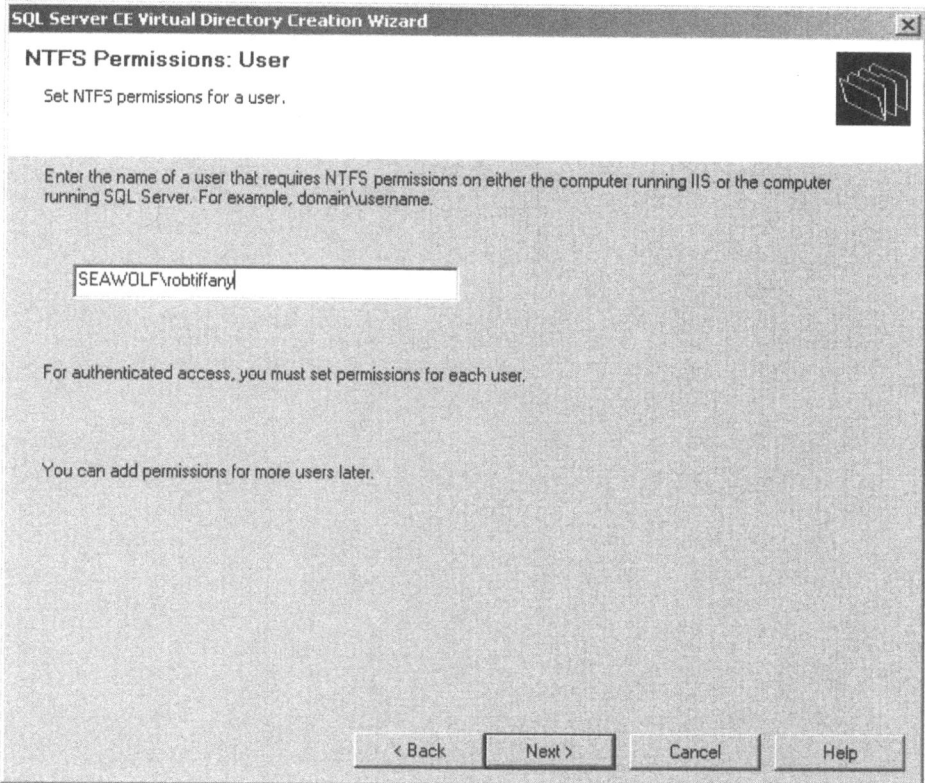

Figure 9-7. NTFS user permissions

The final screen, as shown in Figure 9-9, gives you a quick summary of the choices you made. Make sure and review what the screen displays so that you don't have any unexpected surprises when you make your first attempt to use your RDA application.

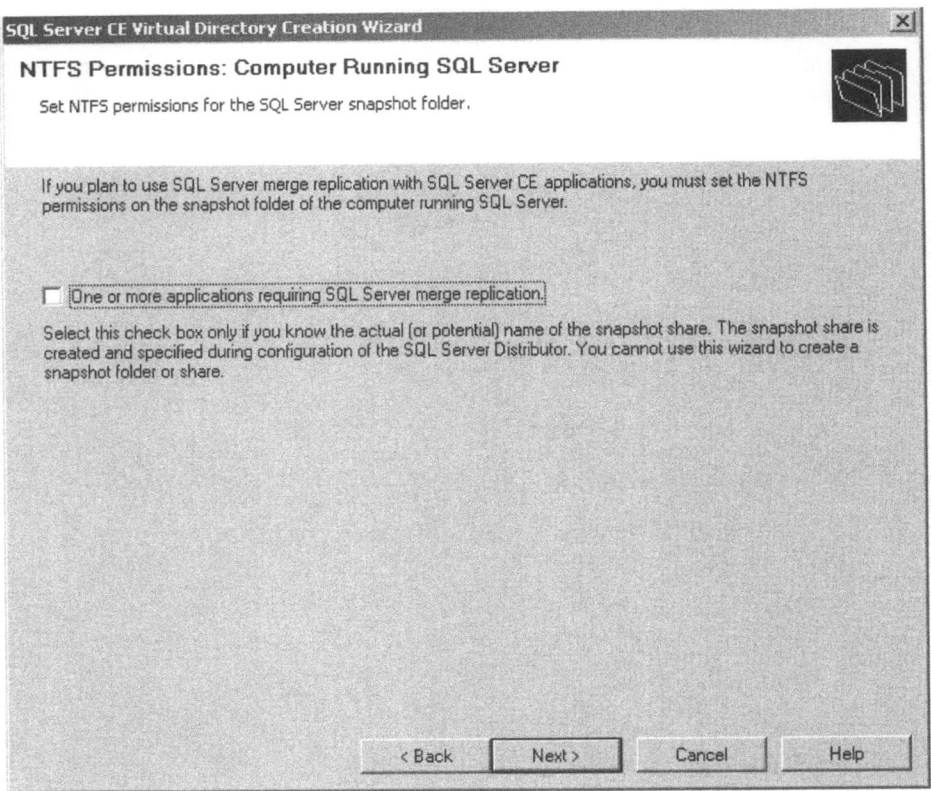

Figure 9-8. NTFS permissions for SQL Server snapshot folders

Now that you've finished the wizard, there are a few things you can do before you execute any code to ensure that everything was set up correctly. First of all, bring up the Windows Explorer on your IIS machine and make sure that a folder called FieldAgentRDA was created in your C:\ drive, if that's where you chose to put it. Next, you need to do the all-important test to make sure that your Pocket PC device can see the Server Agent in your virtual directory. With your Pocket PC connected to your IIS computer via either a network or ActiveSync, bring up Pocket Internet Explorer and point it to `http://<servername or serverIP>/fieldagentrda/ sscesa20.dll`. Hopefully, you'll be presented with a screen that looks like the one shown in Figure 9-10.

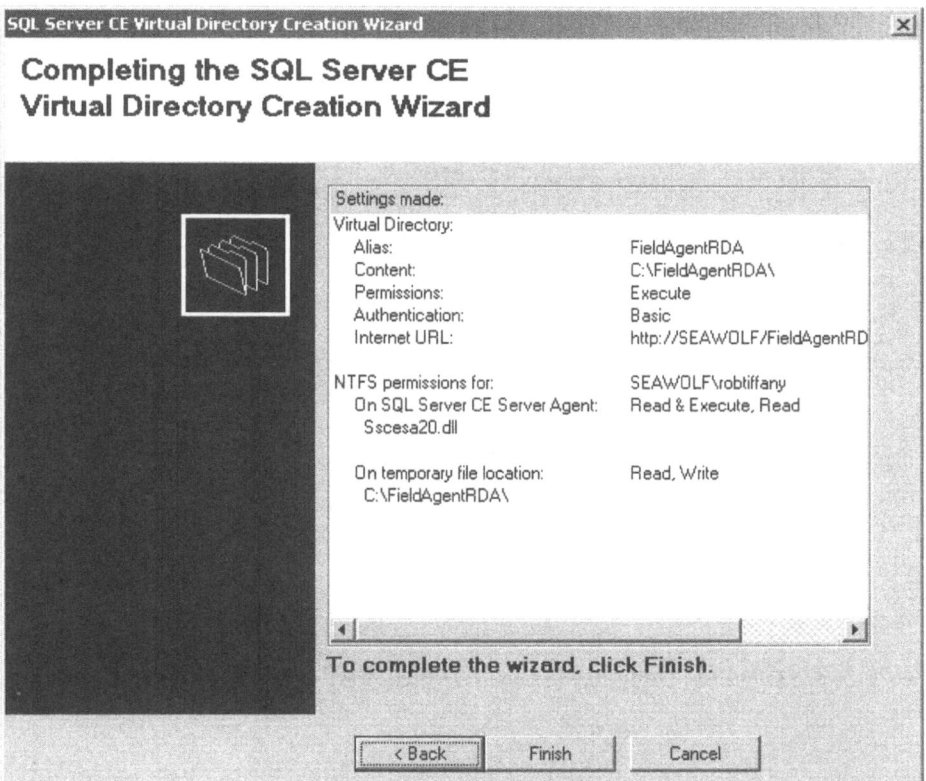

Figure 9-9. Completion of SQL Server CE Virtual Directory Creation Wizard

Remember when you chose Basic Authentication for your virtual directory? This screen is a reflection of that choice since you're being asked to provide a username and password that will be sent to IIS via clear text. If you had chosen Anonymous Access, you wouldn't have been prompted for anything, because IIS wouldn't have cared who you were. The same lack of prompting would have occurred if you chose Integrated Windows Authentication, just as long as you were logged onto a Windows Domain. When you enter the username and password for the user you chose in the wizard, you should be presented with a Web page for SQL Server CE Server Agent, like the one in Figure 9-11.

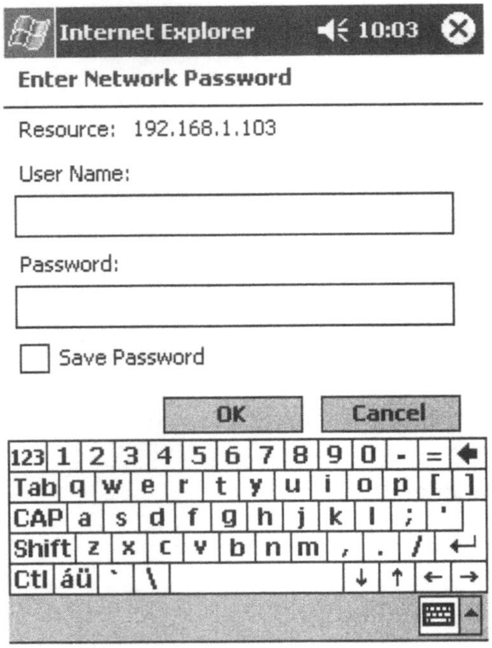

Internet Explorer ◀€ 10:03 ⊗

Enter Network Password

Resource: 192.168.1.103

User Name:

Password:

☐ Save Password

| OK | Cancel |

123	1	2	3	4	5	6	7	8	9	0	-	=	←
Tab	q	w	e	r	t	y	u	i	o	p	[	]
CAP	a	s	d	f	g	h	j	k	l	;	'
Shift	z	x	c	v	b	n	m	,	.	/	↵
Ctl	áü	`	\			↓	↑	←	→

Figure 9-10. Pocket Internet Explorer prompting for credentials

Internet Explorer ◀€ 10:04 ⊗

http://192.168.1.103/FieldAgentRD ▼ ⟳

SQL Server CE Server Agent

View Tools ← 🔄 🏠 🗁 🔂   ⌨ ▲

Figure 9-11. Successfully viewing the Server Agent from Pocket Internet Explorer

Securing Your Connection

You've tested your connection to the Server Agent and everything works great, so you're probably thinking that now it's time to write some RDA code and deploy the application. Wrong answer. Unless you want everyone on the Internet to see your username and password along with the sensitive memos sent in from field agents, you had better do something about encrypting that data stream. The correct answer in this situation is Secure Sockets Layer or SSL. In order to do this, you're going to get a little help from VeriSign, since it allows you to download trial SSL Server IDs for free. Head on over to http://www.verisign.com and click the SSL Trial ID link on the home page. At this point you'll be presented with a page asking for some personal information in order to help out their marketing folks. Once you submit that information, you'll be presented with a page that provides you with some info before you get started. Go ahead and click Continue so you can get started generating your Certificate Signing Request or CSR.

Generating a CSR

To illustrate all the steps required to get up and running with your Web server certificate, I'm going to show you how to do so using Windows 2000 and IIS 5.0, since this is currently the most popular combination in the Windows world. I'm sure Windows Server 2003 will take the lead in a few years from now. To get started, navigate to the Administrative Tools on your Start menu and then select Internet Services Manager. Right-click the Default Web Site and select Properties to bring up the Default Web Site Properties dialog box as shown in Figure 9-12.

Select the Directory Security tab and then click the Server Certificate button in order to bring up the Web Server Certificate Wizard as shown in Figure 9-13.

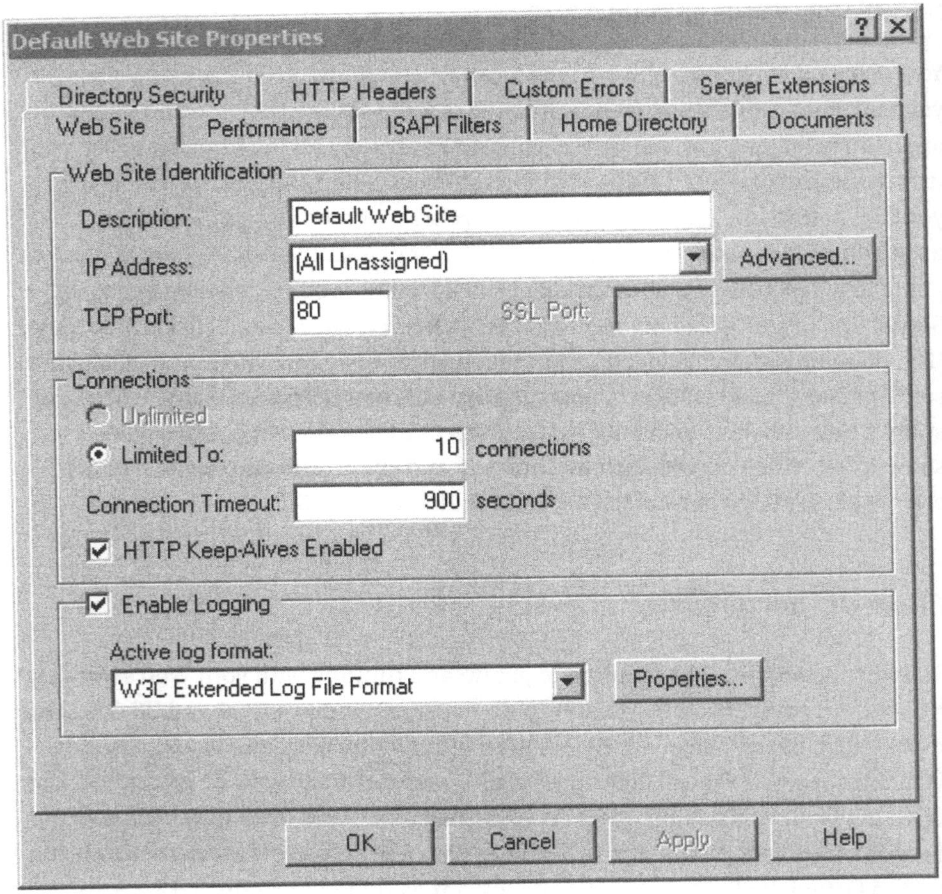

Figure 9-12. Default Web Site Properties dialog box

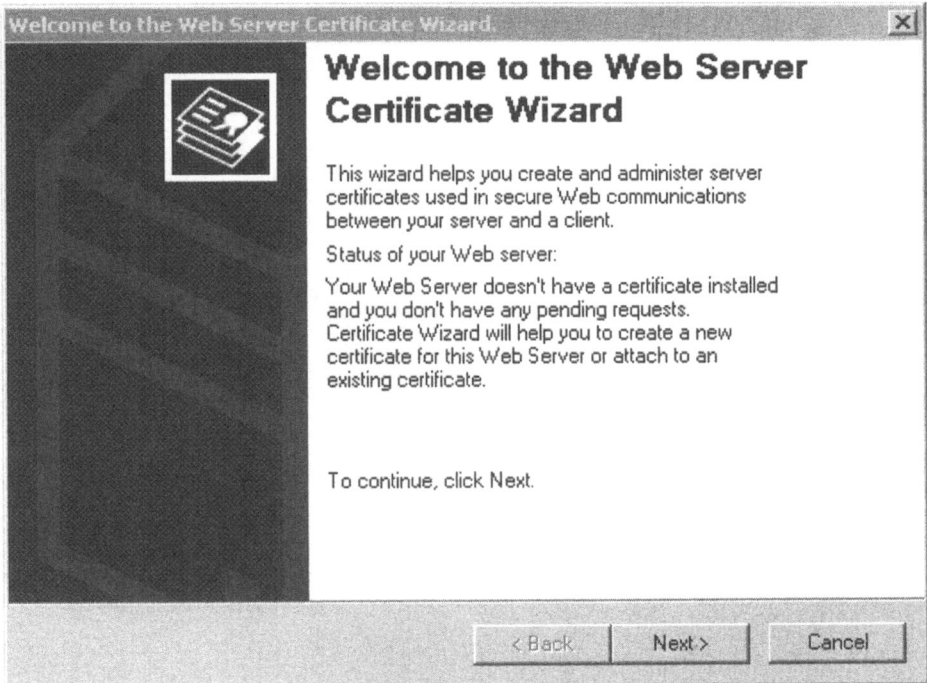

Figure 9-13. Web Server Certificate Wizard

Click Next and then select Create a new certificate as shown in Figure 9-14; now click Next again.

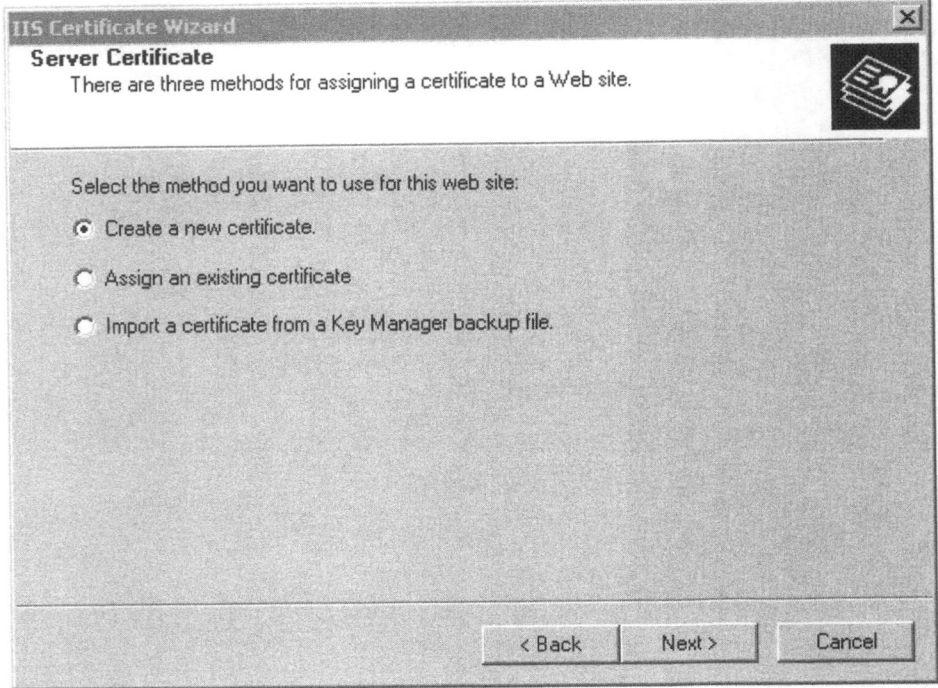

Figure 9-14. Creating a new certificate

On the next screen, ensure that the "Prepare the request now, but send it later" option is selected, as shown in Figure 9-15, and then click Next.

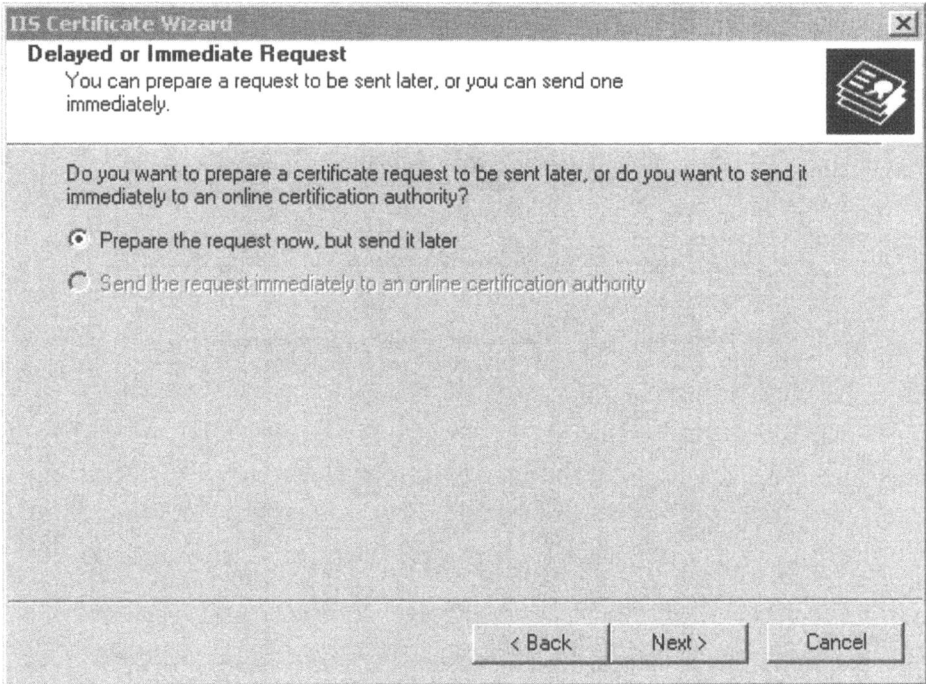

Figure 9-15. Specifying a delayed or immediate request

On this next screen, you get to specify the certificate name and strength as shown in Figure 9-16. Enter FieldAgentRDA as the name and set the bit length to an encryption strength of no more than 1024 so that you don't degrade the performance of your application.

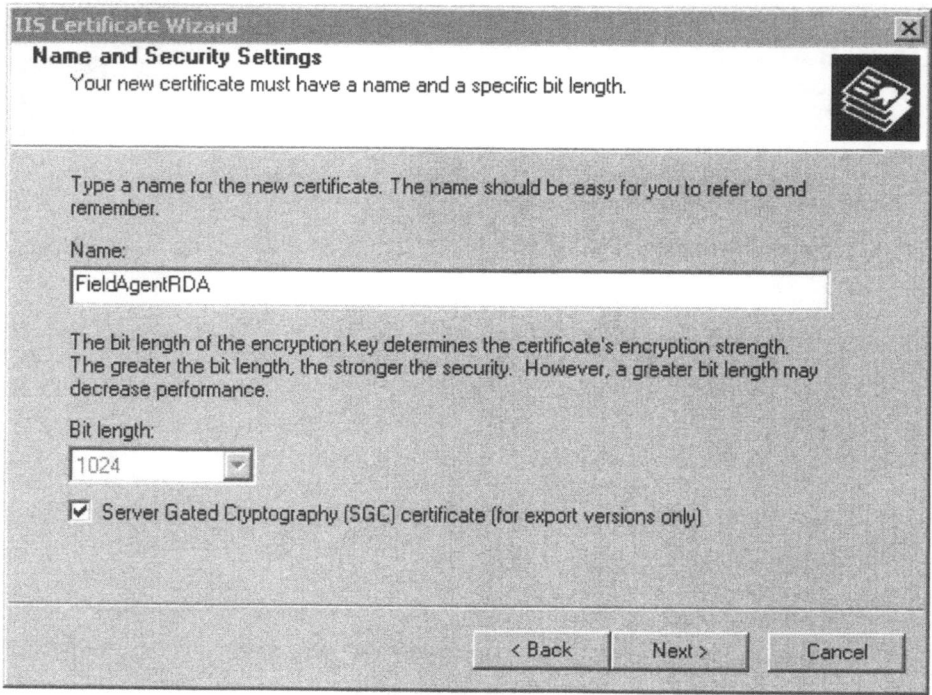

Figure 9-16. Name and security settings

Over the next several screens, you'll begin entering information that will identify you as the owner of the certificate that you're going to generate. On this first screen, you'll need to enter the real or made up name of your organization along with an organizational unit inside your company or organization as shown in Figure 9-17.

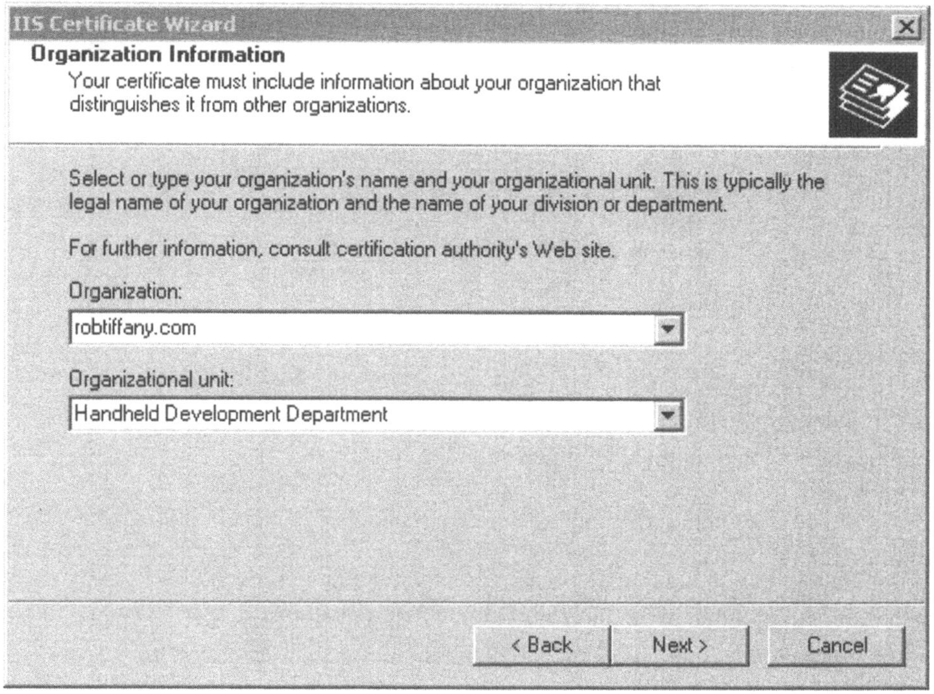

Figure 9-17. Organization information

On the next screen you're asked to provide a common name for your Web site. Normally, this would be a fully qualified DNS name that includes the name of the host computer. An example might be server1.microsoft.com. A more unorthodox approach that works with Windows servers in a Microsoft-based intranet is to enter just the computer's NetBIOS name. For the purposes of this book, that's exactly what I want you to enter. You'll probably be setting up this example on your desktop PC or laptop. The likelihood that you'll be able to get your Pocket PC to resolve your desktop PC via a valid DNS name is low in a situation where ActiveSync and a USB cable are the only providers of your connectivity. Luckily, the Your Site's Common Name screen defaults to your computer's NetBIOS name as shown in Figure 9-18. As you can see, my laptop is called seawolf, named such because I used to drive submarines for a living.

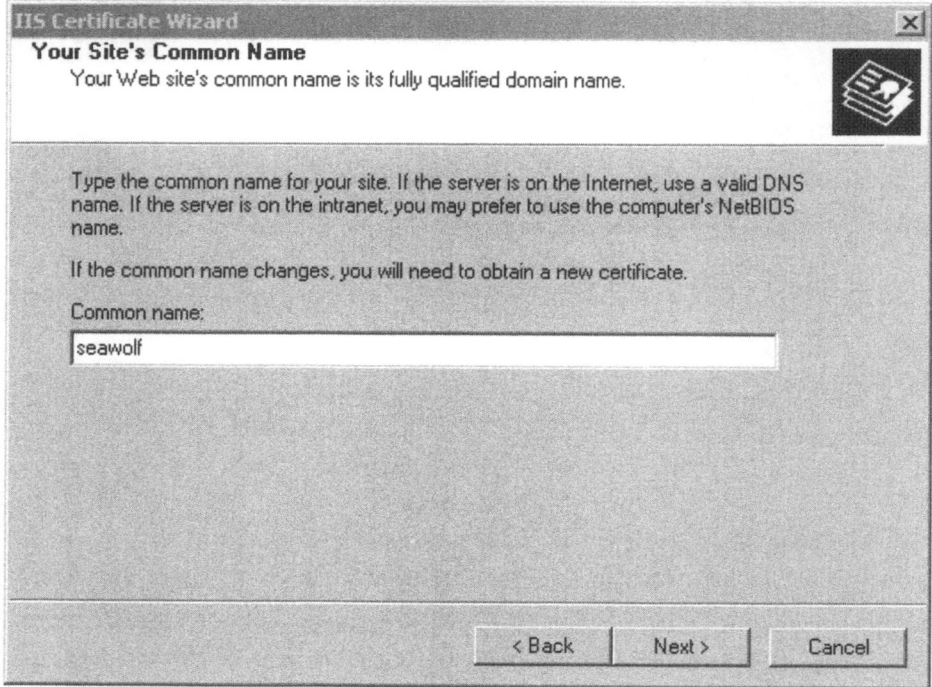

Figure 9-18. Your site's common name

The next screen requires geographical information as shown in Figure 9-19. Enter your country, state, and city and then click Next.

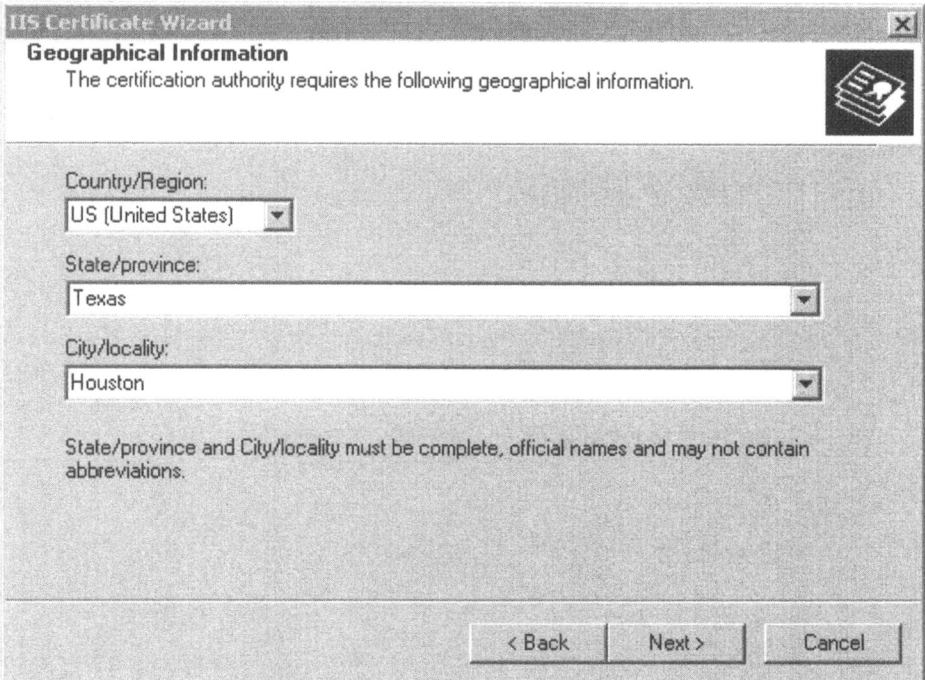

Figure 9-19. Geographical information

On the next screen you'll need to enter a path and filename as shown in Figure 9-20 since your certificate request is saved as a text file.

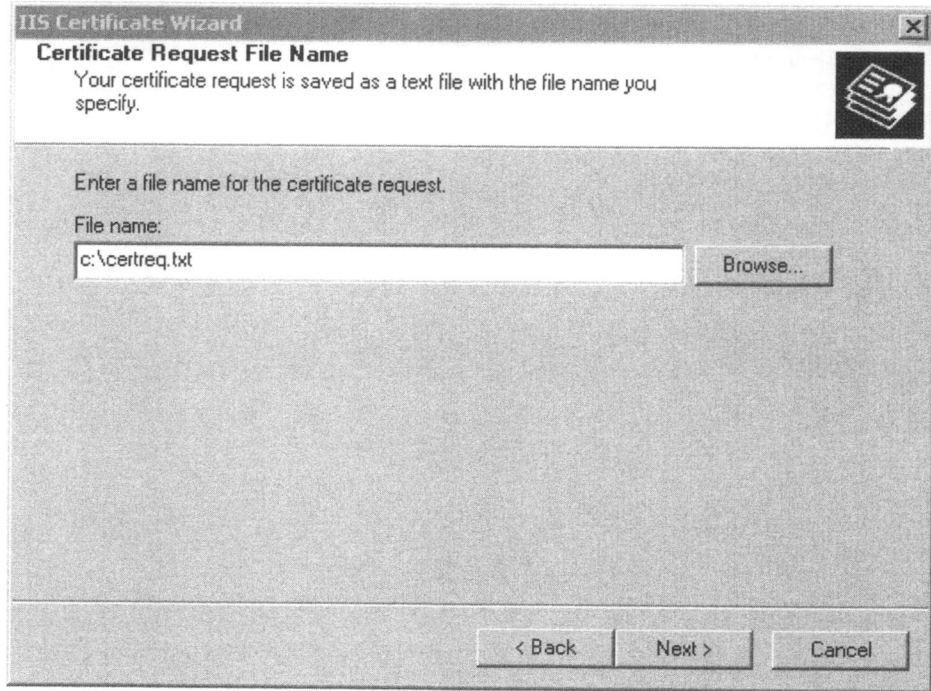

Figure 9-20. Certificate request filename

The next screen provides you with a summary of your choices. Click Next to move on to the final page where you can click Finish—and then you're done.

Submit Your CSR

Click the Continue button on the VeriSign Web site in order to move on to step 2 of 5 through which you'll get to submit your CSR. Navigate to wherever you saved your certificate request text file on your hard drive and open it in Notepad. Choose Select All from the Notepad menu and then select Copy. Now go back to the Web page and paste your information into the text area as shown in Figure 9-21 and then click Continue.

 **Enrollment**

Step 2 of 5: Submit CSR

Before you Start   Step 3: Complete Application

Step 1: Generate CSR   Step 4: Install Test CA Root

♦ Step 2: Submit CSR   Step 5: Install your Test Server ID

Submit CSR

When you generated the CSR in Step 1: Generate CSR, your server software either e-mailed the CSR to you, or created a request file on your hard disk (such as key.req). Open the CSR file with an ASCII text editor such as NotePad. (Do not use a word processor such as Word that inserts formatting or control characters.)

This is an example CSR file:

```
-----BEGIN NEW CERTIFICATE REQUEST----
MIIBCTCBtAIBADBPMQswCQYDVQQGEwJVUzEQMA4GA1UECBMHRmxvcmlkYTEYMBYG
A1UEChMPRX11cyBvbiBUaGUgV2ViMRQwEgYDVQQDFAt3d3cuZXR3Lm51dDBcMA0G
CSqGSIb3DQEBAQUAA0sAMEgCQQCeojtjnHqgOGTxp+XZ56RaSeliZWpumXjU6Sx7
v1FdXzsY1oLOQa09OJtnu1WsQRHhOyDS+45oncjKm1zCG/IZAgMBAAGgADANBgkq
hkiG9w0BAQQFAANBAFBj9g+NiUh8YWPrFGntgf4miUd/wqUshptjJy4PjdsD3ugy
5avvuh3G//PpGh2aYXIjHpJXTUBQyzxSEIINYtc=
-----END NEW CERTIFICATE REQUEST-----
```

Description	
Enter CSR Information: Copy the entire contents of the CSR file including the lines that contain the begin and end statements into the field on the right.	bgBuAGUAbAAgAEMAcgB5AHAAdABvAGcAcgBhAHAAaABpA ▲ ZAB1AHIDgYkAUL9Rtrw1nPb5Ys6tk8N+R/ABN/KEC++h4 vLGCmQrAdxNc/gcC5nvDUoaciLlI4dIAcZh/ew4jhNqM7 XIqGaJihWa5KciQvIwF9Nhtw3cii1yQQR8M+iseGxgc+S ADANBgkqhkiG9w0BAQUFAAOBgQCuB8x1rscQLGVyQGpyM 5TpUmFyC/NKrKQMI7DaKteNphi7FzD1Cuf2tNHYuikt85 uPVc/1IEvvDgbjy7JFYf1O2jK8VtwB7Bd5MJzvpeLJK56 sIGUzw== -----END NEW CERTIFICATE REQUEST----- ▼ ◄ ►

 Click the CONTINUE button to submit the CSR and proceed with the Test Server ID enrollment.   [**Continue**]

You're now on step 3 of 5 through which you get to review and complete your application with VeriSign. Double-check the data in the Distinguished Name box, enter technical contact information in the box below and then click the Accept button. You will then be presented with a Web page telling you that VeriSign is now processing your request and will be sending you an e-mail in the next hour that contains your trial Server ID and instructions for installation. This is probably a good time to go take a break; I know I would.

Okay, the hour's up and your e-mail from VeriSign should have arrived by now. At the bottom of this e-mail is your certificate response from VeriSign. To get things going, create a new text file on your hard drive called certres.txt. Then copy and paste the certificate response found at the bottom of your e-mail. Make sure to include BEGIN CERTIFICATE and END CERTIFICATE in the text file. Once you've closed and saved this certificate response text file, reopen the Internet Services Manager, right-click the Default Web Site, and select Properties as you've done before. Select the Directory Security tab and then click the Server Certificate button. This will bring up the familiar Web Server Certificate Wizard in which you'll need to click Next to proceed. On the Pending Certificate Request screen, shown in Figure 9-22, you'll need to select "Process the pending request and install the certificate" and then click Next.

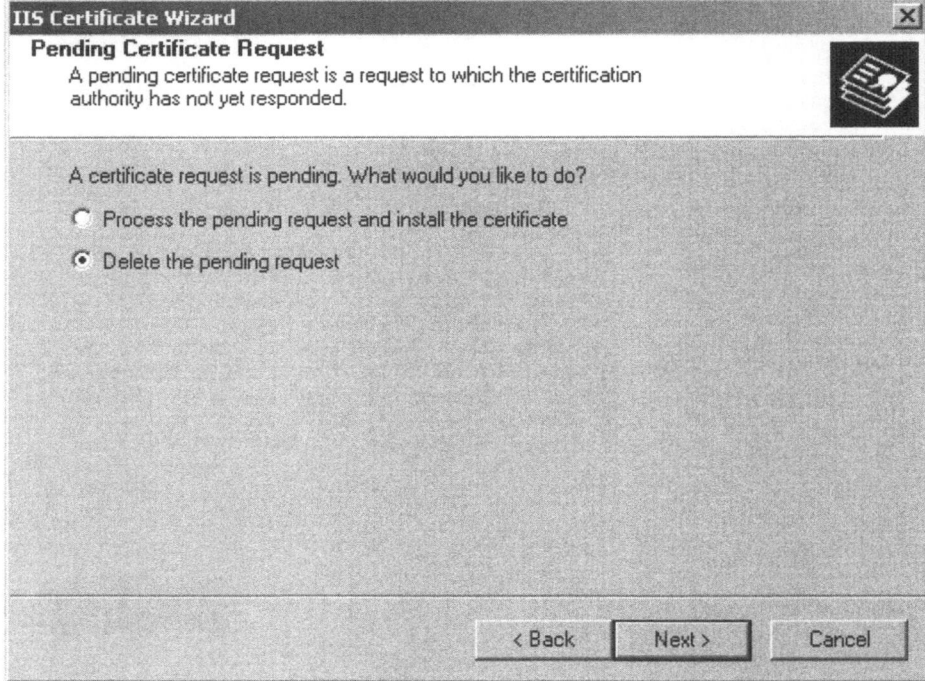

Figure 9-22. Pending certificate request

On the Process a Pending Request screen shown in Figure 9-23, click the Browse button to navigate to the certres.txt file you just created and click Next on this and the following screen.

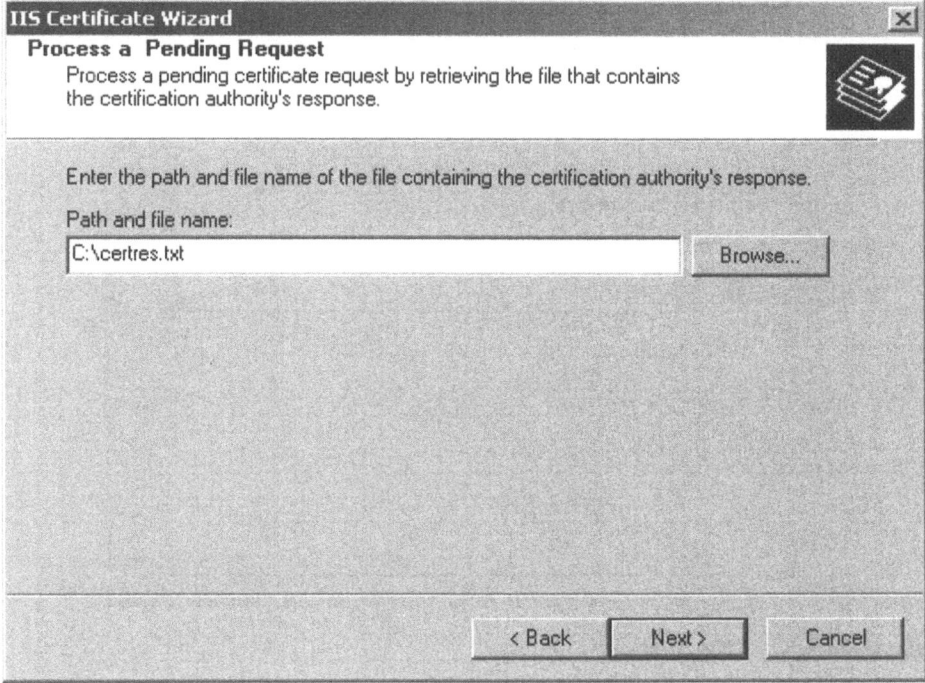

Figure 9-23. Processing a pending request

Your certificate is now installed on IIS. The next step is to enable SSL for your FieldAgentRDA Web site. To do this, right-click FieldAgentRDA while still inside Internet Information Services, and select Properties. Select the Directory Security tab and click the Edit button in the Secure Communications area. In the Secure Communications dialog box shown in Figure 9-24, check the Require secure channel (SSL) checkbox, and then click OK.

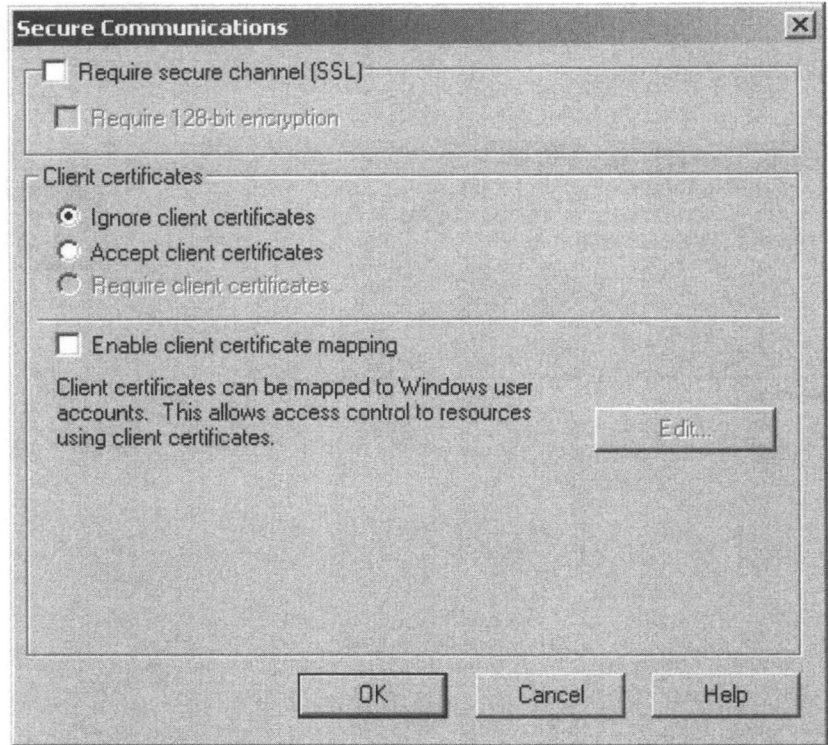

Figure 9-24. Securing communications

By now you've probably lost all patience and you're dying to see if you can hit your FieldAgentRDA Web site via Pocket Internet Explorer. Keep in mind that VeriSign made it abundantly clear that you'll need to download a Test CA Root in order for you to view the site without receiving some kind of an invalid certificate error. Just for fun, enter `https://servername/fieldagentrda/sscesa20.dll` in Pocket Internet Explorer to view this certificate error as shown in Figure 9-25.

Figure 9-25. Security error

If you click Yes in this Security dialog box, you should be able to enter your Basic Authentication username and password and view the site securely. Obviously, this isn't good enough. In order to have things operate smoothly, you will need to download and install the VeriSign Test CA Root. Navigate your desktop browser to `http://www.verisign.com/server/trial/faq/index.html`, click the Accept button, and download the file called getcacert.cer to your hard drive. Additionally, you need to download a Pocket PC program call AddRootCert from Microsoft at `http://download.microsoft.com/download/pocketpc/addroot/1.0/wce/en-us/AddRootCert.exe`. This program is used to add additional certificates to your Pocket PC. It comes as a self-extracting WinZip EXE that you'll need to unzip into a temporary directory on your desktop. Once you've unzipped it, look inside a folder called Armrel in order to find the actual AddRootCert.exe program that you're looking for. Once that's been accomplished, copy both getcacert.cer and AddRootCert.exe to the /My Documents directory of your Pocket PC via the Explore feature of ActiveSync. Once those files are copied over, open the File Explorer on your Pocket PC and tap AddRootCert.exe. Once the application is running, click the File menu, and select Open in order to search for your VeriSign certificate. Once found, click getcacert and the AddRootCert application will look like Figure 9-26.

Figure 9-26. AddRootCert Powertoy

Click the Install Certificate button to add the certificate to your device. Now comes the moment of truth. After making sure that Pocket Internet Explorer has been removed from memory, relaunch it and navigate to the FieldAgentRDA Web site. If your installation has gone well, you won't see an invalid certificate warning on your device and you'll be good to go for secure communications via both RDA and merge replication.

Creating the Field Memo Database

One of the great things about RDA, and merge replication for that matter, is that you can design your SQL Server CE database on the desktop or server using SQL Server's Enterprise Manager. I'm sure you'll find this much easier than using either Query Analyzer or DDL on the handheld. All aspects of the database structure you create are faithfully downloaded and reproduced on your Pocket PC. The first thing you need to do to get started with this RDA project is to build the database that will contain the memos sent in from the field. Even though you can use SQL Server 6.5 or 7.0 for this task, I'd prefer you use SQL Server 2000, since you'll use the same database in Chapter 10's examples. On that note, fire up Enterprise Manager and create a database called IntelligenceData.

A Table, Columns, and Indexes

I'm going to make things real easy for you when it comes to creating this database application. For starters, there's only one table with nine columns, so there's not much to think about. In the Enterprise Manager, right-click your IntelligenceData database and select New Table. This table will be called FieldMemos, and its columns are described in Table 9-4.

Table 9-4. FieldMemos

COLUMNNAME	DATATYPE	LENGTH	NULLS	PRIMARY KEY	INDEXED	DEFAULT VALUE
MemoID	uniqueidentifier	16	No	Yes	Yes	newid()
MemoTo	nvarchar	50	Yes	No	Yes	
MemoFrom	nvarchar	50	Yes	No	Yes	
MemoDateTime	datetime	8	Yes	No	Yes	
MemoCity	nvarchar	50	Yes	No	Yes	
MemoState	nvarchar	2	Yes	No	Yes	
MemoSubject	nvarchar	50	Yes	No	Yes	
MemoPriority	int	4	Yes	No	Yes	
MemoBody	ntext	16	Yes	No	Yes	

Figure 9-27 gives you the design view of the FieldMemos table inside Enterprise Manager.

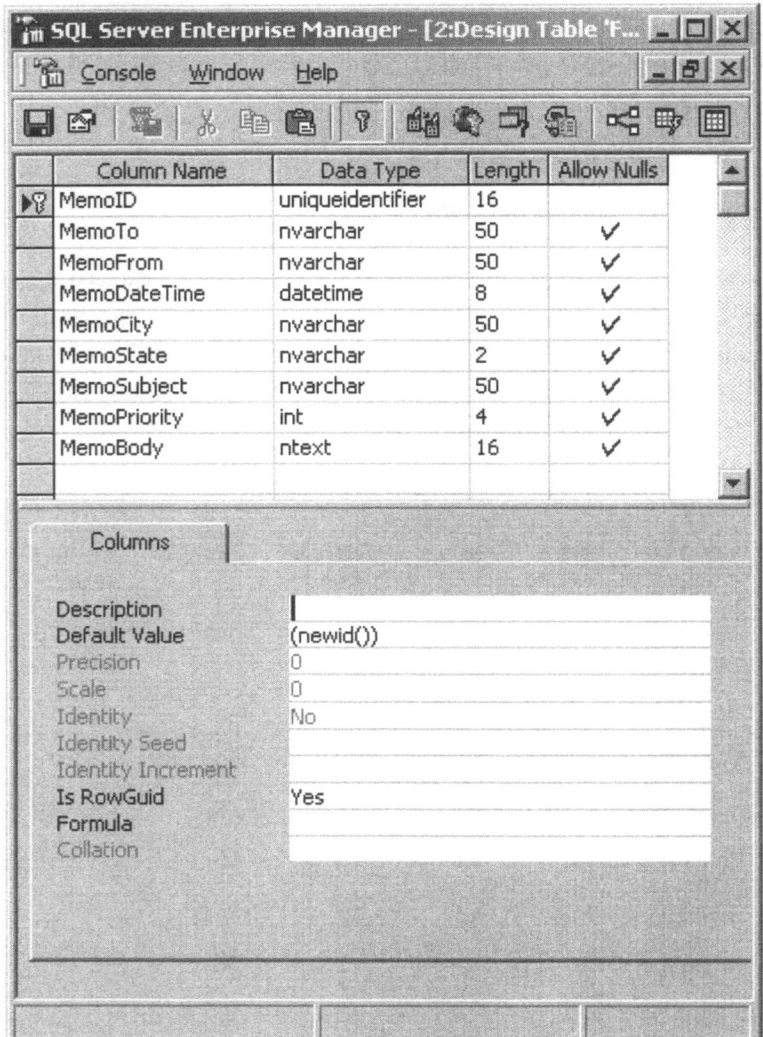

Figure 9-27. Field memos in design mode

Primary Key Concerns

The first strange thing you probably noticed is that my primary key column, MemoID, is a uniqueidentifier. You're probably accustomed to using the integer data type along with an IDENTITY constraint in order to have an auto-incrementing primary key column. In a situation where multiple clients are all making inserts to the same table, this is perfectly acceptable. Just think about the RDA architecture for a moment. Multiple users are pulling down copies of the same table for offline use in the field. RDA is using optimistic concurrency so none of the pulled records are locked on the server. Offline users are making numerous inserts of new data to their offline tables. If IDENTITY columns are being employed for the primary keys of those offline tables, you'd have lots of MemoIDs incrementing along to their heart's content. With each new memo added to the offline database, the primary key is incremented one, two, three, four, five, etc. Can you imagine thousands of users all sharing the same values for their MemoID column? Everything is cool until these users attempt to push their new rows of data back to the primary SQL Server database. SQL exceptions will be flying when all those identical primary keys collide as SQL Server tries to merge these field memos into the database. Therefore, this method of trying to keep all your new rows unique is flawed, because you can't guarantee their uniqueness across multiple offline SQL Server CE databases. The only way to guarantee complete uniqueness in any situation is to employ globally unique identifiers as your primary key data type. When coupled with the newid() function as your default value to generate new GUIDs each time a row is added to the table, your row's uniqueness is ensured.

Table Structure Explanation

A quick glance at the structure of this table reveals that it looks like the fields found in an e-mail. The MemoTo field is usually filled with "Office of the Director", whereas the MemoFrom field is filled in with the name of the agent in the field. The MemoDateTime field will contain a system-generated timestamp; and the MemoCity and MemoState fields will reveal where the memo is coming from. The MemoSubject field is pretty self-explanatory and the MemoPriority field will contain 1, 2, or 3 to denote the priority level. In the MemoBody field, I chose to use the ntext data type since these field memos can be quite detailed and lengthy, and I didn't want to limit the length of the content to 255 characters by using the nvarchar data type.

Creating the RDA Client

After all this IIS, security, and SQL Server configuration, you finally get to write some code and work with the RDA object model. Luckily, all this up-front work you just completed is utilized by merge replication so you won't have to do this all over again in Chapter 10. Earlier in this chapter, I gave you a quick overview of the Pull, Push, and SubmitSQL methods of the SqlCeRemoteDataAccess class. In fact, they're the only three methods you'll find in the class, so there's no danger of things getting too complicated. This class has a number of properties as described in

Table 9-5 whose values are essential to the smooth execution of the three different methods.

Table 9-5. SqlCeRemoteDataAccess Properties

PROPERTY	DESCRIPTION
InternetLogin	IIS login name used when connecting to the SQL Server CE Server Agent
InternetPassword	IIS password used when connecting to the SQL Server CE Server Agent
InternetProxyLogin	Login name used when connecting to a proxy server that requires authentication
InternetProxyPassword	Password used when connecting to a proxy server that requires authentication
InternetProxyServer	The proxy server to use when accessing the HTTP resource specified in the InternetUrl property
InternetUrl	The URL used to connect to the SQL Server CE Server Agent
LocalConnectionString	The OLE DB connection string for the SQL Server CE database residing on the handheld

InternetLogin and InternetPassword correlate to the Basic Authentication credentials you have to send to IIS in order to access the SQL Server CE Server Agent. If you're using a proxy server in your network, then you'll specify it in the InternetProxyServer property. If that proxy server requires authentication, you'll take care of that using the InternetProxyLogin and InternetProxyPassword properties. Remember how I had you point to the sscesa20.dll file in the FieldAgentRDA virtual directory? Well, the InternetUrl property is where you assign that URL. I find the LocalConnectionString property a little strange in that it wants you to use an OLE DB connection string to communicate with your SQL Server CE database rather than using ADO.NET. I'm sure that will change in future versions of the RDA technology.

Time to Code

Bring up Visual Studio .NET 2003 and create a Smart Device Application in either C# or Visual Basic .NET. In the spirit of keeping things simple, I want you to add just four buttons to your form as described in Table 9-6.

Table 9-6. Buttons

NAME	TEXT
btnPull	Pull
btnAddMemo	Add Memo
btnPush	Push
btnSubmitSQL	Submit SQL

You can place these buttons anywhere on the form that you like. The purpose of these buttons is to illustrate how to pull data down to your device, add new rows of data to SQL Server CE, push the data back up to the server, and submit queries for execution on SQL Server. The code to make all this possible will be placed in the click events of these four buttons. Before you write any code, make sure to add a reference to both System.Data.Common and System.Data.SqlServerCe. At the top of your form class, add

```
using System.Data.SqlServerCe;
```

and

```
using System.IO;
```

if you're doing a C# project.

If you're creating a Visual Basic .NET project, add

```
Imports System.Data.SqlServerCe
```

and

```
Imports System.IO
```

Pull

You already know that the Pull method will retrieve tables, indexes, and data from SQL Server and transfer it to SQL Server CE on your Pocket PC. What you don't know is that the Pull method has several important arguments that are critical to making the retrieval go off without a hitch, and these are shown in Table 9-7.

Table 9-7. Pull Method Arguments

ARGUMENT	DESCRIPTION
LocalTableName	Name of the SQL Server CE table that will be created and populated with data as a result of the Pull operation
SqlSelectString	Query that determines which rows and columns are retrieved from SQL Server
OLEDBConnection String	An OLE DB–based connection string needed to connect to the proper remote SQL Server database
TrackOption	Indicates to the SQL Server CE Database Engine whether or not to track changes made to the local tables and whether or not to re-create the indexes that the tables contain in SQL Server
ErrorTable	Name of the SQL Server CE table used for error purposes

Usually, LocalTableName will be the same name as the name of the table you're pulling from on SQL Server. If you wish to retrieve all the data from a given SQL Server table, then you'll use a SELECT * statement. OLEDBConnectionString will take you back in time to the days of classic ADO. You'll specify SQLOLEDB as the provider, the data source will be the name of the server that SQL Server is running on, the initial catalog will be the name of the actual database, and the user ID and password are the required credentials based on SQL Server Authentication.

There are potentially two other things you need to concern yourself with before setting the RDA properties and calling the Pull method. It's usually a good idea to check whether your SQL Server CE database even exists before attempting this operation. The reason is that an RDA Pull method is usually relied upon to populate Pocket PC devices with databases and tables to help streamline deployment. Even though the Pull method only creates tables, it's a good idea to check for the existence of a database and then create one if it isn't there. If, on the other hand, the database already exists, it's possible that the table that the Pull method is about to create is already present in the database. Since the Pull method is somewhat destructive in that it isn't designed to merge server data with your handheld, you need to drop the local table before running the Pull method, or an error will occur. The following example that resides in the click event of the Pull

button illustrates these issues and shows you how to properly run the Pull method
in order to create the FieldMemos table in your local database.

Visual Basic .NET

```vbnet
Private Sub btnPull_Click(ByVal sender As System.Object, & _
                        ByVal e As System.EventArgs) Handles btnPull.Click


Dim cn As SqlCeConnection
Dim rda As SqlCeRemoteDataAccess
Dim sqlEngine As SqlCeEngine

Try
    btnPull.Enabled = False

    ' Create database if it doesn't already exist
    If (Not File.Exists("\My Documents\IntelligenceData.sdf")) Then
        sqlEngine = New SqlCeEngine
        sqlEngine.LocalConnectionString = & _
            "Data Source=\My Documents\IntelligenceData.sdf;" & _
            "Password=apress;" & _
            "Encrypt Database=True"
        sqlEngine.CreateDatabase()
        sqlEngine.Dispose()
    Else
        ' Open the connection to the database
        cn = New SqlCeConnection("Data Source=\My Documents" & _
                            "\IntelligenceData.sdf;Password=apress")
        cn.Open()
        Dim cmd As SqlCeCommand = cn.CreateCommand()

        ' Drop the FieldMemos table
        cmd.CommandText = "DROP TABLE FieldMemos"
        cmd.ExecuteNonQuery()

        ' Close the connection
        If cn.State <> ConnectionState.Closed Then
            cn.Close()
        End If
    End If

    ' Instantiate the RDA Object
    rda = New SqlCeRemoteDataAccess
```

```
                     ' Connection String to the SQL Server.
                     Dim remoteConnectString As String = "Provider=SQLOLEDB;" & _
                                               "Data Source=seawolf;" & _
                                               "Initial Catalog=IntelligenceData;" & _
                                               "User Id=sa;" & _
                                               "Password=apress"


                     rda.InternetLogin = "robtiffany"
                     rda.InternetPassword = "pinnacle"
                     rda.InternetUrl = "https://seawolf/fieldagentrda/sscesa20.dll"
                     rda.LocalConnectionString = "Data Source=\My Documents\" & _
                                       "IntelligenceData.sdf;" & _
                                       "SSCE:Database Password=apress"


                     rda.Pull("FieldMemos", "Select * from FieldMemos", remoteConnectString, & _
                             RdaTrackOption.TrackingOnWithIndexes, "FieldMemosErrorTable")

         Catch sqlex As SqlCeException
             Dim sqlError As SqlCeError
             For Each sqlError In sqlex.Errors
                 MessageBox.Show(sqlError.Message)
             Next
         Catch ex As Exception
             MessageBox.Show(ex.Message)
         Finally
             rda.Dispose()
             btnPull.Enabled = True
         End Try
     End Sub
```

C#

```csharp
private void btnPull_Click(object sender, System.EventArgs e)
{
    SqlCeConnection cn = null;
    SqlCeRemoteDataAccess rda = null;
    SqlCeEngine sqlEngine = null;

    try
    {
        btnPull.Enabled = false;
```

```
// Create database if it doesn't already exist
if (!File.Exists("\\My Documents\\IntelligenceData.sdf"))
{
    sqlEngine = new SqlCeEngine();
    sqlEngine.LocalConnectionString = "Data Source=\\My  Documents\\" +
                                      "IntelligenceData.sdf;" +
                                      "Password=apress;" +
                                      "Encrypt Database=True";
    sqlEngine.CreateDatabase();
    sqlEngine.Dispose();
}
else
{
    // Open the connection to the database
    cn = new SqlCeConnection("Data Source=\\My Documents\\" +
                             "IntelligenceData.sdf;Password=apress");
    cn.Open();
    SqlCeCommand cmd = cn.CreateCommand();

    // Drop the FieldMemos table
    cmd.CommandText = "DROP TABLE FieldMemos";
    cmd.ExecuteNonQuery();

    // Close the connection
    if (cn.State != ConnectionState.Closed)
    {
        cn.Close();
    }
}


// Instantiate the RDA Object
rda = new SqlCeRemoteDataAccess();

// Connection String to the SQL Server.
string remoteConnectString = "Provider=SQLOLEDB;" +
                             "Data Source=seawolf;" +
                             "Initial Catalog=IntelligenceData;" +
                             "User Id=sa;" +
                             "Password=apress";


rda.InternetLogin = "robtiffany";
rda.InternetPassword = "pinnacle";
rda.InternetUrl = "https://seawolf/fieldagentrda/sscesa20.dll";
rda.LocalConnectionString = "Data Source=\\My Documents\\" +
```

```
                                                   "IntelligenceData.sdf;" +
                                                   "SSCE:Database Password=apress";


            rda.Pull("FieldMemos",
                     "Select * from FieldMemos",
                     remoteConnectString,
                     RdaTrackOption.TrackingOnWithIndexes,
                     "FieldMemosErrorTable");
        }
        catch(SqlCeException sqlex)
        {
            foreach(SqlCeError sqlError in sqlex.Errors)
            {
                MessageBox.Show(sqlError.Message, "Error");
            }
        }
        catch(Exception ex)
        {
            MessageBox.Show(ex.Message, "Error");
        }
        finally
        {
            rda.Dispose();
            btnPull.Enabled = true;
        }
}
```

Add Memo

Once you have a database, table, and indexes created on your Pocket PC, you need to start adding your field memos to it. The following example resides inside the click event of the AddMemo button and shows you how to insert your memo data into the database. You could even build a full-blown graphical application with text boxes tied to the parameters of the SqlCeCommand object to drive this insert statement rather than use the static information I've included.

Visual Basic .NET

```
Private Sub btnAddMemo_Click(ByVal sender As System.Object, & _
                        ByVal e As System.EventArgs) Handles btnAddMemo.Click


Dim cn As SqlCeConnection
```

```
Try
    btnAddMemo.Enabled = False
    cn = New SqlCeConnection("Data Source=\My
    Documents\IntelligenceData.sdf;Password=apress")
    cn.Open()

    Dim cmd As SqlCeCommand = cn.CreateCommand()

    ' Insert Memo data
    cmd.CommandText = "INSERT INTO FieldMemos (" & _
                    "MemoTo, " & _
                    "MemoFrom, " & _
                    "MemoDateTime, " & _
                    "MemoCity, " & _
                    "MemoState, " & _
                    "MemoSubject, " & _
                    "MemoPriority, " & _
                    "MemoBody) " & _
                    "VALUES " & _
                    "(?, ?, ?, ?, ?, ?, ?, ?)"
    cmd.Parameters.Add("@MemoTo", "Office of the Director")
    cmd.Parameters.Add("@MemoFrom", "Agent 99")
    cmd.Parameters.Add("@MemoDateTime", System.DateTime.Now)
    cmd.Parameters.Add("@MemoCity", "Houston")
    cmd.Parameters.Add("@MemoState", "TX")
    cmd.Parameters.Add("@MemoSubject", "Suspicious Activity 2")
    cmd.Parameters.Add("@MemoPriority", 1)
    cmd.Parameters.Add("@MemoBody", "Observed a suspicious meeting")
    cmd.Prepare()
    cmd.ExecuteNonQuery()

Catch sqlex As SqlCeException
    Dim sqlError As SqlCeError
    For Each sqlError In sqlex.Errors
        MessageBox.Show(sqlError.Message)
    Next
Catch ex As Exception
    MessageBox.Show(ex.Message)
Finally
    If cn.State <> ConnectionState.Closed Then
        cn.Close()
    End If
    btnAddMemo.Enabled = True
End Try
End Sub
```

C#

```csharp
private void btnAddMemo_Click(object sender, System.EventArgs e)
{
    SqlCeConnection cn = null;

    try
    {
        btnAddMemo.Enabled = false;
        cn = new SqlCeConnection("Data Source=\\My Documents\\" +
                                "IntelligenceData.sdf;Password=apress");
        cn.Open();

        SqlCeCommand cmd = cn.CreateCommand();

        // Insert Memo data
        cmd.CommandText = "INSERT INTO FieldMemos (" +
                    "MemoTo, " +
                    "MemoFrom, " +
                    "MemoDateTime, " +
                    "MemoCity, " +
                    "MemoState, " +
                    "MemoSubject, " +
                    "MemoPriority, " +
                    "MemoBody) " +
                    "VALUES " +
                    "(?, ?, ?, ?, ?, ?, ?, ?)";
        cmd.Parameters.Add("@MemoTo", "Office of the Director");
        cmd.Parameters.Add("@MemoFrom", "Agent 86");
        cmd.Parameters.Add("@MemoDateTime", System.DateTime.Now);
        cmd.Parameters.Add("@MemoCity", "Houston");
        cmd.Parameters.Add("@MemoState", "TX");
        cmd.Parameters.Add("@MemoSubject", "Suspicious Activity");
        cmd.Parameters.Add("@MemoPriority", 1);
        cmd.Parameters.Add("@MemoBody", "Observed a suspicious meeting");
        cmd.Prepare();
        cmd.ExecuteNonQuery();
    }
    catch (SqlCeException sqlex)
    {
        foreach(SqlCeError sqlError in sqlex.Errors)
        {
            MessageBox.Show(sqlError.Message, "Error");
        }
```

```
    }
    catch(Exception ex)
    {
        MessageBox.Show(ex.Message, "Error");
    }
    finally
    {
        if(cn.State != ConnectionState.Closed)
        {
            cn.Close();
        }
        btnAddMemo.Enabled = true;
    }
}
```

Push

Calling the Push method doesn't require nearly as much coding as the Pull method. There are no databases to create or tables to drop in this case. The Push method only has three arguments that you need to concern yourself with, as described in Table 9-8.

Table 9-8. Push Method Arguments

ARGUMENT	DESCRIPTION
LocalTableName	Name of the previously pulled and tracked table whose data needs to be sent back to SQL Server for updates.
OLEDBConnection String	An OLE DB–based connection string needed to connect to the proper remote SQL Server database.
BatchOption	You specify BatchingOn or BatchingOff to control whether to treat all the rows of data being sent to SQL Server as a single transaction or to process each row individually

The following example that resides inside the click event of the Push button shows you how to send the new field memos that you generated back to SQL Server for analysis. I use the BatchingOn option in the Push method because I want all the rows of data in the Push operation to either succeed or fail as a single transaction.

Visual Basic .NET

```vbnet
Private Sub btnPush_Click(ByVal sender As System.Object, _
ByVal e As System.EventArgs) Handles btnPush.Click

Dim rda As SqlCeRemoteDataAccess

Try

    btnPush.Enabled = False

    'Instantiate the RDA Object
    rda = New SqlCeRemoteDataAccess

    'Connection String to the SQL Server.
    Dim remoteConnectString As String = "Provider=SQLOLEDB;" & _
    "Data Source=seawolf;" & _
    "Initial Catalog=IntelligenceData;" & _
    "User Id=sa;" & _
    "Password=apress"

    rda.InternetLogin = "robtiffany"
    rda.InternetPassword = "pinnacle"
    rda.InternetUrl = "https://seawolf/fieldagentrda/sscesa20.dll"
    rda.LocalConnectionString = & _
    "Data Source=\My Documents\IntelligenceData.sdf;" & _
    "SSCE:Database Password=apress"

    rda.Push("FieldMemos", remoteConnectString, RdaBatchOption.BatchingOn)

Catch sqlex As SqlCeException
    Dim sqlError As SqlCeError
    For Each sqlError In sqlex.Errors
        MessageBox.Show(sqlError.Message)
    Next
Catch ex As Exception
    MessageBox.Show(ex.Message)
Finally
    rda.Dispose()
    btnPush.Enabled = True
End Try
End Sub
```

C#

```csharp
private void btnPush_Click(object sender, System.EventArgs e)
{
    SqlCeRemoteDataAccess rda = null;

    try
    {
        btnPush.Enabled = false;

        // Instantiate the RDA Object
        rda = new SqlCeRemoteDataAccess();

        // Connection String to the SQL Server.
        string remoteConnectString = "Provider=SQLOLEDB;" +
                                "Data Source=seawolf;" +
                                "Initial Catalog=IntelligenceData;" +
                                "User Id=sa;" +
                                "Password=apress";

        rda.InternetLogin = "robtiffany";
        rda.InternetPassword = " pinnacle";
        rda.InternetUrl = "https://seawolf/fieldagentrda/sscesa20.dll";
        rda.LocalConnectionString = "Data Source=\\My Documents\\" +
                                "IntelligenceData.sdf;" +
                                "SSCE:Database Password=apress";

        rda.Push("FieldMemos", remoteConnectString, RdaBatchOption.BatchingOn);
    }
    catch(SqlCeException sqlex)
    {
        foreach(SqlCeError sqlError in sqlex.Errors)
        {
            MessageBox.Show(sqlError.Message, "Error");
        }
    }
    catch(Exception ex)
    {
        MessageBox.Show(ex.Message, "Error");
    }
    finally
```

```
    {
        rda.Dispose();
        btnPush.Enabled = true;
    }
}
```

Submit SQL

The SubmitSQL method doesn't have much to do with synchronizing data between a handheld and a server. I personally think it was just thrown in there for good measure since the architecture already exists to support the remote execution of SQL statements against SQL Server. You're allowed to execute any kind of query or stored procedure, as long as it doesn't involve the returning of rows back to the Pocket PC. Table 9-9 explains the usage of the two arguments for the SubmitSQL method.

Table 9-9. SubmitSQL Method Arguments

ARGUMENT	DESCRIPTION
SQLString	Any valid SQL statement that doesn't return rows
OLEDBConnection String	An OLE DB–based connection string needed to connect to the proper remote SQL Server database

In the following example that resides inside the click event of the Submit SQL button, I use the same insert statement that I showed you back in the Add Memo example to submit the field memo directly into SQL Server without first saving it to the local SQL Server CE database. Keep in mind that this method only works in a reliable, network-connected state. It's definitely not as robust a solution as the offline design of Pull and Push.

Visual Basic .NET

```
Private Sub btnSubmitSQL_Click(ByVal sender As System.Object, & _
                ByVal e As System.EventArgs) Handles submitSQL.Click

Dim rda As SqlCeRemoteDataAccess

Try
    btnSubmitSQL.Enabled = False
```

```vbnet
        ' Instantiate the RDA Object
        rda = New SqlCeRemoteDataAccess

        ' Connection String to the SQL Server.
        Dim remoteConnectString As String = "Provider=SQLOLEDB;" & _
                                    "Data Source=seawolf;" & _
                                    "Initial Catalog=IntelligenceData;" & _
                                    "User Id=sa;" & _
                                    "Password=apress"

        rda.InternetLogin = "robtiffany"
        rda.InternetPassword = "pinnacle"
        rda.InternetUrl = "https://seawolf/fieldagentrda/sscesa20.dll"
        rda.LocalConnectionString = "Data Source=\My Documents\" & _
                            "IntelligenceData.sdf;" & _
                            "SSCE:Database Password=apress"

        Dim remoteSQL As String = "INSERT INTO FieldMemos (" & _
                            "MemoTo, " & _
                            "MemoFrom, " & _
                            "MemoDateTime, " & _
                            "MemoCity, " & _
                            "MemoState, " & _
                            "MemoSubject, " & _
                            "MemoPriority, " & _
                            "MemoBody) " & _
                            "VALUES " & _
                            "('Office of the Director', " & _
                            "'Agent 99', " & _
                            "'" + System.DateTime.Now + "', " & _
                            "'Houston', " & _
                            "'TX', " & _
                            "'Suspicious Activity 3', " & _
                            "'1', " & _
                            "'Observed a suspicious meeting')"

        rda.SubmitSql(remoteSQL, remoteConnectString)

Catch sqlex As SqlCeException
        Dim sqlError As SqlCeError
        For Each sqlError In sqlex.Errors
            MessageBox.Show(sqlError.Message)
        Next
Catch ex As Exception
```

```
                MessageBox.Show(ex.Message)
        Finally

                rda.Dispose()
                btnSubmitSQL.Enabled = True
        End Try
        End Sub
```

C#

```csharp
private void btnSubmitSQL_Click(object sender, System.EventArgs e)
{
    SqlCeRemoteDataAccess rda = null;

    try
    {
        btnSubmitSQL.Enabled = false;

        // Instantiate the RDA Object
        rda = new SqlCeRemoteDataAccess();

        // Connection String to the SQL Server.
        string remoteConnectString = "Provider=SQLOLEDB;" +
                            "Data Source=seawolf;" +
                            "Initial Catalog=IntelligenceData;" +
                            "User Id=sa;" +
                            "Password=apress";

        rda.InternetLogin = "robtiffany";
        rda.InternetPassword = "pinnacle";
        rda.InternetUrl = "https://seawolf/fieldagentrda/sscesa20.dll";
        rda.LocalConnectionString = "Data Source=\\My Documents\\" +
                            "IntelligenceData.sdf;" +
                            "SSCE:Database Password=apress";

    string remoteSQL = "INSERT INTO FieldMemos (" +
                    "MemoTo, " +
                    "MemoFrom, " +
                    "MemoDateTime, " +
                    "MemoCity, " +
                    "MemoState, " +
                    "MemoSubject, " +
                    "MemoPriority, " +
                    "MemoBody) " +
```

```
                    "VALUES " +
                    "('Office of the Director', " +
                    "'Agent 99', " +
                    "'" + System.DateTime.Now + "', " +
                    "'Houston', " +
                    "'TX', " +
                    "'More Suspicious Activity', " +
                    "'1', " +
                    "'Observed another suspicious meeting')";

        rda.SubmitSql(remoteSQL, remoteConnectString);
    }
    catch (SqlCeException sqlex)
    {
        foreach(SqlCeError sqlError in sqlex.Errors)
        {
            MessageBox.Show(sqlError.Message, "Error");
        }
    }
    catch (Exception ex)
    {
        MessageBox.Show(ex.Message, "Error");
    }
    finally
    {
        rda.Dispose();
        btnSubmitSQL.Enabled = true;
    }
}
```

Run the Pull, AddMemo, and Push operations several times in succession while changing the memo data each time. Take a look at the changes in data rows on the server with Enterprise Manager and on the Pocket PC with Query Analyzer. I think you'll find that this is a very effective method of working with, adding to, and updating offline data and synchronizing it with SQL Server.

Conclusion

It probably seems like setting up and executing an RDA solution is a lot of work for an object that only has three methods. I hope that by taking you step by step through each configuration process at a granular level, you'll come away with a better understanding of how RDA works. It was also very important for you to learn the process of securing your RDA system with SSL, since this step is usually overlooked but extremely important. I'm sure you're glad to see that you can design your SQL Server CE databases at the SQL Server level inside Enterprise Manager and then download the results to your handheld. That sure beats using DDL or Query Analyzer on your Pocket PC to do the same thing. The next and final chapter covers the synchronization of your field memo table using merge replication. Luckily, all the work you've done in this chapter to create HTTPS connectivity between your Pocket PC and IIS will be reused with merge replication. With a little more configuration required on SQL Server but significantly less code on the client, I'm sure you'll find this technology to be very interesting.

CHAPTER 10
Replication

WELCOME TO PART TWO of our miniseries on connecting SQL Server CE on the Pocket PC to SQL Server. In last night's episode, you learned the tale of two SQL Servers that exchanged data with each other via a technology called RDA. Tonight you're going to learn about another way to skin the same cat with SQL Server merge replication. Long before SQL Server CE was born, big brother SQL Server 7 and 2000 implemented a method of distributing data amongst remote servers called merge replication. Essentially this means that one SQL Server can make the contents of its databases and tables available to other SQL Servers by publishing those objects and the data contained in them. Other SQL Servers subscribe to those publications in order to create replicas of those objects and their data on their own servers. This is a great way to move the data that people need closer to them. One common example of this technology is a branch office that replicates with a home office so that branch users won't have to run queries over the WAN. Today, SQL Server CE can take advantage of this same technology by subscribing to publications found in SQL Server. The replicated data can be added to, updated, and deleted, and then remerged back into SQL Server. This makes for a powerful alternative to RDA and will certainly help your field agents get their memos merged together in a unified SQL Server database back at headquarters.

Merge Replication Architecture

Almost all of the merge replication architecture is identical to the architecture found in RDA. It uses many of the same client-side and server-side components to allow SQL Server CE devices to communicate with SQL Server 2000. Again, IIS brokers HTTP and HTTPS requests between the Pocket PC and the server. If all this talk about publishing and subscribing has you thinking about Microsoft Message Queue, you're not too far off the mark. Like any reliable messaging system, if a communications link fails, merge replication will resume transmitting its data right after the last successfully broadcast message buffer—until the set timeout value is reached. Keep in mind that, unlike RDA, merge replication technology only works on SQL Server 2000.

Client Agent

The SQL Server CE Client Agent runs on your Pocket PC and sits in between your
.NET Compact Framework application and the SQL Server CE Database Engine. It
exposes all the properties and methods that your application will use to control
merge replication. Based on the methods you call, the Client Agent will manipulate the Database Engine and communicate with the SQL Server CE Server Agent
via IIS and HTTP/S. The four methods that do all the work for your merge replication application are found in the SqlCeReplication class and include
AddSubscription, Synchronize, ReinitializeSubscription, and DropSubscription.

AddSubscription

This method is used to create a subscription to a published database. Additionally,
it can also create a new SQL Server CE database for you on your handheld device.

Synchronize

This method is used to kick off the merge replication operation between the
subscriber on the Pocket PC and the publisher on the server.

ReinitializeSubscription

This method is used to mark a subscription for reinitialization. This action
re-creates the snapshot of the published database on the publishing server.

DropSubscription

This method is used to remove a subscription to a publication. You're also given
the option to persist or delete the local SQL Server CE subscription database.

Database Engine

The SQL Server CE Database Engine is designed to manage the data store on your
Pocket PC. The Database Engine tracks all records that are inserted, updated, and
deleted in subscription databases.

Server Agent

As you learned in Chapter 9, the SQL Server CE Server Agent runs as an ISAPI DLL on your IIS server, where it handles HTTP/S requests made by the Client Agent and then makes calls to the SQL Server CE Replication Provider to fulfill those requests. The ISAPI extension is called sscesa20.dll and it resides in the special IIS virtual directory that you create for your merge replication application.

SQL Server Reconciler

The only new player in this game is the SQL Server Reconciler. It works in concert with the SQL Server CE and SQL Server Replication Providers when synchronization occurs to resolve any data or metadata conflicts that might arise during the process.

Creating a Publication

In order for your Pocket PC to replicate with SQL Server, it needs a publication that it can subscribe to. In preparation for this, go ahead and bring up Enterprise Manager on your desktop or server and navigate to the FieldMemos table of your IntelligenceData database. I need you to open the FieldMemos table in design mode and delete the MemoID column. Next, reinsert MemoID into the table as the primary key with an int data type. Additionally, make MemoID an identity column with a seed and increment of one. SQL Server won't let you directly convert a uniqueidentifier to an int, and that's why you have to jump through all these hoops. After last chapter's diatribe over the evils of identity columns and the potential for colliding keys, you're probably wondering why I want you to make this change. The answer is so you can try out the Identity Ranges feature of merge replication that gives each Pocket PC its own block of integers for its identity columns. I'll explain more about this in a moment.

There are just two other things I want you to check on before proceeding further. First off, if your Enterprise Manager is connected to your SQL Server and the registered name is (local), you will be required to delete that server registration and re-register it with the actual server name. The other thing you need to do is to ensure that both SQL Server and the SQL Server Agent services are not running under the LocalSystem account. If your SQL Server needs to reach out and touch another server on the network, the LocalSystem account credentials won't cut it. Running under a Domain account with privileges on other servers will do the trick.

Now that your database change has been made, I want you to right-click the FieldMemos table icon and first select All tasks, and then select Create new publication. You will be presented with the first screen of the Create Publication Wizard as shown in Figure 10-1.

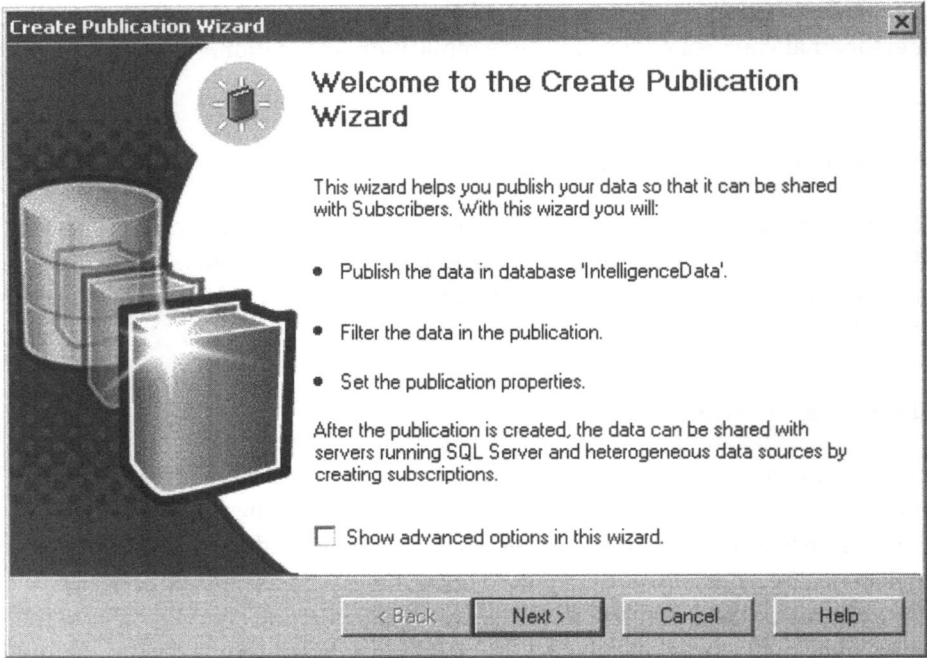

Figure 10-1. Create Publication Wizard

Click Next to get started with the Select Distributor screen as shown in Figure 10-2. On this screen you get to choose a SQL Server on your network to be the distributor. The job of the distributor is to synchronize data between the SQL Servers that publish data and subscribers that consume the data. For simplicity's sake, select the first radio button to make your publishing SQL Server a distributor as well. Having SQL Server double up as a publisher and a distributor is very common, except where extreme scalability is required.

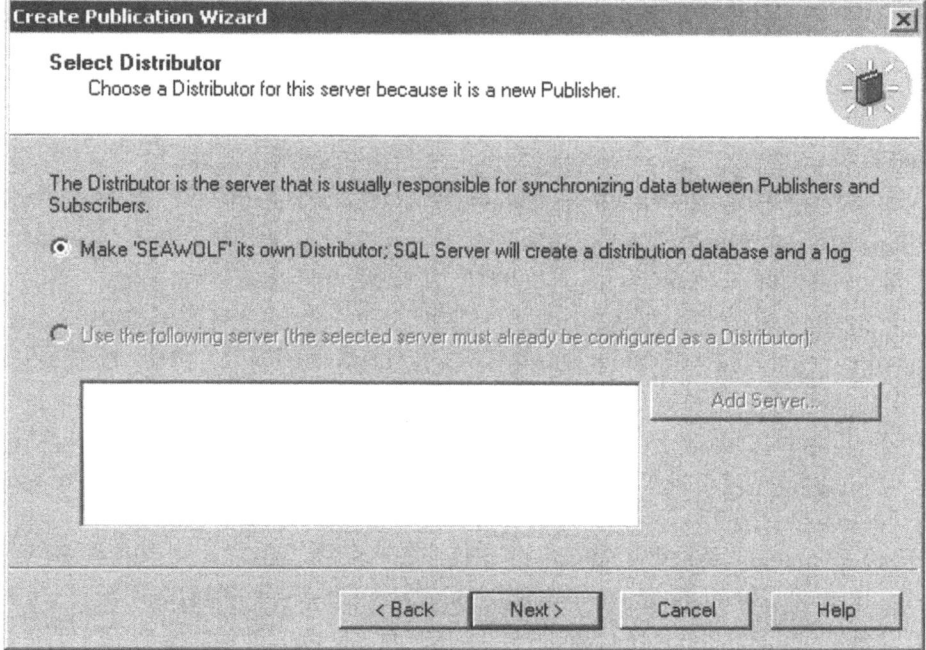

Figure 10-2. Selecting a distributor

On the next screen you get to select whether to have the SQL Server Agent service start up automatically or whether you want to start it manually as specified in the screen in Figure 10-3. I recommend you select the radio button to have it start automatically, since it's needed at all times so the replication agents can synchronize their subscriptions whenever they want.

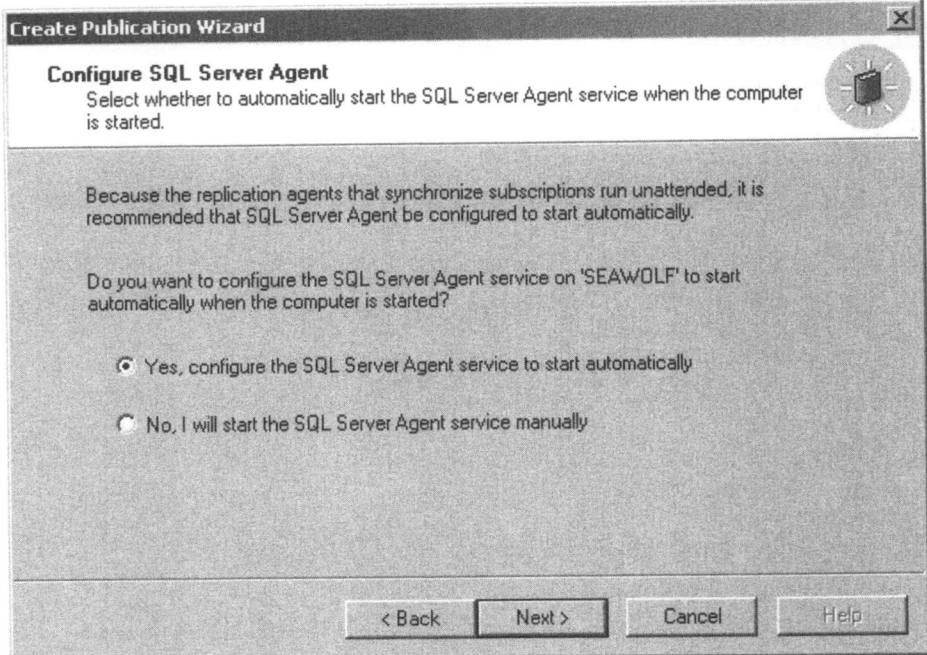

Figure 10-3. Configuring SQL Server Agent

On the next screen you get to specify a snapshot folder. This folder will hold so-called snapshot files from SQL Server that contain the schema and data for the tables you publish. It's important that this folder is shared so that it can be used by SQL Server and IIS whether they're on the same computer or not. The UNC path presented to you on this screen points to an administrative (C$) share by default. Microsoft recommends that you disregard this share and create a new one of your own with the appropriate permissions. Therefore, I want you to go to the Windows Explorer, create a new folder called SnapshotShare, and then share it as Snapshot-Share. As far as this folder's permissions are concerned, grant full control to the account that the SQL Server service and SQL Server Agent service are running under. Since you'll be connecting to IIS via Basic Authentication, grant read permissions to the account of the connecting user. With the new share created with appropriate permissions, click the Browse button on the Specify Snapshot Folder screen and navigate to your new share so that the screen looks something like Figure 10-4.

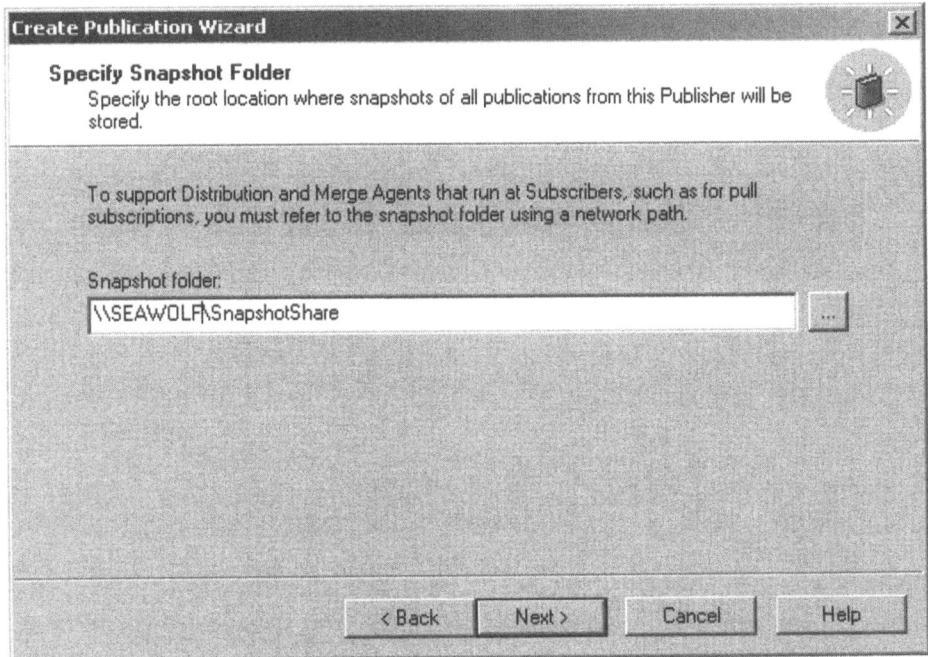

Figure 10-4. Specifying a snapshot folder

On the next screen you get to choose which database you'd like to publish as shown in Figure 10-5. Select the IntelligenceData database and click Next.

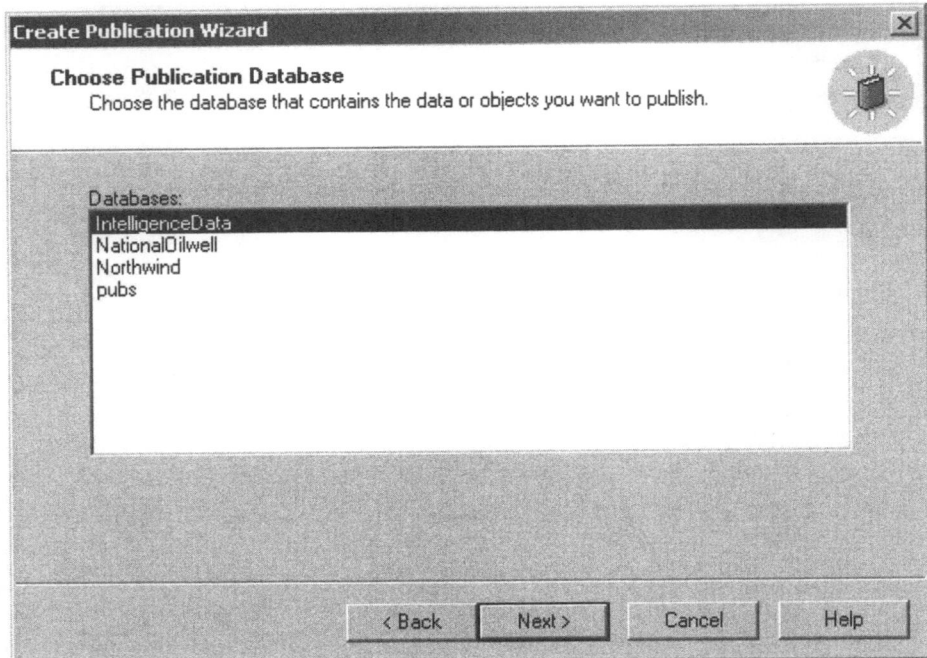

Figure 10-5. Choosing a publication database

The next screen asks you to select what kind of publication type to use. Make sure you select Merge publication as shown in Figure 10-6 so that data can be updated by the publisher and mobile subscribers.

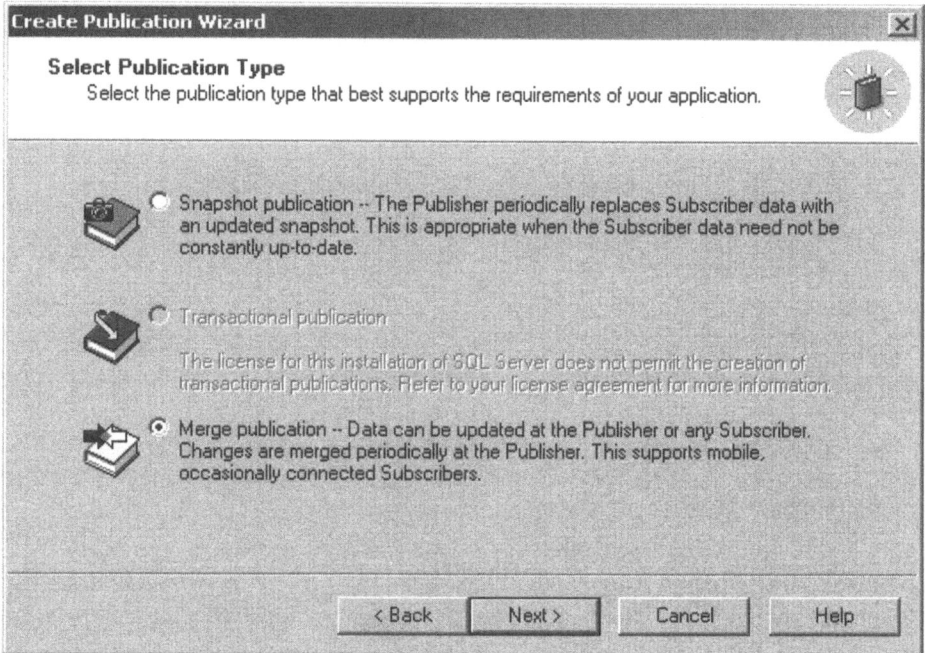

Figure 10-6. Selecting the publication type

The next screen, shown in Figure 10-7, allows you to select the types of subscribers you expect to consume data from your publication. For the purposes of this example, just check Devices running SQL Server CE, and then click Next.

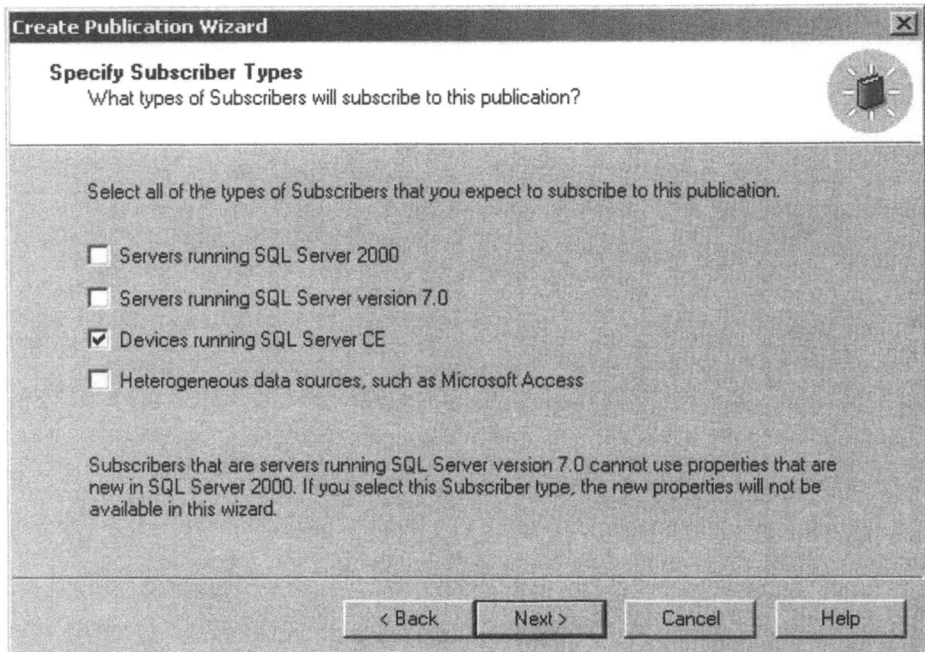

Figure 10-7. Specifying subscriber types

On the next screen you get to specify which articles you want to make available in your publication. Typically, an article can be a stored procedure, a view, or a table. In this case, just check the checkbox to the left of the FieldMemos object as shown in Figure 10-8.

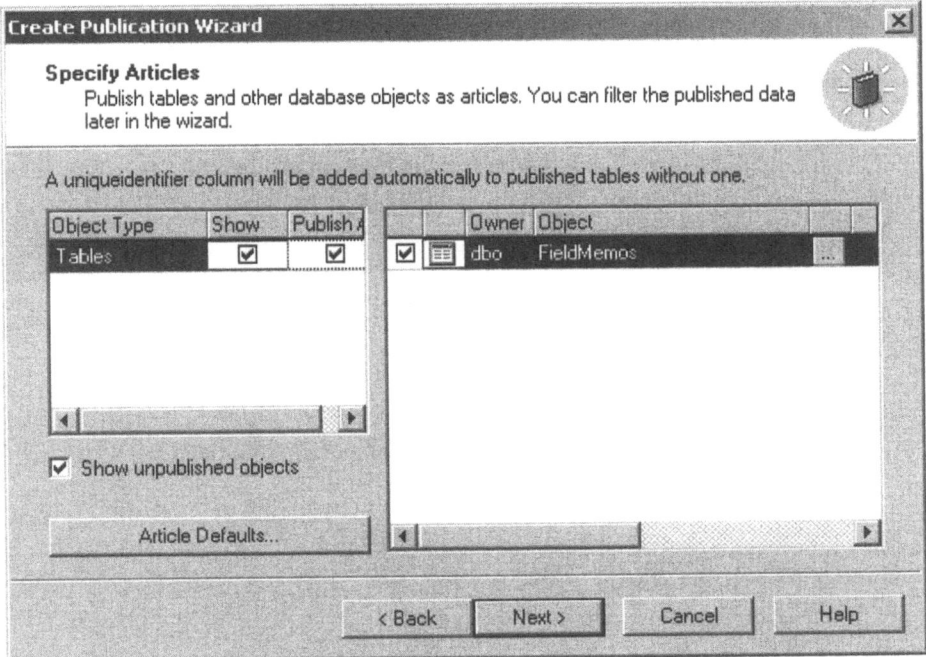

Figure 10-8. Specifying articles

You probably noticed that once you checked the checkbox, an ellipsis button appeared to the right of the FieldMemos object. Click this button in order to bring up the Table Article Properties dialog box. Now select the Identity Range tab and check the "Automatically assign and maintain a unique identity range for each subscription" checkbox as shown in Figure 10-9.

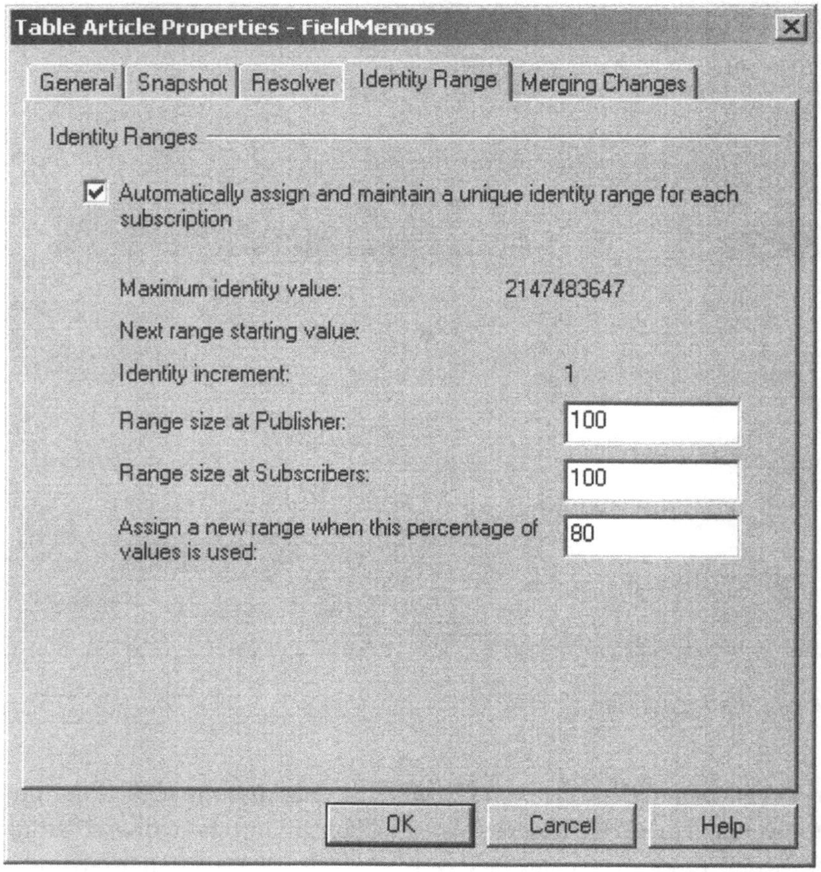

Figure 10-9. Specifying the identity range

You'll remember back at the beginning of this section, I had you convert your uniqueidentifier primary key into an int identity column. By default, the Identity Ranges feature of merge replication means SQL Server will pass out blocks of 100 numbers to itself and to each individual subscriber. SQL Server's own first block might be 1–100. Your Pocket PC might be given 400–500. Another device might be given 600–700. Each device will be able to increment its identity columns by 1 until it reaches 80 percent of the block that it was given. At that point an error will be thrown. The remedy for this situation is to replicate with SQL Server. It will recognize that you've hit the 80 percent mark and will give you a new and unique block of 100 numbers to work with. This will go on until all the subscribers have pushed the number to just over 2 billion.

Click OK in the Table Article Properties dialog box and then click Next in the Specify Articles screen. The next screen displays a list of issues or problems that the wizard has with your article as shown in Figure 10-10. The screen also shows a description of the issue, the potential problems caused by the issue, and what SQL Server is going to do about them.

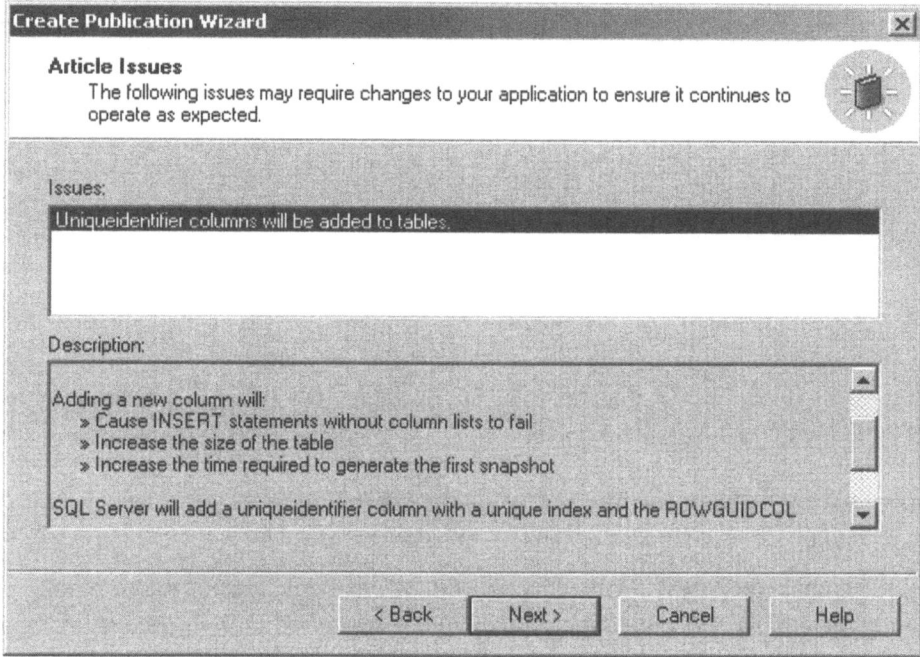

Figure 10-10. Article issues

On the next screen you get to select the publication name and the publication description. By default, your database name is inserted into the Publication name textbox. Go ahead and change it to IntelligenceDataPublication as shown in Figure 10-11, and then click Next.

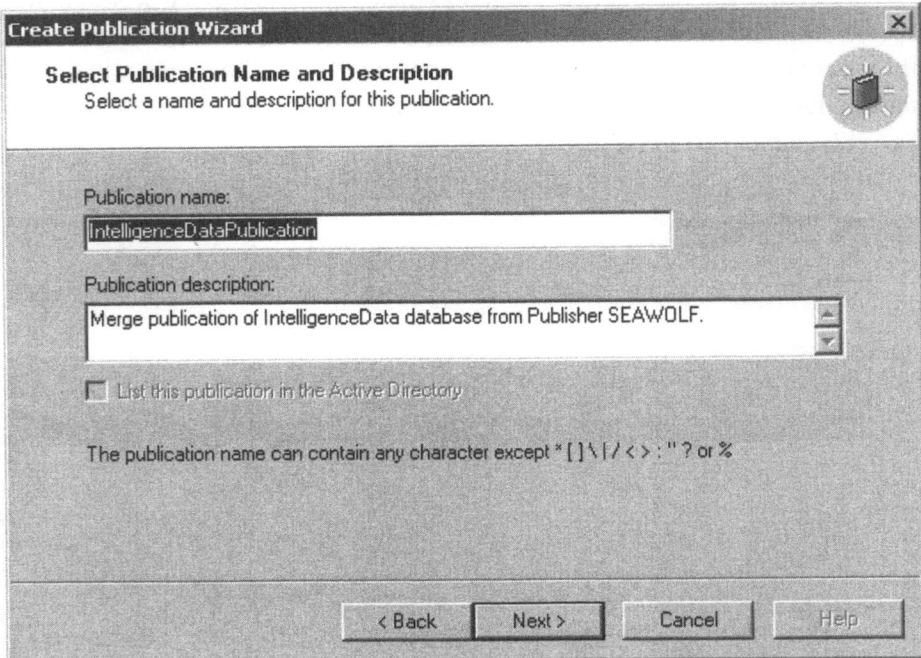

Figure 10-11. Selecting the publication name and description

The next screen gives you a review of the choices you made for your publication. Select the "No, create the publication as specified" radio button as shown in Figure 10-12, and then click Next. Click Finish on the next screen to complete the creation of your publication. With the publication created, it's now just a matter of setting up network connectivity and creating the necessary client code to go live with merge replication.

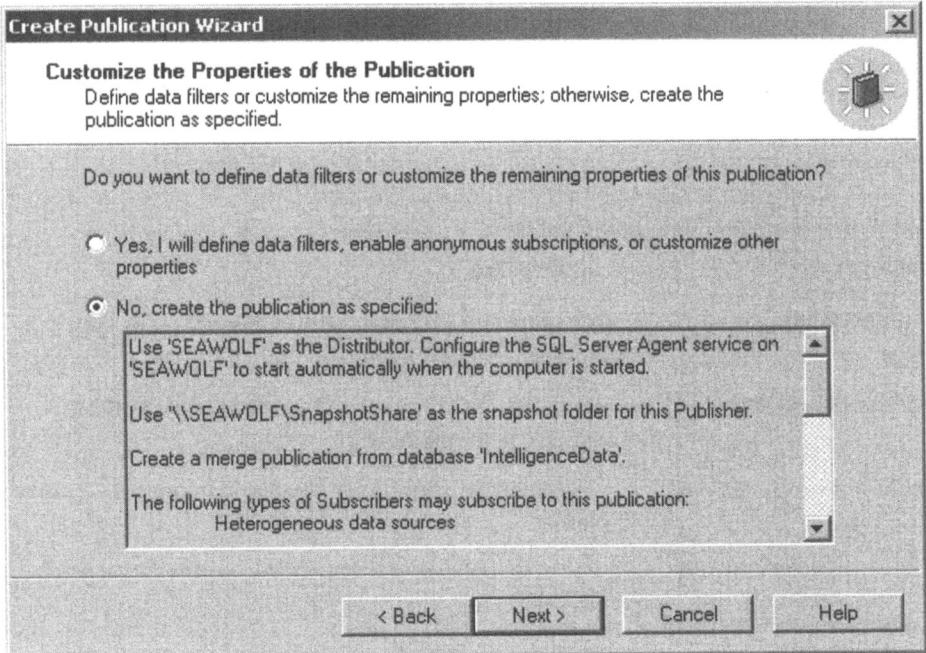

Figure 10-12. Customizing the properties of the publication

Making the Connection

If you're expecting a big section on getting IIS configured for connectivity and security, you're in for a big disappointment. Remember all the IIS configuration work you did in the last chapter? Nothing new is required for merge replication, so it's safe to say that you're already done. You'll just continue to use the Field-AgentRDA virtual directory along with SSL to communicate with SQL Server via the SQL Server CE Server Agent (sscesa20.dll). You've already created the snapshot share with all the appropriate permissions, so there's nothing else to do but build the client application. That was easy.

Creating the Replication Client

In the same way that you created a client with RDA in the last chapter, so will you do with merge replication in this chapter. It's now time to build the .NET Compact Framework client that your field agents will use to capture and replicate their important memos back to headquarters. To do so, you're provided with the SqlCeReplication class that includes a number of properties and methods to help you get the job done. I already went over the methods available to you earlier in the architecture section of this chapter. Take a look at Table 10-1 in order to get a handle on the properties you'll be using in conjunction with those methods.

Table 10-1. SqlCeReplication Properties

PROPERTY	DESCRIPTION
InternetLogin	Specifies the IIS login name needed to access the SQL Server CE Server Agent
InternetPassword	Specifies the IIS password needed to access the SQL Server CE Server Agent
InternetProxyLogin	Specifies the login name needed to connect to a proxy server
InternetProxyPassword	Specifies the password needed to connect to a proxy server
InternetProxyServer	Specifies the name or IP address of the proxy server used to access the IIS server specified in the InternetURL property
InternetURL	Specifies the URL needed to connect to the SQL Server CE Server Agent
Publication	Specifies the publication name that has been enabled for anonymous merge subscriptions
Publisher	Specifies the name of the server running the SQL Server that contains the publication
PublisherDatabase	Specifies the name of the database that is being published
PublisherLogin	Specifies the login name used when connecting to the publisher
PublisherPassword	Specifies the password used when connecting to the publisher
Subscriber	Specifies the name of the subscriber (this can be any name you choose)
SubscriberConnectionString	Database connection string needed to connect to SQL Server CE

Other properties exist besides the ones displayed in Table 10-1, but these are the ones most commonly used. As you might imagine, the InternetURL, Internet-Login, InternetPassword, InternetProxyServer, InternetProxyLogin, and InternetProxyPassword properties all serve the exact same functions as their counterparts in the SqlCeRemoteDataAccess class. Additionally, the Subscriber-ConnectionString property for merge replication works the same way as the LocalConnectionString property in RDA.

Your Last Chance to Code

It's time to build the final examples you'll see in this book. These examples are designed to illustrate and reinforce what you've learned about merge replication so far. So once again, fire up Visual Studio .NET 2003 and create a Smart Device Application in either C# or Visual Basic .NET. Just as you did in the last chapter, I want you to add five buttons to your form as described in Table 10-2.

Table 10-2. Buttons

NAME	TEXT
btnCreateSubscription	Create Subscription
btnSynchronize	Synchronize
btnAddMemo	Add Memo
btnReinitializeSubscription	Reinitialize Subscription
btnDropSubscription	Drop Subscription

You can place these buttons anywhere on the form that you like. The purpose of these buttons is to illustrate how to create a new subscription database on your device, replicate data and metadata from SQL Server to this new subscription database, add new rows of data to SQL Server CE, re-create a snapshot, and remove your subscription to the publication. The code to make all this possible will be placed in the click events of these five buttons. Before you write any code, make sure to add a reference to both System.Data.Common and System.Data.SqlServerCe. At the top of your form class, add

```
using System.Data.SqlServerCe;
```

and

```
using System.IO;
```

if you're doing a C# project.

If you're creating a Visual Basic .NET project, add

```
Imports System.Data.SqlServerCe
```

and

```
Imports System.IO
```

Create Subscription

The creation of a new subscription is accomplished through the use of the AddSubscription method of the SqlCeReplication object. Additionally, this method will also create a new SQL Server CE database on your Pocket PC if you choose the AddOption.CreateDatabase parameter of the AddSubscription method. To make sure that a database with the same name doesn't get overwritten, make sure to test for the existence of the database that the AddSubscription method is about to create. The following example resides in the click event handler of the Create Subscription button, and shows you how to properly run the AddSubscription method in order to create the IntelligenceData database on your Pocket PC.

Visual Basic .NET

```
Private Sub btnCreateSubscription_Click(ByVal sender As System.Object, & _
                ByVal e As System.EventArgs) Handles btnCreateSubscription.Click

Dim rep As SqlCeReplication

Try
    btnCreateSubscription.Enabled = False
    rep = New SqlCeReplication()

    ' This is the connection string to your local SQL Server CE database file
    rep.SubscriberConnectionString = "Data Source=\My Documents\" & _
                                     "IntelligenceData.sdf;" & _
                                     "SSCE:Database Password=apress"
    ' If database doesn't exist then...
    If Not File.Exists("\My Documents\IntelligenceData.sdf") Then
        ' Add a subscription and create the local database
        rep.AddSubscription(AddOption.CreateDatabase)
    End If
```

```
Catch sqlex As SqlCeException
    Dim sqlError As SqlCeError
    For Each sqlError In sqlex.Errors
        MessageBox.Show(sqlError.Message, "Error")
    Next
Catch ex As Exception
    MessageBox.Show(ex.Message, "Error")
Finally
    rep.Dispose()
    btnCreateSubscription.Enabled = True
End Try

End Sub
```

C#

```
private void btnCreateSubscription_Click(object sender, System.EventArgs e)
{
    SqlCeReplication rep = null;

    try
    {
        btnCreateSubscription.Enabled = false;
        rep = new SqlCeReplication();

        // This is the connection string to your local SQL Server CE database file
        rep.SubscriberConnectionString = "Data Source=\\My Documents\\" +
                                         "IntelligenceData.sdf;" +
                                         "SSCE:Database Password=apress";

        // If database doesn't exist then...
        if (!File.Exists("\\My Documents\\IntelligenceData.sdf"))
        {
            // Add a subscription and create the local database
            rep.AddSubscription(AddOption.CreateDatabase);
        }
    }
    catch (SqlCeException sqlex)
    {
        foreach (SqlCeError sqlError in sqlex.Errors)
        {
            MessageBox.Show(sqlError.Message, "Error");
```

```
        }
    }
    catch(Exception ex)
    {
        MessageBox.Show(ex.Message, "Error");
    }
    finally
    {
        rep.Dispose();
        btnCreateSubscription.Enabled = true;
    }
}
```

Synchronize

The Synchronize method is used to retrieve data and metadata from SQL Server in order to populate the newly created subscription database. Once this database has data added to it, the Synchronize method will send that information back to SQL Server to be merged with the publication. You also get to set all the properties you just learned about. The following example resides inside the click event of the Synchronize button and shows you how to replicate data between SQL Server and SQL Server CE.

Visual Basic .NET

```vbnet
Private Sub btnSynchronize_Click(ByVal sender As System.Object, & _
              ByVal e As System.EventArgs) Handles btnSynchronize.Click


Dim rep As SqlCeReplication

Try
    btnSynchronize.Enabled = False

    rep = New SqlCeReplication()

    ' This is the URL that points to sscesa20.dll running on IIS
    rep.InternetUrl = "https://seawolf/fieldagentrda/sscesa20.dll"

    ' This is your Basic Authentication username
    rep.InternetLogin = "robtiffany"

    ' This is your Basic Authentication password
    rep.InternetPassword = "pinnacle"
```

```vbnet
        ' This is the name of the server running SQL Server
        rep.Publisher = "seawolf"

        ' This is the name of the actual database that you're publishing
        rep.PublisherDatabase = "IntelligenceData"

        ' This is your SQL Server username
        rep.PublisherLogin = "sa"

        ' This is your SQL Server password
        rep.PublisherPassword = "apress"

        ' This is the name that you give to your publication during the wizard setup
        rep.Publication = "IntelligenceDataPublication"

        ' This anonymous subscriber name can be anything you want it to be
        rep.Subscriber = "Subscriber"

        ' This is the connection string to your local SQL Server CE database file
        rep.SubscriberConnectionString = "Data Source=\My Documents\" & _
                                    "IntelligenceData.sdf;" & _
                                    "SSCE:Database Password=apress"

        ' If database already exists then...
        If File.Exists("\My Documents\IntelligenceData.sdf") Then
            ' Synchronize with SQL Server
            rep.Synchronize()
        Else
            MessageBox.Show("You must first create a database", "Error")
        End If

    Catch sqlex As SqlCeException
        Dim sqlError As SqlCeError
        For Each sqlError In sqlex.Errors
            MessageBox.Show(sqlError.Message, "Error")
        Next
    Catch ex As Exception
        MessageBox.Show(ex.Message, "Error")
    Finally
        rep.Dispose()
        btnSynchronize.Enabled = True
    End Try

End Sub
```

C#

```csharp
private void btnSynchronize_Click(object sender, System.EventArgs e)
{
    SqlCeReplication rep = null;

    try
    {
        btnSynchronize.Enabled = false;
        rep = new SqlCeReplication();

        // This is the URL that points to sscesa20.dll running on IIS
        rep.InternetUrl = "https://seawolf/fieldagentrda/sscesa20.dll";

        // This is your Basic Authentication username
        rep.InternetLogin = "robtiffany";

        // This is your Basic Authentication password
        rep.InternetPassword = "pinnacle";

        // This is the name of the server running SQL Server
        rep.Publisher = "seawolf";

        // This is the name of the actual database that you're publishing
        rep.PublisherDatabase = "IntelligenceData";

        // This is your SQL Server username
        rep.PublisherLogin = "sa";

        // This is your SQL Server password
        rep.PublisherPassword = "apress";

        // This is the name that you give to your publication
        // during the wizard setup
        rep.Publication = "IntelligenceDataPublication";

        // This anonymous subscriber name can be anything you want it to be
        rep.Subscriber = "Subscriber";

        // This is the connection string to your local SQL Server CE database file
        rep.SubscriberConnectionString = "Data Source=\\My Documents\\" +
                                    "IntelligenceData.sdf;" +
                                    "SSCE:Database Password=apress";
```

```csharp
        // If database already exists then...
        if (File.Exists("\\My Documents\\IntelligenceData.sdf"))
        {
            // Synchronize with SQL Server
            rep.Synchronize();
        }
        else
        {
            MessageBox.Show("You must first create a database", "Error");
        }
    }
    catch (SqlCeException sqlex)
    {
        foreach (SqlCeError sqlError in sqlex.Errors)
        {
            MessageBox.Show(sqlError.Message, "Error");
        }
    }
    catch (Exception ex)
    {
        MessageBox.Show(ex.Message, "Error");
    }
    finally
    {
        rep.Dispose();
        btnSynchronize.Enabled = true;
    }
}
```

Add Memo

Once you have a database, table, and indexes created on your Pocket PC, you need to start adding your field memos to it. The following example resides inside the click event of the Add Memo button and shows you how to insert your memo data into the database. Yes, it works just like the Add Memo button you built in Chapter 9.

Visual Basic .NET

```vb
Private Sub btnAddMemo_Click(ByVal sender As System.Object, & _
                        ByVal e As System.EventArgs) Handles btnAddMemo.Click


Dim cn As SqlCeConnection

Try
    btnAddMemo.Enabled = False
    cn = New SqlCeConnection("Data Source=\My Documents\" & _
                        "IntelligenceData.sdf;Password=apress")
    cn.Open()

    Dim cmd As SqlCeCommand = cn.CreateCommand()

    'insert Memo Data
    cmd.CommandText = "INSERT INTO FieldMemos (" & _
                    "MemoTo, " & _
                    "MemoFrom, " & _
                    "MemoDateTime, " & _
                    "MemoCity, " & _
                    "MemoState, " & _
                    "MemoSubject, " & _
                    "MemoPriority, " & _
                    "MemoBody) " & _
                    "VALUES " & _
                    "(?, ?, ?, ?, ?, ?, ?, ?)"
    cmd.Parameters.Add("@MemoTo", "Office of the Director")
    cmd.Parameters.Add("@MemoFrom", "Neo")
    cmd.Parameters.Add("@MemoDateTime", System.DateTime.Now)
    cmd.Parameters.Add("@MemoCity", "Houston")
    cmd.Parameters.Add("@MemoState", "TX")
    cmd.Parameters.Add("@MemoSubject", "Suspicious Activity")
    cmd.Parameters.Add("@MemoPriority", 2)
    cmd.Parameters.Add("@MemoBody", & _
                    "Observed suspicious meeting with Agent Smith")
    cmd.Prepare()
    cmd.ExecuteNonQuery()
Catch sqlex As SqlCeException
    Dim sqlError As SqlCeError
    For Each sqlError In sqlex.Errors
        MessageBox.Show(sqlError.Message, "Error")
    Next
Catch ex As Exception
```

```
        MessageBox.Show(ex.Message, "Error")
Finally
    If cn.State <> ConnectionState.Closed Then
        cn.Close()
    End If
    btnAddMemo.Enabled = True
End Try
End Sub
```

C#

```csharp
private void btnAddMemo_Click(object sender, System.EventArgs e)
{
    SqlCeConnection cn = null;

    try
    {
        btnAddMemo.Enabled = false;
        cn = new SqlCeConnection("Data Source=\\My Documents" +
                                "\\IntelligenceData.sdf;Password=apress");
        cn.Open();

        SqlCeCommand cmd = cn.CreateCommand();

        // Insert Memo Data
        cmd.CommandText = "INSERT INTO FieldMemos (" +
                        "MemoTo, " +
                        "MemoFrom, " +
                        "MemoDateTime, " +
                        "MemoCity, " +
                        "MemoState, " +
                        "MemoSubject, " +
                        "MemoPriority, " +
                        "MemoBody) " +
                        "VALUES " +
                        "(?, ?, ?, ?, ?, ?, ?, ?)";
        cmd.Parameters.Add("@MemoTo", "Office of the Director");
        cmd.Parameters.Add("@MemoFrom", "Trinity");
        cmd.Parameters.Add("@MemoDateTime", System.DateTime.Now);
        cmd.Parameters.Add("@MemoCity", "Los Angeles");
        cmd.Parameters.Add("@MemoState", "CA");
        cmd.Parameters.Add("@MemoSubject", "Strange Activity");
        cmd.Parameters.Add("@MemoPriority", 1);
```

```
            cmd.Parameters.Add("@MemoBody", "Agent Smith seems to be replicating");
            cmd.Prepare();
            cmd.ExecuteNonQuery();
        }
        catch(SqlCeException sqlex)
        {
            foreach (SqlCeError sqlError in sqlex.Errors)
            {
                MessageBox.Show(sqlError.Message, "Error");
            }
        }
        catch(Exception ex)
        {
            MessageBox.Show(ex.Message, "Error");
        }
        finally
        {
            if (cn.State != ConnectionState.Closed)
            {
                cn.Close();
            }
            btnAddMemo.Enabled = true;
        }
}
```

Reinitialize Subscription

Calling the ReinitializeSubscription method marks your SQL Server CE database
subscription for reinitialization. This re-creates the snapshot of the publication
database, which will then be pulled down to your handheld the next time you call
the Synchronize method. The ReinitializeSubscription method also has a Boolean
argument that, if set to true, will upload your latest changes before the re-created
snapshot is applied to your subscription database. The following example resides
inside the click event handler of the Reinitialize Subscription button and shows
you how to mark your subscription for reinitialization.

Visual Basic .NET

```
Private Sub btnReinitializeSubscription_Click(ByVal sender As System.Object, & _
            ByVal e As System.EventArgs) Handles btnReinitializeSubscription.Click

Dim rep As SqlCeReplication
```

```
Try
    btnReinitializeSubscription.Enabled = False
    rep = New SqlCeReplication

    ' This is the URL that points to sscesa20.dll running on IIS
    rep.InternetUrl = "https://seawolf/fieldagentrda/sscesa20.dll"

    ' This is your Basic Authentication username
    rep.InternetLogin = "robtiffany"

    ' This is your Basic Authentication password
    rep.InternetPassword = "pinnacle"

    ' This is the name of the server running SQL Server
    rep.Publisher = "seawolf"

    ' This is the name of the actual database that you're publishing
    rep.PublisherDatabase = "IntelligenceData"

    ' This is your SQL Server username
    rep.PublisherLogin = "sa"

    ' This is your SQL Server password
    rep.PublisherPassword = "apress"

    ' This is the name that you give to your publication during the wizard setup
    rep.Publication = "IntelligenceDataPublication"

    ' This anonymous subscriber name can be anything you want it to be
    rep.Subscriber = "Subscriber"

    ' This is the connection string to your local SQL Server CE database file
    rep.SubscriberConnectionString = "Data Source=\My Documents\" & _
                                     "IntelligenceData.sdf;" & _
                                     "SSCE:Database Password=apress"

    ' If database already exists then...
    If File.Exists("\My Documents\IntelligenceData.sdf") Then
        ' This uploads your changes and then marks the
        ' subscription for reinitialization
        rep.ReinitializeSubscription(True)

        ' Synchronize with SQL Server
```

```
            rep.Synchronize()
        Else
            MessageBox.Show("You must first create a database", "Error")
        End If
Catch sqlex As SqlCeException
    Dim sqlError As SqlCeError
    For Each sqlError In sqlex.Errors
        MessageBox.Show(sqlError.Message, "Error")
    Next
Catch ex As Exception
    MessageBox.Show(ex.Message, "Error")
Finally
    rep.Dispose()
    btnReinitializeSubscription.Enabled = True
End Try

End Sub
```

C#

```csharp
private void btnReinitializeSubscription_Click(object sender, System.EventArgs e)
{
    SqlCeReplication rep = null;

    try
    {
        btnReinitializeSubscription.Enabled = false;
        rep = new SqlCeReplication();

        // This is the URL that points to sscesa20.dll running on IIS
        rep.InternetUrl = "https://seawolf/fieldagentrda/sscesa20.dll";

        // This is your Basic Authentication username
        rep.InternetLogin = "robtiffany";

        // This is your Basic Authentication password
        rep.InternetPassword = "pinnacle";

        // This is the name of the server running SQL Server
        rep.Publisher = "seawolf";

        // This is the name of the actual database that you're publishing
        rep.PublisherDatabase = "IntelligenceData";
```

```csharp
        // This is your SQL Server username
        rep.PublisherLogin = "sa";

        // This is your SQL Server password
        rep.PublisherPassword = "apress";

        // This is the name that you give to your publication
        // during the wizard setup
        rep.Publication = "IntelligenceDataPublication";

        // This anonymous subscriber name can be anything you want it to be
        rep.Subscriber = "Subscriber";

        // This is the connection string to your local SQL Server CE database file
        rep.SubscriberConnectionString = "Data Source=\\My Documents\\" +
                                "IntelligenceData.sdf;" +
                                "SSCE:Database Password=apress";

        // If database already exists then...
        if (File.Exists("\\My Documents\\IntelligenceData.sdf"))
        {
            // This uploads your changes and then marks the
            // subscription for reinitialization
            rep.ReinitializeSubscription(true);

            // Synchronize with SQL Server
            rep.Synchronize();
        }
        else
        {
            MessageBox.Show("You must first create a database", "Error");
        }
    }
    catch (SqlCeException sqlex)
    {
        foreach (SqlCeError sqlError in sqlex.Errors)
        {
            MessageBox.Show(sqlError.Message, "Error");
        }
    }
    catch (Exception ex)
    {
        MessageBox.Show(ex.Message, "Error");
```

```
    }
    finally
    {
        rep.Dispose();
        btnReinitializeSubscription.Enabled = true;
    }
}
```

Drop Subscription

When you no longer have any desire to replicate data between your device and
SQL Server, the DropSubscription method is your ticket out of this relationship.
Not only will it put an end to your subscription, but it can also remove the SQL
Server CE database in question from your handheld if you so desire using the
DropOption.DropDatabase argument. The following example resides inside the
click event handler of the Drop Subscription button and shows you how to put an
end to your subscription while leaving your SQL Server CE database intact.

Visual Basic .NET

```
Private Sub btnDropSubscription_Click(ByVal sender As System.Object, & _
            ByVal e As System.EventArgs) Handles btnDropSubscription.Click

Dim rep As SqlCeReplication

Try
    btnDropSubscription.Enabled = False
    rep = New SqlCeReplication()

    ' This is the connection string to your local SQL Server CE database file
    rep.SubscriberConnectionString = "Data Source=\My Documents\" & _
                                "IntelligenceData.sdf;" & _
                                "SSCE:Database Password=apress"

    ' If database already exists then...
    If File.Exists("\My Documents\IntelligenceData.sdf") Then
        ' This drops the subscription but leaves the database
        rep.DropSubscription(DropOption.LeaveDatabase)
    Else
        MessageBox.Show("You must first create a database", "Error")
    End If
Catch sqlex As SqlCeException
```

```vb
        Dim sqlError As SqlCeError
        For Each sqlError In sqlex.Errors
            MessageBox.Show(sqlError.Message, "Error")
        Next
    Catch ex As Exception
        MessageBox.Show(ex.Message, "Error")
    Finally
        rep.Dispose()
        btnDropSubscription.Enabled = True
    End Try

End Sub
```

C#

```csharp
private void btnDropSubscription_Click(object sender, System.EventArgs e)
{
    SqlCeReplication rep = null;

    try
    {
        btnDropSubscription.Enabled = false;
        rep = new SqlCeReplication();

        // This is the connection string to your local SQL Server CE database file
        rep.SubscriberConnectionString = "Data Source=\\My Documents\\" +
                                "IntelligenceData.sdf;" +
                                "SSCE:Database Password=apress";

        // If database already exists then...
        if (File.Exists("\\My Documents\\IntelligenceData.sdf"))
        {
            // This drops the subscription and deletes the database
            rep.DropSubscription(DropOption.LeaveDatabase);
        }
        else
        {
            MessageBox.Show("You must first create a database", "Error");
        }
    }
    catch (SqlCeException sqlex)
    {
        foreach (SqlCeError sqlError in sqlex.Errors)
```

```
        {
            MessageBox.Show(sqlError.Message, "Error");
        }
    }
    catch (Exception ex)
    {
        MessageBox.Show(ex.Message, "Error");
    }
    finally
    {
        rep.Dispose();
        btnDropSubscription.Enabled = true;
    }
}
```

Run the Add Subscription, Synchronize, and Add Memo operations in order to get a database with data onto your handheld. Now run Synchronize and Add Memo several times in succession and take a look at how the data has changed on the server with Enterprise Manager and on the Pocket PC with Query Analyzer. Now click the Drop Subscription button and go and see how the columns have changed in Query Analyzer as a result of that method call.

Conclusion

Wow, I can't believe it's over. Not only are you concluding a chapter on merge replication, but you've also made it to the end of the book. These last two chapters should leave you well equipped to move any kind of data from the server to the handheld and back again. In some cases, you may even find that a combination of merge replication and RDA gives your application the scalability you're looking for. This kind of technology is perfect not only for your field agents, but for your sales force, your route drivers, police officers, real-estate agents, military personnel, insurance agents, or anyone else who needs to either gather information or have information at their fingertips. When you combine this technology with rugged, barcode-scanning Pocket PCs, you have a powerful new class of inventory management devices to run your warehouse operations and help enable your real-time enterprise. On the other hand, when you combine this technology with credit card readers and portable Bluetooth thermal printers, you can turn the Pocket PC into a mobile point of sale device for retail operations. Wireless Pocket PCs equipped with the .NET Compact Framework and SQL Server CE 2.0 will begin to change the rules of business or any other enterprise that has yet to realize the efficiencies that can be gained by utilizing this powerful technology. Whether you're a loading dock worker scanning in new inventory or a submarine captain monitoring the real-time status of the sonar suite from inside your stateroom, the Pocket PC will be the primary enabler of new possibilities. I certainly hope that I've anticipated and answered all the questions you might have about SQL Server CE 2.0 and how the .NET Compact Framework interacts with it through ADO.NET.

As we move forward into a future of rapid technological change in the mobile/ wireless arena, stay tuned to my Web site, `http://www.hoodcanalsystems.com`, in order to stay abreast of these changes as they happen.

The .NET Compact Framework Class Libraries

IT GOES WITHOUT saying that a runtime that weighs in at just over 1MB won't support all the functionality found in its larger desktop cousin. That being said, I think you'll be pleasantly surprised with all the features you get in such a small package. In order to build Pocket PC applications that take advantage of everything the .NET Compact Framework has to offer, it's important to know what's on the menu. In the tables that follow, you'll see all the namespaces, classes, structures, enumerations, delegates, and interfaces that are available to you.

Microsoft.VisualBasic

Table A-1. The Microsoft.VisualBasic Namespace

OBJECT NAME	OBJECT TYPE
AppWinStyle	Enumeration
Collection	Class
CompareMethod	Enumeration
Constants	Class
ControlChars	Class
Conversion	Class
DateAndTime	Class
DateFormat	Enumeration
DateInterval	Enumeration
DueDate	Enumeration
ErrObject	Class

Table A-1. The Microsoft.VisualBasic Namespace (Continued)

OBJECT NAME	OBJECT TYPE
Financial	Class
FirstDayOfWeek	Enumeration
FirstWeekOfYear	Enumeration
Information	Class
Interaction	Class
MsgBoxResult	Enumeration
MsgBoxStyle	Enumeration
SpcInfo	Structure
Strings	Class
TabInfo	Structure
TriState	Enumeration
VBFixedArrayAttribute	Class
VBFixedStringAttribute	Class
VBMath	Class

Microsoft.VisualBasic.CompilerServices

Table A-2. The Microsoft.VisualBasic.CompilerServices Namespace

OBJECT NAME	OBJECT TYPE
BooleanType	Class
ByteType	Class
CharArrayType	Class
CharType	Class
DateType	Class
DecimalType	Class
DoubleType	Class
ExceptionUtils	Class
FlowControl	Class
HostServices	Class

Table A-2. The Microsoft.VisualBasic.CompilerServices Namespace (Continued)

OBJECT NAME	OBJECT TYPE
IncompleteInitialization	Class
IntegerType	Class
IVBHost	Interface
LongType	Class
ObjectType	Class
OptionCompareAttribute	Class
OptionTextAttribute	Class
ProjectData	Class
ShortType	Class
SingleType	Class
StandardModuleAttribute	Class
StaticLocalInitFlag	Class
StringType	Class
UnsafeNativeMethods+tagDESCKIND	Enumeration
UnsafeNativeMethods+tagFUNCDESC	Structure
UnsafeNativeMethods+tagINVOKEKIND	Enumeration
UnsafeNativeMethods+tagPARAMDESC	Structure
UnsafeNativeMethods+tagSYSKIND	Enumeration
UnsafeNativeMethods+tagTLIBATTR	Structure
UnsafeNativeMethods+tagTYPEDESC	Class
UnsafeNativeMethods+tagTYPEKIND	Class
UnsafeNativeMethods+tagVARDESC	Structure
UnsafeNativeMethods+value tagELEMDESC	Structure
Utils	Class

Microsoft.WindowsCE.Forms

Table A-3. The Microsoft.WindowsCE.Forms Namespace

OBJECT NAME	OBJECT TYPE
InputPanel	Class
MessageStructure	Class
MessageWindow	Class

System

Table A-4. The System Namespace

OBJECT NAME	OBJECT TYPE
Activator	Class
AppDomain	Class
ApplicationException	Class
ArgumentException	Class
ArgumentNullException	Class
ArgumentOutOfRangeException	Class
ArithmeticException	Class
Array	Class
ArrayTypeMismatchException	Class
AsyncCallback	Delegate
Attribute	Class
AttributeTargets	Enumeration
AttributeUsageAttribute	Class
BitConverter	Class
Boolean	Structure
Buffer	Class
Byte	Structure
Char	Structure

Table A-4. The System Namespace (Continued)

OBJECT NAME	OBJECT TYPE
CharEnumerator	Class
CLSCompliantAttribute	Class
Console	Class
Convert	Class
DateTime	Structure
DayOfWeek	Enumeration
DBNull	Class
Decimal	Structure
Delegate	Class
DivideByZeroException	Class
DllNotFoundException	Class
Double	Structure
EntryPointNotFoundException	Class
Enum	Class
Environment	Class
EventArgs	Class
EventHandler	Delegate
Exception	Class
FlagsAttribute	Class
FormatException	Class
GC	Class
Guid	Structure
IAsyncResult	Interface
ICloneable	Interface
IComparable	Interface
IConvertible	Interface
ICustomFormatter	Interface

Table A-4. The System Namespace (Continued)

OBJECT NAME	OBJECT TYPE
IDisposable	Interface
IFormatProvider	Interface
IFormattable	Interface
IndexOutOfRangeException	Class
Int16	Structure
Int32	Structure
Int64	Structure
IntPtr	Structure
InvalidCastException	Class
InvalidOperationException	Class
InvalidProgramException	Class
IServiceProvider	Interface
LocalDataStoreSlot	Class
MarshalByRefObject	Class
Math	Class
MemberAccessException	Class
MissingFieldException	Class
MissingMemberException	Class
MissingMethodException	Class
MulticastDelegate	Class
MulticastNotSupportedException	Class
NonSerializedAttribute	Class
NotFiniteNumberException	Class
NotSupportedException	Class
NullReferenceException	Class
Object	Class
ObjectDisposedException	Class

Table A-4. The System Namespace (Continued)

OBJECT NAME	OBJECT TYPE
ObsoleteAttribute	Class
OutOfMemoryException	Class
OverflowException	Class
ParamArrayAttribute	Class
PlatformID	Enumeration
PlatformNotSupportedException	Class
Random	Class
RankException	Class
RuntimeFieldHandle	Structure
RuntimeMethodHandle	Structure
RuntimeTypeHandle	Structure
SByte	Structure
Single	Structure
StackOverflowException	Class
String	Class
SystemException	Class
TimeSpan	Structure
TimeZone	Class
Type	Class
TypeCode	Enumeration
TypedReference	Structure
TypeLoadException	Class
UInt16	Structure
UInt32	Structure
UInt64	Structure
UIntPtr	Structure
UnauthorizedAccessException	Class

Table A-4. The System Namespace (Continued)

OBJECT NAME	OBJECT TYPE
Uri	Class
UriFormatException	Class
UriHostNameType	Enumeration
UriPartial	Enumeration
ValueType	Class
Version	Class
Void	Structure
WeakReference	Class

System.Collections

Table A-5. The System.Collections Namespace

OBJECT NAME	OBJECT TYPE
ArrayList	Class
BitArray	Class
CaseInsensitiveComparer	Class
CaseInsensitiveHashCodeProvider	Class
CollectionBase	Class
Comparer	Class
DictionaryEntry	Structure
Hashtable	Class
ICollection	Interface
IComparer	Interface
IDictionary	Interface
IDictionaryEnumerator	Interface
IEnumerable	Interface
IEnumerator	Interface
IHashCodeProvider	Interface
IList	Interface

Table A-5. The System.Collections Namespace (Continued)

OBJECT NAME	OBJECT TYPE
Queue	Class
Stack	Class

System.Collections.Specialized

Table A-6. The System.Collections.Specialized Namespace

OBJECT NAME	OBJECT TYPE
BitVector32	Structure
BitVector32+Section	Structure
HybridDictionary	Class
ListDictionary	Class
NameObjectCollectionBase	Class
NameObjectCollectionBase+KeysCollection	Class
NameValueCollection	Class

System.ComponentModel

Table A-7. The System.ComponentModel Namespace

OBJECT NAME	OBJECT TYPE
AttributeCollection	Class
CancelEventArgs	Class
CancelEventHandler	Delegate
CollectionChangeAction	Enumeration
CollectionChangeEventArgs	Class
CollectionChangeEventHandler	Delegate
Component	Class
ComponentResourceManager	Class
Container	Class
DefaultValueAttribute	Class

Table A-7. The System.ComponentModel Namespace (Continued)

OBJECT NAME	OBJECT TYPE
DesignerCategoryAttribute	Class
EditorBrowsableAttribute	Class
EditorBrowsableState	Enumeration
EventDescriptor	Class
EventDescriptorCollection	Class
EventHandlerList	Class
IBindingList	Interface
IComponent	Interface
IContainer	Interface
ICustomTypeDescriptor	Interface
IDataErrorInfo	Interface
IEditableObject	Interface
IListSource	Interface
ISite	Interface
ITypedList	Interface
ListChangedEventArgs	Class
ListChangedEventHandler	Delegate
ListChangedType	Enumeration
ListSortDirection	Enumeration
MarshalByValueComponent	Class
MemberDescriptor	Class
PropertyChangedEventArgs	Class
PropertyChangedEventHandler	Delegate
PropertyDescriptor	Class
PropertyDescriptorCollection	Class
TypeConverter	Class
TypeDescriptor	Class
Win32Exception	Class

System.Configuration.Assemblies

Table A-8. The System.Configuration.Assemblies Namespace

OBJECT NAME	OBJECT TYPE
AssemblyHashAlgorithm	Enumeration
AssemblyVersionCompatibility	Enumeration

System.Data

Table A-9. The System.Data Namespace

OBJECT NAME	OBJECT TYPE
AcceptRejectRule	Enumeration
CommandBehavior	Enumeration
CommandType	Enumeration
ConnectionState	Enumeration
Constraint	Class
ConstraintCollection	Class
ConstraintException	Class
DataColumn	Class
DataColumnChangeEventArgs	Class
DataColumnChangeEventHandler	Delegate
DataColumnCollection	Class
DataException	Class
DataRelation	Class
DataRelationCollection	Class
DataRow	Class
DataRowAction	Enumeration
DataRowBuilder	Class
DataRowChangeEventArgs	Class
DataRowChangeEventHandler	Delegate
DataRowCollection	Class

Table A-9. The System.Data Namespace (Continued)

OBJECT NAME	OBJECT TYPE
DataRowState	Enumeration
DataRowVersion	Enumeration
DataRowView	Class
DataSet	Class
DataTable	Class
DataTableCollection	Class
DataView	Class
DataViewManager	Class
DataViewRowState	Enumeration
DataViewSetting	Class
DataViewSettingCollection	Class
DBConcurrencyException	Class
DbType	Enumeration
DeletedRowInaccessibleException	Class
DuplicateNameException	Class
EvaluateException	Class
FillErrorEventArgs	Class
FillErrorEventHandler	Delegate
ForeignKeyConstraint	Class
IColumnMapping	Interface
IColumnMappingCollection	Interface
IDataAdapter	Interface
IDataParameter	Interface
IDataParameterCollection	Interface
IDataReader	Interface
IDataRecord	Interface
IDbCommand	Interface
IDbConnection	Interface

Table A-9. The System.Data Namespace (Continued)

OBJECT NAME	OBJECT TYPE
IDbDataAdapter	Interface
IDbDataParameter	Interface
IDbTransaction	Interface
InRowChangingEventException	Class
InternalDataCollectionBase	Class
InvalidConstraintException	Class
InvalidExpressionException	Class
IsolationLevel	Enumeration
ITableMapping	Interface
ITableMappingCollection	Interface
MappingType	Enumeration
MissingMappingAction	Enumeration
MissingPrimaryKeyException	Class
MissingSchemaAction	Enumeration
NoNullAllowedException	Class
ParameterDirection	Enumeration
PropertyAttributes	Enumeration
PropertyCollection	Class
ReadOnlyException	Class
RowNotInTableException	Class
Rule	Enumeration
SchemaType	Enumeration
SqlDbType	Enumeration
StateChangeEventArgs	Class
StateChangeEventHandler	Delegate
StatementType	Enumeration
StrongTypingException	Class
SyntaxErrorException	Class

Table A-9. The System.Data Namespace (Continued)

OBJECT NAME	OBJECT TYPE
UniqueConstraint	Class
UpdateRowSource	Enumeration
UpdateStatus	Enumeration
VersionNotFoundException	Class
XmlReadMode	Enumeration
XmlWriteMode	Enumeration

System.Data.Common

Table A-10. The System.Data.Common Namespace

OBJECT NAME	OBJECT TYPE
DataAdapter	Class
DataColumnMapping	Class
DataColumnMappingCollection	Class
DataTableMapping	Class
DataTableMappingCollection	Class
DbDataAdapter	Class
DbDataRecord	Class
DbEnumerator	Class
RowUpdatedEventArgs	Class
RowUpdatingEventArgs	Class

System.Data.SqlClient

Table A-11. The System.Data.SqlClient Namespace

OBJECT NAME	OBJECT TYPE
SqlCommand	Class
SqlCommandBuilder	Class
SqlConnection	Class

Table A-11. The System.Data.SqlClient Namespace (Continued)

OBJECT NAME	OBJECT TYPE
SqlDataAdapter	Class
SqlDataReader	Class
SqlError	Class
SqlErrorCollection	Class
SqlException	Class
SqlInfoMessageEventArgs	Class
SqlInfoMessageEventHandler	Delegate
SqlParameter	Class
SqlParameterCollection	Class
SqlRowUpdatedEventArgs	Class
SqlRowUpdatedEventHandler	Delegate
SqlRowUpdatingEventArgs	Class
SqlRowUpdatingEventHandler	Delegate
SqlTransaction	Class

System.Data.SqlServerCe

Table A-12. The System.Data.SqlServerCe Namespace

OBJECT NAME	OBJECT TYPE
AddOption	Enumeration
DbRangeOptions	Enumeration
DbSeekOptions	Enumeration
DropOption	Enumeration
ExchangeType	Enumeration
NetworkType	Enumeration
RdaBatchOption	Enumeration

Table A-12. The System.Data.SqlServerCe Namespace (Continued)

OBJECT NAME	OBJECT TYPE
RdaTrackOption	Enumeration
SecurityType	Enumeration
SqlCeCommand	Class
SqlCeCommandBuilder	Class
SqlCeConnection	Class
SqlCeDataAdapter	Class
SqlCeDataReader	Class
SqlCeEngine	Class
SqlCeError	Class
SqlCeErrorCollection	Class
SqlCeException	Class
SqlCeInfoMessageEventArgs	Class
SqlCeInfoMessageEventHandler	Delegate
SqlCeParameter	Class
SqlCeParameterCollection	Class
SqlCeRemoteDataAccess	Class
SqlCeReplication	Class
SqlCeRowUpdatedEventArgs	Class
SqlCeRowUpdatedEventHandler	Delegate
SqlCeRowUpdatingEventArgs	Class
SqlCeRowUpdatingEventHandler	Delegate
SqlCeTransaction	Class
ValidateType	Enumeration

System.Data.SqlTypes

Table A-13. The System.Data.SqlTypes Namespace

OBJECT NAME	OBJECT TYPE
INullable	Interface
SqlBinary	Structure
SqlBoolean	Structure
SqlByte	Structure
SqlCompareOptions	Enumeration
SqlDateTime	Structure
SqlDecimal	Structure
SqlDouble	Structure
SqlGuid	Structure
SqlInt16	Structure
SqlInt32	Structure
SqlInt64	Structure
SqlMoney	Structure
SqlNullValueException	Class
SqlSingle	Structure
SqlString	Structure
SqlTruncateException	Class
SqlTypeException	Class

System.Diagnostics

Table A-14. The System.Diagnostics Namespace

OBJECT NAME	OBJECT TYPE
ConditionalAttribute	Class
Debug	Class
DebuggableAttribute	Class
Debugger	Class
DebuggerStepThroughAttribute	Class
DefaultTraceListener	Class
Trace	Class
TraceListener	Class
TraceListenerCollection	Class

System.Drawing

Table A-15. The System.Drawing Namespace

OBJECT NAME	OBJECT TYPE
Bitmap	Class
Brush	Class
Color	Structure
ContentAlignment	Enumeration
Font	Class
FontFamily	Class
FontStyle	Enumeration
Graphics	Class
GraphicsUnit	Enumeration
Icon	Class
Image	Class
Pen	Class
Point	Structure

Table A-15. The System.Drawing Namespace (Continued)

OBJECT NAME	OBJECT TYPE
Rectangle	Structure
RectangleF	Structure
Region	Class
Size	Structure
SizeF	Structure
SolidBrush	Class
SystemColors	Class

System.Drawing2D

Table A-16. The System.Drawing2D Namespace

OBJECT NAME	OBJECT TYPE
CombineMode	Enumeration

System.Drawing.Imaging

Table A-17. The System.Drawing.Imaging Namespace

OBJECT NAME	OBJECT TYPE
ImageAttributes	Class

System.Globalization

Table A-18. The System.Globalization Namespace

OBJECT NAME	OBJECT TYPE
Calendar	Class
CalendarWeekRule	Enumeration
CompareInfo	Class
CompareOptions	Enumeration
CultureInfo	Class
CultureTypes	Enumeration

Table A-18. The System.Globalization Namespace (Continued)

OBJECT NAME	OBJECT TYPE
DateTimeFormatInfo	Class
DateTimeStyles	Enumeration
DaylightTime	Class
GregorianCalendar	Class
GregorianCalendarTypes	Enumeration
JapaneseCalendar	Class
KoreanCalendar	Class
NumberFormatInfo	Class
NumberStyles	Enumeration
RegionInfo	Class
StringInfo	Class
TaiwanCalendar	Class
TextElementEnumerator	Class
TextInfo	Class
ThaiBuddistCalendar	Class
UnicodeCategory	Enumeration

System.IO

Table A-19. The System.IO Namespace

OBJECT NAME	OBJECT TYPE
BinaryReader	Class
BinaryWriter	Class
Directory	Class
DirectoryInfo	Class
DirectoryNotFoundException	Class
EndOfStreamException	Class
File	Class
FileAccess	Enumeration

Table A-19. The System.IO Namespace (Continued)

OBJECT NAME	OBJECT TYPE
FileAttributes	Enumeration
FileInfo	Class
FileMode	Enumeration
FileNotFoundException	Class
FileShare	Enumeration
FileStream	Class
FileSystemInfo	Class
IOException	Class
MemoryStream	Class
Path	Class
PathTooLongException	Class
SeekOrigin	Enumeration
Stream	Class
StreamReader	Class
StreamWriter	Class
StringReader	Class
StringWriter	Class
TextReader	Class
TextWriter	Class

System.Net

Table A-20. The System.Net Namespace

OBJECT NAME	OBJECT TYPE
AuthenticationManager	Class
Authorization	Class
Dns	Class
EndPoint	Class
GlobalProxySelection	Class

Table A-20. The System.Net Namespace (Continued)

OBJECT NAME	OBJECT TYPE
HttpContinueDelegate	Delegate
HttpStatusCode	Enumeration
HttpVersion	Class
HttpWebRequest	Class
HttpWebResponse	Class
IAuthenticationModule	Interface
ICertificatePolicy	Interface
ICredentials	Interface
IPAddress	Class
IPEndPoint	Class
IPHostEntry	Class
IrDAEndPoint	Class
IWebProxy	Interface
IWebRequestCreate	Interface
NetworkCredential	Class
ProtocolViolationException	Class
ServicePoint	Class
ServicePointManager	Class
SocketAddress	Class
WebException	Class
WebExceptionStatus	Enumeration
WebHeaderCollection	Class
WebProxy	Class
WebRequest	Class
WebResponse	Class

System.Net.Sockets

Table A-21. The System.Net.Sockets Namespace

OBJECT NAME	OBJECT TYPE
AddressFamily	Enumeration
IrDACharacterSet	Enumeration
IrDAClient	Class
IrDADeviceInfo	Class
IrDAHints	Enumeration
IrDAListener	Class
LingerOption	Class
MulticastOption	Class
NetworkStream	Class
ProtocolFamily	Enumeration
ProtocolType	Enumeration
SelectMode	Enumeration
Socket	Class
SocketException	Class
SocketFlags	Enumeration
SocketOptionLevel	Enumeration
SocketOptionName	Enumeration
SocketShutdown	Enumeration
SocketType	Enumeration
TcpClient	Class
TcpListener	Class
UdpClient	Class

System.Reflection

Table A-22. The System.Reflection Namespace

OBJECT NAME	OBJECT TYPE
AmbiguousMatchException	Class
Assembly	Class
AssemblyAlgorithmIdAttribute	Class
AssemblyCompanyAttribute	Class
AssemblyConfigurationAttribute	Class
AssemblyCopyrightAttribute	Class
AssemblyCultureAttribute	Class
AssemblyDefaultAliasAttribute	Class
AssemblyDelaySignAttribute	Class
AssemblyDescriptionAttribute	Class
AssemblyFlagsAttribute	Class
AssemblyInformationalVersionAttribute	Class
AssemblyKeyFileAttribute	Class
AssemblyKeyNameAttribute	Class
AssemblyName	Class
AssemblyNameFlags	Enumeration
AssemblyProductAttribute	Class
AssemblyTitleAttribute	Class
AssemblyTrademarkAttribute	Class
AssemblyVersionAttribute	Class
Binder	Class
BindingFlags	Enumeration
CallingConventions	Enumeration
ConstructorInfo	Class

Table A-22. The System.Reflection Namespace (Continued)

OBJECT NAME	OBJECT TYPE
CustomAttributeFormatException	Class
DefaultMemberAttribute	Class
EventAttributes	Enumeration
EventInfo	Class
FieldAttributes	Enumeration
FieldInfo	Class
ICustomAttributeProvider	Interface
MemberInfo	Class
MemberTypes	Enumeration
MethodAttributes	Enumeration
MethodBase	Class
MethodImplAttributes	Enumeration
MethodInfo	Class
Missing	Class
Module	Class
ParameterAttributes	Enumeration
ParameterInfo	Class
ParameterModifier	Structure
PropertyAttributes	Enumeration
PropertyInfo	Class
TargetInvocationException	Class
TargetParameterCountException	Class
TypeAttributes	Enumeration

System.Resources

Table A-23. The System.Resources Namespace

OBJECT NAME	OBJECT TYPE
IResourceReader	Interface
MissingManifestResourceException	Class
NeutralResourcesLanguageAttribute	Class
ResourceManager	Class
ResourceReader	Class
ResourceSet	Class
SatelliteContractVersionAttribute	Class

System.Runtime.CompilerServices

Table A-24. The System.Runtime.CompilerServices Namespace

OBJECT NAME	OBJECT TYPE
AccessedThroughPropertyAttribute	Class
CustomConstantAttribute	Class
DateTimeConstantAttribute	Class
DecimalConstantAttribute	Class
IndexerNameAttribute	Class
MethodCodeType	Enumeration
MethodImplAttribute	Class
MethodImpOptions	Enumeration
RuntimeHelpers	Class

System.RuntimeInteropServices

Table A-25. The System.RuntimeInteropServices Namespace

OBJECT NAME	OBJECT TYPE
CallingConvention	Enumeration
CharSet	Enumeration
ComVisibleAttribute	Class
DispIdAttribute	Class
DllImportAttribute	Class
ExternalException	Class
GCHandle	Structure
GCHandleType	Enumeration
GuidAttribute	Class
InAttribute	Class
LayoutKind	Enumeration
Marshal	Class
OutAttribute	Class
StructLayoutAttribute	Class
UnmanagedType	Enumeration

System.Security

Table A-26. The System.Security Namespace

OBJECT NAME	OBJECT TYPE
SecurityException	Class
VerificationException	Class

System.Cryptography.X509Certificates

Table A-27. The System.Cryptography.X509Certificates Namespace

OBJECT NAME	OBJECT TYPE
X509Certificate	Class

System.Security.Policy

Table A-28. The System.Security.Policy Namespace

OBJECT NAME	OBJECT TYPE
Evidence	Class

System.Text

Table A-29. The System.Text Namespace

OBJECT NAME	OBJECT TYPE
ASCIIEncoding	Class
Decoder	Class
Encoder	Class
Encoding	Class
MLangCodePageEncoding	Class
StringBuilder	Class
UnicodeEncoding	Class
UTF7Encoding	Class
UTF8Encoding	Class

System.Text.RegularExpressions

Table A-30. The System.Text.RegularExpressions Namespace

OBJECT NAME	OBJECT TYPE
Capture	Class
CaptureCollection	Class
Group	Class
GroupCollection	Class
Match	Class
MatchCollection	Class
MatchEvaluator	Delegate
Regex	Class
RegexOptions	Enumeration
RegexRunner	Class
RegexRunnerFactory	Class

System.Threading

Table A-31. The System.Threading Namespace

OBJECT NAME	OBJECT TYPE
AutoResetEvent	Class
Interlocked	Class
ManualResetEvent	Class
Monitor	Class
Mutex	Class
Thread	Class
ThreadPool	Class
ThreadPriority	Class
ThreadStart	Delegate
ThreadStateException	Class
Timeout	Class

Table A-31. The System.Threading Namespace (Continued)

OBJECT NAME	OBJECT TYPE
Timer	Class
TimerCallback	Delegate
WaitCallback	Delegate
WaitHandle	Class

System.Web.Services

Table A-32. The System.Web.Services Namespace

OBJECT NAME	OBJECT TYPE
WebMethodAttribute	Class
WebServiceBindingAttribute	Class

System.Web.Services.Description

Table A-33. The System.Web.Services.Description Namespace

OBJECT NAME	OBJECT TYPE
SoapBindingUse	Enumeration

System.Web.Services.Protocols

Table A-34. The System.Web.Services.Protocols Namespace

OBJECT NAME	OBJECT TYPE
HttpWebClientProtocol	Class
LogicalMethodInfo	Class
LogicalMethodTypes	Enumeration
SoapClientMessage	Class
SoapDocumentMethodAttribute	Class
SoapDocumentServiceAttribute	Class
SoapException	Class
SoapExtension	Class
SoapExtensionAttribute	Class

Table A-34. The System.Web.Services.Protocols Namespace (Continued)

OBJECT NAME	OBJECT TYPE
SoapHeader	Class
SoapHeaderAttribute	Class
SoapHeaderCollection	Class
SoapHeaderDirection	Enumeration
SoapHeaderException	Class
SoapHttpClientProtocol	Class
SoapMessage	Class
SoapMessageStage	Enumeration
SoapParameterStyle	Enumeration
SoapRpcMethodAttribute	Class
SoapServiceRoutingStyle	Enumeration
SoapUnknownHeader	Class
WebClientAsyncResult	Class
WebClientProtocol	Class

System.Windows.Forms

Table A-35. The System.Windows.Forms Namespace

OBJECT NAME	OBJECT TYPE
Application	Class
BaseCollection	Class
Binding	Class
BindingContext	Class
BindingManagerBase	Class
BindingMemberInfo	Structure
BindingsCollection	Class
BorderStyle	Enumeration
Button	Class
ButtonBase	Class

Table A-35. The System.Windows.Forms Namespace (Continued)

OBJECT NAME	OBJECT TYPE
CheckBox	Class
CheckState	Enumeration
ColumnClickEventArgs	Class
ColumnClickEventHandler	Delegate
ColumnHeader	Class
ColumnHeaderStyle	Enumeration
ComboBox	Class
ComboBox.ObjectCollection	Class
ComboBoxStyle	Enumeration
CommonDialog	Class
ContainerControl	Class
ContextMenu	Class
Control	Class
Control+ControlCollection	Class
ControlBindingsCollection	Class
ConvertEventArgs	Class
ConvertEventHandler	Delegate
CurrencyManager	Class
Cursor	Class
Cursors	Class
DataGrid	Class
DataGrid+HitTestInfo	Class
DataGrid+HitTestType	Enumeration
DataGridCell	Structure
DataGridColumnStyle	Class
DataGridTableStyle	Class
DataGridTexBoxColumn	Class
DialogResult	Enumeration

Table A-35. The System.Windows.Forms Namespace (Continued)

OBJECT NAME	OBJECT TYPE
DomainUpDown	Class
DomainUpDown+DomainUpDownItem Collection	Class
FileDialog	Class
Form	Class
FormBorderStyle	Enumeration
FormWindowState	Enumeration
GridColumnStylesCollection	Class
GridTableStylesCollection	Class
HorizontalAlignment	Enumeration
HScrollBar	Class
ImageList	Class
ImageList+ImageCollection	Class
ItemActivation	Enumeration
ItemChangedEventArgs	Class
ItemChangedEventHandler	Delegate
KeyEventArgs	Class
KeyEventHandler	Delegate
KeyPressEventArgs	Class
KeyPressEventHandler	Delegate
Keys	Enumeration
Label	Class
ListBox	Class
ListBox+ObjectCollection	Class
ListControl	Class
ListView	Class
ListView+ColumnHeaderCollection	Class
ListView+ListViewItemCollection	Class
ListView+SelectedIndexCollection	Class

Table A-35. The System.Windows.Forms Namespace (Continued)

OBJECT NAME	OBJECT TYPE
ListViewItem	Class
ListViewItem+ListViewSubItem	Class
ListViewItem+ListViewSubItemCollection	Class
MainMenu	Class
Menu	Class
Menu+MenuItemCollection	Class
MenuItem	Class
MessageBox	Class
MessageBoxButtons	Enumeration
MessageBoxDefaultButton	Enumeration
MessageBoxIcon	Enumeration
MouseButtons	Enumeration
MouseEventArgs	Class
MouseEventHandler	Delegate
NumericUpDown	Class
OpenFileDialog	Class
Orientation	Enumeration
PaintEventArgs	Class
PaintEventHandler	Delegate
Panel	Class
PictureBox	Class
PictureBoxSizeMode	Enumeration
ProgressBar	Class
PropertyManager	Class
RadioButton	Class
SaveFileDialog	Class
Screen	Class
ScrollableControl	Class

Table A-35. The System.Windows.Forms Namespace (Continued)

OBJECT NAME	OBJECT TYPE
ScrollBar	Class
ScrollBars	Enumeration
StatusBar	Class
SystemInformation	Class
TabControl	Class
TabControl+TabPageCollection	Class
TabPage	Class
TextBox	Class
TextBoxBase	Class
Timer	Class
ToolBar	Class
ToolBar+ToolBarButtonCollection	Class
ToolBarButton	Class
ToolBarButtonClickEventArgs	Class
ToolBarButtonClickEventHandler	Delegate
ToolBarButtonStyle	Enumeration
TrackBar	Class
TreeNode	Class
TreeNodeCollection	Class
TreeView	Class
TreeViewAction	Enumeration
TreeViewCancelEventArgs	Class
TreeViewCancelEventHandler	Delegate
TreeViewEventArgs	Class
TreeViewEventHandler	Delegate
UpDownBase	Class
View	Enumeration
VScrollBar	Class

System.Xml

Table A-36. The System.Xml Namespace

OBJECT NAME	OBJECT TYPE
EntityHandling	Enumeration
Formatting	Enumeration
IXmlLineInfo	Interface
NameTable	Class
ReadState	Enumeration
WhitespaceHandling	Enumeration
WriteState	Enumeration
XmlAttribute	Class
XmlAttributeCollection	Class
XmlCDataSection	Class
XmlCharacterData	Class
XmlComment	Class
XmlConvert	Class
XmlDeclaration	Class
XmlDocument	Class
XmlDocumentFragment	Class
XmlElement	Class
XmlEntityReference	Class
XmlException	Class
XmlImplementation	Class
XmlLinkedNode	Class
XmlNamedNodeMap	Class
XmlNamespaceManager	Class
XmlNameTable	Class
XmlNode	Class
XmlNodeChangedAction	Enumeration
XmlNodeChangedEventArgs	Class

Table A-36. The System.Xml Namespace (Continued)

OBJECT NAME	OBJECT TYPE
XmlNodeChangedEventHandler	Delegate
XmlNodeList	Class
XmlNodeReader	Class
XmlNodeReaderNavigator+VirtualAttribute	Structure
XmlNodeType	Enumeration
XmlParserContext	Class
XmlProcessingInstruction	Class
XmlQualifiedName	Class
XmlReader	Class
XmlResolver	Class
XmlSignificantWhitespace	Class
XmlSpace	Enumeration
XmlText	Class
XmlTextReader	Class
XmlTextWriter	Class
XmlUrlResolver	Class
XmlWhitespace	Class
XmlWriter	Class

System.Xml.Schema

Table A-37. The System.Xml.Schema Namespace

OBJECT NAME	OBJECT TYPE
XmlSchema	Class
XmlSchemaException	Class
XmlSchemaObject	Class

System.Xml.Serialization

Table A-38. The System.Xml.Serialization Namespace

OBJECT NAME	OBJECT TYPE
IXmlSerializable	Interface
SoapAttributeAttribute	Class
SoapElementAttribute	Class
SoapEnumAttribute	Class
SoapIgnoreAttribute	Class
SoapIncludeAttribute	Class
SoapTypeAttribute	Class
XmlAnyAttributeAttribute	Class
XmlAnyElementAttribute	Class
XmlArrayAttribute	Class
XmlArrayItemAttribute	Class
XmlAttributeAttribute	Class
XmlChoiceIdentifierAttribute	Class
XmlElementAttribute	Class
XmlEnumAttribute	Class
XmlIgnoreAttribute	Class
XmlIncludeAttribute	Class
XmlNamespaceDeclarationsAttribute	Class
XmlRootAttribute	Class
XmlSerializerNamespaces	Class
XmlTextAttribute	Class
XmlTypeAttribute	Class

Index

G